McGraw-Hill Education
Preparation for the
TASC Test

Test Assessing Secondary Completion™

McGraw-Hill Education

Preparation for the
TASC Test

Test Assessing Secondary Completion™

Second Edition

Kathy A. Zahler

Diane Zahler

Stephanie Muntone

Thomas A. Evangelist

New York Chicago San Francisco Athens London Madrid
Mexico City Milan New Delhi Singapore Sydney Toronto

1 2 3 4 5 6 7 8 9 10   QVS/QVS   1 2 1 0 9 8 7 6 5

ISBN   978-0-07-184387-4
MHID   0-07-184387-6

e-ISBN   978-0-07-184388-1
e-MHID   0-07-184388-4

Library of Congress Control Number 2014952595

"TASC Test Assessing Secondary Completion," and the associated "tree" logo are trademarks of McGraw-Hill School Education Holdings LLC.

McGraw-Hill Education is not affiliated with The After-School Corporation, which is known as TASC. The After-School Corporation has no affiliation with the Test Assessing Secondary Completion ("TASC test") offered by McGraw-Hill Education, and has not authorized, sponsored or otherwise approved of any of McGraw-Hill Education's products and services, including the TASC test.

McGraw-Hill Education products are available at special quantity discounts to use as premiums and sales promotions or for use in corporate training programs. To contact a representative, please visit the Contact Us pages at www.mhprofessional.com.

Contents

Introducing the TASC Test 1

The TASC Language Arts–Reading Test 19

3 The TASC Language Arts–Writing Test 75

4 The TASC Mathematics Test 133

5   The TASC Social Studies Test   231

6 The TASC Science Test   315

Appendix   393

Introducing the TASC Test

1

HOW TO USE THIS CHAPTER

» Read "Why a New Test Now?" and "What Is the Common Core?" to learn basic information about the TASC test.

» Read "New Formats" and "About the Test" to find out about the different test sections and to see some sample questions.

» Review "Test-Taking Strategies" to discover some effective ways to get your best score.

Why a New Test Now?

CTB/McGraw-Hill designed the Test Assessing Secondary Completion (TASC) to meet the demand of many states for a new, affordable high school equivalency assessment. States wanted a test that was easily accessible to adult learners and provided options for administering the exam. By 2015–2016, the test will also offer a degree of rigor not found on earlier equivalency tests. This level of rigor is now required for high school graduation in states that have adopted the Common Core State Standards.

Like the high school equivalency exams that have existed since the 1940s, the TASC test compares your achievement to that of graduating high school seniors across the United States. In addition, it measures your readiness for college and the workforce as defined by the Common Core State Standards. Unlike other high school equivalency exams, the TASC test is reasonably priced, and it is available as a paper-and-pencil test as well as online. This allows states to phase in computer-based testing at a reasonable pace.

The TASC test assesses knowledge and skills in English language arts (including reading and writing), math, science, and social studies.

It is available in English and Spanish and in large-print, braille, and audio versions.

In states that recognize and use the TASC test, passing the TASC test may help you get a job, advance in a current job, apply for college, or qualify for military service. Successful test-takers will receive both Career and College Readiness (CCR) and passing scores. Passing the TASC test with a satisfactory CCR score means that your skills compare to those of students who graduate from America's high schools. It means that you are well prepared for college or career.

What Is the Common Core?

The Common Core State Standards provide a consistent, clear understanding of what students are expected to learn so teachers and parents know what they need to do to help them. The Standards are designed to be robust and relevant to the real world, reflecting the knowledge and skills that our young people need for success in college and careers. With American students fully prepared for the future, our communities will be best positioned to compete successfully in the global economy.

—Common Core State Standards Initiative

For nearly a decade, states had been hearing from community colleges that students were entering unprepared for college work. Community colleges had to provide remedial courses at enormous cost. Even so, most remedial students failed to earn a degree, even after up to eight years. Meanwhile, businesses reported that young people entering the workforce lacked critical-thinking, problem-solving, and communication skills that their bosses considered crucial. Many new employees could not write or do basic arithmetic at an acceptable level.

At the same time, US students continued to do poorly when measured against students from other nations. On international tests, high school students from the United States tested about mid-range in reading. They tested below average in math. America's place in the global economy was challenged because American students could not compete with international standards.

In 2009, a group of states, territories, the National Governors Association, and the Council of Chief State School Officers came together to form the Common Core State Standards Initiative. Their first task was to define college and career readiness. They would use that definition to prepare a new set of standards for US K–12 education. This group worked together to develop and release the College and Career Readiness Standards in September of that year.

Next, the Initiative formed English language arts (ELA) and Mathematics teams. Each team was made up of teachers and professors, curriculum and assessment experts, educational organizations, and parents. Those teams began to work on common standards. They started with the College and Career Readiness Standards. They added bits and pieces from the best standards from their respective states. In June of 2010, they released Common Core State Standards for ELA, Content Area Literacy, and Mathematics.

The point of the Standards was to provide goals that were "fewer, clearer, and higher" than what states had provided in the past. Instead of a curriculum that was "a mile high and an inch deep," the new Standards require in-depth knowledge of some key ideas. Instead of using educational jargon, the new Standards are understandable by students and parents as well as by educators. Instead of focusing on a lowest common denominator, the new Standards raise the bar for all students.

So what does that mean for someone taking the TASC test?

1. It means that the test will be rigorous. Starting in 2015, some TASC test questions will require you to write or construct your response in addition to answering multiple-choice questions.
2. It means that the test will focus on skills that are critical to the Common Core. Here are some changes you are likely to see.

Changes in Focus with the Common Core

In Reading and Writing	Increased complexity in texts
	Emphasis on informational texts
	Writing arguments and informative/explanatory essays
	Locating evidence in texts
	Focus on academic vocabulary
In Mathematics	Real-world problems
	Modeling with mathematics
	Constructing arguments and critiquing reasoning
In Social Studies	Text-based questions
	Analysis of author's claims
	Analysis of societal issues and events through the lens of civics, geography, economics, and history
	Comparisons of primary and secondary sources
In Science	Emphasis on scientific practices
	Real-world problems
	Inclusion of technology and engineering concepts

In other words, whereas former high school equivalency tests might have asked you to read a lot of fiction and poetry, now you will read more nonfiction. Where earlier tests might have asked you to write about a place or event, now you will write and support an opinion about an idea. You may see math problems that ask you to analyze someone else's response to a problem. You may face science questions that ask about steps in the experimental process or social studies questions that require you to compare and contrast writings from two different eras.

The good news is that this kind of questioning will better prepare you for the world of work or college. To help you get there, the TASC test will move gradually from current standards to the Common Core State Standards. Beginning in 2015, TASC test exams will feature more Common Core–related questions in multiple formats. By 2016, technology-enhanced items such as those used to test the Common Core State Standards in high schools will be a standard feature of the online TASC tests.

New Formats

Beginning in 2015, the TASC test will start to feature a variety of formats. As you can imagine, a computer-based test offers more options for questions and responses. You will find interactive demonstrations of these new formats on the website www.tasctest.com. Here are some examples.

Constructed Response

A constructed-response item is a short-answer question. Instead of choosing or manipulating given answers, you have to come up with an answer on your own.

At the bake sale, students sold x items at 15¢ apiece, y items at 25¢ apiece, and z items at 50¢ apiece. After paying back their advisor $12 for ingredients, they were left with $45. Write an expression to represent the value of the items sold.

Correct Answer: $0.15x + 0.25y + 0.50z = \$57$. The total raised was $45 + $12, or $57. Each variable is represented by a letter and the amount a single item was worth.

Multiple-Select Response

This type of question is just like a multiple-choice question, except that instead of a single correct answer, there is more than one possible answer. On a computer-based test, you may need to click on each response.

Which two American presidents had as a goal the annexation of Texas?

(A) Jefferson
(B) Madison
(C) Tyler
(D) Grant
(E) Polk
(F) Johnson

Correct Answers: C and E. The annexation took place in 1845, just prior to the inauguration of President Polk, who had campaigned on a promise to see it through. President Tyler worked with his soon-to-be successor to develop a joint resolution for annexation.

Evidence-Based Selected Response

This is a format you may see on a reading test. In the first part, Part A, you analyze a text and choose a conclusion from four options. In the second part, Part B, you choose evidence from the text to support your conclusion in Part A. The second part may be in multiple-choice format, or it may be a multiple-select response.

Read this text. Then answer the questions.

Excerpt from *Rose in Bloom*

Louisa May Alcott

Three young men stood together on a wharf one bright October day awaiting the arrival of an ocean steamer with an impatience which found a vent in lively skirmishes with a small lad, who pervaded the premises like a will-o'-the-wisp and afforded much amusement to the other groups assembled there.

"They are the Campbells, waiting for their cousin, who has been abroad several years with her uncle, the doctor," whispered one lady to another as the handsomest of the young men touched his hat to her as he passed, lugging the boy, whom he had just rescued from a little expedition down among the piles.

"Which is that?" asked the stranger.

"Prince Charlie, as he's called a fine fellow, the most promising of the seven, but a little fast, people say," answered the first speaker with a shake of the head.

"Are the others his brothers?"

"No, cousins. The elder is Archie, a most exemplary young man. He has just gone into business with the merchant uncle and bids fair to be an honor to his family. The other, with the eyeglasses and no gloves, is Mac, the odd one, just out of college."

"And the boy?"

"Oh, he is Jamie, the youngest brother of Archibald, and the pet of the whole family. Mercy on us; he'll be in if they don't hold on to him!"

Part A

Which word <u>best</u> describes young Jamie?

Ⓐ quarrelsome
Ⓑ rambunctious
Ⓒ good-looking
Ⓓ praiseworthy

Part B

Which three phrases from the text provide evidence that supports the answer to Part A?

Ⓐ awaiting the arrival of an ocean steamer
Ⓑ pervaded the premises like a will-o'-the-wisp
Ⓒ rescued from a little expedition down among the piles
Ⓓ the most promising of the seven
Ⓔ with the eyeglasses and no gloves
Ⓕ the pet of the whole family
Ⓖ he'll be in if they don't hold on to him

<u>Correct Answers:</u> **Part A: B.** Every description of Jamie indicates that he is a lively, high-spirited boy who makes trouble for his brothers. **Part B: B, C, and G.** Choices D and E apply to other cousins, and choices A and F don't support Jamie's rambunctiousness. Choices B, C, and G show how troublesome and wild he is.

Drag and Drop

You may have seen formats like this on video games. In this case, you drag and drop the correct responses to complete the number line. In the print edition of this book, you will simply draw lines to match answers to spaces.

Drag and drop each number into its correct place on the number line.

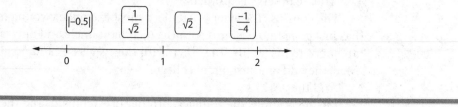

$$|{-0.5}| \qquad \frac{1}{\sqrt{2}} \qquad \sqrt{2} \qquad \frac{-1}{-4}$$

<u>Correct Answer:</u> In order, negative 1 over negative 4, or ¼, should appear a quarter of a unit to the right of 0; the absolute value of −0.5 should appear halfway between 0 and 1; 1 divided by the square root of 2 (about 0.7) should appear a little farther along between 0 and 1; and the square root of 2 (1.414)

should appear slightly less than halfway between 1 and 2. For the purposes of this number line, neither the square root of 2 nor 1 over the square root of 2 can be negative numbers.

About the Test

The TASC test features test items in five areas: Language Arts–Reading, Language Arts–Writing, Social Studies, Science, and Mathematics. Here is the breakdown by approximate number of items and time for each section.

Breakdown of TASC Test Sections

SUBJECT	DOMAIN	TIME IN MINUTES (ENGLISH)	TIME IN MINUTES (SPANISH)	NUMBER OF ITEMS
Language Arts—Reading	Informational Reading & Language Literary Reading & Language	75	80	50
Language Arts—Writing	Language Writing	105	110	50 1 essay
Mathematics	Number & Quantity Algebra Functions Geometry Statistics & Probability	50 calculator 55 no calculator	55 calculator 60 no calculator	40 12 gridded response
Social Studies	US History World History Civics & Government Geography Economics	75	80	47
Science	Physical Sciences Life Sciences Earth & Space Sciences (Engineering, Technology & Application of Science plus Scientific & Engineering Practices are integrated throughout.)	85	90	47

The Language Arts–Reading Section

50 items, 75 minutes

On the Language Arts–Reading section of the test, you will read passages and answer a series of questions about each passage. Beginning in 2015, this section will include multiple-choice, constructed-response, multiple-select response, and evidence-based selected response items. See page 4 for more about those formats.

Questions in the Language Arts–Reading section will typically emphasize these skills:

» Drawing and supporting conclusions
» Determining the main idea
» Summarizing a text
» Analyzing how ideas or events develop
» Interpreting words and phrases
» Analyzing structure of texts
» Assessing point of view and purpose
» Evaluating arguments
» Demonstrating understanding of figurative language
» Clarifying meaning of unknown or multiple-meaning words
» Analyzing how two texts address similar themes or topics

Here is an example of a passage and Reading question. Most of the reading passages on the TASC test will be nonfiction.

Read this text. Then answer the question.

Excerpt from "The Man with the Muck-Rake"

Theodore Roosevelt

April 15, 1906

Over a century ago Washington laid the corner-stone of the Capitol in what was then little more than a tract of wooded wilderness here beside the Potomac. We now find it necessary to provide great additional buildings for the business of the government. This growth in the need for the housing of the government is but a proof and example of the way in which the nation has grown and the sphere of action of the National Government has grown. We now administer the affairs of a nation in which the extraordinary growth of population has been outstripped by the growth of wealth and the growth in complex interests.

The material problems that face us to-day are not such as they were in Washington's time, but the underlying facts of human nature are the same now as they were then. Under altered external form we war with the same tendencies toward evil that were evident in Washington's time, and are helped by the same tendencies for good.

It is about some of these that I wish to say a word to-day. In Bunyan's *Pilgrim's Progress* you may recall the description of the Man with the Muck-Rake, the man who could look no way but downward, with the muck-rake in his hand; who was offered a celestial crown for his muck-rake, but who would neither look up nor regard the crown he was offered, but continued to rake to himself the filth of the floor.

In *Pilgrim's Progress* the Man with the Muck-Rake is set forth as the example of him whose vision is fixed on carnal instead of on spiritual things. Yet he also typifies the man who in this life consistently refuses to see aught that is lofty, and fixes his eyes with solemn intentness only on that which is vile and debasing. Now, it is very necessary that we should not flinch from seeing what is vile and debasing. There is filth on the floor and it must be scraped up with the muck-rake; and there are times and places where this service is the most needed of all the services that can be performed. But the man who never does anything else, who never thinks or speaks or writes, save of his feats with the muck-rake, speedily becomes, not a help to society, not an incitement to good, but one of the most potent forces for evil.

Why does Roosevelt refer to the character from *Pilgrim's Progress*?

Ⓐ to show how the nation and its government have grown over time
Ⓑ to suggest that always looking for the worst may be destructive
Ⓒ to illustrate that spirituality is part of the American essence
Ⓓ to clarify the importance of seeing the bad as well as the good

Correct Answer: B. Roosevelt says that the Man with the Muck-Rake never looks up, but continues to rake the filth of the floor. Although he acknowledges that "we should not flinch from seeing what is vile and debasing," his main point is that the Man with the Muck-Rake can be too blind to the good and therefore may be "one of the most potent forces for evil." Although the passage refers to choice A, it is not in the context of the character from *Pilgrim's Progress*. Choice D reverses Roosevelt's point.

The Language Arts–Writing Section

50 items, 55 minutes	1 essay, 50 minutes

The Language Arts–Writing section of the TASC test features two separate parts. The first part deals with language skills—spelling, grammar, capitalization, and punctuation. Beginning in 2015, this section may include multiple-choice, constructed-response, multiple-select response, and drag-and-drop items. See page 4 for more on those formats. The second part is an essay. You will write a response to a passage or passages.

Here are the skills you should expect to see tested in the Language Arts–Writing section:

》 Identifying and correcting errors in grammar, usage, capitalization, punctuation, and spelling
》 Revising text to improve clarity, precision, organization, and style
》 Writing arguments to support claims
》 Writing informative/explanatory texts

There are many possible formats for language skills questions. Here is just one example.

Read this sentence.

> Because nobody was receiving the invitation by the date of the party, attendance being minimal.

Which of these is the <u>most</u> grammatical and clearest revision to the sentence?

(A) Because nobody has received the invitation by the date of the party, it was minimal attendance.

(B) When nobody received the invitation by the date of the party, minimal attendance was had.

(C) Nobody having received the invitation by the date of the party, there were minimal attendance.

(D) Because nobody had received the invitation by the date of the party, attendance was minimal.

Correct Answer: D. The problem in the original sentence lies with the verbs. Choice D corrects the first verb to fix the time of the action and adjusts the second verb to agree with its subject and avoid the passive voice. Reading the sentences aloud may help you choose the best one.

The essay part of the Writing section will require you to evaluate and respond to an author's argument or to examine a topic and present related information. Here is an example.

Write an essay to support or contradict Teddy Roosevelt's notion that the muckraker can be a force for evil. Base your ideas on the excerpt from Roosevelt's speech "The Man with the Muck-Rake" and this dictionary definition of *muckraker*.

Muckraker: one who searches for and publicly exposes real or apparent misconduct of a prominent official or business

As you reread the speech, think about what details from the text you might use. Think about Roosevelt's point of view as a public official. Think about how muckrakers work today.

After reading the texts, create a plan for your essay. Consider the argument you wish to make. Do you agree or disagree with Roosevelt? Why? What facts and details can you use to support your argument?

Now, write your essay. Be sure to:

>> Include specific details or quotations from the speech.
>> Make clear whether you support or dispute Roosevelt's point of view.
>> Support your own argument with facts and details.
>> Use transition words and phrases to organize your ideas.
>> Choose words that are precise and clear.
>> Provide a concluding statement that follows from your argument.

Your essay will receive a score of 0 to 4, based on a reader's assessment of your argument and its support, your organization, your use of precise and powerful words, your transitions, your tone, the strength of your conclusion, and your correct use of standard English.

The Mathematics Section

52 items, 105 minutes

Beginning in 2015, Mathematics will feature multiple-choice, constructed-response, and drag-and-drop items. See page 4 for more about those formats. In addition, the no-calculator part of the test will feature gridded responses.

As you study for the Mathematics section of the TASC test, concentrate on these areas:

>> Polynomials and rational expressions
>> Equations and inequalities
>> Interpreting functions
>> Linear, quadratic, and exponential models
>> Geometric measurement in three dimensions

» Triangles
» Congruence and similarity
» Basics of trigonometry
» Real numbers
» Making inferences from data
» Interpreting data

You may also see occasional questions on circles, trigonometric functions, complex numbers, and the rules of probability.

On most of the Mathematics section, you will be allowed to use a calculator. On one section, calculators are not permitted. The directions will tell you whether or not to use a calculator.

Here is an example of a question that requires a gridded response.

Find the measure of ∠*a* in the following triangle.

2.5 *a*

a   *a*

Mark your answer in the answer grid.

Correct Answer: 40. The angles of any triangle add up to 180 degrees, so this question may be solved easily algebraically: $a + a + 2.5a = 180$. $4.5a = 180$. $a = 40$. On the grid, you would write 4 and 0 in any two adjoining columns (it's best to start at the far left and work toward the right) and then fill in the bubbles for 4 and 0 below each numeral you wrote:

4	0			
	⊘	⊘	⊘	
⊙	⊙	⊙	⊙	⊙
⓪	●	⓪	⓪	⓪
①	①	①	①	①
②	②	②	②	②
③	③	③	③	③
●	④	④	④	④
⑤	⑤	⑤	⑤	⑤
⑥	⑥	⑥	⑥	⑥
⑦	⑦	⑦	⑦	⑦
⑧	⑧	⑧	⑧	⑧
⑨	⑨	⑨	⑨	⑨

The Social Studies Section

47 items, 75 minutes

Many questions in the Social Studies section will be based on a passage, a map, a chart, a graph, or a cartoon. There may be a few stand-alone questions, but most questions will be in sets. Starting in 2015, questions may be multiple-choice, constructed-response, multiple-select, or drag-and-drop. See page 4 for more on those formats.

Expect to see questions in this section that focus on these areas:

» US Constitution
» Foundations of American politics
» Industrialization
» Civil War and Reconstruction
» Great Depression and World War II
» Postwar United States
» Government and economics
» Civic life and politics
» Microeconomics
» Macroeconomics
» Places and regions
» Environment and society

» Age of revolutions
» Twentieth-century world history

To a lesser degree, the TASC test may test other eras in US history, early civilizations, classical traditions, major religions, empires and exploration, trade and international politics, and physical systems.

Here is an example of a Social Studies question based on a graph.

Look at the graph. Then answer the question that follows.

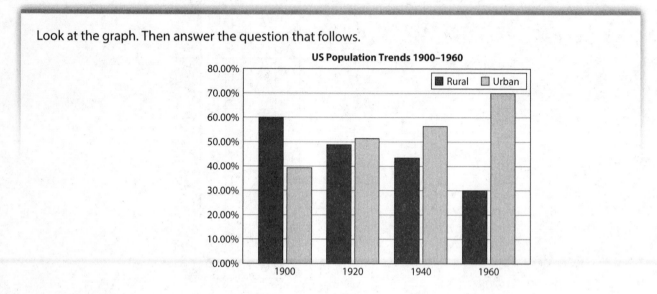

The trend shown in the graph was <u>mainly</u> affected by which two of these elements?

Ⓐ employment opportunities
Ⓑ climate change
Ⓒ World War II
Ⓓ famine in Ireland
Ⓔ decline of family farming
Ⓕ improvements in birth control

<u>**Correct Answers: A and E.**</u> To answer this multiple-select question, you must first identify the trend. It may be stated simply as, "Rural population declined, whereas urban population increased." That trend was under way long before World War II (choice C), and immigration from Ireland took place long before the change began (choice D). The best answer is that jobs were available in the cities, and that is where the population moved, whether up from the rural South to northern cities, into eastern cities from Eastern Europe and other foreign lands, or simply from the farms of the central states to the cities of the Midwest or West. Because of poor soil, the Dust Bowl of the 1930s, and increased industrialization, family farms failed regularly or were bought out by larger concerns, and those displaced people moved where the jobs were, making choice E another potential cause.

The Science Section

47 items, 85 minutes

Like the Social Studies section, the Science section will feature several sets of questions that may refer to a passage, a diagram, a table, and so on. Science items are likely to be multiple-choice, multiple-select response, or drag-and-drop. See page 4 for more about those formats.

Most Science questions will focus on these areas, with equal emphasis on physics, life sciences, and earth and space sciences:

» Matter and its interactions
» Force and motion
» Energy
» Waves
» Structures and processes of molecules and organisms
» Ecosystems
» Heredity and genetics
» Biological evolution
» Earth's systems
» Earth and the universe
» Human activity on Earth

Woven throughout the Science questions will be principles of science and engineering, including such concepts as cause and effect, system models, proportions, problem solving, and evaluating design solutions.

Here is an example of a drag-and-drop Science question based on a diagram. When you answer drag-and-drop questions in this book, you may simply draw lines to match answers to spaces. When you answer them on a computer-based test, you will drag and drop using a mouse or touch pad.

Look at the diagram. Then drag the tiles to the correct boxes.

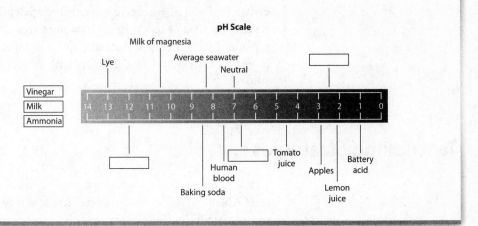

Correct Answer: ammonia, milk, vinegar. Milk is essentially neutral, lying typically between 6 and 7 on the pH scale. On this diagram, that places it near the middle. Ammonia is basic and should appear in the left-hand box at pH 12. Vinegar is acidic and should appear at pH 2.5.

Scoring the Test

On the TASC test, multiple-choice and gridded response items are each worth 1 score point. Multiple-response questions may be scored differently. In reading questions with a Part A and Part B, you must successfully answer Part B to get credit for the question as a whole.

The essay that you will write in the Language Arts–Writing section of the test is worth a total of 8 score points. Your essay will be read by two readers, each of whom will score it from 0 to 4 score points. If those readers each give your essay the same score, or if their scores differ by only one point, then the two scores will be added together for your final essay score. If the two scores differ by more than one point, a third reader will read and score your essay.

There is no penalty for wrong answers, so it is a good idea to try to answer every question, even if you have to guess. When you need to guess, try to eliminate one or more answer choices. The more choices you eliminate, the better your chance of picking the correct answer.

TASC test raw scores are converted to scaled scores through a statistical process. The scaling is done so that scores on each version of the test are equivalent to scores on all other versions. You will see your scaled scores on the score report that you receive. You will receive a scaled score in each of the five TASC test subject areas, as well as an English Language Arts score that is the average of your scores in Reading and Writing. You will also receive an overall scaled score that is an average of the five subject-area scores.

Passing scores are set for each TASC subject area test. To pass, you must achieve a scaled score of 500 on each section and at least 2 out of 8 on the essay. You will also receive a second score, called the College and Career Readiness (CCR) score, in each subject area. Based on statistical studies, a student who meets or exceeds the CCR passing score would be expected to earn a C or better in credit-bearing college courses in the relevant subject.

Test-Taking Strategies

Can you do anything to improve your chances of scoring well on the TASC test? Absolutely! The methods you use to study, prepare, and take the test can make all the difference.

You will receive scores for your computer-based test within 24 hours. Scores for paper-and-pencil test may take up to 10 business days.

Study Strategies

» **Know what to expect.** This book will help you recognize how the test will look, what the directions may be, and what kinds of questions you might see on the TASC test. "About the Test" on pages 7–16 shows you which topics are likely to appear on the TASC test.

» **Know where you stand.** Each of the subject review chapters in this book begins with a pretest. Take each pretest to see where you are right now. Did you test well in Reading but poorly in Mathematics? That means that you should spend your time reviewing math skills and concepts. The review sections in this book will help, but you should also plan to use old textbooks, books from the library, and online resources to improve your skills before you take the TASC test.

» **Test your improvement.** Once you have taken the pretests and reviewed the skills that you missed, take each of the full-length tests in Chapters 2 through 6. Time yourself so you are spending the correct amount of time on each section. Compare your work there to your scores on the pretests. Did you improve after your review? Do you need to review more before you take the TASC test? Do you need to keep better track of your time when you face the real thing?

Tips for Taking the Test

» **Answer all the questions, but go back if you have time.** Your time is limited on each section of the test, so try to answer each question as you go. If you have time at the end of the section, go back and double-check any questions that gave you trouble.

» **Use the process of elimination.** You might not know the right answer out of the four choices, but you can probably eliminate one or two just by using your head. Once you do that, your odds of choosing the right answer improve. There is no penalty for guessing, so guess if you must. If you do not guess, your odds of getting the answer right go down to zero.

» **Beware of answer choices that look reasonable but are not correct.** More than one of the multiple-choice options may look correct at first glance. Read carefully to make sure you are choosing the best answer.

Tips for Test Day

» **Sleep well.** The TASC test is long! You will have breaks during the day, but to do your best, you will need plenty of energy. Do not cram the night before. Plan to get a full night's sleep, with ample time for a good breakfast on the morning of the test.

» **Mark carefully.** If you are taking the pencil-and-paper test, fill in the answer ovals completely. Do not cross anything out, and erase any stray marks completely. Be sure that the answer space you are marking matches the number of the question you are answering. If you skip a question, skip the corresponding space on the answer sheet. Use your finger to track your place, if it helps.

» **Watch the time.** Wear a watch and check yourself from time to time. If you have timed yourself on the full-length tests, you should be pretty good at estimating the time you have left as you progress through the TASC test.

The TASC Language Arts–Reading Test

HOW TO USE THIS CHAPTER

» Read the Overview to learn what the TASC Language Arts–Reading Test covers.

» Take the TASC Language Arts–Reading Pretest to preview your knowledge and skills.

» Study the TASC Language Arts–Reading Test Review to refresh your knowledge of TASC test reading skills.

» Take the TASC Language Arts–Reading Practice Test to sharpen your skills and get ready for test day.

Overview

The TASC Language Arts–Reading Test is based on the Common Core English Language Arts State Standards, which you may review at http://www.corestandards.org/ELA-Literacy. The twelve standards for high school reading are as follows:

Key Ideas and Details

1. **CCSS.ELA-Literacy.CCRA.R.1** Read closely to determine what the text says explicitly and to make logical inferences from it; cite specific textual evidence when writing or speaking to support conclusions drawn from the text.
2. **CCSS.ELA-Literacy.CCRA.R.2** Determine central ideas or themes of a text and analyze their development; summarize the key supporting details and ideas.
3. **CCSS.ELA-Literacy.CCRA.R.3** Analyze how and why individuals, events, or ideas develop and interact over the course of a text.

LA·CC
Standards

Craft and Structure

4. **CCSS.ELA-Literacy.CCRA.R.4** Interpret words and phrases as they are used in a text, including determining technical, connotative, and figurative meanings, and analyze how specific word choices shape meaning or tone.
5. **CCSS.ELA-Literacy.CCRA.R.5** Analyze the structure of texts, including how specific sentences, paragraphs, and larger portions of the text (e.g., a section, chapter, scene, or stanza) relate to each other and the whole.
6. **CCSS.ELA-Literacy.CCRA.R.6** Assess how point of view or purpose shapes the content and style of a text.

Integration of Knowledge and Ideas

7. **CCSS.ELA-Literacy.CCRA.R.7** Integrate and evaluate content presented in diverse media and formats, including visually and quantitatively, as well as in words.
8. **CCSS.ELA-Literacy.CCRA.R.8** Delineate and evaluate the argument and specific claims in a text, including the validity of the reasoning as well as the relevance and sufficiency of the evidence.
9. **CCSS.ELA-Literacy.CCRA.R.9** Analyze how two or more texts address similar themes or topics in order to build knowledge or to compare the approaches the authors take.

Vocabulary Acquisition and Use

10. **CCSS.ELA-Literacy.CCRA.L.4** Determine or clarify the meaning of unknown and multiple-meaning words and phrases by using context clues, analyzing meaningful word parts, and consulting general and specialized reference materials, as appropriate.
11. **CCSS.ELA-Literacy.CCRA.L.5** Demonstrate understanding of figurative language, word relationships, and nuances in word meanings.
12. **CCSS.ELA-Literacy.CCRA.L.6** Acquire and use accurately a range of general academic and domain-specific words and phrases sufficient for reading, writing, speaking, and listening at the college and career readiness level; demonstrate independence in gathering vocabulary knowledge when encountering an unknown term important to comprehension or expression.

You can expect to see questions on the TASC test in any and all of these areas. The Standards ask you to exhibit the capacities of a literate reader, using these skills:

1. Reading closely and citing textual evidence
2. Determining central themes and ideas
3. Analyzing text structure and development
4. Interpreting and analyzing words and phrases
5. Assessing author's point of view and purpose
6. Evaluating content from diverse media
7. Evaluating arguments, claims, and evidence

TASC Language Arts–Reading Pretest

Use the items that follow to preview your knowledge of reading concepts and skills. Answers appear on page 29.

Read this text. Then answer the questions.

Excerpt from *Life on the Mississippi*

Mark Twain (Samuel Clemens)

The Mississippi is well worth reading about. It is not a commonplace river, but on the contrary is in all ways remarkable. Considering the Missouri its main branch, it is the longest river in the world—four thousand three hundred miles. It seems safe to say that it is also the crookedest river in the world, since in one part of its journey it uses up one thousand three hundred miles to cover the same ground that the crow would fly over in six hundred and seventy-five. It discharges three times as much water as the St. Lawrence, twenty-five times as much as the Rhine, and three hundred and thirty-eight times as much as the Thames. No other river has so vast a drainage-basin: it draws its water supply from twenty-eight States and Territories; from Delaware, on the Atlantic seaboard, and from all the country between that and Idaho on the Pacific slope—a spread of forty-five degrees of longitude. The Mississippi receives and carries to the Gulf water from fifty-four subordinate rivers that are navigable by steamboats, and from some hundreds that are navigable by flats and keels . . .

It is a remarkable river in this: that instead of widening toward its mouth, it grows narrower; grows narrower and deeper. From the junction of the Ohio to a point half way down to the sea, the width averages a mile in high water: thence to the sea the width steadily diminishes, until, at the 'Passes,' above the mouth, it is but little over half a mile. At the junction of the Ohio the Mississippi's depth is eighty-seven feet; the depth increases gradually, reaching one hundred and twenty-nine just above the mouth . . .

An article in the New Orleans 'Times-Democrat,' based upon reports of able engineers, states that the river annually empties four hundred and six million tons of mud into the Gulf of Mexico—which brings to mind Captain Marryat's rude name for the Mississippi—'the Great Sewer.' This mud, solidified, would make a mass a mile square and two hundred and forty-one feet high.

The Mississippi is remarkable in still another way—its disposition to make prodigious jumps by cutting through narrow necks of land, and thus straightening and shortening itself. More than once it has shortened itself thirty miles at a single jump! These cut-offs have had curious effects: they have thrown several river towns out into the rural districts, and built up sand bars and forests in front of them. The town of Delta used to be three miles below Vicksburg: a recent cutoff has radically changed the position, and Delta is now two miles above Vicksburg.

Both of these river towns have been retired to the country by that cut-off. A cut-off plays havoc with boundary lines and jurisdictions: for instance, a man is living in the State of Mississippi to-day, a cut-off occurs to-night, and to-morrow the man finds himself and his land over on the other side of the river, within the boundaries and subject to the laws of the State of Louisiana! Such a thing, happening in the upper river in the old times, could have transferred a slave from Missouri to Illinois and made a free man of him.

1. Which of these statements from the text supports the idea that the Mississippi River is exceptional?
   Ⓐ It has changed the location of several towns from riverside to rural.
   Ⓑ It is eighty-seven feet deep at the junction of the Ohio River.
   Ⓒ It is half a mile wide in the area near the "Passes."
   Ⓓ It empties into the Gulf of Mexico.

2. Read this excerpt from the text.

   The Mississippi receives and carries to the Gulf water from fifty-four subordinate rivers that are navigable by steamboats, and from some hundreds that are navigable by flats and keels.

   As used in the passage, the word *navigable* is closest in meaning to
   Ⓐ seafaring
   Ⓑ dark blue
   Ⓒ passable
   Ⓓ blocked

3. Read this excerpt from the text.

   A cut-off plays havoc with boundary lines and jurisdictions: for instance, a man is living in the State of Mississippi to-day, a cut-off occurs to-night, and to-morrow the man finds himself and his land over on the other side of the river, within the boundaries and subject to the laws of the State of Louisiana! Such a thing, happening in the upper river in the old times, could have transferred a slave from Missouri to Illinois and made a free man of him.

   Why does the author write that "Such a thing, happening in the upper river in the old times, could have transferred a slave from Missouri to Illinois and made a free man of him"?
   Ⓐ to explain that the river passes through both slave and free territory
   Ⓑ to show that the river's cut-offs could have a dramatic effect
   Ⓒ to stress that he is writing after the end of the Civil War
   Ⓓ to make an implicit criticism of slavery

4. What detail from the text tells you that the Mississippi River is exceptionally crooked?

   (A) Its depth increases gradually from eighty-seven to one hundred and twenty-nine feet.

   (B) It discharges twenty-five times as much water as the Rhine.

   (C) One part of it is over twice as long as it would be as the crow flies.

   (D) It draws its water from twenty-eight states and territories.

5. The author mentions Captain Marryat, who calls the Mississippi River "the Great Sewer." This phrase refers to

   (A) the remarkable amount of mud the river discharges

   (B) the fact that the river is unusually polluted

   (C) the lack of respect that river captains have for the river

   (D) the idea that people discharge a remarkable amount of sewage into the river

6. Read this excerpt from the text.

   The Mississippi is remarkable in still another way—its disposition to make prodigious jumps by cutting through narrow necks of land, and thus straightening and shortening itself.

   The author uses the word *prodigious* to show

   (A) his bewilderment at the river's twists and turns

   (B) his concern for the river's unpredictability

   (C) his fear of the river's instability

   (D) his admiration for the river's jumps

7. The author creates a picture of a remarkable river by

   (A) showing the causes and effects of the river's size

   (B) providing facts and examples about the river

   (C) explaining the problems the river has created

   (D) describing the beauty of the river and its surroundings

Read this poem. Then answer the questions.

Excerpt from *Poems, Three Series, Complete*

Emily Dickinson

VI.

If you were coming in the fall,
I'd brush the summer by
With half a smile and half a spurn,
As housewives do a fly.

If I could see you in a year,
I'd wind the months in balls,
And put them each in separate drawers,
Until their time befalls.

If only centuries delayed,
I'd count them on my hand,
Subtracting till my fingers dropped
Into Van Diemen's land.

If certain, when this life was out,
That yours and mine should be,
I'd toss it yonder like a rind,
And taste eternity.

But now, all ignorant of the length
Of time's uncertain wing,
It goads me, like the goblin bee,
That will not state its sting.

8. Why does the poet start four of the poem's stanzas with the word *if*?

   (A) to ask a question about why the beloved has gone
   (B) to show the randomness of life
   (C) to stress the uncertainty of the beloved's return
   (D) to reveal the unpredictability of love

9. Select two major themes of the poem.

   (A) heaven
   (B) separation
   (C) fear
   (D) insects
   (E) time
   (F) rebirth

10. How does the tone of the last stanza differ from the previous four stanzas?

   (A) It is more unsure and chilling.
   (B) It is dreamier and happier.
   (C) It is more anticipatory.
   (D) It is less unhappy.

11. Reread the final stanza.

> But now, all ignorant of the length
> Of time's uncertain wing,
> It goads me, like the goblin bee,
> That will not state its sting.

In what way is time like a "goblin bee"? Explain in your own words what the poet means by using this simile. Write your answer in the box.

12. Over the five stanzas, the speaker becomes

Ⓐ comfortable

Ⓑ impatient

Ⓒ calm

Ⓓ indifferent

13. The person whom the speaker addresses is

Ⓐ herself

Ⓑ someone who is threatened by bees

Ⓒ someone she loves who is away

Ⓓ someone who has died

Read this text. Then answer the questions.

Tulip Mania!

Diane Zahler

We're used to considering certain objects valuable —works by well-known artists, for example, or diamonds, designer clothing, and cars made by a handful of specialized companies. But for a brief, outrageous time in the 1600s, there was a commodity considered so valuable it was almost priceless: tulips.

Tulips came to Europe from Turkey in the 1550s, when the Sultan of Turkey sent tulip bulbs, from which the flowers grow, to Vienna. The colorful flowers took well to the cold northern climate, and almost immediately Europeans, and especially the Dutch, went wild for them. To the Dutch, tulips became a symbol of the new and the exciting.

The delicate, beautiful blooms became a kind of currency. Bulbs of new kinds of tulips could fetch absurdly high prices. The most popular tulips in the 1630s were those with streaks or stripes on their petals. The Dutch didn't know it, but those stripes were caused by a virus. The virus weakened the plant, making it less likely to bloom well in years to come. Although these bulbs were the most valuable, they also became the least likely to pay off in beautiful flowers or future sales. The value of these exotic flowers rose and rose, and the bulbs themselves became a kind of money. Merchants of all sorts became involved in the tulip trade, and speculation, in which buyers purchase risky investments that present the possibility of large profits, but also pose a higher-than-average possibility of loss, caused prices to rise still more. There was a report in 1635 of a sale of 40 tulip bulbs bought for 100,000 florins. That was nearly ten times what a skilled laborer would earn in a year.

In that year, the tulip trade changed. Up until then, tulips were bought and sold in summer, after the flower had bloomed. The bulb would be dug from the ground, wrapped up, and kept dry and safe indoors. Sellers sold the bulbs when they were dug up, and buyers paid for them when they were delivered. However, in 1635, sellers began to sell tulips by weight while the bulbs were still in the ground, with a note for the buyer describing the bulb, including its weight at planting and when it would be dug up. Only the paper notes were sold; the bulbs themselves could not be delivered for months to come. This "futures market" in tulips resulted in the paper notes being sold and resold, always at higher prices. People began to wonder if the bulbs would actually be worth the money they were costing. At the same time, tulip farmers were planting more and more bulbs, which made the tulips worth less money, as they were becoming less rare.

The combination of investor worry and an oversupply of tulips led the tulip market to crash in February of 1637. The price of tulips could go no higher. Most tulips that ended up actually being sold were purchased for about five percent of what had been promised, and many merchants were utterly ruined. Tulip mania, a bizarre and short-lived phenomenon, was over.

14.

Part A

Which word <u>best</u> describes the tulips as portrayed in the passage?

Ⓐ overvalued
Ⓑ hardy
Ⓒ scarce
Ⓓ profitable

Part B

Which detail <u>best</u> supports your response to Part A?

Ⓐ To the Dutch, tulips became a symbol of the new and the exciting.
Ⓑ There was a report in 1635 of a sale of 40 tulip bulbs bought for 100,000 florins.
Ⓒ The most popular tulips in the 1630s were those with streaks or stripes on their petals.
Ⓓ Sellers sold the bulbs when they were dug up, and buyers paid for them when they were delivered.

15. The Dutch created an exaggerated market for tulip bulbs because

 Ⓐ they had no currency of their own

 Ⓑ they had always valued flowers over money

 Ⓒ they were drawn to the newness and excitement of tulips

 Ⓓ there were few markets for their other goods

16. Read this excerpt from the text.

> However, in 1635, sellers began to sell tulips by weight while the bulbs were still in the ground, with a note for the buyer describing the bulb, including its weight at planting and when it would be dug up. Only the paper notes were sold; the bulbs themselves could not be delivered for months to come. This "futures market" in tulips resulted in the paper notes being sold and resold, always at higher prices.

Based on the passage, what is a "futures market"?

 Ⓐ the sale of something that will be available in the future

 Ⓑ selling something that will be paid for in the future

 Ⓒ a flower market that will be set up in the future

 Ⓓ a store where people arrange to pay in the future

17. Which of these events led to the eventual crash of the tulip market?

 Ⓐ Tulips were bought and sold in summer.

 Ⓑ There was an oversupply of tulips.

 Ⓒ Many merchants were ruined.

 Ⓓ Tulips sold for five percent of what they had been worth.

18. The author's use of the words *outrageous*, *bizarre*, and *absurdly* shows that she thinks

 Ⓐ tulip mania is amusing

 Ⓑ tulips are worthless

 Ⓒ tulip mania is baffling

 Ⓓ the Dutch are interesting

19. Read this excerpt from the text.

> But for a brief time in the 1600s, there was a commodity considered so valuable it was almost priceless: tulips.

Based on this sentence, what does the word *commodity* mean?

Ⓐ ordinarily
Ⓑ money
Ⓒ sale
Ⓓ product

20. The third and fourth paragraphs of the text explain how

Ⓐ the Dutch became so fond of tulips
Ⓑ greed contributed to the overvaluing of tulips
Ⓒ people began to doubt the worth of tulips
Ⓓ tulips came to northern Europe

This is the end of the TASC Language Arts–Reading Pretest.

TASC Language Arts–Reading Pretest Answers

1. **A** Review 1. Read Closely to Make Inferences, Cite Evidence, and Draw Conclusions (pp. 30–32).

2. **C** Review 10. Determine Word Meanings (pp. 47–48).

3. **B** Review 6. Assess Point of View or Purpose (pp. 39–41).

4. **C** Review 2. Determine Themes or Central Ideas; Summarize Supporting Details and Ideas (pp. 32–34).

5. **A** Review 1. Read Closely to Make Inferences, Cite Evidence, and Draw Conclusions (pp. 30–32).

6. **D** Review 4. Interpret and Analyze Words and Phrases (pp. 35–37).

7. **B** Review 8. Delineate and Evaluate Argument and Claims in a Text (p. 44).

8. **C** Review 6. Assess Point of View or Purpose (pp. 39–41).

9. **B and E** Review 2. Determine Themes or Central Ideas; Summarize Supporting Details and Ideas (pp. 32–34).

10. **A** Review 5. Analyze the Structure of Texts (pp. 37–39).

11. **Possible answer: Time is like a goblin bee because it torments and can harm the speaker.** Review 11. Understand Figurative Language, Word Relationships, and Nuances (pp. 48–50).

12. **B** Review 3. Analyze How and Why Individuals, Events, or Ideas Develop and Interact (pp. 34–35).

13. **C** Review 1. Read Closely to Make Inferences, Cite Evidence, and Draw Conclusions (pp. 30–32).

14. **Part A: A; Part B: B** Review 2. Determine Themes or Central Ideas; Summarize Supporting Details and Ideas (pp. 32–34).

15. **C** Review 1. Read Closely to Make Inferences, Cite Evidence, and Draw Conclusions (pp. 30–32).

16. **A** Review 4. Interpret and Analyze Words and Phrases (pp. 35–37).

17. **B** Review 3. Analyze How and Why Individuals, Events, or Ideas Develop and Interact (pp. 34–35).

18. **C** Review 6. Assess Point of View or Purpose (pp. 39–41).

19. **D** Review 12. Use Academic and Domain-Specific Words and Phrases (pp. 50–51).

20. **B** Review 5. Analyze the Structure of Texts (pp. 37–39).

TASC Language Arts–Reading Test Review

The pages that follow briefly review each of the twelve Common Core State Standards listed in the Overview. To learn more about each standard, look online at www.corestandards.org.

 ## Read Closely to Make Inferences, Cite Evidence, and Draw Conclusions

Reading closely means looking carefully at the author's words to determine what the text is about.

KEY TERMS: conclusions, evidence, inferences

Inferences

You make inferences all the time. When you hear a fire truck siren, you infer that there is a fire somewhere. When people in an audience get to their feet, clapping, you infer that they liked the performance. When you read to make an inference for the TASC test, follow these steps:

1. Look closely at information in the text.
2. Ask yourself, "What does it mean?"
3. Use the information you have to make an educated guess.

Monique was pale and trembling, and every time thunder cracked, she jumped.

INFERENCE: Monique is afraid of storms.

Evidence

When you make an inference from your reading, you must be able to support it with evidence. **Evidence** includes **facts**, **reasons**, and **examples**.

Superstorm Sandy did terrible damage on the East Coast. Over 8 million people lost power in the storm.

EVIDENCE: Over 8 million people lost power.

Conclusions

A **conclusion** is similar to an inference. It is an educated guess that is supported by evidence and by your own experience. To draw a conclusion from your reading, follow these steps:

1. Look closely at the evidence in your reading.
2. Apply your own experience or knowledge.
3. Make an educated guess based on the information you have gathered.

Evidence: Over 8 million people lost power in Superstorm Sandy. My own experience: It's hard to live and work without power.

CONCLUSION: Millions of people had trouble living and working during Superstorm Sandy.

CHALLENGE

Read Closely to Make Inferences, Cite Evidence, and Draw Conclusions

Read the passage. Then choose the word or phrase that makes each sentence true.

From *In the Maine Woods*

Henry David Thoreau

The note of the white-throated sparrow, a very inspiriting but almost wiry sound, was the first heard in the morning, and with this all the woods rang. This was the prevailing bird in the northern part of Maine. The forest generally was all alive with them at this season, and they were proportionally numerous and musical about Bangor. They evidently breed in that State. Though commonly unseen, their simple ah, te-te-te, te-te-te, te-te-te, so sharp and piercing, was as distinct to the ear as the passage of a spark of fire shot into the darkest of the forest would be to the eye. I thought that they commonly uttered it as they flew. I hear this note for a few days only in the spring, as they go through Concord, and in the fall see them again going southward, but then they are mute. We were commonly aroused by their lively strain very early. What a glorious time they must have in that wilderness, far from mankind and election day!

1. The author's evidence that the bird singing is a white-throated sparrow is **(its sound/ its appearance)**.

2. When the author says, *What a glorious time they must have in that wilderness, far from mankind and election day!* you can infer that he **(prefers/does not prefer)** the wilderness.

3. From the information the author provides about nature, you can conclude that his feelings about nature are **(negative/positive)**.

CHALLENGE ANSWERS

Read Closely to Make Inferences, Cite Evidence, and Draw Conclusions

1. **its sound:** The author writes that the bird is "commonly unseen."

2. **prefers:** The author calls the wilderness "glorious," implying that he prefers it.

3. **positive:** The author seems to enjoy gathering and possessing his knowledge; someone who enjoys getting information about something generally feels positive about it.

Determine Themes or Central Ideas; Summarize Supporting Details and Ideas

Finding the theme or central idea in a text gives you more information about what the text is about and why it is important.

KEY TERMS: central idea, summarize, supporting details, theme

Theme

The **theme** of a text is the overall idea that the author wants readers to understand. Often the theme will convey a deeper meaning about the human experience. Sometimes the theme is stated directly, as in a fable by Aesop where the theme is the story's moral. More often, the theme is implied. To identify the theme, follow these steps:

1. Think about the characters' actions and words.
2. Think about the events of the work.
3. Ask, "What message or idea does the author want to convey?"

COMMON THEMES: the power of love, the importance of family, sacrifice can bring rewards, death is part of life

---

Central Ideas

The **central idea**, or main idea, of a paragraph or text is its most important idea. You can determine a central idea by asking, "What is this paragraph or text mostly about?"

Supporting Details

Supporting details are those details that help explain the main idea. Supporting details can include the following:

» Facts and statistics
» Evidence
» Examples
» Anecdotes
» Descriptions

Summarize

A **summary** of a text is a brief statement that includes its most important details. When you summarize a work, follow these steps:

1. Find the main idea of the text.
2. Find the details in the text that are necessary to understanding the main idea.
3. Include the main idea and the important details in your summary.

The red panda is very different from the black-and-white panda bear we usually imagine when we hear the word *panda*. In fact, it's not even a bear. It is more closely related to raccoons, weasels, and skunks.

MAIN IDEA: The red panda is not the same as the panda bear.

SUPPORTING DETAILS: It is closely related to raccoons, weasels, and skunks.

SUMMARY: The red panda is not a bear. It is closely related to raccoons, weasels, and skunks.

CHALLENGE

Determine Themes or Central Ideas; Summarize Supporting Details and Ideas

Read the passage. Then answer the question or choose the word or phrase that makes each sentence true.

Dying of Thirst

It's easy enough to say, "I'm dying of thirst!" In many places around the globe, though, people actually are dying for lack of clean drinking water. About 1 out of every 6 people in the world do not have enough access to clean water. Dirty water causes diseases such as diarrhea, which kills thousands of children every day. One of the greatest challenges of the twenty-first century is providing enough water for the needs of Earth's people.

1. Which sentence states the central idea of the passage? Underline it.

2. One supporting detail in the passage is found in the **(first/third)** sentence.

3. In a summary, you would NOT include the **(first/fourth)** sentence.

4. You could state the theme of this passage as **(water is vital to life/people do not have access to clean water)**.

CHALLENGE ANSWERS
Determine Themes or Central Ideas;
Summarize Supporting Details and Ideas

1. One of the greatest challenges of the twenty-first century is providing enough water for the needs of Earth's people.

2. third: The third sentence includes facts and statistics that support the main idea.

3. first: The first sentence is not necessary to understanding the main idea.

4. water is vital to life: This statement conveys a deeper meaning about human experience.

Analyze How and Why Individuals, Events, or Ideas Develop and Interact

As a text progresses, it is important to figure out exactly what is happening and why. On the TASC test, you might be asked to explain the order of events and how events build or change.

KEY TERM: sequence of events

Sequence of Events

Many texts are organized by time order. The **sequence of events** in a text is the order in which events take place. In a nonfiction text, the sequence might include steps in a process. In a fiction text, the sequence of events would be the actions that occur as part of the plot. Sequence is sometimes indicated by time-order words, such as *first, next, then, last,* and *finally.* When you determine the sequence of events for the TASC test, look for time-order words that tell you the order of events.

To delete cookies, which allow websites to identify your computer, you should first search the drive for a folder labeled "cookies." When you find it, open the folder and look for files that read *user@sitename.* Next, highlight those cookies you want to delete. Finally, hit the "delete" button.

SEQUENCE OF EVENTS
1. Find the "cookies" folder.
2. Open the folder.
3. Find the cookies files.
4. Highlight them.
5. Press "delete."

Analyze How and Why Individuals, Events, or Ideas Develop and Interact

Read the passage. Then choose the word or phrase that makes each sentence true.

The Seventeen-Year Cicada

Every seventeen years, summer nights become horrifically noisy in certain places in the eastern United States. The seventeen-year cicadas emerge, live their brief lives, reproduce, and die. These insects hatch out as nymphs, then burrow underground, where they feed on tree roots, growing slowly over the years. Then in early spring of the seventeenth year, they begin to tunnel upward. When the soil reaches 63 degrees Fahrenheit, the insects emerge, all at the same time. They climb upward into the vegetation, mate, and finally, within six weeks, all die.

1. The final event in this sequence is the cicadas' **(tunneling/mating/death)**.

2. The author develops the events to explain **(the cicada life cycle/the impact of the cicada)**.

CHALLENGE ANSWERS

Analyze How and Why Individuals, Events, or Ideas Develop and Interact

1. **death:** The author uses the time-order word *finally* to show the last event in the cicada life cycle.

2. **the cicada life cycle:** The author mentions the effect of the cicadas' noise, but the main purpose of the passage is to explain the cicada life cycle.

 Interpret and Analyze Words and Phrases

The way authors use language can help you understand the texts you read. On the TASC test, you might be asked to identify forms of figurative language or specific word meanings.

KEY TERMS: connotative, figurative, tone

Figurative Language

Figurative language is words or phrases that describe one thing in terms of another. Figurative language is not meant to be understood literally. Instead, it uses comparison to create unusual, imaginative descriptions. When you interpret figurative language for the TASC test, think about what is being compared and what the comparison tells you.

» Simile: a comparison using *like* or *as*

Example: *My love is like a red, red rose.*

» Metaphor: a comparison that does not use *like* or *as*

Example: *All the world's a stage.*

» Personification: a comparison giving a nonhuman thing human qualities

Example: *Death be not proud.*

Connotation

Connotative language includes all the meanings, emotions, and associations that a word suggests. A word's dictionary definition is its denotation. Its **connotation** includes emotions and linked meanings.

Word: home

DENOTATION: the place where someone lives

CONNOTATION: the place where someone feels a sense of belonging, peace, family, even happiness

---

Tone

The **tone** of a text is the attitude a writer takes toward the reader, the subject, or a character. The writer expresses tone through word choice and details. Possible tones include *humorous, angry, sarcastic, sentimental, matter-of-fact, compassionate, playful.* When you analyze a writer's tone for the TASC test, think about how the writer reveals what he or she feels.

It wasn't easy being the worst goalie in the history of the game of soccer, but Marnie managed it almost effortlessly.

TONE: humorous

CHALLENGE Interpret and Analyze Words and Phrases

Read the poem. Then choose the word or phrase that makes each sentence true.

Excerpt from "Rhapsody on a Windy Night"

T. S. Eliot

Twelve o'clock.
Along the reaches of the street
Held in a lunar synthesis,
Whispering lunar incantations
Dissolve the floors of memory
And all its clear relations,
Its divisions and precisions,
Every street lamp that I pass
Beats like a fatalistic drum,
And through the spaces of the dark
Midnight shakes the memory
As a madman shakes a dead geranium.

1. The type of figurative language in the ninth line is **(personification/simile)**.

2. One connotation of the word *whispering* is **(secrecy/speech)**.

3. The poet's tone is **(whimsical/uneasy)**.

CHALLENGE ANSWERS

Interpret and Analyze Words and Phrases

1. simile: The author compares streetlights to drums, using the word *like*.

2. secrecy: The word *whispering* means "speaking softly," but it suggests secrecy.

3. uneasy: The author uses menacing words such as *fatalistic* and *madman*, creating an uneasy tone.

 ## Analyze the Structure of Texts

The parts of texts, such as sentences, paragraphs, chapters, stanzas, or acts, contribute to the text as a whole. Understanding how the parts of texts, including arguments, are organized can help you understand the whole text.

KEY TERMS: argument, structure

Argument

An **argument** is a written work that includes the following:

» A claim or statement the author wants to prove
» Supporting evidence that is relevant and verifiable
» An explanation of how the evidence supports the claim
» Counterarguments that acknowledge differing claims

When you analyze an argument for the TASC test, think about the author's claim and how it is supported.

One of the greatest threats to elephant survival is the black market in ivory, which is taken from the elephants' tusks. While ivory trading was banned in 1989, there are huge numbers of elephants killed by poachers for their tusks. This practice must be stopped.

CLAIM: One of the greatest threats to elephant survival is the black market in ivory, which is taken from the elephants' tusks.

EVIDENCE: Huge numbers of elephants are killed by poachers for their tusks.

Structure

Recognizing the way an author has structured a text can help you understand it more fully. The **structure** of an informational text is based on its method of organization. Methods of organization include the following:

» Cause/effect
» Comparison/contrast
» Problem/solution
» Sequence of events

The **structure** of a fictional text is the way the author has organized the plot. It includes the following:

» The exposition, or introduction
» The rising action
» The climax, or point of greatest excitement or suspense
» The falling action
» The resolution, which may be comedic (funny) or tragic (sad)

When you analyze the structure of a work for the TASC test, consider its organization and how it helps convey the author's ideas.

When most people picture elephants, they see an image of the African elephant, with its enormous, floppy ears and thick tusks. There is another species of the animal, though—the Asian elephant. The biggest difference between the two animals is the size and shape of their ears, with the African elephant's ears being much larger, reaching farther up its head.

STRUCTURE: compare/contrast

CHALLENGE Analyze the Structure of Texts

Read the passage. Then answer the question or choose the word or phrase that makes each sentence true.

I Sing the Auto Electric

It's vitally important that people start buying more electric cars. This will help us become less dependent on oil imports and will reduce the amount of carbon dioxide we put into the atmosphere. However, many consumers say that one of the things that keeps them from purchasing an electric car is the difficulty of finding a place to charge its battery. One way to address this problem is by installing free or low-charge personal charging stations in homes, or by providing tax breaks so people can afford their own.

1. Which sentence states the author's claim? Underline it.

2. The structure the author uses is **(comparison–contrast/problem–solution)**.

CHALLENGE ANSWERS

Analyze the Structure of Texts

1. It's vitally important that people start buying more electric cars.

2. **problem–solution:** The author describes a problem people have with electric cars and proposes a solution.

 ## Assess Point of View or Purpose

Being able to identify an author's attitude and reason for writing can help you figure out the meaning of the text. On the TASC test, you might be asked to identify aspects of a text's style and content.

KEY TERMS: irony, point of view, purpose, sarcasm, satire, style, understatement

Point of View

The author's **point of view** is his or her attitude toward the subject. An author may express point of view directly by stating opinions or indirectly through word choice and tone. Authors may reveal their point of view through satire, sarcasm, irony, or understatement. When you consider an author's point of view for the TASC test, think about the author's attitude and how he or she reveals it.

Satire	Writing that makes fun of human weakness, often in an attempt to change behavior
Sarcasm	Writing that is sharp, biting, or cutting; often humorous in effect
Irony	A difference between what is expected and what is real. There are three kinds of irony: • Verbal irony, in which a speaker says something but means the opposite • Situational irony, in which something occurs that is the opposite of what is expected or what is appropriate • Dramatic irony, in which the audience or reader knows something that a character doesn't know
Understatement	Writing that deliberately makes an event or situation seem less serious than it is

Purpose

An author's **purpose** is his or her reason for writing. Common purposes include:

» To inform
» To entertain
» To persuade

Authors may have more than one purpose for writing. For example, an editorial writer might want to persuade readers to think a certain way and to entertain them, too.

Ladies and gentlemen, we are here today to celebrate the work of the Brother and Sister Organization—and to raise money for it. This worthy group has helped thousands of young people by matching them with adult mentors who can help them navigate their way through school, work, and life. And we want the organization to keep doing its good work.

PURPOSE: to inform, entertain, and persuade

Style

A writer's **style** is the way he or she chooses words and puts sentences and paragraphs together. Style includes several elements.

ELEMENT OF STYLE	SENTENCE STRUCTURE	WORD CHOICE	TONE	VOICE	MECHANICS
Definition	The length of sentences, the variety of sentence types, and the order of words within sentences	The choice of formal or informal words, the connotations of words chosen, and the use of figurative language	The attitude toward the subject	The sound of the author's words	The choice of punctuation

CHALLENGE Assess Point of View or Purpose

Read the passage. Then choose the word or phrase that makes each sentence true.

Excerpt from "How the Animals of the Wood Sent Out a Scientific Expedition"

Mark Twain

Once the creatures of the forest held a great convention and appointed a commission consisting of the most illustrious scientists among them to go forth, clear beyond the forest and out into the unknown and unexplored world, to verify the truth of the matters already taught in their schools and colleges and also to make discoveries. It was the most imposing enterprise of the kind the nation had ever embarked in. True, the government had once sent Dr. Bull Frog, with a picked crew, to hunt for a northwesterly passage through the swamp to the right-hand corner of the wood, and had since sent out many expeditions to hunt for Dr. Bull Frog; but they never could find him, and so government finally gave him up and ennobled his mother to show its gratitude for the services her son had rendered to science. And once government sent Sir Grass Hopper to hunt for the sources of the rill that emptied into the swamp; and afterward sent out many expeditions to hunt for Sir Grass, and at last they were successful—they found his body, but if he had discovered the sources meantime, he did not let on. So government acted handsomely by deceased, and many envied his funeral.

1. The author uses (**satire/understatement**) to reveal his point of view.

2. The author's purpose is to (**persuade/inform/entertain**).

3. The author's tone is (**serious/humorous**).

CHALLENGE ANSWERS

Assess Point of View or Purpose

1. **satire:** The author is making fun of scientific expeditions by describing an expedition of animals.

2. **entertain:** The passage doesn't include information or try to persuade. It is amusing and is intended to entertain.

3. **humorous:** The author uses satire to amuse and entertain the reader.

7 Evaluate Content Presented in Diverse Media and Formats

It is important to be able to read, judge, and understand content in a variety of formats, from book to magazine to website.

KEY TERMS: evaluate, format

Evaluate

When you **evaluate** text and media, you judge its value, quality, and importance. To evaluate informative text or other media, ask yourself these questions:

» Is this source reliable? If the content appears biased or inaccurate, you can't be sure that the information you are reading is true.
» Is this source consistent? If you don't know whether you can trust the source, you can't rely on its evidence.
» Is this source up-to-date? If you are gathering facts and statistics, you want a source to be as recent as possible.

To evaluate multiple versions of a story, drama, or poem, ask yourself these questions:

» How are the versions similar? How are they different?
» How do the versions relate to the original source?

Top Ten Cities in the United States by Population, 2000

RANK	CITY	POPULATION
1	New York, NY	8,008,279
2	Los Angeles, CA	3,694,820
3	Chicago, IL	2,896,016
4	Houston, TX	1,953,631
5	Philadelphia, PA	1,517,550
6	Phoenix, AZ	1,321,045
7	San Diego, CA	1,223,400
8	Dallas, TX	1,188,580
9	San Antonio, TX	1,144,646
10	Detroit, MI	951,270

EVALUATION: The statistics are out of date. A census is taken every ten years, so there must have been another census since 2000, and more recent figures must be available.

Format

The **format** of a work is the structure in which it is presented. Format might include the following:

>> Novels
>> Short stories
>> Plays
>> Poetry
>> Charts
>> Tables
>> Diagrams
>> Maps
>> Websites

When you read a work for the TASC test, it might appear in any of these formats.

CHALLENGE Evaluate Content Presented in Diverse Media and Formats

Read the passage. Then choose the word or phrase that makes each sentence true.

Anneliese Watkins would be a terrible choice for Supervisor. She has been on the Town Board for only two years, which is obviously not enough time for her to get to know the problems our town faces. Her background as a lawyer is not appropriate for the position, and since she has missed two meetings, it is clear she is not committed to the town.

1. A word in the editorial that helps you evaluate its content is (**terrible/background**).

2. The content of the editorial appears to be (**unbiased/biased**).

CHALLENGE ANSWERS

Evaluate Content Presented in Diverse Media and Formats

1. **terrible:** The word *terrible* is emotional, is not rational, and is not supported by facts or evidence.

2. **biased:** The author clearly has strong feelings against the subject that aren't well supported.

Delineate and Evaluate Argument and Claims in a Text

Many nonfiction and informative works are written as arguments. They present a claim and support it with reasons, facts, and evidence. You may be asked to explain and evaluate, or judge, the strength of an argument on the TASC test.

KEY TERM: premise

Premise

The **premise** of an argument is the claim that forms the basis of an argument. To find an argument's premise, ask yourself, "What is the author claiming?"

A recent study showed that young people from ages 8 to 18 spend an average of 7.5 hours a day on electronic media. As people spend more and more time on electronic media, their attention spans grow shorter.

PREMISE: People's attention spans shorten as they spend more time on electronic media.

CHALLENGE Delineate and Evaluate Argument and Claims in a Text

Read the passage. Then answer the question or choose the word or phrase that makes each sentence true.

Malaria, a disease transmitted by mosquitoes, is one of the most serious health threats in the world. In 2010, it infected more than 200 million people, and more than a million died from it. Many of them were children. It is vital that we fund anti-malaria programs as fully as possible so we can keep working toward control of this disease.

1. Which sentence states the premise of the argument? Underline it.

2. The argument is supported by **(facts/opinions)**.

CHALLENGE ANSWERS
Delineate and Evaluate Argument and Claims in a Text

1. It is vital that we fund anti-malaria programs as fully as possible so we can keep working toward control of this disease.

2. facts: The argument includes the number of people infected and the number who died.

⑨ Analyze How Two or More Texts Address Similar Themes or Topics

On the TASC test, you may be asked to look at two or more texts that have similar themes or topics. You can compare them, or find the similarities, and contrast them, or find the differences. To do this, you should look closely at the elements of the texts to determine the approaches the authors take.

KEY TERM: rhetorical features

Rhetorical Features

A work's **rhetorical features** are the aspects of its style and structure that make it unique. Look back at points 5 and 6 to find definitions of style and structure. When you analyze two or more works, it is helpful to look at their rhetorical features and ask yourself, "What makes this work unique?"

Editorial from *The North Star*

Frederick Douglass

THE RIGHTS OF WOMEN.—One of the most interesting events of the past week, was the holding of what is technically styled a Woman's Rights Convention at Seneca Falls. The speaking, addresses, and resolutions of this extraordinary meeting were almost wholly conducted by women; and although they evidently felt themselves in a novel position, it is but simple justice to say that their whole proceedings were characterized by marked ability and dignity. No one present, we think, however much he might be disposed to differ from the views advanced by the leading speakers on that occasion, will fail to give them credit for brilliant talents and excellent dispositions. In this meeting, as in other deliberative assemblies, there were frequent differences of opinion and animated discussion; but in no case was there the slightest absence of good feeling and decorum.

> **RHETORICAL FEATURES:** The text structure is an editorial. Its style is formal, with long sentences and an admiring tone.

Analyze How Two or More Texts Address Similar Themes or Topics

Read the passages. Then choose the word or phrase that makes each sentence true.

Excerpt from *Paul Revere's Three Accounts of His Famous Ride*

Paul Revere

I returned at Night thro Charlestown; there I agreed with a Col. Conant, and some other Gentlemen, that if the British went out by Water, we would shew two Lanthorns in the North Church Steeple; and if by Land, one, as a Signal; for we were aprehensive it would be difficult to Cross the Charles River, or git over Boston neck.

Excerpt from "The Midnight Ride of Paul Revere"

Henry Wadsworth Longfellow

He said to his friend, "If the British march
By land or sea from the town to-night,
Hang a lantern aloft in the belfry-arch
Of the North Church tower as a signal light,—
One, if by land, and two, if by sea;
And I on the opposite shore will be,
Ready to ride and spread the alarm
Through every Middlesex village and farm,
For the country folk to be up and to arm."

1. The structure of the second work is a **(drama/poem)**.

2. The style of the first work is **(formal/informal)**.

3. Both works mention **(the lanterns/the Charles River)**.

CHALLENGE ANSWERS
Analyze How Two or More Texts Address
Similar Themes or Topics

1. **poem:** The work is arranged in stanzas and includes rhyme and regular rhythm.

2. **formal:** The author uses long sentences and formal words and phrases.

3. **the lanterns:** The warning lanterns are included in both works.

Determine Word Meanings

Knowing word meanings and how words are used is vital to understanding the texts you read. You may be asked to define words and name their parts of speech on the TASC test.

KEY TERMS: context, etymology, part of speech

Context

The **context** of a word is the words, phrases, or passages that come before and after it. You can often determine a word's meaning by looking at the words around it, or its context.

The accused man stood up and made a strong *avowal* of his innocence, his words and facial expression so convincing that even his accusers felt uncertain.

CONTEXT: The context of *avowal* includes the words and phrases *of his innocence*, *words*, and *convincing*. They hint that the meaning of *avowal* is "frank statement."

Part of Speech

A word's **part of speech** is the grammatical category into which it falls, based on how it is used in a sentence.

The Parts of Speech

PART OF SPEECH	FUNCTION	EXAMPLES
Noun	Names a person, place, thing, or idea	boy, lake, wagon, fear
Pronoun	Takes the place of a noun	she, them, mine, somebody
Verb	Expresses action or state of being	scream, jump, are, seemed
Adjective	Modifies a noun or pronoun	huge, first, several, the
Adverb	Modifies a verb, adjective, or adverb	there, soon, cleverly, far
Preposition	Shows relationships	behind, after, toward, prior to
Conjunction	Joins words or groups of words	and, but, or, neither/nor
Interjection	Expresses emotion	hey, wow, oh, ugh

Etymology

The history and origins of a word are its **etymology**. Many of the words we use today in English have their etymology in other languages. You can find a word's etymology in most dictionaries. A word's etymology can show you how it is linked to other words that share its origins.

Etymology of *logic*: from the Greek word *logos* (word, speech, topic, treatise, reasoning)

LINKED WORDS: analogy, biology, logarithm

CHALLENGE Determine Word Meanings

Read the passage. Then choose the word or phrase that makes each sentence true.

Excerpt from *The Autobiography of Benjamin Franklin*

Benjamin Franklin

There was a salt-marsh that bounded part of the mill-pond, on the edge of which, at high water, we used to stand to fish for minnows. By much trampling, we had made it a mere quagmire.

1. The meaning of *quagmire* in the second sentence is **(swamp/situation)**.

2. A context word that helps you define *quagmire* is **(minnows/trampling)**.

3. The word *quagmire* is a **(noun/verb/pronoun)**.

CHALLENGE ANSWERS

Determine Word Meanings

1. **swamp:** The author describes a marshy area that has become a quagmire when boys trampled it.

2. **trampling:** The context word *trampling* indicates the marsh has been walked on and squashed.

3. **noun:** A quagmire is a thing or a place, which is named by a noun.

 Understand Figurative Language, Word Relationships, and Nuances

Defining words is vital to comprehension, but words can have meanings that reach beyond their dictionary definitions. Learning the ways authors use words can help you better understand their work.

KEY TERMS: hyperbole, paradox, word relationships

Hyperbole

You've already learned that figurative language can include simile, metaphor, and personification. **Hyperbole,** or deliberate exaggeration, is another form of figurative language. Writers often use it for humorous effect.

Excerpt from *The Marvelous Exploits of Paul Bunyan*

W. B. Laughead

The year of the Two Winters they had winter all summer and then in the fall it turned colder.

Paradox

A **paradox** is a statement that appears to contradict itself but may in fact be true. When writers use paradox, they often intend to surprise or amuse their readers.

Excerpt from *Walden*

Henry David Thoreau

The swiftest traveler is he that goes afoot.

Word Relationships

Word relationships include the following:

» Synonyms: words that have similar meanings
» Antonyms: words with opposite meanings
» Homophones: words with the same sound but different meanings

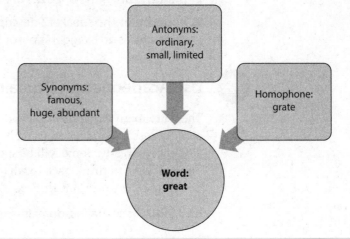

Understand Figurative Language, Word Relationships, and Nuances

Read the passage. Then choose the word or phrase that makes each sentence true.

Excerpt from *The Paradox*

Paul Laurence Dunbar

White are my hands as the snowdrop;
Swart are my fingers as clay;
Dark is my frown as the midnight,
Fair is my brow as the day.

Battle and war are my minions,
Doing my will as divine;
I am the calmer of passions,
Peace is a nursling of mine.

1. The color of the speaker's hands and fingers is a (**hyperbole/paradox**).

2. In the poem, the antonym of *war* is (**peace/battle**).

3. The description of the speaker's frown is a (**synonym/hyperbole**).

CHALLENGE ANSWERS

Understand Figurative Language, Word Relationships, and Nuances

1. **paradox:** The speaker's hands are both white and "swart," or dark—a paradox.

2. **peace:** *Peace* is the opposite of *war*.

3. **hyperbole:** The speaker's description of his frown as dark "as the midnight" is an exaggeration, or hyperbole.

 ## Use Academic and Domain-Specific Words and Phrases

There are many different ways to define and use words. Some words you'll come across in your reading can be defined in context; many of them you will know already. Some will be specific to a certain field of study, however. You will have to think back to what you have learned or read in that field to determine the words' meanings.

KEY TERMS: academic, domain-specific

Academic Words

General **academic words** often represent subtle or precise ways to say relatively simple things—*saunter* instead of *walk*, for example. They can frequently be defined in context.

Domain-Specific Words

Domain-specific words are terms that are connected with a specific field of study, such as literature, science, mathematics, or history. They must often be defined using a dictionary or glossary.

Academic words are underlined once. Domain-specific words are underlined twice.

The release of methane into the atmosphere causes a sudden shift in carbon isotopes.

| CHALLENGE | Use Academic and Domain-Specific Words and Phrases |

Read the passage. Then choose the word or phrase that makes each sentence true.

Excerpt from *The Deep Space Network*

. . . NASA established the concept of the Deep Space Network as a separate Earth-based communications facility that would support many space flight missions simultaneously, thereby avoiding the impractical duplication of a specialized space communications network for each flight project. The Network was given responsibility for its own research, development, and operation in support of all its users. Under this concept, it has become a world leader in the development of low-noise receivers, tracking, telemetry, and command systems, digital signal processing, and deep space radio navigation.

1. Using context, you can determine that the meaning of the word *simultaneously* is **(alone/at the same time)**.

2. One word that is domain-specific is **(telemetry/impractical)**.

CHALLENGE ANSWERS
Use Academic and Domain-Specific Words and Phrases

1. **at the same time:** The word *many* tells you that the Network would support more than one mission; the phrase "avoiding the impractical duplication" suggests that the support of the missions would happen at the same time.

2. **telemetry:** *Telemetry* is a term specific to the communications industry. It is the science of collecting data at remote sites and transmitting it to receiving equipment for monitoring.

TASC Language Arts–Reading Practice Test

50 questions, 70 minutes

The following test is designed to simulate a real TASC Language Arts–Reading Test section in terms of question formats, number, and degree of difficulty. To get a good idea of how you will do on the real exam, take this test under actual exam conditions. Complete the test in one session and follow the given time limit. Answers and explanations begin on page 73.

Read this text. Then answer the questions.

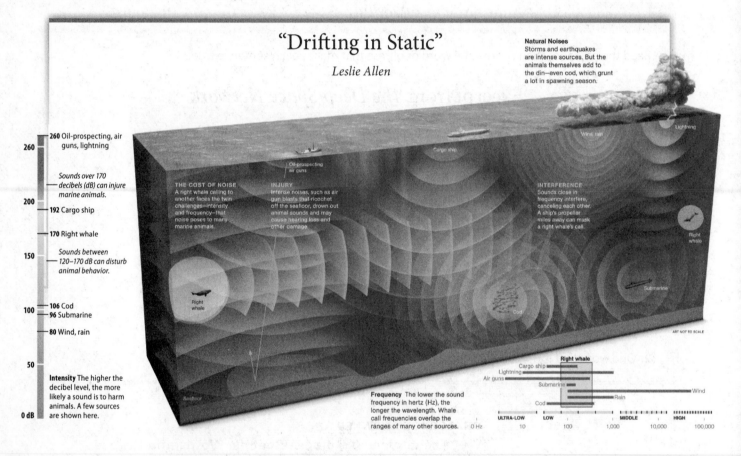

"Drifting in Static"

Leslie Allen

A rising tide of man-made noise is disrupting the lives of marine animals.

The deep is dark, but not silent; it's alive with sounds. Whales and other marine mammals, fish, and even some invertebrates depend on sound, which travels much farther in water than light does. The animals use sound to find food and mates, to avoid predators, and to communicate. They face a growing problem: Man-made noise is drowning them out. "For many of these animals it's as if they live in cities," says marine scientist Brandon Southall, former director of the National Oceanic and Atmospheric Administration's (NOAA) ocean acoustics program.

Two years ago the problem made it to the U.S. Supreme Court, in a case that might have been called *U.S. Navy v. Whales.* The Court's decision protected the right of naval vessels to test submarine-hunting sonar systems, whose intense sound pulses have been linked to several mass whale strandings. But the Navy is not the lone villain. Oil company ships towing arrays of air guns fire round-the-clock fusillades loud enough to locate oil buried under the seafloor—and also to be heard hundreds of miles away. Undersea construction operations drive piles into the seafloor and blast holes in it with explosives.

And most of the rising tide of noise—a hundred-fold increase since 1960, in many areas—is created simply by the dramatic growth in shipping traffic. "Shipping noise is always there," Southall says. "It doesn't have to be lethal to be problematic over time." The problem is getting steadily worse for another reason. As we're making more noise, we're also making the ocean better at transmitting it. Seawater is absorbing less sound as carbon dioxide from fossil-fuel burning seeps into the ocean and acidifies it.

Noise drives many species of whales, dolphins, and other marine animals to change their behavior markedly—their calling, foraging, and migration patterns—even when it's not enough to drive them onto a beach. Cod and haddock in the Barents Sea have been found to flee the area when air guns start firing, drastically reducing fish catches for days. Large baleen whales are of special concern. They communicate over vast distances in the same frequencies, around the lowest C on a piano, that ship propellers and engines generate. On most days, says Christopher W. Clark, director of the bioacoustics research program at Cornell University, the area over which whales in coastal waters can hear one another shrinks to only 10 to 20 percent of its natural extent.

Clark studies endangered northern right whales, whose habitat includes busy shipping lanes for the port of Boston. In 2007 he and his colleagues deployed a network of seafloor recorders and automated listening buoys in Massachusetts Bay. From three years of continuous recordings, they then compiled a complete underwater "noise budget." Color animations of the data show the calls of right whales getting all but obliterated as ships pass. "The whales' social network is constantly being ripped and reformed," Clark says. Unable to communicate, individual whales have trouble finding each other and spend more time on their own.

The ten listening buoys now bobbing in Massachusetts Bay could actually help the animals. The researchers are sharing their real-time data on whale locations, transmitted from the buoys via satellite, with tanker captains, who can then slow down their ships or alter course to avoid whales. It's a small note of hope in the din. "Science can only help in so many ways," Clark says. "Then we have to decide whether the animals are important to us."

TEXT BY LESLIE ALLEN / ILLUSTRATION BY STEFAN FICHTE / NATIONAL GEOGRAPHIC CREATIVE

1. According to the text, what two elements combine to make marine noise a problem?

   Ⓐ shipping noise
   Ⓑ migration patterns
   Ⓒ listening buoys
   Ⓓ seafloor recorders
   Ⓔ acidified seawater
   Ⓕ whale stranding

2. Which of these statements includes a central idea from the text?

   Ⓐ The ten listening buoys now bobbing in Massachusetts Bay could actually help the animals.
   Ⓑ Unable to communicate, individual whales have trouble finding each other and spend more time on their own.
   Ⓒ The animals use sound to find food and mates, to avoid predators, and to communicate.
   Ⓓ A rising tide of man-made noise is disrupting the lives of marine animals.

3. According to the graphic at the top of the text, which of these is most likely to cause damage to marine animals' hearing?

   Ⓐ submarines
   Ⓑ air guns
   Ⓒ wind
   Ⓓ cargo ships

4. Read the excerpt from "Drifting in Static."

   > Cod and haddock in the Barents Sea have been found to flee the area when air guns start firing, drastically reducing fish catches for days.

   How does the author use this statement to develop the argument that noise causes marine animals to change their behavior?

   Ⓐ She supplies a contrast to the ways land animals behave.
   Ⓑ She explains the behavior of animals in quiet areas.
   Ⓒ She provides an example that supports the argument.
   Ⓓ She criticizes the levels of noise in the Barents Sea.

5. From the author's argument, you can infer that one way to help reduce marine noise from <u>all</u> sources would be to

   Ⓐ stop using air guns
   Ⓑ burn less fossil fuel
   Ⓒ end marine oil drilling
   Ⓓ change shipping routes

6. Read the excerpt from "Drifting in Static."

> On most days, says Christopher W. Clark, director of the bioacoustics research program at Cornell University, the area over which whales in coastal waters can hear one another shrinks to only 10 to 20 percent of its natural extent.

The most likely meaning of *bioacoustics* is

Ⓐ the study of noise made by humans
Ⓑ the analysis of animal senses
Ⓒ the study of underwater organisms and habitats
Ⓓ the science of sounds that affect living creatures

7. The author's description of the depths of the sea in the second paragraph demonstrates the

Ⓐ magnitude of undersea noise
Ⓑ extent of the silence of deep water
Ⓒ fact that deep-water noise is generated by humans
Ⓓ dangers facing marine animals in deep water

8. The author's main purpose in this article is to

Ⓐ explain why whales have become endangered
Ⓑ argue that humans should make less deep-sea noise
Ⓒ persuade people to burn less fossil fuel
Ⓓ explain the problems caused by deep-sea noise

Read these texts. Then answer the questions.

Excerpt from *Sir Gawain and the Green Knight*

Anonymous, fourteenth century

Thus the king sat before the high tables, and spake of many things; and there good figure Sir Gawain was seated by Guinevere the present queen, and on her other side sat Agravain, both were the king's sister's sons and full gallant knights. And at the end of the table was Bishop Bawdewyn, and Ywain, King Urien's son, sat at the other side alone. These were worthily served on the dais, and at the lower tables sat many valiant knights. Then they bare the first course with the blast of trumpets and waving of banners, with the sound of drums and pipes, of song and lute, that many a heart was uplifted at the melody. Many were the dainties, and rare the meats, so great was the plenty they might scarce find room on the board to set on the dishes. Each helped himself as he liked best, and to each two were twelve dishes, with great plenty of beer and wine.

Excerpt from *A Connecticut Yankee in King Arthur's Court*

Mark Twain

In the middle of this groined and vaulted public square was an oaken table which they called the Table Round. It was as large as a circus-ring; and around it sat a great company of men dressed in such various and splendid colors that it hurt one's eyes to look at them. They wore their plumed hats, right along, except that whenever one addressed himself directly to the king, he lifted his hat a trifle just as he was beginning his remark. Mainly they were drinking—from entire ox horns; but a few were still munching bread or gnawing beef bones. There was about an average of two dogs to one man; and these sat in expectant attitudes till a spent bone was flung to them, and then they went for it by brigades and divisions, with a rush, and there ensued a fight which filled the prospect with a tumultuous chaos of plunging heads and bodies and flashing tails, and the storm of bowlings and barkings deafened all speech for the time; but that was no matter, for the dog-fight was always a bigger interest anyway; the men rose, sometimes, to observe it the better and bet on it, and the ladies and the musicians stretched themselves out over their balusters with the same object; and all broke into delighted ejaculations from time to time. In the end, the winning dog stretched himself out comfortably with his bone between his paws, and proceeded to growl over it, and gnaw it, and grease the floor with it, just as fifty others were already doing; and the rest of the court resumed their previous industries and entertainments.

9. Both texts describe King Arthur's court. How do the tones of the texts differ?

(A) The first is mocking, while the second is suspenseful.
(B) The first is serious, while the second is humorous.
(C) The first is ironic, while the second is gloomy.
(D) The first is informal, while the second is formal.

10. What impression does the author create of the court in *Sir Gawain and the Green Knight*?

(A) an impression of simplicity and modesty
(B) an impression of cheerfulness and anticipation
(C) an impression of darkness and danger
(D) an impression of splendor and celebration

11. Gawain and Agravaine are described as "full gallant knights" in *Sir Gawain and the Green Knight*. From this description, you can infer that they are

Ⓐ brave
Ⓑ large
Ⓒ graceful
Ⓓ impolite

12. Why does Twain choose to describe the dogs at court in *A Connecticut Yankee in King Arthur's Court*?

Ⓐ to suggest that the dogs are more civilized than the humans
Ⓑ to suggest that the court is not very civilized
Ⓒ to show how important dogs are to the court
Ⓓ to show that the court is refined but exciting

13. Read this excerpt from *A Connecticut Yankee in King Arthur's Court*.

It was as large as a circus-ring; and around it sat a great company of men dressed in such various and splendid colors that it hurt one's eyes to look at them.

What tone does the author's use of hyperbole create?

Ⓐ a gloomy tone
Ⓑ a realistic tone
Ⓒ a threatening tone
Ⓓ a comical tone

14. Read this excerpt from *Sir Gawain and the Green Knight*.

Many were the dainties, and rare the meats, so great was the plenty they might scarce find room on the board to set on the dishes.

The phrase "rare the meats" implies that

Ⓐ there was only meat at the table
Ⓑ the meats were not well cooked
Ⓒ the meats were costly and unusual
Ⓓ there were several kinds of meat

15. The author's description of the setting in *A Connecticut Yankee in King Arthur's Court* suggests that the story will be

Ⓐ tragic
Ⓑ comic
Ⓒ adventurous
Ⓓ suspenseful

Read this text. Then answer the questions.

Olympic Upset

Diane Zahler

In 1936, the summer Olympic Games were held in Berlin, Germany. These Games were significant in a number of ways. They were the first to be televised; they were the first to feature the torch relay, in which the Olympic torch was carried by runners from Olympia in Greece; they were the first to hold competitions in basketball, canoeing, and field handball. And they were the first Games held after Adolph Hitler's rise to power in Germany.

The Games were awarded to Germany before the National Socialist, or Nazi, party came to power in 1933, and as the Nazis' racist views became evident, the Olympic committee grew worried that other countries might boycott the Games. The Nazis assured the committee that they would not use the Olympics to promote Nazi ideology, but Hitler planned to utilize the Games to advance the Nazi political agenda. The official Nazi newspaper, the *Völkischer Beobachter*, published editorials stating that Jewish and black athletes should not be allowed to compete. There was a huge, worldwide outcry against this, however, and the Nazis, to ensure that the Games weren't cancelled, did not bar athletes from other countries. They allowed only one Jewish athlete on their own team, though—Helene Mayer, an award-winning fencer whose father was Jewish. The Nazis' greatest hopes rested on Carl Ludwig (Luz) Long, a German long jumper whose looks and great strength exemplified the Nazi physical ideal—the blond-haired, blue-eyed Aryans whom the Nazis called the master race.

The Germans built a huge stadium and over 100 other buildings; everything was completed in time for the Games. Estimates are that the cost to the government was at least $30 million. Anti-Semitic posters and flyers were taken down from all around the city; Berlin was readied for the influx of nearly 4,000 athletes from 49 countries as well as spectators and journalists from all over the world. The opening ceremonies went off without a hitch, and it quickly became clear that the Germans would win many medals. In the track and field competition, however, where Luz Long was predicted to excel, there was an unexpected challenge: Jesse Owens.

Jesse Owens was an African American from Alabama, a runner and long jumper who, by the time of the Berlin Olympics, had already broken several world records. Owens was immediately an audience favorite, even among the Germans. His initial attempts in the qualifying competition for the long jump were problematic, though. A leap that he thought was a practice jump was actually his first official attempt.

On his second try, he foot-faulted. He only had one more chance. It wasn't until his third try that he qualified for the finals.

Jesse Owens won gold medals in the 100-meter run (10.3 seconds, an Olympic record), the 200-meter run (20.7 seconds, a world record), and the 4 × 100-meter relay (39.8 seconds), and he beat Luz Long handily in the long jump (8.06 meters [26.4 feet]). Long was the first to congratulate Owens on his win, and the two athletes embraced—in front of Adolph Hitler, watching in the stands.

While the German athletes won the greatest total number of medals, Owens had the best individual performance, putting the lie to the Nazis' theories of the racial inferiority of blacks. Ironically, he and Luz Long remained friends after the Games, and though Long was killed in World War II, Owens continued to correspond with his family for years afterward.

16. Read this excerpt from "Olympic Upset."

Anti-Semitic posters and flyers were taken down from all around the city; Berlin was readied for the influx of nearly 4,000 athletes from 49 countries as well as spectators and journalists from all over the world.

What can you infer from this statement?

Ⓐ The Nazis were ashamed of their anti-Semitism.
Ⓑ The Nazis had changed their minds about anti-Semitism.
Ⓒ The Nazis had barred all Jewish and black athletes from the Games.
Ⓓ The Nazis wanted the world to be impressed by Berlin.

17. Read this excerpt from "Olympic Upset."

While the German athletes won the greatest total number of medals, Owens had the best individual performance, putting the lie to the Nazis' theories of the racial inferiority of blacks.

What does the phrase "putting the lie to the Nazis' theories" mean? Write your answer in the box.

18. What is the effect of the author's description of Jesse Owens's difficulties in qualifying for the long-jump finals?

Ⓐ It creates suspense.
Ⓑ It provides humor.
Ⓒ It sets the scene.
Ⓓ It foreshadows his loss.

19. Luz Long's embrace of Jesse Owens after Owens's win at the long jump showed

Ⓐ a long-standing friendship
Ⓑ courage and good sportsmanship
Ⓒ his hatred of Nazi ideals
Ⓓ fear of the authorities

20. The Nazis' most probable feelings about Luz Long after the Olympics were

Ⓐ pride and respect
Ⓑ disappointment and betrayal
Ⓒ suspicion and uncertainty
Ⓓ fear and contempt

21. Read this excerpt from "Olympic Upset."

> The Nazis assured the committee that they would not use the Olympics to promote Nazi ideology, but Hitler planned to utilize the Games to advance the Nazi political agenda.

The most likely meaning of *ideology* is

Ⓐ history of ideas
Ⓑ study of identity
Ⓒ system of beliefs
Ⓓ science of heredity

22. Which of these statements best summarizes the text?

Ⓐ Jesse Owens helped show the world that the Nazi ideology was flawed.
Ⓑ Luz Long proved that the Nazis were wrong about Jewish and black athletes.
Ⓒ The 1936 Berlin Olympics marked the beginning of World War II.
Ⓓ Even in the 1930s, American athletes were superior to other athletes.

Read this poem. Then answer the questions.

Forget Me Not

Ann Plato

When in the morning's misty hour,
When the sun beems gently o'er each flower;
When thou dost cease to smile benign,
And think each heart responds with thine,
When seeking rest among divine,
Forget me not.

When the last rays of twilight fall,
And thou art pacing yonder hall;
When mists are gathering on the hill,
Nor sound is heard save mountain rill,
When all around bids peace be still,
Forget me not.

When the first star with brilliance bright,
Gleams lonely o'er the arch of night;
When the bright moon dispels the gloom,
And various are the stars that bloom,
And brighten as the sun at noon,
Forget me not.

When solemn sighs the hollow wind,
And deepen'd thought enraps the mind;
If e'er thou doest in mournful tone,
E'er sigh because thou feel alone,
Or wrapt in melancholy prone,
Forget me not.

When bird does wait thy absence long,
Nor tend unto its morning song;
While thou art searching stoic page,
Or listening to an ancient sage,
Whose spirit curbs a mournful rage,
Forget me not.

Then when in silence thou doest walk,
Nor being round with whom to talk;
When thou art on the mighty deep,
And do in quiet action sleep;
If we no more on earth do meet,
Forget me not.

When brightness round thee long shall bloom,
And knelt remembering those in gloom;
And when in deep oblivion's shade,
This breathless, mouldering form is laid,
And thy terrestrial body staid,
Forget me not.

"Should sorrow cloud thy coming years,
And bathe thy happiness in tears,
Remember, though we're doom'd to part,
There lives one fond and faithful heart,
That will forget thee not."

23. A theme of the poem is

Ⓐ the sorrows of death

Ⓑ how love can endure separation

Ⓒ the difficulties of travel

Ⓓ family bonds and their importance

24. You can infer that the speaker in the poem is addressing a

Ⓐ sister

Ⓑ parent

Ⓒ child

Ⓓ loved one

25.

Part A

The first three stanzas of the poem describe

Ⓐ the passing of time

Ⓑ the loss of love

Ⓒ the death of a beloved

Ⓓ the power of love

Part B

Which lines from the poem provide support for the answer to Part A? Choose all that apply.

Ⓐ When in the morning's misty hour

Ⓑ And think each heart responds with thine

Ⓒ When the last rays of twilight fall

Ⓓ When all around bids peace be still

Ⓔ When the first star with brilliance bright

Ⓕ When the bright moon dispels the gloom

Ⓖ When solemn sighs the hollow wind

26. Why does the poet change the refrain in the last stanza of the poem?

Ⓐ to show that the speaker forgives her beloved

Ⓑ to demonstrate that the speaker will remain faithful

Ⓒ to reveal a surprise about the speaker

Ⓓ to indicate the vast difference between the speaker and her beloved

27. Read this stanza from "Forget Me Not."

> When brightness round thee long shall bloom,
> And knelt remembering those in gloom;
> And when in deep oblivion's shade,
> This breathless, mouldering form is laid,
> And thy terrestrial body staid,
> Forget me not.

What is the speaker asking?

(A) to be buried beside her beloved
(B) to be remembered in brightness and in gloom
(C) for her beloved to remember her even after death
(D) for her beloved not to die

28. Read this stanza from "Forget Me Not."

> When solemn sighs the hollow wind,
> And deepen'd thought enraps the mind;
> If e'er thou doest in mournful tone,
> E'er sigh because thou feel alone,
> Or wrapt in melancholy prone,
> Forget me not.

Which three words help create a tone of sorrow?

(A) solemn
(B) enraps
(C) e'er
(D) alone
(E) mournful
(F) melancholy

29. What is the meaning of the word *dispels* in the third stanza?

(A) brings together
(B) destroys
(C) chases away
(D) scorns

Read this text. Then answer the questions.

Inaugural Address of Andrew Johnson, after the assassination of Abraham Lincoln on April 14, 1865

(From the Sunday Morning Chronicle, *Washington, April 16, 1865, and* The Sun, *Baltimore, April 17, 1865.)*

GENTLEMEN: I must be permitted to say that I have been almost overwhelmed by the announcement of the sad event which has so recently occurred. I feel incompetent to perform duties so important and responsible as those which have been so unexpectedly thrown upon me. As to an indication of any policy which may be pursued by me in the administration of the Government, I have to say that that must be left for development as the Administration progresses. The message or declaration must be made by the acts as they transpire. The only assurance that I can now give of the future is reference to the past. The course which I have taken in the past in connection with this rebellion must be regarded as a guaranty of the future. My past public life, which has been long and laborious, has been founded, as I in good conscience believe, upon a great principle of right, which lies at the basis of all things. The best energies of my life have been spent in endeavoring to establish and perpetuate the principles of free government, and I believe that the Government in passing through its present perils will settle down upon principles consonant with popular rights more permanent and enduring than heretofore. I must be permitted to say, if I understand the feelings of my own heart, that I have long labored to ameliorate and elevate the condition of the great mass of the American people. Toil and an honest advocacy of the great principles of free government have been my lot. Duties have been mine; consequences are God's. This has been the foundation of my political creed, and I feel that in the end the Government will triumph and that these great principles will be permanently established.

In conclusion, gentlemen, let me say that I want your encouragement and countenance. I shall ask and rely upon you and others in carrying the Government through its present perils. I feel in making this request that it will be heartily responded to by you and all other patriots and lovers of the rights and interests of a free people.

April 15, 1865

30. What is the "sad event" to which Andrew Johnson refers? Write your answer in the box.

```
┌─────────────────────────────────────────────────────────┐
│                                                         │
│                                                         │
│                                                         │
│                                                         │
│                                                         │
└─────────────────────────────────────────────────────────┘
```

31.

Part A

How does Johnson attempt to calm his listeners' fears?

Ⓐ by stating that any aggressors shall be punished

Ⓑ by reminding them of his reputation for prudence and insight

Ⓒ by suggesting that he will continue the government's existing policies

Ⓓ by revealing a list of plans for America's future direction

Part B

Which of these statements most strongly supports your response to Part A?

Ⓐ I feel incompetent to perform duties so important and responsible as those which have been so unexpectedly thrown upon me.

Ⓑ The course which I have taken in the past in connection with this rebellion must be regarded as a guaranty of the future.

Ⓒ I must be permitted to say, if I understand the feelings of my own heart, that I have long labored to ameliorate and elevate the condition of the great mass of the American people.

Ⓓ I shall ask and rely upon you and others in carrying the Government through its present perils.

32. What is President Johnson's main purpose in this address?

Ⓐ to inform the audience that he will reunite the North and South

Ⓑ to explain to the audience why he will not be as good a president as Lincoln

Ⓒ to defend his past record in government to the audience

Ⓓ to assure the audience that he will do his best for the country

33. What does President Johnson mean when he refers to his "political creed"?

Ⓐ the political party to which he belongs

Ⓑ his writings about government

Ⓒ his beliefs about government

Ⓓ his political enemies

34. How do you think Andrew Johnson feels about becoming president? Use evidence from the text to support your analysis. Write your answer in the box.

35. Read this excerpt from the address.

> My past public life, which has been long and laborious, has been founded, as I in good conscience believe, upon a great principle of right, which lies at the basis of all things.

What is the most likely meaning of *laborious*?

- (A) requiring much effort
- (B) causing physical pain
- (C) difficult to explain
- (D) done in a laboratory

36. In the final paragraph, what hope does President Johnson express about his government?

- (A) that it will be better than Lincoln's government
- (B) that it will reject the demands of the South
- (C) that it will survive the Civil War
- (D) that it will ban slavery

Read this text. Then answer the questions.

Excerpt from "On Memory"

Jerome K. Jerome

Life altogether is but a crumbling ruin when we turn to look behind: a shattered column here, where a massive portal stood; the broken shaft of a window to mark my lady's bower; and a moldering heap of blackened stones where the glowing flames once leaped, and over all the tinted lichen and the ivy clinging green.

For everything looms pleasant through the softening haze of time. Even the sadness that is past seems sweet. Our boyish days look very merry to us now, all nutting, hoop, and gingerbread. The snubbings and toothaches and the Latin verbs are all forgotten—the Latin verbs especially. And we fancy we were very happy when we were hobbledehoys and loved; and we wish that we could love again. We never think of the heartaches, or the sleepless nights, or the hot dryness of our throats, when she said she could never be anything to us but a sister—as if any man wanted more sisters!

Yes, it is the brightness, not the darkness, that we see when we look back. The sunshine casts no shadows on the past. The road that we have traversed stretches very fair behind us. We see not the sharp stones. We dwell but on the roses by the wayside, and the strong briers that stung us are, to our distant eyes, but gentle tendrils waving in the wind. God be thanked that it is so—that the ever-lengthening chain of memory has only pleasant links, and that the bitterness and sorrow of to-day are smiled at on the morrow.

It seems as though the brightest side of everything were also its highest and best, so that as our little lives sink back behind us into the dark sea of forgetfulness, all that which is the lightest and the most gladsome is the last to sink, and stands above the waters, long in sight, when the angry thoughts and smarting pain are buried deep below the waves and trouble us no more.

It is this glamour of the past, I suppose, that makes old folk talk so much nonsense about the days when they were young. The world appears to have been a very superior sort of place then, and things were more like what they ought to be. Boys were boys then, and girls were very different. Also winters were something like winters, and summers not at all the wretched-things we get put off with nowadays. As for the wonderful deeds people did in those times and the extraordinary events that happened, it takes three strong men to believe half of them.

I like to hear one of the old boys telling all about it to a party of youngsters who he knows cannot contradict him. It is odd if, after awhile, he doesn't swear that the moon shone every night when he was a boy, and that tossing mad bulls in a blanket was the favorite sport at his school.

It always has been and always will be the same. The old folk of our grandfathers' young days sang a song bearing exactly the same burden; and the young folk of to-day will drone out precisely similar nonsense for the aggravation of the next generation. "Oh, give me back the good old days of fifty years ago," has been the cry ever since Adam's fifty-first birthday. Take up the literature of 1835, and you will find the poets and novelists asking for the same impossible gift as did the German Minnesingers long before them and the old Norse Saga writers long before that. And for the same thing sighed the early prophets and the philosophers of ancient Greece. From all accounts, the world has been getting worse and worse ever since it was created. All I can say is that it must have been a remarkably delightful place when it was first opened to the public, for it is very pleasant even now if you only keep as much as possible in the sunshine and take the rain good-temperedly.

37. In the first paragraph, what is the effect of the author's use of hyperbole?

Ⓐ It builds a sense of threat.
Ⓑ It creates a humorous tone.
Ⓒ It introduces an element of suspense.
Ⓓ It creates a serious tone.

38. Read this excerpt from the text.

> I like to hear one of the old boys telling all about it to a party of youngsters who he knows cannot contradict him. It is odd if, after awhile, he doesn't swear that the moon shone every night when he was a boy, and that tossing mad bulls in a blanket was the favorite sport at his school.

What is the author saying about older people and their memories of the past?

Ⓐ They tend to exaggerate or make up stories.
Ⓑ They become more specific over time.
Ⓒ They remember only the amusing incidents.
Ⓓ They only like to relate their memories to youngsters.

39. The author believes that the past looks good to us because

Ⓐ we suffer more when we get older
Ⓑ the present is full of strife and difficulty
Ⓒ we forget the pain and exaggerate the pleasures of the past
Ⓓ we are more likely to love when we are younger

40. In which two paragraphs does the author treat memory and time seriously?

Ⓐ the first paragraph
Ⓑ the second paragraph
Ⓒ the third paragraph
Ⓓ the fourth paragraph
Ⓔ the fifth paragraph
Ⓕ the sixth paragraph

41. Read this excerpt from the text.

> Yes, it is the brightness, not the darkness, that we see when we look back. The sunshine casts no shadows on the past.

What is the author saying about the past in this excerpt?

Ⓐ The sun shone more often in the past.
Ⓑ We forget the bad things that happened in the past.
Ⓒ The weather was different in the past.
Ⓓ It is difficult to remember the past.

42. Read this excerpt from the text.

> Take up the literature of 1835, and you will find the poets and novelists asking for the same impossible gift as did the German Minnesingers long before them and the old Norse Saga writers long before that. And for the same thing sighed the early prophets and the philosophers of ancient Greece.

What is the "impossible gift" that the author mentions?

- Ⓐ the ability to live a long life
- Ⓑ a life without difficulty or pain
- Ⓒ the ability to remember the past precisely
- Ⓓ the return to a past that didn't really exist

43. In the final paragraph, what feeling does the author express about the present?

- Ⓐ that it is better than the past
- Ⓑ that it is very pleasant
- Ⓒ that it is worse than the past
- Ⓓ that it is unpleasant

Read this text. Then answer the questions.

Food of the Future?

Diane Zahler

When you hear the term *genetically modified food*, what do you picture? A stalk of corn with poison lurking in its kernels? A thick, healthy field of wheat? The practice of genetically modifying crops has been going on for decades, but the controversy surrounding it has only grown stronger over the years.

To create a genetically modified food, scientists introduce changes into the DNA, or genetic material, of a plant. The changes might help the plant resist disease, grow faster or better in bad weather conditions, resist insect infestation, produce extra nutrients, or resist the effects of herbicides. In 1994, tomatoes became the first genetically modified plants to be sold to consumers. Now, the majority of corn, soybean, canola, and cotton seed crops in the United States are genetically modified. Other foods that might be grown or produced with genetic modification include papayas, potatoes, zucchini, sugar from sugar beets, and cheese. Flour, cornstarch, and corn syrup are made from genetically engineered corn. Genetically modified soy products can be found in many prepared foods, as can modified vegetable oils.

There are several major objections to the use of genetically modified foods, according to the World Health Organization (WHO). The first is allergenicity, or the possibility of allergic reactions in people as a result of gene modification. The Food and Agriculture Organization of the United Nations (FAO) and the WHO do some testing of genetically modified foods for allergenicity. So far, they have found no allergic effects.

The second objection involves the transfer of modified genes to cells or bacteria in the body. Some of the modified genes are unaffected by, or resistant to, the drugs known as antibiotics. Transferring these antibiotic-resistant genes to humans is a possibility. Antibiotic resistance is already a problem for human populations. There are many diseases that are becoming or have become resistant to treatment with antibiotics. The WHO has suggested that genetic modification not include antibiotic-resistant genes.

Outcrossing, or the movement of genes from genetically modified plants into other crops or related plants in the wild, is the third problem raising objections. In the United States, this danger has become a reality. A type of genetically modified corn that was approved only for animal feed crossed into corn products raised for human consumption.

A fourth objection involves the effects of genetically modified crops on biodiversity. Because these crops are generally stronger and often faster-growing than other plants, they tend to overtake and push out weaker plants. This leads to a decrease in the variety of plant life. Outcrossing makes this even more of a problem.

Because genetically modified foods have been available only for a short time, the results of long-term testing of their effects in both the human and animal populations and on the environment are not yet available. The American Association for the Advancement of Science, the American Medical Association, the National Academies of Sciences, and the Royal Society of Medicine have stated that there have been no negative health effects on humans proven to date. However, many individuals and groups such as Greenpeace and the Organic Consumers Association protest the use of genetically modified crops. They want foods produced from these crops to be banned until more tests are done. At the very least, they want genetically modified foods to be labeled. The European Union, Australia, New Zealand, China, India, and several other countries require labeling. The United States, however, does not. The question of whether genetically modified food is the answer to food shortages and famine or a threat to people and the environment is still unanswered, and is likely to be controversial for many years to come.

44. According to this article, why might genetically modified food be a threat to the environment? Use evidence from the text to support your analysis. Write your answer in the box.

[ ]

45. Read this excerpt from the text.

> A type of genetically modified corn that was approved only for animal feed crossed into corn products raised for human consumption.

How does the author use this statement to support the argument that genetically modified food might be dangerous?

Ⓐ She provides an example of outcrossing, which might affect people's food.

Ⓑ She provides a contrast to experts' statements that no ill effects have been proven.

Ⓒ She describes a scenario in which genetic modification causes injury.

Ⓓ She raises doubts about whether changes in genes can be controlled.

46. In the fourth paragraph, what does the term *antibiotic resistance* mean?

Ⓐ the ability of humans to refuse antibiotic treatment

Ⓑ the presence of antibiotics in plants and animals

Ⓒ the use of antibiotics to fight disease

Ⓓ the ability of germs to resist antibiotics

47. Which of these sentences <u>best</u> expresses why genetically modified food might be useful?

Ⓐ Because these crops are generally stronger and often faster-growing than other plants, they tend to overtake and push out weaker plants.

Ⓑ The American Association for the Advancement of Science, the American Medical Association, the National Academies of Sciences, and the Royal Society of Medicine have stated that there have been no negative health effects on humans proven to date.

Ⓒ The changes might help the plant resist disease, grow faster or better in bad weather conditions, resist insect infestation, produce extra nutrients, or resist the effects of herbicides.

Ⓓ Because genetically modified foods have only been available for a short time, the results of long-term testing of their effects in both the human and animal populations and on the environment are not yet available.

48.

Part A

In the second paragraph, what is the meaning of the word *modified*?

(A) modernized
(B) improved
(C) strengthened
(D) changed

Part B

Which word in the paragraph gives the <u>best</u> clue to the meaning of *modified*?

(A) genetically
(B) food
(C) changes
(D) material

49. In the sixth paragraph, what is the meaning of *biodiversity*?

(A) the interactions of animals and plants
(B) the variety of organisms in an environment
(C) the ability of organisms to change
(D) the number of plants in an environment

50. What is the <u>most</u> likely reason for the WHO's recommendation that antibiotic-resistant genes not be used in genetically modified food?

(A) They might introduce new diseases into humans.
(B) They might increase the problem of antibiotic resistance in humans.
(C) They might cause humans to become allergic to antibiotics.
(D) They might cause other crops to be antibiotic-resistant.

_____ *This is the end of the TASC Language Arts–Reading Practice Test.*

TASC Language Arts–Reading
Practice Test Explanatory Answers

1. **A and E** The acidified water helps sounds carry farther, which makes shipping noise more of a threat.

2. **D** The main idea of the text is that man-made noise is threatening marine life.

3. **B** The graphic shows that air guns have the highest decibel level.

4. **C** The example of fish fleeing the noise of air guns supports the idea that noise changes animal behavior.

5. **B** The author states that burning fossil fuel acidifies the water, making all noise carry farther; the implication is that burning less fossil fuel would reverse this effect.

6. **D** *Bio* means "living" and *acoustics* is the study of sound.

7. **A** The author contrasts the darkness of the sea depths with the amount of noise and describes the different kinds of noise.

8. **D** The author describes various problems that have resulted from deep-sea noise, including the endangerment of whales; her main purpose is to inform the reader about the problems.

9. **B** *Sir Gawain and the Green Knight* has a serious, formal tone, while the tone of *A Connecticut Yankee in King Arthur's Court* is informal, satiric, and humorous.

10. **D** The description of the music, formal dress, and wondrous food work to create a sense of great celebration and splendor.

11. **A** "Full gallant" implies that the knights possess all the characteristics of a good knight, including courtesy and bravery.

12. **B** The description of the dogs creates an impression of a court that is disorderly and uncivilized.

13. **D** By describing the Round Table as "as large as a circus-ring" and the colors of clothing as so splendid as to hurt the eyes, the author uses exaggeration, or hyperbole, to create a comical tone.

14. **C** *Rare* in this sentence means expensive and unusual.

15. **B** The description of the knights and the actions of the dogs creates a setting that suggests a humorous story will follow.

16. **D** There is no indication that the Nazis had changed their minds about their anti-Semitism or racism, but it is clear from the amount of money they spend that they wanted to impress the world.

17. **Possible answer:** *Putting the lie to* **means "showing that something is a lie." Jesse Owens' success showed that the Nazis' biased way of thinking was based on falsehoods.**

18. **A** The author's description of Jesse Owens's two failures in qualifying for the long jump put his qualification for the finals in doubt, creating suspense.

19. **B** Luz Long's embrace showed that he was both a gracious loser and a brave man, as he defied the precepts of the powerful Nazi party when he hugged Jesse Owens.

20. **B** The Nazis had expected Long to win, so they were probably disappointed in him. Also, they very likely expected him to uphold their beliefs, so they would have felt betrayed when he embraced Jesse Owens.

21. **C** An *ideology* is a system of beliefs, from the Greek roots meaning *ideas* and *study of.*

22. **A** The 1936 Olympics were an opportunity for Jesse Owens to prove to the watching world that a black athlete, contrary to Nazi ideology and propaganda, could excel.

23. **B** The speaker describes how she is separated from her beloved and begs him not to forget her.

24. **D** In the last two stanzas, the poet makes it clear that the speaker is addressing someone she loves; she refers to their deaths and states that she will remain faithful.

25. **Part A: A; Part B: A, C, E, and F** The first stanza describes the morning, the second describes the evening, and the third describes the night; together they depict the passage of time.

26. B In the previous stanzas, the speaker asks her beloved to remember her, but in the last stanza she stresses that she, at least, will remain faithful and will remember him.

27. C The speaker refers both to her own death and to the death of her beloved, asking him to remember her even afterward.

28. A, E, and F The words *solemn*, *mournful*, and *melancholy* have connotations of sorrow.

29. C To *dispel* means to drive something away or to rid the mind of something.

30. Possible answer: He is referring to the death of President Lincoln. As the note with the title states, President Lincoln was assassinated a day earlier; Johnson became president at his death.

31. Part A: C; Part B: B President Johnson refers to his actions in the past, when he was part of President Lincoln's administration, and states that they will inform his future acts, implying that he will continue the government's existing policies.

32. D President Johnson states that he will continue the work of his predecessor and believes "that in the end the Government will triumph and that these great principles will be permanently established," thus assuring the audience that he will do his best for the country.

33. C A *creed* is a system of beliefs or principles; a political creed would include beliefs or principles concerning government.

34. Possible answer: The use of the words *overwhelmed* and *incompetent* indicate that Johnson feels uneasy about his new and unexpected position as president.

35. A The noun *labor* means "hard work," so the adjective form, *laborious*, means "requiring much effort."

36. C The president states that he wants to "carry the government through its present perils," referring to the Civil War. He is telling the audience that he wants to help the country survive the war.

37. B The author exaggerates, calling the past a "crumbling ruin" and "moldering heap" of stones, which creates a humorous tone that continues throughout the essay.

38. A The older people, who "swear that the moon shone every night" and tell stories of tossing mad bulls in blankets, are prone to stories that feature exaggeration or fabrication.

39. C The author states that we see the "brightness, not the darkness" when we look back—we remember the good things, not the bad things, and tend to exaggerate what was best.

40. C and D The third and fourth paragraphs treat memory and time with more seriousness than the rest of the essay, describing how painful memories fade over time and good memories become brighter.

41. B The author uses the metaphor of sunshine and darkness to stress that we tend to recall the positive and forget the negative, or dark memories.

42. D The author is saying that writers and other people who lived long ago wanted the same thing that people today do—a past without pain, which is a past that never existed.

43. B The author states, "for it is very pleasant even now if you only keep as much as possible in the sunshine and take the rain good-temperedly." He is referring to the world of the present.

44. Possible answer: The author suggests that genetically modified food might decrease plant variety and lead to the lessening of biodiversity. Such a change could threaten the environment.

45. A The author provides an example that helps support the idea that genetically modified foods might be dangerous.

46. D The word *resistance* has *resist* as its base word, which means "to withstand." *Antibiotic resistance* is the ability of germs to resist, or withstand, the use of antibiotics.

47. C The sentence provides a number of positive effects of genetic modification.

48. Part A: D; Part B: C The context of the word *modified* makes it clear that its meaning is "altered."

49. B The root *bio* means "life," and *diversity* means "variety," so *biodiversity* means "the variety of life in an environment."

50. B The fourth paragraph states that antibiotic-resistant genes might increase the problem of antibiotic resistance in humans, making it the most likely reason for the WHO to recommend against using them.

The TASC Language Arts– Writing Test

3

HOW TO USE THIS CHAPTER

» Read the Overview to learn what the TASC Language Arts–Writing Test covers.

» Take the TASC Language Arts–Writing Pretest to preview your knowledge and skills.

» Study the TASC Language Arts–Writing Test Review to refresh your knowledge of TASC test writing skills.

» Take the TASC Language Arts–Writing Practice Test to sharpen your skills and get ready for test day.

Overview

The TASC Language Arts–Writing Test is divided into two parts. The first part deals with your understanding of standard English. You will be asked to correct or revise existing sentences or paragraphs to improve or elaborate them. The second part requires you to write an essay in response to a prompt.

The TASC Language Arts–Writing Test is based on the Common Core State Standards for Language and Writing. You can see these standards at www.corestandards.org/ELA-Literacy. The main standards covered by the TASC test include the following:

Conventions of Standard English

1. CCSS.ELA-Literacy.CCRA.L.1 Demonstrate command of the conventions of standard English grammar and usage when writing or speaking.

Writing CC Standard

2. **CCSS.ELA-Literacy.CCRA.L.2** Demonstrate command of the conventions of standard English capitalization, punctuation, and spelling when writing.

Knowledge of Language

3. **CCSS.ELA-Literacy.CCRA.L.3** Apply knowledge of language to understand how language functions in different contexts, to make effective choices for meaning or style, and to comprehend more fully when reading or listening.

Text Types and Purposes

4. **CCSS.ELA-Literacy.CCRA.W.1** Write arguments to support claims in an analysis of substantive topics or texts using valid reasoning and relevant and sufficient evidence.
5. **CCSS.ELA-Literacy.CCRA.W.2** Write informative or explanatory texts to examine and convey complex ideas and information clearly and accurately through the effective selection, organization, and analysis of content.

Production and Distribution of Writing

6. **CCSS.ELA-Literacy.CCRA.W.4** Produce clear and coherent writing in which the development, organization, and style are appropriate to task, purpose, and audience.
7. **CCSS.ELA-Literacy.CCRA.W.5** Develop and strengthen writing as needed by planning, revising, editing, rewriting, or trying a new approach.

Research to Build and Present Knowledge

8. **CCSS.ELA-Literacy.CCRA.W.9** Draw evidence from literary or informational texts to support analysis, reflection, and research.

In general, the first part of the Language Arts–Writing section will focus on the first three standards previously listed, and the second part will focus on the remaining five standards—but there is some crossover. For example, you might be given a multiple-choice question that asks you to choose the best concluding statement for a given paragraph. That is a subskill under Text Types and Purposes.

The argument writing that you may do on the TASC test is similar but not identical to opinion writing you may have done in the past. Pages 100–102 of the Review will show you some specific rules for argument writing.

TASC Language Arts–Writing Pretest

Use the items that follow to preview your knowledge of language and writing.
Answers appear on page 85.

Part 1: Language

1. Read this sentence.

   Before she participates in the recital, Bridget is been putting in hours of practice.

   Which of these is the <u>most</u> accurate and effective revision to the sentence?

   Ⓐ Before she participates in the recital, Bridget will put in hours of practice.
   Ⓑ Bridget been putting in hours of practice before participating in the recital.
   Ⓒ Having participated in the recital, Bridget putting in hours of practice.
   Ⓓ Participating in the recital, Bridget will be putting in hours of practice.

2. Which two sentences include a misspelled word?

   Ⓐ The photographer asked the bridal party to align themselves along the stone wall.
   Ⓑ His camera was profesional quality, of course; he makes a living taking pictures.
   Ⓒ The groom, a lawyer by occupation, towered over his diminutive bride.
   Ⓓ Groomsmen in tuxedos accompanied a bevy of elegant bridesmaids.
   Ⓔ The ivy twining up the wall made a charming backdrop.
   Ⓕ The bride held a bouquet wholy made up of white roses.

3. Read the paragraph.

The right to vote is something we often take for granted in our free society. Rest assured that people in newly democratized nations take it far more seriously. After the end of apartheid, some South African voters waited patiently for 12 hours to cast their first vote for a multiracial slate of candidates.

Which sentence best concludes this paragraph?

Ⓐ The voting process must be changed to accommodate urban voters.

Ⓑ South Africa's National Assembly is made up of 400 representatives.

Ⓒ There are many arguments about which nation is the world's oldest democracy.

Ⓓ On Election Day, we would do well to remember how crucial a right this is.

4. Which of these sentences is punctuated correctly?

Ⓐ The New Visions program, offers high school seniors a non-traditional year of study.

Ⓑ New Visions offers courses in two areas: Life Sciences, and Health and Medical Careers.

Ⓒ Students in New Visions earn concurrent enrollment credits, with the local community college.

Ⓓ Selection into New Visions is based upon grades, recommendations, an interview, and essays.

5. Read this sentence.

It was not surprising that we had all awoken at the same instant, since the crowing of the rooster was not something that most of us, being from the city, were used to.

Which revision of the sentence best expresses the idea precisely and concisely?

Ⓐ Unsurprising that we had all awoken at the same instant, being that the rooster's crowing was not something we were used to, being from the city.

Ⓑ Since the crowing of the rooster was unfamiliar to us city-dwellers, it was not surprising that we all awoke at the same instant.

Ⓒ Given that we were from the city and therefore unused to the crowing of a rooster, it was unsurprising that we had all awoken at the same instant.

Ⓓ Waking at the same instant was unsurprising for us who were from the city, unused to crowing roosters.

6. Which two sentences correctly use hyphens?

(A) Mr. Penn's course on writing fiction was well-attended.

(B) He liked to break-down the writing process into steps.

(C) All thirty-two of the students wrote fiction weekly.

(D) Mr. Penn had to grade all of those cleverly-written stories.

(E) He marked the papers with a distinctive, red ball-point pen.

(F) He preferred to grade papers in a quiet, off-campus cafe.

Read this excerpt of a draft of an essay. Then answer questions 7 and 8.

[1]Manga are Japanese comics, illustrated in a particular style that goes back over a century. [2]Although they have been popular in Japan for decades, manga have only recently become a worldwide phenomenon.

[3]Anime such as *Sailor Moon* introduced manga characters to new fans in the United States. [4]The popular *Pokemon* anime drew in young viewers and readers. [5]More mature anime such as the *Ghost in the Shell* series appealed to an older audience. [6]Today, Japanese artists are not the only ones creating manga; many American and European cartoonists have adopted the distinctive style.

---

7. Which sentence would be the <u>most</u> effective addition to the end of the first paragraph?

(A) Since the late 1900s, graphic novels have become increasingly popular.

(B) The author of a manga is known as a *mangaka*; most mangaka are professional artists.

(C) People outside Japan often first encountered manga through its animated form, anime.

(D) Manga may be serialized in comic books or published in longer graphic novels.

8. How could sentences 4 and 5 <u>best</u> be combined?

(A) The popular *Pokemon* anime drew in young viewers and readers, whereas more mature anime such as the *Ghost in the Shell* series appealed to an older audience.

(B) Because the popular *Pokemon* anime drew in young viewers and readers, more mature anime such as the *Ghost in the Shell* series appealed to an older audience.

(C) The popularity of *Pokemon* anime and the appeal of more mature anime such as the *Ghost in the Shell* series drew in young viewers and readers as well as an older audience.

(D) Drawn to *Pokemon* anime were younger viewers and readers; older audiences were appealed to by more mature anime such as the *Ghost in the Shell* series.

9. Read the paragraph.

They include familiar metals such as gold, silver, platinum, and copper; but they also include less well-known metals—rhodium, ruthenium, palladium, osmium, and iridium. These noble metals are relatively rare, and many are therefore precious.

Which sentence would best open the paragraph to introduce the topic?

(A) The noble metals, unlike base metals, do not corrode or rust.

(B) The English chemist William Hyde Wollaston discovered two noble metals.

(C) Platinum and gold, being resistant to tarnish, make fine jewelry.

(D) A metal may be an element, a compound, or an alloy.

10. Read this sentence.

Emmanuel Vargas, a recent arrival from Spain, gave us a rousing speech.

How could you revise the sentence to stress the quality of the speech?

(A) A recent arrival from Spain named Emmanuel Vargas gave us a rousing speech.

(B) We heard a rousing speech from Emmanuel Vargas, a recent arrival from Spain.

(C) Emmanuel Vargas gave us a rousing speech; he is a recent arrival from Spain.

(D) A recent arrival from Spain, Emmanuel Vargas, gave us a rousing speech.

11. Which of these sentences contains an error or errors in capitalization?

(A) Did your English class read *To Kill a Mockingbird* this spring?

(B) You should definitely read Harper Lee's masterwork more than once.

(C) Young children enjoy the story of Scout, her brother, and their friend Dill.

(D) Older readers understand the underlying themes of Racism and Empathy.

Read this excerpt of a draft of an essay. Then answer questions 12–14.

[1]State lotteries are popular games in all but six of the United States. [2]_____ they are an important source of revenue for those states, they appeal most to those people who can least afford the cost of a ticket.

[3]Lotteries also contribute to the gambling epidemic. [4]Many people in Gamblers Anonymous report relying on the weekly purchase of lottery tickets to fulfill their craving. [5]It is not uncommon for such gamblers to spend $50 a week on tickets. [6]The odds of winning a lottery are astronomical; it is truly a sucker's game. [7]The odds of winning a game with 6 numbers drawn out of 49 are 1 in 13,983,816. [8]There is even a website on which you can plug in numbers to determine your odds in any given game.

12. Drag the correct word to the blank in sentence 2 to clarify the transition between ideas.

| Since |
| Nonetheless |
| Although |
| Assuming |

13. Which sentence would be the most effective addition to the end of the first paragraph?

Ⓐ Usually, the higher the cost of a lottery ticket, the more money can be collected by the lucky winner.

Ⓑ Lotteries are often called "a tax on the poor" because households with the lowest incomes spend as much as 5 percent of their earnings on tickets.

Ⓒ There are ample stories, true or exaggerated, about lottery winners who blew through their winnings and lost everything.

Ⓓ Some people use birthdates to pick their lucky numbers; others simply let the lottery machine randomly pick for them.

14. Where might the author add a paragraph break to better organize the text?

Ⓐ between sentences 4 and 5
Ⓑ between sentences 5 and 6
Ⓒ between sentences 6 and 7
Ⓓ between sentences 7 and 8

15. Read this sentence.

> When I took the algebra test, I was a bit concerned beforehand because I had not taken a course in algebra (or used the skill, actually) for at least a year.

Which of these is the <u>most</u> accurate and effective revision to the sentence?

Ⓐ In taking the algebra test, I was concerned a bit beforehand due to not having taken an algebra course or used the actual skill for at least a year.

Ⓑ Before taking the algebra test, I was a bit concerned, having not taken a course in algebra or actually not used the skill for at least a year.

Ⓒ Not taking an algebra course or using the skill for about a year made me concerned beforehand on taking the algebra test.

Ⓓ I was a bit concerned before taking the algebra test because I had neither taken an algebra course nor used the skill for at least a year.

16. Which of these sentences contains a misspelled word?

Ⓐ Devin knew that attendance at a good college was something worth pursuing.

Ⓑ His principal concern was financial; college would be expensive!

Ⓒ He luckily landed a job as a maintainance worker at his former school.

Ⓓ The salary was more than adequate, and Devin could work evenings and nights.

17. Read this sentence.

> Wanda has always lived in the city ☐ for that reason ☐ she does not yet have a driver's license ☐

Drag each punctuation mark to its correct position in the sentence.

> ☐.
> ☐,
> ☐;

18. Read this sentence.

> An award for "most-improved writer" was given to Jabez by the committee.

Which revision of the sentence is <u>most</u> correct and concise?

Ⓐ By the committee was given an award for "most-improved writer" to Jabez.

Ⓑ Jabez received from the committee an award for "most-improved writer."

Ⓒ The committee gave Jabez an award for "most-improved writer."

Ⓓ The award by the committee for "most-improved writer" was given to Jabez.

19. Read the paragraph.

If "chance favors the prepared mind," as Louis Pasteur once said, it may not really matter whether you study with a specific career in mind. By getting a sound, basic, well-rounded education, you will prepare your mind to be ready for any opportunity. It is not easy to predict today what careers will be available four or five years from now.

Write a concluding sentence that logically follows from the information given in this paragraph. Write your sentence in the box.

20. Which of these sentences contains a grammatical error?

Ⓐ Either Danielle or her sisters are planning the event.

Ⓑ Marianne and Felicia have the list of invited guests.

Ⓒ Danielle and she will arrange for all of the food.

Ⓓ You should respond to she or Marianne this week.

Part 2: Writing

Write an essay to explain how a writer may use specific facts and data to make a point. Base your ideas on the excerpt from Mark Twain's *Life on the Mississippi* and the essay "Olympic Upset" that you read on pages 21 and 58.

Before you begin planning and writing, reread the texts.

As you read the texts, think about how authors use data—and numbers in particular—to make a point about their subjects. You may take notes or highlight the details as you read.

After reading the texts, create a plan for your essay. Think about the quotes or examples you want to use. Think about how you will introduce your topic and what the main topic will be for each paragraph.

Now, write your essay. Be sure to:

» Use information from the texts so that your article includes important details. Introduce the topic clearly, provide a focus, and organize information in a way that makes sense.
» Develop the topic with facts, definitions, details, quotations, or other information and examples related to the topic.
» Use appropriate and varied transitions to create cohesion.
» Clarify the relationship among ideas and concepts.
» Use clear language and vocabulary to inform about the topic.
» Provide a conclusion that follows the information presented.

This is the end of the TASC Language Arts–Writing Pretest.

TASC Language Arts–Writing Pretest Answers

1. **A** Review 1. Conventions of Standard English Grammar and Usage (pp. 88–94); Review 7. Develop and Strengthen Writing (pp. 106–108).

2. **B and F** Review 2. Conventions of Standard English Capitalization, Punctuation, and Spelling (pp. 94–98).

3. **D** Review 4. Write Arguments to Support Claims (pp. 100–102); Review 6. Produce Clear and Coherent Writing (pp. 104–106).

4. **D** Review 2. Conventions of Standard English Capitalization, Punctuation, and Spelling (pp. 94–98).

5. **B** Review 1. Conventions of Standard English Grammar and Usage (pp. 88–94); Review 7. Develop and Strengthen Writing (pp. 106–108).

6. **C and F** Review 2. Conventions of Standard English Capitalization, Punctuation, and Spelling (pp. 94–98).

7. **C** Review 5. Write Informative or Explanatory Texts (pp. 102–104); Review 6. Produce Clear and Coherent Writing (pp. 104–106).

8. **A** Review 5. Write Informative or Explanatory Texts (pp. 102–104); Review 7. Develop and Strengthen Writing (pp. 106–108).

9. **A** Review 5. Write Informative or Explanatory Texts (pp. 102–104); Review 6. Produce Clear and Coherent Writing (pp. 104–106).

10. **B** Review 3. Apply Knowledge of Language (pp. 98–99).

11. **D** Review 2. Conventions of Standard English Capitalization, Punctuation, and Spelling (pp. 94–98).

12. **Although** Review 4. Write Arguments to Support Claims (pp. 100–102); Review 6. Produce Clear and Coherent Writing (pp. 104–106).

13. **B** Review 4. Write Arguments to Support Claims (pp. 100–102); Review 6. Produce Clear and Coherent Writing (pp. 104–106).

14. **B** Review 4. Write Arguments to Support Claims (pp. 100–102); Review 6. Produce Clear and Coherent Writing (pp. 104–106).

15. **D** Review 1. Conventions of Standard English Grammar and Usage (pp. 88–94); Review 7. Develop and Strengthen Writing (pp. 106–108).

16. **C** Review 2. Conventions of Standard English Capitalization, Punctuation, and Spelling (pp. 94–98).

17. Wanda has always lived in the city; for that reason, she does not yet have a driver's license. Review 2. Conventions of Standard English Capitalization, Punctuation, and Spelling (pp. 94–98).

18. **C** Review 1. Conventions of Standard English Grammar and Usage (pp. 88–94).

19. **Possible answer: Studying a broad range of subjects may prepare you best for any eventuality.** Review 4. Write Arguments to Support Claims (pp. 100–102); Review 6. Produce Clear and Coherent Writing (pp. 104–106).

20. **D** Review 1. Conventions of Standard English Grammar and Usage (pp. 88–94).

Essay

Here are the scoring rubrics that the test-makers at CTB have provided to show how to assess TASC test essay writing. Use them to score your own essay for the pretest, or give your essay to a friend to score for you.

Informative Essay

SCORE	SCORING CRITERIA
4	The response is a well-developed essay that examines a topic and presents related information. • Effectively introduces the topic to be examined • Uses specific facts, details, definitions, examples, and/or other information to develop topic fully • Uses an organizational strategy to present information effectively • Uses precise and purposeful word choice • Uses words, phrases, and/or clauses that effectively connect and show relationships among ideas • Uses and maintains an appropriate tone • Provides a strong concluding statement or section that logically follows from the ideas presented • Has no errors in usage and conventions that interfere with meaning
3	The response is a complete essay that examines a topic and presents information. • Clearly introduces the topic to be examined • Uses multiple pieces of relevant information to develop topic • Uses an organizational structure to group information • Uses clear word choice • Uses words and/or phrases to connect ideas • Uses an appropriate tone • Provides a concluding statement or section that follows from the ideas presented • Has few, if any, errors in usage and conventions that interfere with meaning
2	The response is an incomplete or oversimplified essay that examines a topic. • Attempts to introduce a topic • Develops topic, sometimes unevenly, with mostly relevant information • Attempts to use an organizational structure • Uses simple language, which sometimes lacks clarity • Provides a weak concluding statement or section • May have errors in usage and conventions that interfere with meaning
1	The response provides evidence of an attempt to write an essay that examines a topic. • May not introduce a topic, or topic must be inferred • Provides minimal information to develop the topic • May be too brief to demonstrate an organizational structure • Uses words that are inappropriate, overly simple, or unclear • Provides a minimal or no concluding statement or section • Has errors in usage and conventions that interfere with meaning
0	The response is completely irrelevant or incorrect, or there is no response.

Argumentative Essay

SCORE	SCORING CRITERIA
4	The response is a well-developed essay that develops and supports an argument. • Effectively introduces a claim • Uses logical, credible, and relevant reasoning and evidence to support a claim • Uses an organizational strategy to present reasons and relevant evidence • Acknowledges and counters opposing claims, as appropriate • Uses precise and purposeful word choice • Uses words, phrases, and/or clauses that effectively connect and show relationships among ideas • Uses and maintains an appropriate tone • Provides a strong concluding statement or section that logically follows from the ideas presented • Has no errors in usage and conventions that interfere with meaning
3	The response is a complete essay that develops and supports an argument. • Clearly introduces a claim • Uses multiple pieces of evidence to support the claim • Uses an organizational strategy to present reasons and evidence • Uses clear word choice • Uses words and phrases to connect ideas • Uses an appropriate tone • Provides a concluding statement or section that follows from the ideas presented • Has few, if any, errors in usage and conventions that interfere with meaning
2	The response is an incomplete or oversimplified essay that develops an argument. • Attempts to introduce a claim • Supports the claim, sometimes unevenly, with mostly relevant evidence • Attempts to use an organizational structure • Uses simple language, which sometimes lacks clarity • Provides a weak concluding statement or section • May have errors in usage and conventions that interfere with meaning
1	The response provides evidence of an attempt to write an essay that develops an argument. • May not introduce a claim, or claim must be inferred • Provides minimal evidence to support the claim • May be too brief to demonstrate an organizational structure • Uses words that are inappropriate, overly simple, or unclear • Provides a minimal or no concluding statement or section • Has errors in usage and conventions that interfere with meaning
0	The response is completely irrelevant or incorrect, or there is no response.

Review 4. Write Arguments to Support Claims (pp. 100–102); Review 6. Produce Clear and Coherent Writing (pp. 104–106); Review 7. Develop and Strengthen Writing (pp. 106–108); Review 8. Draw Evidence from Texts (pp. 108–111)

TASC Language Arts–Writing Test Review

The pages that follow briefly review each of the eight standards listed in the Overview. To learn more about grammar, usage, mechanics, and writing, find books on those topics in the library or look for instructional webinars online.

 ## Conventions of Standard English Grammar and Usage

Grammar is the system and structure of a language. Usage is the way in which the parts of a language are used—how sentences are put together, how words agree with each other, and so on.

KEY TERMS: active voice, agreement, antecedent, clause, compound, misplaced modifier, parallel structure, parts of speech, passive voice, phrase, plural, singular, subject, tense, verb

Parts of Speech

Every word in a sentence plays a particular role. There are eight parts of speech.

The Parts of Speech

PART OF SPEECH	FUNCTION	EXAMPLES
Noun	Names a person, place, thing, or idea	boy, lake, wagon, fear
Pronoun	Takes the place of a noun	she, them, mine, somebody
Verb	Expresses action or state of being	scream, jump, are, seemed
Adjective	Modifies a noun or pronoun	huge, first, several, the
Adverb	Modifies a verb, adjective, or adverb	there, soon, cleverly, far
Preposition	Shows relationships	behind, after, toward, prior to
Conjunction	Joins words or groups of words	and, but, or, neither/nor
Interjection	Expresses emotion	hey, wow, oh, ugh

Subjects and Verbs

A sentence is composed of at least one subject and one verb. The **subject** is the part of the sentence about which something is being said. The **verb** tells what the subject is or does.

The tiny <u>insect</u> <u>buzzes</u> furiously over the flowering plant.

Insect is the subject about which something is being said. *Buzzes* is the verb that tells what the insect does.

Subjects and verbs may be simple, as shown, or **compound**, as shown here.

The tiny <u>insect</u> and its <u>mate</u> <u>swoop</u> and <u>buzz</u> furiously over the flowering plant.

This sentence has two subjects and two verbs. Notice that the verbs change form to match the compound subject.

Phrases

A **phrase** is a group of related words used as a single part of speech. Phrases do not contain a sentence's subject and verb.

Types of Phrases

TYPE OF PHRASE	DESCRIPTION	EXAMPLES
Prepositional	Begins with a preposition and ends with a noun or pronoun; may act as an adjective or adverb	into the woods, after the long winter, like me
Participial	Contains the *-ing* or *-ed* form of a verb; acts as an adjective	skipping happily, kept under wraps, collecting his thoughts
Gerund	Contains the *-ing* form of a verb; acts as a noun	your essay writing, flying a plane, clever storytelling
Infinitive	Contains the *to* form of a verb; acts as a noun, adjective, or adverb	needed <u>to sleep</u>, a day <u>to remember</u>, happy <u>to help</u>
Appositive	Contains a noun or pronoun and any modifiers; renames or explains another noun or pronoun	Our coach, <u>this year's teacher of the year</u>, is a wonderful mentor. We will meet on Friday, <u>the last day in June</u>.

Clauses

A **clause** is a group of words that contains a subject and verb and is used as part or all of a sentence. An **independent clause** expresses a complete thought and can stand on its own as a sentence.

<u>Fairy tales are common worldwide</u>.

<u>Fairy tales are common worldwide</u>; <u>many stories share similar plots and characters</u>.

The first sentence is composed of a single independent clause. The second is a compound sentence made up of two independent clauses separated by a semicolon.

A **dependent (subordinate) clause** does not express a complete thought and cannot stand on its own as a sentence. Dependent clauses may be used as adjectives or adverbs.

Types of Dependent Clauses

Adjective	Let the student who finishes first collect the papers.
	The only flavor that I liked was the ginger-lemon blend.
Adverb	Before you leave, remind me to give you that book.
	Joe will loan me the money if I pay it back promptly.

Adjective clauses typically begin with relative pronouns *who, whom, whose, which,* and *that.* Adverb clauses begin with subordinating conjunctions such as *after, although, as if, because, before, if, since, so that, unless, until, whenever, where,* and *while.*

Subject-Verb Agreement

Nouns and pronouns may be **singular**, referring to one person, place, thing, or idea. They may be **plural**, referring to more than one. In standard English, verbs agree with subjects in number. Singular subjects require singular verbs, and plural subjects require plural verbs.

The banjo is a popular stringed instrument. (singular)
Banjos are popular stringed instruments. (plural)

Michele plays several instruments in a jug band. (singular)
Michele and her sister play several instruments in a jug band. (plural)

Everyone looks forward to their concerts. (singular)
We look forward to their concerts. (plural)

Pronoun-Antecedent Agreement

Pronouns take the place of nouns. The noun to which the pronoun refers is its **antecedent**. A pronoun must agree with its antecedent both in number and in gender.

The library in Danville usually opens its doors at ten.

Before people can check out books, they need a card.

Everybody must show ID before receiving his or her card.

Singular antecedents joined by *or* or *nor* should be referred to by a singular pronoun. Singular antecedents joined by *and* should be referred to by a plural pronoun.

Neither Jasmine nor Hallie remembered her library card.

Both Charlie and I offered to share our books with the girls.

Consistent Tense

The **tense** of a verb tells when the action takes place.

Verb Tenses

TENSE	EXAMPLES
Present	is, goes, practices
Past	was, went, practiced
Future	will be, will go, will practice
Present perfect	has been, has gone, has practiced
Past perfect	had been, had gone, had practiced
Future perfect	will have been, will have gone, will have practiced

Sentences and paragraphs should not shift from one tense to another.

INCONSISTENT:	Writing is my hobby, and it became my profession as well.
	Writing is my hobby, and it will have been my profession as well.
CONSISTENT:	Writing is my hobby, and it has become my profession as well.
	Writing is my hobby, and it is becoming my profession as well.

So-called perfect tenses express action that is finished. You can use perfect tenses to show the relationship between actions.

I <u>wrote</u> about many people whom I <u>had encountered</u>.

I <u>will write</u> about many people whom I <u>have encountered</u>.

In the examples, the encountering of people is an action that is finished. The use of the perfect form shows that the finished action precedes the action of writing.

Active and Passive Voice

When a subject performs an action, the sentence is in **active voice**. When an action is performed upon a subject, the sentence is in **passive voice**. Active voice is preferable, especially in formal writing.

PASSIVE VOICE:	The heavy doors were pushed open by Hector.
ACTIVE VOICE:	Hector pushed open the heavy doors.
PASSIVE VOICE:	A loud alarm was heard.
ACTIVE VOICE:	We heard a loud alarm.

Pronoun Usage

Personal pronouns come in three cases. They may be subjects, objects, or possessive words. In addition, the pronoun *who* is a subject pronoun. The pronoun *whom* is an object pronoun.

Pronoun Cases

SUBJECT	OBJECT	POSSESSIVE
I	me	my, mine
you (singular or plural)	you	your, yours
he, she, it	him, her, it	his, her, hers, its
we	us	our, ours
they	them	their, theirs
who	whom	whose

Use subject pronouns as sentence subjects or after a linking verb.

I enjoyed the new restaurant.

He and she ordered the ribs.

The most polite dinner guest was she.

Who is the chef here?

Use object pronouns as direct objects, indirect objects, or the objects of prepositions.

The owner invited him and me. (direct object)

Please hand us some napkins. (indirect object)

For whom was that sandwich named? (object of a preposition)

Misplaced Modifiers

Phrases and clauses that modify other words in a sentence should appear as close as possible to the words they modify.

MISPLACED: At the age of 12, Mr. Purdue started giving me lessons.

CORRECT: At the age of 12, I started lessons with Mr. Purdue.

MISPLACED: The violin belongs to Marla that has the rich tone.

CORRECT: The violin that has the rich tone belongs to Marla.

Parallel Structure

Use the same pattern of words to show that ideas have similar levels of importance.

NOT PARALLEL: Yvonne likes knitting, crocheting, and to quilt.

PARALLEL: Yvonne likes knitting, crocheting, and quilting.

   Yvonne likes to knit, crochet, and quilt.

NOT PARALLEL: My instructor told me that I should buy the best wool possible, that I should take my time, and that mistakes are to be expected at first.

PARALLEL: My instructor told me that I should buy the best wool possible, that I should take my time, and that I should expect to make mistakes at first.

   My instructor told me that I should buy the best wool possible, take my time, and expect to make mistakes at first.

CHALLENGE   Conventions of Standard English Grammar and Usage

Choose the word or phrase that makes each sentence correct.

1. After Martha has completed her Spanish course, she **(graduated/will graduate)** in May.

2. Her parents invited my friends and **(I, me)** to Martha's graduation party.

3. Although I **(has/have)** not seen much of Martha recently, she was once my best friend.

4. I will buy her a gift, bring some flowers, and **(I will go to her party/attend her party)**.

5. Remembering our friendship, **(my heart is full/I have a full heart)**.

CHALLENGE ANSWERS

Conventions of Standard English Grammar and Usage

1. **will graduate:** Martha has not yet completed the course, but when she does complete it, she will graduate. The graduation is in the future, not the past.

2. **me:** The pronoun is being used as an object, so *me* is the correct form.

3. **have:** This is the form of the verb that goes with the subject *I*.

4. **attend her party:** To make the sentence parallel in structure, all three parts should start with a verb and end with an object.

5. **I have a full heart:** It is I who is doing the remembering, not my heart. The modifying phrase should be close to the subject.

 ## Conventions of Standard English Capitalization, Punctuation, and Spelling

We often refer to capitalization, punctuation, and spelling as the *mechanics* of writing. They are the practical details that make our language run smoothly. In this brief discussion, we will review only those rules you are most likely to face on the TASC test.

KEY TERMS: colon, hyphen, independent clause, nonessential, proper adjective, proper noun, quotation, semicolon, series

Capitalization

Capitalize the first word in a sentence, the pronoun *I*, and proper nouns and adjectives. **Proper nouns** name particular people, places, or things. **Proper adjectives** are formed from proper nouns.

Have **I** told you the story of my trip to the **Turkish** border near **Syria**?

In the title of a text, capitalize the first, last, and all important words.

A Tale of Two Cities

"The Charge of the Light Brigade"

Do not capitalize the names of seasons, school subjects (except foreign languages or specific course names), or ideas, unless they are being used in examples of personification.

This spring, I hope to take another course in economics.

Last fall, I enrolled in **Microeconomics I.**

I am especially interested in ethics and fiscal policy.

"It was not **Death**, for I stood up . . ."

Commas

Use commas to separate words or phrases in a **series**, to separate **independent clauses** when conjunctions are used, and to set off **nonessential** clauses or phrases that are not critical to the main idea of a sentence.

I have volunteered at Suicide Prevention, at the Food Pantry, and at Home Builders. (series)

Suicide Prevention is a difficult place to work, but its work is invaluable. (independent clauses)

The Food Pantry, which opened in the 1980s, serves hundreds of families each week. (nonessential clause)

Home Builders, run by two former contractors, constructs houses for low-income families. (nonessential phrase)

Use commas after introductory participial phrases, long prepositional phrases or series of prepositional phrases, and introductory adverb clauses. Use commas to set off appositive phrases.

Finding her voice at last, Greta responded to the customer. (participial phrase)

After her explanation of the situation, the man seemed satisfied. (prepositional phrases)

Until her manager returned, Greta was in charge of the department. (adverb clause)

The manager, a graduate of Tufts, had ten years of experience. (appositive phrase)

Use commas between city and state or between city and country. Add a comma after the city and state in a sentence.

The family recently moved from Tyrone, New York, to Pittsburgh, Pennsylvania.

Semicolons

Use a **semicolon** to separate independent clauses that are not joined by conjunctions or independent clauses that are joined by transitional words such as *for example* or *therefore*. Use a semicolon to separate independent clauses that are joined by conjunctions when commas appear within the independent clauses.

Last night's game was a heartbreaker; our team lost in overtime.

It was the end of our season; nevertheless, we felt content.

We were impressed by the play of Larry, Dwayne, and Joe; and Leon had his best game ever.

Use semicolons between items in a series when the items already contain commas.

> The plane will land in Omaha, Nebraska; Atlanta, Georgia; and then Miami, Florida.

Colons

Use a **colon** to introduce a list of items or before a long or formal quotation.

> My favorite American novelists include the following: William Faulkner, Willa Cather, and Alice Walker.
>
> In *O Pioneers!*, perhaps her greatest novel, Willa Cather once wrote: "There are only two or three human stories, and they go on repeating themselves as fiercely as if they had never happened before; like the larks in this country, that have been singing the same five notes over for thousands of years."

Hyphens

Use a **hyphen** to divide a word at the end of a line of text. Always divide a word between syllables.

> INCORRECT HYPHENATION: Jason collected tickets at yesterday's basketball tournam-ent.
>
> CORRECT HYPHENATION: Jason collected tickets at yesterday's basketball tourna-ment.

Use a hyphen with compound numbers and with fractions used as adjectives—but not as nouns.

> twenty-five, eighty-four, one hundred fifty-six
>
> one-eighth Norwegian, two-thirds majority, three fourths of a cup

Use a hyphen with certain prefixes: *ex-*, *self-*, and *all*; plus all prefixes that precede a proper noun or proper adjective. You may use a hyphen to avoid confusion when a prefix ends with the same letter as the base word.

> ex-husband, self-evident, all-encompassing
>
> mid-August, pre-Columbian
>
> anti-imperialist, pre-election

Spelling

A number of so-called spelling demons may end up on the TASC test. These are words that do not follow particular spelling rules but simply must be recognized and memorized. Here are just a few.

Spelling Demons

absence	acceptable	accessible	accommodate	achieve	acknowledge
acquire	adolescent	aggravate	amateur	anxious	apparent
attempt	awhile	balance	believe	beneficial	brilliant
business	category	ceiling	cemetery	changeable	college
committee	conceive	conscience	conscious	courageous	criticize
decision	dependent	desperate	dilemma	discipline	doubt
ecstasy	eligible	embarrass	endeavor	exaggerate	exhilarate
existence	fierce	fulfill	gauge	genuine	grievous
guilty	harass	height	humorous	hypocrite	immigrant
infinite	interrupt	irrelevant	judgment	knowledge	laboratory
license	lieutenant	literature	maintenance	maneuver	marriage
miscellaneous	mischievous	misspell	necessary	noticeable	obedience
occurrence	omitted	original	parallel	paralyze	perceive
permanent	personnel	physical	pleasant	precede	prejudice
prestige	prevalent	privilege	prodigy	profession	quantity
receipt	referred	renowned	repetition	rhythm	sacrifice
salary	schedule	seize	separate	sergeant	siege
similar	soldier	sophomore	stature	strength	subtle
success	supersede	surprise	susceptible	technique	thorough
tragedy	transferred	truly	unnecessary	vacuum	vengeance
villain	visible	waive	weird	wholly	yacht

Conventions of Standard English Capitalization, Punctuation, and Spelling

CHALLENGE

Edit each sentence to fix two errors in capitalization, punctuation, and/or spelling.

1. The Cuyahoga river runs from Hambden, Ohio to Lake Erie.

2. Local tribes named the river "Cuyahoga" which means "crooked river" in an iroquoian dialect.

3. In mid June of 1969 a portion of the river's surface famously burst into flames.

4. This was not an uncommon occurance a much worse fire had taken place in the 1950s.

5. A reporter for *Time* wrote "The river is a constant fire hazard because of quantaties of oil deposited in it by numerous industries in the Cleveland area."

CHALLENGE ANSWERS

Conventions of Standard English Capitalization, Punctuation, and Spelling

1. The Cuyahoga River runs from Hambden, Ohio, to Lake Erie.

   Cuyahoga River **is the complete proper noun, and a comma must appear after the state name in the sentence.**

2. Local tribes named the river "Cuyahoga," which means "crooked river" in an Iroquoian dialect.

   A comma belongs between the clauses, and *Iroquoian* **is a proper adjective.**

3. In mid-June of 1969, a portion of the river's surface famously burst into flames.

   Mid-June **requires a hyphen, and a comma belongs after the introductory prepositional phrase.**

4. This was not an uncommon occurrence; a much worse fire had taken place in the 1950s.

   Occurrence **was misspelled, and a semicolon should separate the independent clauses.**

5. A reporter for *Time* wrote: "The river is a constant fire hazard because of quantities of oil deposited in it by numerous industries in the Cleveland area."

   Use a colon (or a comma) to introduce the quotation, and spell *quantities* **correctly.**

 Apply Knowledge of Language

In high school, this Common Core skill has to do with making effective word choices for meaning or style. You might be asked to choose the best word for a given purpose or to rearrange a sentence to achieve a given effect.

KEY TERMS: shade of meaning, syntax

Word Choice

Selecting a word with a particular **shade of meaning** may change the nature of a sentence, as in these examples.

Fred <u>resisted</u> his father's suggestions.

Fred <u>defied</u> his father's suggestions.

Fred <u>attacked</u> his father's suggestions.

Syntax

Syntax is the arrangement of words and phrases in a sentence. Different arrangements may emphasize different parts of the sentence and thus affect meaning.

In these sentences, changing one word changes meaning.

Wiley insists that only he knows the entry code. (Wiley is the only one who knows it.)

Wiley only insists that he knows the entry code. (Wiley insists just one thing.)

Wiley insists that he knows only the entry code. (Wiley knows just one thing.)

In these sentences, changing the syntax changes the focus of the sentence.

Although we trust her expertise, Renee can be unreliable.

Renee can be unreliable, although we trust her expertise.

The first sentence is more positive than the second, because it emphasizes our trust rather than Renee's unreliable qualities.

CHALLENGE Apply Knowledge of Language

Choose the word or arrangement of words that makes each sentence more negative.

1. After the party, the four friends (**discussed/disputed**) its success.

2. Becky enjoyed herself despite the bad music./Despite the bad music, Becky enjoyed herself.

3. Connor wondered whether the DJ was simply (**ignorant/inexperienced**).

4. The friends had clearly (**requested/demanded**) a blend of old and new dance music.

5. Instead, the DJ had delivered a (**jumble/blend**) of country and hip-hop.

CHALLENGE ANSWERS

Apply Knowledge of Language

1. **disputed:** The word *disputed* connotes a sort of argument.

2. **Despite the bad music, Becky enjoyed herself.:** Mentioning the bad music first stresses that negative feature of the party.

3. **ignorant:** To be ignorant is worse than to be inexperienced.

4. **demanded:** *Demanded* is a word that implies pressure.

5. **jumble:** A jumble is a messy mixture; a blend is a balanced mixture.

Write Arguments to Support Claims

An **argument** is a logical appeal to a reader or listener. In an argument, you state your ideas and support them. Your goal is to be convincing and clear.

KEY TERMS: argument, claim, conclusion, counterclaim, evidence, style, tone, transitions

Claims

The first part of an argument is the **claim**. In argument writing, your claim may state that something is true or not true. It may state that something is good or not good. It may state that one course of action is better or worse than another. A claim should be arguable, or debatable. In other words, not everyone should instantly agree with it.

ARGUABLE:	In North America, winters and summers are steadily getting hotter.
NOT ARGUABLE:	In North America, winters tend to be colder than summers.

Counterclaims

The best arguments anticipate counterclaims. A **counterclaim** is what someone might say to oppose a claim.

CLAIM:	In North America, winters and summers are steadily getting hotter.
COUNTERCLAIM:	North America goes through cycles of hot years and cooler years.

Evidence

No claim or counterclaim has value unless it is supported by evidence. **Evidence** includes the facts, examples, and data that lead logically to the claim. You may need to name the source of your evidence.

CLAIM:	In North America, winters and summers are steadily getting hotter.
EVIDENCE:	The continental United States has warmed by 1.3°F over 100 years. (*Climate Central*)
	The 9 warmest years in 132 years have occurred since 2000. (NASA)
	Extreme cold temperatures are less frequent in the Northwest. (*Climatic Change*)

Transitions

A good argument includes clear **transitions** that connect one part of the argument to the next. Here are some helpful transition words and phrases to use as you write.

Transition Words and Phrases

addition	besides, furthermore, in addition, moreover
contrast	conversely, however, in spite of, nevertheless, on the other hand, whereas
comparison	also, likewise, similarly
details	especially, including, namely, specifically
examples	for example, for instance, in other words, to illustrate
result	accordingly, as a result, consequently, due to, for this reason, therefore
summary	finally, in conclusion, so, thus

Style and Tone

Your writing **style** should be formal, and your **tone** should be objective. In other words, you should use standard English that conforms to the rules of college or career writing. You should not insert your own biases into the argument but should maintain a fairly neutral tone. Your goal is to impart facts and evidence, not beliefs and feelings.

INFORMAL:	It's wild how fast temperatures in the desert have risen.
FORMAL:	Temperatures in the desert have risen especially fast.
SUBJECTIVE:	People who continue to argue about climate change have lost it.
OBJECTIVE:	Occasionally, people still argue about the sources of climate change.

Conclusion

As with any formal writing, your argument should include a concluding statement or section that supports the argument that preceded it. A solid **conclusion** connects back to the original claim.

So if winters seem milder and summers hotter than ever, those impressions may be accurate. The data appear to support an overall increase in temperatures throughout the Northern Hemisphere.

CHALLENGE | Write Arguments to Support Claims

In this paragraph, underline the claim. Circle each piece of evidence that supports the claim. Draw two lines under the counterclaim.

Better zoning in Middleburg will make our village cleaner and more welcoming. The village of Redding saw a major improvement in civic pride when it created zoning laws restricting the number of vehicles allowed per yard. Zoning restrictions kept industrial waste from polluting nearby Tripptown. Some will say that new laws just limit our freedom. However, if freedom means pollution and trash, perhaps some limitation is needed.

CHALLENGE ANSWERS
Write Arguments to Support Claims

Better zoning in Middleburg will make our village cleaner and more welcoming. The village of Redding saw a major improvement in civic pride when it created zoning laws restricting the number of vehicles allowed per yard. Zoning restrictions kept industrial waste from polluting nearby Tripptown. Some will say that new laws just limit our freedom. However, if freedom means pollution and trash, perhaps some limitation is needed.

 Write Informative or Explanatory Texts

Informative or explanatory writing is nonfiction writing that provides information about a topic or explains a process or event. Your goal in informative or explanatory writing is to explain complex material in a simple and organized way.

KEY TERMS: analogy, relevant, topic

Topic

The **topic**, or central focus, of your writing on the TASC test will be provided for you. As you write, make sure that topic is front and center and is obvious to the reader. You may do this with a topic sentence to start the essay. Your topic sentence may repeat some of the language in the TASC test prompt.

One good example of a community activity with learning potential is our town's annual Community Read.

Organization

Your writing should be organized to create a unified whole. Introduce your topic first; then use transition words and phrases to add information that builds from one element to the next.

There are many possible organizational structures to use for informative or explanatory writing.

- >> Description
- >> Cause/effect
- >> Problem/solution
- >> Definition/example
- >> Classification
- >> Time order
- >> Compare/contrast

Developing the Topic

You may develop your essay using facts, definitions, details, quotations, and/or examples. Choose details that are **relevant**—that apply directly to your topic and do not wander off and confuse the reader.

RELEVANT:	Last year, the entire community read or reread *To Kill a Mockingbird*. This 1961 Pulitzer Prize–winner deals with serious issues of inequality and morality that are universal and timely fifty years later.
IRRELEVANT:	The author of *To Kill a Mockingbird* never wrote another novel. One of her best friends was the author of *In Cold Blood*.

Language and Vocabulary

When you write about science, math, history, or literature, use vocabulary that is appropriate for those subjects. A comparison technique such as the **analogy** can help you link ideas.

To have parents and children, teachers and students, bosses and workers all read the same text is to create a common language for the entire community.

Reading *To Kill a Mockingbird* can feel like taking a trip back in time to an earlier America, one where children roam freely from morning to night.

Conclusion

The conclusion of informative or explanatory writing should tell why the topic is important and of interest. It may suggest effects of the topic.

A Community Read can be a remarkable learning experience for all members of a community and a way to unite many factions in an activity that leads to insight and common purpose.

CHALLENGE Write Informative or Explanatory Texts

In this paragraph, cross out an irrelevant detail. Underline the analogy the writer used. Then circle the type of organization the writer used.

If your engine is backfiring, you probably have too much oxygen in the exhaust system. Think of it as a burp from the guts of the car. Start by inspecting the exhaust system for leaks, checking the muffler, the catalytic converter, and the pipes. Catalytic converters convert harmful pollutants to cleaner emissions. Look carefully at the gaskets. You may need to disconnect the air injection system to see whether it is operating properly. If all else fails, take the car to your mechanic.

Cause/effect   Problem/solution   Compare/contrast

CHALLENGE ANSWERS

Write Informative or Explanatory Texts

If your engine is backfiring, you probably have too much oxygen in the exhaust system. <u>Think of it as a burp from the guts of the car.</u> Start by inspecting the exhaust system for leaks, checking the muffler, the catalytic converter, and the pipes. ~~Catalytic converters convert harmful pollutants to cleaner emissions.~~ Look carefully at the gaskets. You may need to disconnect the air injection system to see whether it is operating properly. If all else fails, take the car to your mechanic.

Cause/effect   (Problem/solution)   Compare/contrast

 Produce Clear and Coherent Writing

When you write for the TASC test, you will be expected to produce clear and coherent (logical and consistent) writing that matches the prompt and is appropriate for your purpose and audience.

KEY TERMS: audience, purpose

Responding to a Prompt

Whenever you respond to a prompt, use this RAFTS strategy:

R = Role. What role are you asked to take as a writer? Are you writing as yourself or as an expert in a subject?

A = Audience. For whom are you writing? Does the prompt tell you?

F = Format. What kind of response are you asked to give? Are you writing an argument? Are you writing an explanation? How can you tell?

T = Task. Use the verbs in the prompt to decide what you must do. Look for specific actions you are being asked to take.

S = Strong key words. Find key words in the prompt that you can use to start your response.

Setting a Purpose

Your **purpose** for writing is the reason you are writing. You may write a story to entertain a friend. You may write an essay to explain a concept. You may write a poem to describe a place. You may write an argument to express an opinion. Keep your purpose clearly in mind as you write for the TASC test.

Audience

The **audience**, or readership, for your writing is important for several reasons. When you write for children, you write differently than you do when you write for adults. Your word choice is different, your sentences are shorter, and even the ideas you include may be simpler. When you write for someone you do not know, you write differently than you do when you write for a friend. You may use formal language and avoid contractions and slang.

When you write for the TASC test, assume that you are writing for readers you do not know. Maintain a formal style and a serious tone.

CHALLENGE Produce Clear and Coherent Writing

Read the prompt. Then answer the questions.

Reread the two letters to the editor about constructing a pedestrian overpass. Imagine that you are a legislator in the town in which the letter-writers live. Which of the letters offers the better-reasoned argument? What other questions would you want to ask before making a decision?

Write a response to your constituents from the point of view of a legislator. Suggest which way you are leaning as you decide on how to rule on the pedestrian overpass bill. Explain what in each letter has caused you to move in that direction. Conclude by suggesting some other pieces of data you might like to see before voting.

1. What role are you asked to take as a writer?

2. Who is your audience?

3. What is your task?

CHALLENGE ANSWERS

Produce Clear and Coherent Writing

1. the role of a legislator in the town where the letter-writers live (See sentence 2.)

2. constituents in that town (See paragraph 2.)

3. My task is to explain which way I am leaning on the pedestrian overpass bill, based on the information in the letters that I find most logical. I must also include ideas for other information I would need to make up my mind. (See paragraph 2.)

 Develop and Strengthen Writing

Although you have a limited time in which to write your TASC test essay, you will be expected to revise it as needed to create the best piece of writing you can. When you develop and strengthen writing, you use a plan to begin your writing, and you use revision skills to improve your work.

KEY TERMS: editing, revising

The Writing Process

Even for a short, timed essay, you can use a process like the one shown to develop and strengthen your work.

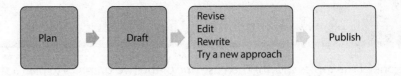

Planning

When you plan your writing, you may use any of these strategies.

>> List your purpose and task.
>> Take notes.
>> Make an outline.
>> Draw a picture.
>> Freewrite or brainstorm.
>> Cluster ideas.

Revising and Editing

Revising may involve moving words, sentences, and paragraphs around to improve your organization. It may involve adding information or removing information that is not relevant. **Editing** includes proofreading your work to fix errors in grammar, usage, mechanics, word choice, and syntax. See Reviews 1–3 on pages 88–99 for the kinds of language errors you might look for in the editing process.

Rewriting or Trying a New Approach

Sometimes you may find that you "write yourself into a corner"—that no amount of revising will get you to where you want to be. At such times, you may need to cross out what you have done and rewrite it. You might even try a new approach to the prompt; for example, taking the opposite side of an argument from the one you started with. Rewriting takes time, of course, so use your judgment. If you have already worked for half an hour on a one-hour essay, try to revise what you have instead of starting over from scratch.

CHALLENGE Develop and Strengthen Writing

Choose one of the topics shown. Then use one of the two graphics to plan a short essay.

TOPICS
How to study for a test
How to dress for an interview
How to balance a checkbook
How to impress an employer

I. _____

   A. _____

   B. _____

II. _____

   A. _____

   B. _____

III. _____

   A. _____

   B. _____

CHALLENGE ANSWERS

Develop and Strengthen Writing

Answers will vary. If you chose the first graphic, your main idea or key word should be in the center, with related ideas in the ovals surrounding it. If you chose the second graphic, your main ideas should appear as I, II, and III, with related ideas as A and B below each Roman numeral.

8 Draw Evidence from Texts

One of the most important skills you will use as you write for the TASC test is being able to draw evidence from texts to support your writing. This is a combination of reading and writing skills, and it is a strategy that you will use whether you go on from here to college or to a career.

KEY TERMS: citing, evidence, paraphrase

Evidence from Informational Texts

You may be asked to analyze a piece of writing for a TASC test essay. Use **evidence**—facts, examples, and data—to support your analysis. You can do this by **citing**—quoting or referring to—specific references from the text that address what you are saying. Here are some examples.

RESTATING AND QUOTING: Here the writer states Paine's argument in her own words and follows with a direct quotation from the text.

> Thomas Paine argues that one should form a new government carefully and thoughtfully, saying, "It is infinitely wiser and safer, to form a constitution of our own in a cool deliberate manner, while we have it in our power, than to trust such an interesting event to time and chance."

PARAPHRASING: When you **paraphrase**, you restate information in your own words.

> Thoreau makes it clear to his readers that he moved to the simple life in the woods not to resign from reality but instead to trim away everything that was not necessary.

DIRECTING THE READER'S ATTENTION TO AN ASPECT OF THE TEXT: You may not wish to quote directly but simply to show a reader where a citation may be found.

> Jefferson did not declare independence without cause. Following paragraph 2 of his Declaration of Independence, he listed the many wrongdoings of the king of Great Britain that led the patriots to such a declaration.

Evidence from Literary Texts

The evidence you draw from literary texts may address the author's style or use of literary elements as well as his or her argument or the theme of the text.

RESTATING AND QUOTING: Here the writer uses a quotation from *The Great Gatsby* to illustrate a point about theme.

> Fitzgerald emphasizes the excesses of the upper class at the expense of the lower class with simple images like this one: "There was a machine in the kitchen which could extract the juice of two hundred oranges in half an hour if a little button was pressed two hundred times by a butler's thumb."

PARAPHRASING: This writer paraphrases a passage from *A Raisin in the Sun* to support a statement about characterization.

> Mama proves herself the moral center of the play with her lecture to Beneatha in Act III, declaring that the time to love someone most is when that person is at his worst.

DIRECTING THE READER'S ATTENTION TO AN ASPECT OF THE TEXT: The writer here refers to lines from "Ode on a Grecian Urn" to point out a particular stylistic feature.

Punctuation is a critical aspect of the poem, providing both meaning and meter. Keats applies apostrophes to words in lines 1 and 5 of the first stanza and to other words throughout the poem to show how those words should be pronounced to achieve the intended rhythm.

CHALLENGE **Draw Evidence from Texts**

Directions: Read the excerpt from a speech by a famous women's suffragist. Then follow the directions.

Excerpt from "The Crisis"

Carrie Chapman Catt

September 7, 1916

Let us then take measure of our strength. Our cause has won the endorsement of all political parties. Every candidate for the presidency is a suffragist. It has won the endorsement of most churches; it has won the hearty approval of all great organizations of women. It was won the support of all reform movements; it has won the progressives of every variety. The majority of the press in most States is with us. Great men in every political party, church and movement are with us. The names of the greatest men and women of art, science, literature and philosophy, reform, religion and politics are on our lists. We have not won the reactionaries of any party, church or society, and we never will. From the beginning of things, there have been Antis. The Antis drove Moses out of Egypt; they crucified Christ who said, "Love thy neighbor as thyself"; they have persecuted Jews in all parts of the world; they poisoned Socrates, the great philosopher; they cruelly persecuted Copernicus and Galileo, the first great scientists; they burned Giordano Bruno at the stake because he believed the world was round; they burned Savonarola who warred upon church corruption; they burned Eufame McIlyane because she used an anaesthetic; they burned Joan d'Arc for a heretic; they have sent great men and women to Siberia to eat their hearts out in isolation; they burned in effigy William Lloyd Garrison; they egged Abbie Kelley and Lucy Stone and mobbed Susan B. Anthony. Yet, in proportion to the enlightenment of their respective ages, these Antis were persons of intelligence and honest purpose. They were merely deaf to the call of Progress and were enraged because the world insisted upon moving on. Antis male and female there still are and will be to the end of time. Give to them a prayer of forgiveness for they know not what they do; and prepare for the forward march.

1. Underline the sentence in the speech that supports this statement: "The cause of women's suffrage has extended to presidential campaigns."

2. Draw two lines under the sentence in the speech that supports this statement: "Those who work against our cause act out of anger and insensitivity."

CHALLENGE ANSWERS

Draw Evidence from Texts

1. "Every candidate for the presidency is a suffragist."

   Clearly, then, the cause extends to presidential campaigns.

2. "They were merely deaf to the call of Progress and were enraged because the world insisted upon moving on."

   Catt means that the Antis of any age are angry and insensitive rather than stupid or dishonest.

TASC Language Arts–Writing Practice Test

50 questions, 55 minutes

The following test is designed to simulate a real TASC Language Arts–Writing Test section in terms of question formats, number, and degree of difficulty. To get a good idea of how you will do on the real exam, take this test under actual exam conditions. Complete the test in one session and follow the given time limit. Answers and explanations begin on page 127.

Part 1: Language

1. Which of these sentences is punctuated correctly?
   (A) Leonardo filled out the application for a loan; which requested information about his finances.
   (B) Having copied the data from his last three years of tax forms, Leonardo felt confident about his prospects.
   (C) His job was stable and his income was steadily climbing; making him a likely candidate for the loan.
   (D) Leonardo signed the application; dated it; and finally sealed it in the envelope, provided by the bank.

2. Read the paragraph.

   Out of thousands of petitions each year, the Supreme Court usually requests oral argument in fewer than 100. From October until April, the Court hears arguments for two weeks each month. Opposing counsel have no more than half an hour apiece to present their case.

   Which sentence best concludes this paragraph?
   (A) Each Supreme Court justice has law clerks to research cases and draft opinions.
   (B) Justices are appointed by the president and confirmed by the Senate.
   (C) At that time, the case is submitted for decision, which is done by majority vote.
   (D) To argue before the Supreme Court, lawyers must be admitted to that Court's bar.

3. Which two sentences include a misspelled word?

(A) Although students may not drive on campus, they are eligible for parking permits.

(B) Acquiring a permanent parking place is useful if one wants to drive on weekends.

(C) Olivia will take the test for her licence before leaving for college this autumn.

(D) Her only qualms concern the portion of the test that involves parallel parking.

(E) She does not think that her recent attempts at parking are exceptable.

(F) She is conscious that she needs to practice until she feels ready.

4. Read this sentence.

After completing the puzzle, Mario feeling rather proud.

Which of these is the most accurate and effective revision to the sentence?

(A) After completing the puzzle, Mario felt rather proud.

(B) After having completed the puzzle, Mario has felt rather proud.

(C) After completed the puzzle, Mario felt rather proud.

(D) After he completes the puzzle, Mario feeling rather proud.

5. Read this sentence.

We admired the view of vineyards and beautiful roses from our balcony.

Which revision of the sentence best expresses the idea correctly and precisely?

(A) From our balcony we admired the view of vineyards and beautiful roses.

(B) We admired the view of vineyards from our balcony and beautiful roses.

(C) We admired the view from our balcony of vineyards and beautiful roses.

(D) Admiring the view of vineyards and beautiful roses, we did from our balcony.

6. Which of these sentences is punctuated correctly?

(A) This outdoor display from the 1700s is well-kept.

(B) The cannonballs are of pre-Revolutionary vintage.

(C) The cannon itself was used in seventeen-seventy-six.

(D) It has been restored to immaculately-clean condition.

7. Read the paragraph.

It is spoken as the primary language in parts of Switzerland, Belgium, and Canada; Monaco; and of course, France. It is a major language in Gabon, Algeria, Senegal, and several other countries of West Africa. It remains the official language of United Nations agencies and of the Olympics.

Which sentence would <u>best</u> open the paragraph to introduce the topic?

Ⓐ Louisiana and Maine are two states with a substantial number of French-speaking citizens.

Ⓑ French uses the same alphabet as English, although several vowels may include diacritical marks.

Ⓒ Although it has lost some of its dominance to English, French is still an important language internationally.

Ⓓ French, Italian, Portuguese, and Spanish are the main languages that derived from the Latin of the Roman Empire.

Read this excerpt of a draft of an essay. Then answer questions 8 and 9.

[1]Formula One racing started as Grand Prix motor racing in France. [2]As early as the 1890s, cars raced on roads from one town to another. [3]Today, of course, Formula One cars go far faster, with some achieving speeds of 220 miles per hour. [4]The races are also far longer. [5]Most take place on a track rather than on the open road. [6]Racing has become big business. [7]Millions of dollars are spent by each team on improving cars, especially on engine development.

---

8. Which sentence would be the <u>most</u> effective addition to the end of the first paragraph?

Ⓐ The first such race was sponsored by a Parisian newspaper.

Ⓑ In those days, drivers rarely reached a speed of 15 miles per hour.

Ⓒ Both drivers and onlookers were frequently injured or killed.

Ⓓ A mechanic often rode along with the driver in the racecar.

9. Which revision <u>most</u> effectively combines the ideas of sentences 4 and 5 into one sentence?

Ⓐ The races being far longer, most take place on a track rather than on the open road.

Ⓑ Although the races are also far longer, most take place on a track rather than on the open road.

Ⓒ The races are also far longer; in fact, most take place on a track rather than on the open road.

Ⓓ The races are also far longer, and most take place on a track rather than on the open road.

10. Which two sentences contain an error or errors in capitalization?

(A) Every Autumn, the residents of Plattesville organize a road cleanup.

(B) They start on Main Street and work outward to the north, south, east, and west.

(C) One group cleans along Route 225 all the way to the town line.

(D) Another works eastward toward the boundary with Clark County.

(E) The mayor and his council members often join in the fun.

(F) By Mid-October, the town is fresh-looking and free of trash.

11. Read these sentences.

> Experienced racers drink water regularly for several days before the event, stopping about an hour or two prior to the start. This hydration process is ⬚ for healthy racing.

In the blank, drop the word that best stresses the importance of hydration.

| useful |
| vital |
| effective |
| handy |

12. Read this sentence.

> After unpacking all of the produce boxes, Randall's boss had given him a short break.

Which of these is the most correct and concise revision to the sentence?

(A) Having unpacked all of the produce boxes, Randall's boss gave Randall a short break.

(B) After Randall unpacked all of the produce boxes, his boss gave him a short break.

(C) Once he had unpacked all of the produce boxes, Randall's boss gave him a short break.

(D) Randall's boss, once Randall unpacked all of the produce boxes, had given him a short break.

13. Which of these sentences contains a misspelled word?

(A) Justin transfered from his community college to a four-year university.

(B) Although he enjoyed his literature courses, he hoped to major in finance.

(C) In his opinion, success in business courses would make him eligible for a good job.

(D) Justin hoped to achieve financial independence shortly after graduation.

14. Read this sentence.

> Serena loved the city, it's mad pace, and the many people she met there.

What change should be made to correct the sentence's punctuation?

A Change the first comma to a semicolon.
B Change the second comma to a semicolon.
C Eliminate the apostrophe.
D Eliminate both commas.

15. Which of these sentences contains a grammatical error?

A Either Martha or Greg is in charge of the trip.
B Greg, Martha, and I have arranged for tickets.
C If you see Martha or him, give me a call.
D Neither he nor she have the maps we need.

16. Read this sentence.

> A wonderful new website design was presented to the board by our company.

Which of these is the <u>most</u> accurate and effective revision to the sentence?

A To the board was presented a wonderful new website design by our company.
B Our company to the board presented a wonderful new website design.
C A wonderful new website design by our company was presented to the board.
D Our company presented a wonderful new website design to the board.

17. Read the paragraph.

> The village council met to discuss the problem of deer overpopulation. Several recent car-deer accidents have caused injuries and property damage. In addition, deer are destroying many of the new plantings around village hall and the golf course.

Write a concluding sentence that logically follows from the information given in this paragraph.

Read this excerpt of a draft of a report. Then answer questions 18–20.

[1]The Tunguska event took place in central Russia in 1908. [2]It was a gigantic explosion that leveled trees, broke windows, and knocked people off their feet. [3]_____ many theories about the explosion exist, the likeliest is that a comet or small asteroid exploded in the atmosphere over Russia.

[4]For example, some people described seeing a fireball in the sky. [5]Others spoke of a column of blue light. [6]Some mentioned a sound like gunfire. [7]Because the explosion was so destructive, it is lucky that it happened in a remote area. [8]A similar explosion over a city could cost thousands of lives.

18. Drag the correct word to the blank in sentence 3 to clarify the transition between ideas.

    | While |
    | However |
    | Since |
    | Perhaps |

19. Which sentence would be the most effective addition to the beginning of the second paragraph?

    (A) Explosions can be extraordinarily destructive, even in such a forested region.
    (B) Scientists have used eyewitness accounts to piece together what might have happened.
    (C) Asteroids are small, rocky bodies that orbit the sun, ranging in size from tiny to gigantic.
    (D) Craters from previous asteroid impacts appear in the deserts of Mexico and Arizona.

20. Where might the author add a paragraph break to better organize the text?

    (A) between sentences 4 and 5
    (B) between sentences 5 and 6
    (C) between sentences 6 and 7
    (D) between sentences 7 and 8

21. Read this sentence.

I would expect Jasmine perform admirably on that test.

Which of these is the <u>most</u> accurate and effective revision to the sentence?

Ⓐ I expect Jasmine performing admirably on that test.
Ⓑ I would expect Jasmine had perform admirably on that test.
Ⓒ I would expect Jasmine to perform admirably on that test.
Ⓓ I would expect Jasmine performing admirably on that test.

22. Which two sentences contain a misspelled word?

Ⓐ Ed's retirement party acknowledged his years of dedicated service.
Ⓑ His boss offered a humorous look back at all of Ed's sucesses.
Ⓒ Ed received accolades from many of his previous coworkers.
Ⓓ He was visibly touched by the present from the personnel director.
Ⓔ Ed was widely percieved as a tough but fair administrator.
Ⓕ His greatest strength was his thoughtful committee work.

23. Which of these sentences is punctuated correctly?

Ⓐ The Red List, is an inventory of endangered and threatened species.
Ⓑ Threatened species include three categories: Critically Endangered, Endangered, and Vulnerable.
Ⓒ More than 10,000 species of plants, and animals are listed as "vulnerable."
Ⓓ To be labeled "vulnerable" species must be at high risk of endangerment in the wild.

24. Which of these sentences contains an error or errors in capitalization?

Ⓐ Jason enrolled in Comparative Literature I this semester.
Ⓑ His class is currently reading *Notes From Underground*.
Ⓒ This classic work by Dostoyevsky is set in Saint Petersburg.
Ⓓ Needless to say, the class is reading the English translation.

25. The sentences in this paragraph are not in a logical order.

> Hershey, Pennsylvania, is sometimes called "Chocolatetown."

> Buildings and roads around Hershey attest to the company's influence.

> Home to the Hershey Company, it is the epitome of a company town.

> Among these are the Milton Hershey Medical Center and Chocolate Avenue.

Drag and drop the sentences to put them in a logical order from 1 to 4.

①

②

③

④

Read this excerpt of a draft of an essay. Then answer questions 26 and 27.

[1]Ice hockey, as we know it today, derives from a game played in Canada in the 1800s. [2]Whether it is an adaptation of a Native American game, an outgrowth of an Icelandic game, or some combination of the two is hard to determine.
   [3]Montreal hosted the first organized team hockey. [4]Students from McGill University founded the first hockey club. [5]They also established a set of rules. [6]The rules are similar to those used today.

---

26. How could sentences 4 through 6 best be combined?

Ⓐ Students from McGill University founded the first hockey club and established a set of rules similar to those used today.

Ⓑ Students from McGill University founded the first hockey club; and they established a set of rules, rules that are similar to those used today.

Ⓒ Students from McGill University first founded a hockey club, then established a set of rules, and finally the rules were similar to those used today.

Ⓓ A set of rules similar to those used today was created by students from McGill University, who also founded the first hockey club.

27. Which sentence would be the <u>most</u> effective addition to the end of the first paragraph?

(A) Hockey is fast-paced, difficult to master, and frequently dangerous.

(B) Finland, Russia, Sweden, and the Czech Republic all field great hockey teams.

(C) Whatever its origin might be, hockey became Canada's premier winter sport.

(D) The Icelandic game looks a bit like a cross between hockey and lacrosse.

28. Read this sentence.

The softball game ran into extra innings, for that reason we decided to cancel our dinner plans.

Which revision of the sentence <u>best</u> expresses the idea precisely and concisely?

(A) Having the softball game run into extra innings led to deciding on our part to cancel our dinner plans.

(B) The softball game ran into extra innings; after that we decided to cancel our dinner plans.

(C) Being that the softball game ran into extra innings resulted in our cancelling our dinner plans.

(D) Because the softball game ran into extra innings, we decided to cancel our dinner plans.

29. Read the paragraph.

What we now call the Cook Islands were once called *Gente Hermosa,* or "Beautiful People," by the Spaniards who landed there in the early 1600s. When British explorer James Cook arrived in the 1770s, he named them the Hervey Islands. It was not until the 1820s that they were renamed for Captain Cook.

Which sentence would <u>best</u> open the paragraph to introduce the topic?

(A) The Cook Islands have undergone several name changes.

(B) The Cook Islands were first settled by sailors from Tahiti.

(C) The Cook Islands lie in the Pacific, northeast of New Zealand.

(D) The Cook Islands are composed of 15 volcanic islands and two reefs.

30. Which of these sentences is punctuated correctly?

(A) His well-intentioned speech turned out rather badly.

(B) The three-hundred members of the audience were shocked.

(C) At least one-half of them assumed they had heard incorrectly.

(D) He left quickly, avoiding the cross-fire of reporters.

31. Read this sentence.

> A two-story bungalow in the old California style, the home is right on the beach.

Which of these is the <u>most</u> accurate and effective revision to the sentence to emphasize the home's location?

(A) A two-story bungalow right on the beach, the home is in the old California style.

(B) The home, a two-story bungalow in the old California style, is right on the beach.

(C) The beach home is a two-story bungalow in the old California style.

(D) Situated right on the beach, the home is a two-story bungalow in the old California style.

32. Which of these sentences contains a misspelled word?

(A) The factory retains some of its original machinery.

(B) A river runs parallel to the east wing of the building.

(C) There was once apparantly a water wheel alongside that wall.

(D) With the advent of modern electricity, the wheel became unnecessary.

Read this excerpt of a draft of an essay. Then answer questions 33–35.

[1]Wildfires may take place in areas of grassland, forest, or scrubland. [2]The size of a wildfire depends on several factors; _____ are available fuel and weather conditions.

[3]Lightning strikes are one common cause of wildfires. [4]In volcanic settings, lava flow may cause a wildfire. [5]Even falling rocks can lead to sparks that may start a fire. [6]A significant number of wildfires are human-caused. [7]Arson, cigarette butts, and equipment malfunctions can cause such fires. [8]Some years, the number of human-caused wildfires in the United States actually exceeds the number of natural fires.

---

33. Which word or words would <u>best</u> fit in the blank in sentence 2 to clarify the transition between ideas?

(A) such as

(B) for example

(C) including

(D) among these

34. Which sentence would be the <u>most</u> effective addition to the start of the second paragraph?

   Ⓐ Natural wildfires have a variety of possible causes.

   Ⓑ High moisture can limit the spread of wildfires.

   Ⓒ Wildfires may lead to significant financial losses.

   Ⓓ Neglected campfires have been known to start fires.

35. Where might the author add a paragraph break to better organize the text?

   Ⓐ between sentences 4 and 5

   Ⓑ between sentences 5 and 6

   Ⓒ between sentences 6 and 7

   Ⓓ between sentences 7 and 8

36. Which of these sentences is grammatically correct?

   Ⓐ The party will be three weeks away, so we are addressing invitations.

   Ⓑ Several on the guest list is coming from across the country.

   Ⓒ Once we add stamps to that stack of envelopes, we will have completed our task.

   Ⓓ Doctor Pliss's retirement is being a big deal in this community.

37. Read this sentence.

> The café is a popular spot for skiers and hikers at the bottom of the mountain to meet.

Which of these is the <u>most</u> accurate and effective revision to the sentence?

   Ⓐ At the bottom of the mountain, skiers meet hikers in the popular café.

   Ⓑ The popular spot at the bottom of the mountain is a café for skiers and hikers to meet.

   Ⓒ The café at the bottom of the mountain is a popular spot for skiers and hikers to meet.

   Ⓓ The café is a popular spot at the bottom of the mountain to meet skiers and hikers.

38. Read this sentence.

> A tiny puppy wearing a blue collar was found in the garden by my sister and me.

Which revision of the sentence is <u>most</u> correct and concise?

   Ⓐ Wearing a blue collar, my sister and I found a tiny puppy in the garden.

   Ⓑ A tiny puppy wearing a blue collar was found by my sister and me in the garden.

   Ⓒ In the garden, I found a tiny puppy wearing a blue collar with my sister.

   Ⓓ In the garden, my sister and I found a tiny puppy wearing a blue collar.

39. Read this sentence.

Kyle's a strong ☐ fit athlete ☐ he has won the local triathlon twice ☐

Drag each punctuation mark to its correct position in the sentence.

☐ .
☐ ,
☐ ;

40. Read the paragraph.

In 2010, the median annual salary for a young worker with no high school diploma was $21,000. With a high school diploma or its equivalent, that rose to $29,900. A degree from a two-year college raised that amount even further, to $37,000.

Write a concluding sentence that logically follows from the information given in this paragraph.

☐

41. Read this sentence.

Having completed the application, John Robert now waiting for an interview.

Which of these is the most accurate and effective revision to the sentence?

Ⓐ Having completed the application, John Robert must now wait for an interview.

Ⓑ After completing the application, John Robert now waiting for an interview.

Ⓒ Having completed the application, John Robert be waiting for an interview.

Ⓓ After having completed the application, John Robert wait for an interview.

42. Which of these sentences contains an error or errors in capitalization?

Ⓐ Chloe works after school at Jason's Grocery.

Ⓑ The store is the only grocery on College Avenue.

Ⓒ Do they carry products from Blue Heron farm?

Ⓓ Yes, they feature their organic vegetables and Rome apples.

43. Read the paragraph.

Norwegian fjord horses were domesticated by the Vikings thousands of years ago. These stocky, strong horses are still used in farming, especially in western Norway. They are sturdy enough to pull a plow or haul timber.

Which sentence best concludes this paragraph?

Ⓐ Nearly nine out of ten fjord horses are a pale, yellowish-tan color.

Ⓑ A fjord, of course, is a narrow, cliff-lined inlet of the sort found along the Norwegian coast.

Ⓒ As their ancestors did, modern Norwegian farmers recognize the value of these powerful horses.

Ⓓ Clydesdales and Percherons are better-known breeds of draft horses.

44. Which of these sentences contains a misspelled word?

Ⓐ It was an honor and a privilege to attend his ordination.

Ⓑ Ralph had studied for the priesthood for several years.

Ⓒ His goal had been interrupted by several family crises.

Ⓓ Today is the culmanation of Ralph's longtime dream.

45. Read this sentence.

Desiree's plan was to kick off her shoes; curl up with a book, and relax.

What change should be made to correct the sentence's punctuation?

Ⓐ Change the semicolon to a comma.

Ⓑ Change the second comma to a semicolon.

Ⓒ Eliminate the apostrophe.

Ⓓ Eliminate the semicolon.

46. Which two sentences are punctuated correctly?

Ⓐ Without waking the baby, from his nap, the women quietly chatted in the kitchen.

Ⓑ They compared notes on their children, their finances, and their part-time jobs.

Ⓒ Working from home, was proving to be more difficult than Leah had imagined.

Ⓓ Rosa reassured her that "it would be easier once Max was in preschool".

Ⓔ "If I make it that far," said Leah, "it will be a miracle!"

Ⓕ "No, really, Rosa insisted. My life is finally back on track."

47. Read these sentences.

> The cell phone, for years merely a staple of businesspeople worldwide, has morphed into the most important of all devices. It is not at all [blank] to suggest that within a few years, we will need no laptops or tablets at all. We will simply carry our phones and plug them into one peripheral after another as we go about our day.

In this blank, drop the word that makes the sentence best stress the reasonableness of the suggestion.

| challenging |
| far-fetched |
| rational |
| injurious |

Read this excerpt of a draft of an essay. Then answer questions 48–50.

> [1]It is hard to believe today, but during her lifetime, Emily Dickinson was barely known. [2]She wrote hundreds of poems; _____, she published very few.
>
> [3]Her poems were short. [4]They used unusual punctuation. [5]They often dealt with dark topics.
>
> [6]Today we might diagnose Dickinson as depressed. [7]She was terribly troubled by the early deaths of her cousins and friends. [8]Many of her best-known poems are reflections on Death.

48. Which word would best fit in the blank in sentence 2 to clarify the transition between ideas?

Ⓐ despite
Ⓑ instead
Ⓒ subsequently
Ⓓ however

49. Which sentence would be the most effective addition to the start of the second paragraph?

Ⓐ Dickinson's poems differed from the typical poetry of the day.
Ⓑ Dickinson lived in New England and studied at Mount Holyoke.
Ⓒ Few know that Dickinson studied botany and was an avid gardener.
Ⓓ Dickinson's sister discovered Emily's poems after her death in 1886.

50. Write a sentence that combines sentences 3 through 5 without changing their meanings. Write your answer in the box.

```


```

Part 2: Writing

Write an essay that assesses the usefulness of research mentioned by an author. Base your ideas on two texts you have read: the article titled "Drifting in Static" on page 52 and "Food of the Future?" on page 69. The first article ends with a description of 10 listening buoys, part of a Cornell University research study. The second calls for more testing of genetically modified foods. If you knew that there were limited funds, which of these studies would you support, and why?

Before you begin planning and writing, reread the texts.

As you read the texts, think about the facts presented that you might use in your essay. What else would you like to know about the topics? You may take notes or highlight the details as you read.

After reading the texts, create a plan for your essay. Choose any quotes or information from the articles that might support or counter your argument. Think about how you will introduce your topic and what the main topic will be for each paragraph. You will have 50 minutes to write your essay.

Now, write your essay. Be sure to:

>> Use information from the texts so that your essay includes important details. Introduce the topic clearly, provide a focus, and organize information in a way that makes sense.
>> Develop the topic with facts, definitions, details, quotations, or other information and examples related to the topic.
>> Use appropriate and varied transitions to create cohesion.
>> Clarify the relationship among ideas and concepts.
>> Use clear language and vocabulary to inform about the topic.
>> Provide a conclusion that follows the information presented.

**This is the end of the TASC Language Arts–Writing Practice Test.**

Writing Practice Answer

TASC Language Arts–Writing
Practice Test Explanatory Answers

1. B In this sentence, the comma correctly follows an introductory clause. The other sentences incorrectly include semicolons that do not separate independent clauses.

2. C The paragraph is in time order, describing the process by which the Supreme Court hears arguments and makes decisions. Only choice C provides a next step in the sequence.

3. C and E The correct spellings are *l-i-c-e-n-s-e* and *a-c-c-e-p-t-a-b-l-e*.

4. A The action of completing the puzzle is over, so the other verb should be in the past tense.

5. A The original sentence makes it seem as though the roses were from the balcony. Choice C is not entirely awkward, but choice A is clearer.

6. B *Well-kept* (choice A) would only require a hyphen if it preceded the word it described. The correct way to write out *1776* (choice C) is *seventeen seventy-six*. No hyphen is needed in choice D. However, a hyphen always connects *pre* and a proper noun or proper adjective, making choice B correct.

7. C The opening sentence must present the topic and lead naturally into the remaining sentences. Only choice C does this.

8. B Paragraph 2 starts abruptly with a statement about today's cars going "far faster." The first paragraph needs a sentence against which that speed can be measured, and choice B is a good example.

9. D The two sentences do not oppose each other, as choice B would suggest. Instead, the second sentence just adds more information, making the use of *and* the simplest way to combine the two.

10. A and F The names of the seasons are not capitalized. The prefix "mid-" is also not capitalized.

11. vital The other choices imply that drinking water is useful. The word *vital* implies that it is absolutely necessary.

12. B Who unpacked the produce boxes? Presumably, Randall did, but sentences A and C make it seem as though his boss did the work.

13. A To form the past tense of *transfer*, double the *r* before adding *ed*. The word should be *transferred*.

14. C The apostrophe makes the possessive pronoun *its* into *it's*, meaning "it is" or "it has."

15. D In compound subjects joined by *either* and *or* or *neither* and *nor*, the verb must agree with the subject nearer to the verb. In this case, it is the singular pronoun *she*, so the sentence should read, "Neither he nor she has the maps we need."

16. D As written, the original sentence is in the passive voice. Choice D corrects that and makes the sentence active.

17. Possible answer: The council hopes to come up with a plan to minimize damage by deer. The paragraph is about the village council's meeting to discuss a problem, so it makes sense for the paragraph to conclude with a sentence about that meeting.

18. While The relationship between the first part of the sentence ("many theories about the explosion exist") and the second part ("the likeliest is that . . .") is one of contrast. Many theories exist, but one is most likely. The word from the choices that shows this contrast is *While*.

19. B As it stands, the first three sentences of paragraph 2 describe what witnesses saw and heard. These descriptions should be introduced with an explanation that they are eyewitness descriptions.

20. C Sentences 4 through 6 belong together, but sentence 7 starts a new thought. Adding a break between sentences 6 and 7 would clarify that change.

21. C You are asked to choose the correct verb form; in this case, it is the infinitive ("to") form.

22. B and E The correct spellings are *s-u-c-c-e-s-s-e-s* and *p-e-r-c-e-i-v-e-d*.

23. B Choice B correctly uses the colon to introduce a series.

24. B You do not capitalize prepositions in the middle of titles. The correct title is *Notes from Underground.*

25. 1. Hershey, Pennsylvania, is sometimes called "Chocolatetown." 2. Home to the Hershey Company, it is the epitome of a company town. 3. Building and roads around Hershey attest to the company's influence. 4. Among these are the Milton Hershey Medical Center and Chocolate Avenue.

26. A Choice A correctly connects all three sentences in the simplest, most active way. Reading the choices aloud may help you determine the best solution.

27. C The sentences that precede it discuss hockey's possible origin, so choice C leads most naturally from those.

28. D Choice A is awkward, choice B suggests a time sequence that is not indicated by the original sentence, and choice C is ungrammatical.

29. A The paragraph is about the Cook Islands, but particularly it is about their former names, making choice A logical.

30. A Numbers in the hundreds do not require hyphens (B), *one-half* only takes a hyphen when it is used as an adjective (C), and *crossfire* is a single word, not a hyphenated one (D). When an adjective that starts with *well* precedes a noun, it takes a hyphen, making choice A correct.

31. D You are asked to emphasize the location, which is "on the beach." Choice D does that while de-emphasizing the other details.

32. C The correct spelling is *a-p-p-a-r-e-n-t-l-y.*

33. D Although the choices are similar in meaning, only choice D fits the syntax of the sentence. Read the sentence aloud with the choices in place to hear which one makes sense.

34. A The opening sentences of that paragraph all have to do with natural causes of wildfires, making choice A the best introduction.

35. B Whereas sentences 3 through 5 discuss natural causes, sentences 6 through 8 discuss man-made causes of wildfires. Adding a paragraph break between sentences 5 and 6 would clarify this division.

36. C Sentence C demonstrates a correct use of verbs. Choice A uses an idiom incorrectly; we say "the party *is* three weeks away," not "the party *will be* three weeks away." Choice B has incorrect subject-verb agreement; the verb should be *are.* Sentence D is simply ungrammatical.

37. C The café is at the bottom of the mountain, and it is a popular spot for skiers and hikers to meet. Only choice C makes the relationship of ideas clear.

38. D The original sentence is in the passive voice, as is choice B. Choices A and C misplace modifying phrases. The best correction is choice D.

39. Kyle's a strong**,** fit athlete**;** he has won the local triathalon twice**.**

40. Possible answer: It is clear that earnings increase with years of schooling. All of the sentences in the paragraph lead to the conclusion that earnings increase as schooling increases.

41. A The original sentence lacks a helping verb that would correctly accompany *waiting.* Choices B, C, and D are all ungrammatical. Only choice A uses correct tense and verb form.

42. C The whole name of the farm is Blue Heron Farm, just as the whole name of the grocery in choice A is Jason's Grocery.

43. C The paragraph as a whole is about the usefulness of the horses both in the past and in the present, so this addition follows best as a conclusion.

44. D *Culmination,* meaning "conclusion" or "fulfillment," has an *i,* not an *a.*

45. A The sentence contains three phrases in a series. Separating the three with commas is correct.

46. B and E Choice B contains serial commas used correctly. Choice A does not need the first comma, choice C needs no comma at all, and the quotation marks in choice D are unnecessary, as this is not a direct quotation. Quote marks in choice F are incorrect as well, but they are used correctly in choice E.

47. far-fetched You are asked to find a word that stresses the reasonableness or logic of the suggestion. Since the phrase begins, "It is not at all _____," the word must mean the opposite of *reasonable*. A good antonym is *far-fetched*, meaning "implausible" or "unlikely."

48. D Try substituting the choices in place of the blank. Both choices A and D imply a contradiction, but only *however* fits the structure of the sentence.

49. A The other sentences in the second paragraph describe Dickinson's poetry, naming specific features of her poems. Although choice D also has to do with poetry, choice A forms a better transition.

50. Possible answer: Her poems were short, used unusual punctuation, and often dealt with dark topics. Since the subjects of the sentences are the same, you may easily combine predicates.

Essay

Use the scoring rubric on page 86 to assess your own writing. Presented here are two sample essays, either of which might achieve a score of 4. The first essay considers the research in the first study beneficial. The second essay prefers the study suggested in the second article. Both essays score high because the writers support their arguments with solid details and facts from the texts. Compare them to your own writing to get a sense of where you might improve your work.

Essay 1: In Support of the Whale Study

The research taking place in Massachusetts Bay seems to be genuinely useful and effective. In contrast, studies of genetically modified foods are not clearly defined, are extremely controversial, and would probably cost far more than the whale study.

The original Cornell plan was to collect recordings of underwater noise in the bay. Now the buoys are also being used to help locate whales and to keep them out of the path of tankers.

The Cornell study focuses on one endangered species of whale. Unfortunately, those whales share the ocean with large ships, which produce noise of close to 200 decibels. The noise interferes with the whales' ability to communicate with each other. As a result, the whales become separated and may be disoriented.

Since there is little chance that ships will avoid the bay, and in fact, the traffic there is growing, finding ways to help the whales seems to be a sensible plan. It makes sense to find a way that allows whales and ships to share the channels. Transmitting data on whale locations to ships' captains helps the ships avoid the whales and perhaps save them. This is enough to make the study worthwhile. Unlike any study of genetically modified foods, this study is small, limited in scope, and likely to be cost-effective.

Essay 2: In Support of the Food Study

Of the two studies, the one dealing with modified foods seems worthier of spending time and money on. It is the study that will yield important results for humankind.

Cornell's project, which deployed seafloor recorders and listening buoys in Massachusetts Bay, has not achieved much that will save the endangered northern right whales. Although the buoys proved what scientists already suspected, knowing that noise endangers whales is not enough to protect them.

The whales live and hunt in busy shipping lanes. They communicate with each other using sounds that are similar in frequency to the sounds produced by large ships. Therefore, when there are many ships in the area, the whales can become confused.

Understanding whale communication is interesting for humans, but it is not of much use to the whales. Is the Cornell study calling for changes in the shipping lanes? Is it finding ways to reduce fossil-fuel burning, which acidifies the ocean and makes underwater noises louder?

The goals of studies of modified foods are much clearer. Scientists want to find out their effects on humans, animals, and the environment. The goals are also more important because they deal with critical issues of world hunger and the health of the planet.

Right now, there are serious problems involving genetically modified foods, from allergenicity to outcrossing. If scientists could solve those problems and ensure the safety of modified foods, the effects on health and food availability would be well worth the investment.

The TASC Mathematics Test 4

HOW TO USE THIS CHAPTER

» Read the Overview to learn what the TASC Mathematics Test covers.

» Take the TASC Mathematics Test Pretest to preview your knowledge and skills.

» Study the TASC Mathematics Review to refresh your knowledge of TASC test math skills.

» Take the TASC Mathematics Practice Test to sharpen your skills and get ready for test day.

Overview

On part of the TASC Mathematics Test, you are allowed to use a calculator. For the rest of that section, calculators are not allowed.

The TASC Mathematics Test is based on the Common Core State Standards for Mathematics. You can see these standards at www.core standards.org/Math. The TASC test does not test the most advanced of those standards, which are the ones marked with plus signs. The main standards covered by the TASC test include the following:

Number and Quantity
1. **CCSS.Math.Content.HSN-RN.A.1–2, B.3** The Real Number System
2. **CCSS.Math.Content.HSN-Q.A.1–3** Quantities
3. **CCSS.Math.Content.HSN-CN.A.1–2, C.7** The Complex Number System

Algebra
4. **CCSS.Math.Content.HSA-SSE.A.2** Seeing Structure in Expressions

5. **CCSS.Math.Content.HSA-APR.A.1, B.2–3, C.4, D.6** Arithmetic with Polynomials and Rational Expressions
6. **CCSS.Math.Content.HSA-CED.A.1–4** Creating Equations
7. **CCSS.Math.Content.HSA-REI.A.1–2, B.3–4, C.5–7, D.10–12** Reasoning with Equations and Inequalities

Functions

8. **CCSS.Math.Content.HSF-IF.A.1–3, B.4–6, C.7–9** Interpreting Functions
9. **CCSS.Math.Content.HSF-BF.A.1–2, B.3–4** Building Functions
10. **CCSS.Math.Content.HSF-LE.A.1–4, B.5** Linear, Quadratic, and Exponential Models
11. **CCSS.Math.Content.HSF-TF.A.1–2, B.5, C.8** Trigonometric Functions

Geometry

12. **CCSS.Math.Content.HSG-CO.A.1–5, B.6–8, C.9–11, D.12–13** Congruence
13. **CCSS.Math.Content.HSG-SRT.A.1–3, B.4–5, C.6–8** Similarity, Right Triangles, and Trigonometry
14. **CCSS.Math.Content.HSG-C.A.1–3, B.5** Circles
15. **CCSS.Math.Content.HSG-GPE.A.1–2, B.4–7** Expressing Geometric Properties with Equations
16. **CCSS.Math.Content.HSG-GMD.A.1, 3, B.4** Geometric Measurement and Dimension
17. **CCSS.Math.Content.HSG-MG.A.1–3** Modeling with Geometry

Statistics and Probability

18. **CCSS.Math.Content.HSS-ID.A.1–4, B.5–6, C.7–9** Interpreting Categorical and Quantitative Data
19. **CCSS.Math.Content.HSS-IC.A.1–2, B.3–6** Making Inferences and Justifying Conclusions
20. **CCSS.Math.Content.HSS-CP.A.1–5, B.6–7** Conditional Probability and the Rules of Probability

The Common Core State Standards also feature Standards for Mathematical Practice, which are not tested directly on the TASC test but are featured throughout as a starting point and foundation for the types of questions asked. Those standards are the following:

1. Make sense of problems and persevere in solving them.
2. Reason abstractly and quantitatively.
3. Construct viable arguments and critique the reasoning of others.
4. Model with mathematics.
5. Use appropriate tools strategically.
6. Attend to precision.
7. Look for and make use of structure.
8. Look for and express regularity in repeated reasoning.

TASC Mathematics Pretest

Use the items that follow to preview your knowledge of high school mathematics.
Answers appear on page 144.

Part 1: Calculator Allowed

1. A standard deck of 52 cards holds 4 cards each of twos through aces in four equal-sized suits—hearts, diamonds, clubs, and spades. If you choose a card at random, what is the probability of choosing an ace or a heart? Drag and drop two numerals to make the correct ratio.

1	4	5	13	17	52

2. Which is a simplified version of $((2^{-4})(3^{-3}))^{-2}$?

   Ⓐ $(2^{-8})(3^{-6})$
   Ⓑ $(2^2)(3)$
   Ⓒ $(2^{-6})(3^{-5})$
   Ⓓ $(2^8)(3^6)$

3. Zolar Moving Company drove a truck from Dryden, New York, to Morgantown, West Virginia, at an average rate of 55 miles per hour. If the trip is 396 miles, how long was the truck on the road?

   (Rate $= \dfrac{\text{distance}}{\text{time}}$)

   Ⓐ 6 hours 3 minutes
   Ⓑ 6 hours 20 minutes
   Ⓒ 7 hours 12 minutes
   Ⓓ 7 hours 20 minutes

4. Solve for x: $\log_2 64 = x$.

   Ⓐ 3
   Ⓑ 4
   Ⓒ 5
   Ⓓ 6

5. Density = $\frac{mass}{volume}$. Gold has a density of 19.3 grams per cubic centimeter. What is the mass in kilograms of a bar of gold that measures 10 centimeters by 4 centimeters by 5 centimeters?

Ⓐ 3.67 kg
Ⓑ 3.86 kg
Ⓒ 10.36 kg
Ⓓ 386 kg

6. Julius measured the heights of a random sample of boys in his high school senior class. Here are his results.

DARYL	HUGO	JASPER	PETE	NICO	ANDREW	TAYLOR	DYLAN
5.3 feet	5.5 feet	5.8 feet	6.0 feet	5.8 feet	6.4 feet	5.5 feet	5.5 feet

Which is the <u>most</u> reasonable estimate of the average height of all boys in Julius's high school senior class?

Ⓐ 5.3 feet
Ⓑ 5.5 feet
Ⓒ 5.7 feet
Ⓓ 5.9 feet

7. A team of engineers is drilling a tunnel through a mountain, as shown.

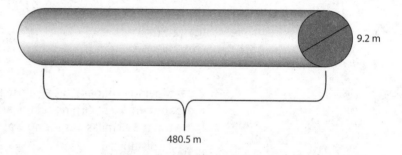

9.2 m

480.5 m

To the nearest cubic meter, how much dirt and rock must be cleared away in order to create the tunnel? Use 3.14 as pi.

Ⓐ 4,421 m³
Ⓑ 13,881 m³
Ⓒ 31,926 m³
Ⓓ 127,702 m³

8. In 1871, most of Chicago was destroyed by fire. This graph shows the population from 1880 until 1910.

Population of Chicago

2,500,000	
2,000,000	
1,500,000	
1,000,000	
500,000	
0	
	1880 1890 1900 1910

Which is the best estimate of the rate of change in population?

(A) 25,000/year

(B) 50,000/year

(C) 100,000/year

(D) 400,000/year

9. The diagram shows a unit circle, a circle with a radius of 1.

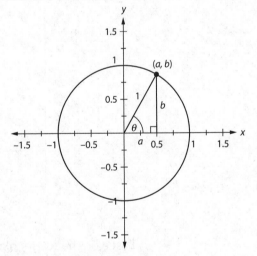

If the cosine of θ in this unit circle is a, what would be true of the cosine of θ in a circle with a radius of 2?

(A) The cosine would be $\frac{a}{2}$.

(B) The cosine would be $2a$.

(C) The cosine would be b.

(D) The cosine would be a.

10. What is the solution to the equation $4(x + 12) = -3x + 6$?

(A) -6

(B) 6

(C) -7.7

(D) $\dfrac{-6}{7}$

11. The cost of a software package, S, is $290 less than the cost of a laptop, L. The total price for both laptop and software is $500. Which system of equations could you use to find the price of each item? Drag and drop the two equations that lead to a solution.

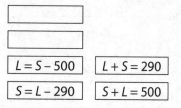

| $L = S - 500$ | $L + S = 290$ |
| $S = L - 290$ | $S + L = 500$ |

12. This scatter plot shows the time between eruptions and the duration of each eruption for Yellowstone Park's Old Faithful Geyser.

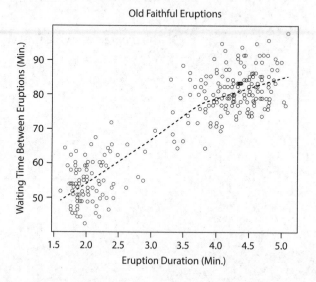

Based on the scatter plot, which types of eruptions are most common?

(A) short wait, long duration eruptions and long wait, long duration eruptions

(B) short wait, short duration eruptions and long wait, long duration eruptions

(C) short wait, short duration eruptions and long wait, short duration eruptions

(D) short wait, long duration eruptions and long wait, short duration eruptions

13. Which two statements are <u>not</u> true?

Ⓐ The product of two irrational numbers is always rational.

Ⓑ The sum of a rational and an irrational number is always irrational.

Ⓒ The product of two rational numbers is always rational.

Ⓓ The product of a rational number (other than zero) and an irrational number is always irrational.

Ⓔ A repeating decimal is not a rational number.

14. Which expression is equivalent to $\frac{x^2}{y^2}$?

Ⓐ $2(xy)$

Ⓑ $\frac{(x^2)^2}{y}$

Ⓒ $\frac{x^8}{y^8}$

Ⓓ $\left(\frac{x}{y}\right)^2$

15. What is the sum of these polynomials?

$$(3x^2y + 6x - 5) + (2x^2y + 4x^2 - 6x)$$

Ⓐ $9x^2y - 5$

Ⓑ $5x^2y + 4x^2 - 5$

Ⓒ $5x^2y + 10x^2 - 6x - 5$

Ⓓ $6x^2y + 4x^2 - 36x - 5$

Part 2: No Calculator Allowed

16. If isosceles triangle *ABC* is similar to isosceles triangle *DEF*, what must the value of *x* be?

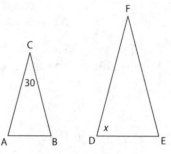

Mark your answer in the grid.

17. What is the greatest whole number that when added to this data set would result in a data set that skews left?

4   7   7   8   9

Mark your answer in the grid.

18. Find the value of $f(-4)$ for the function $f(x) = \frac{1}{2}x + 5$.

Mark your answer in the grid.

19. The function *f*(*x*) is shown on the graph. Find *f*(−3).

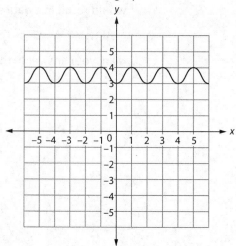

Mark your answer in the grid.

20. Point *O* is the center of this circle. What is the measure of ∠*A*?

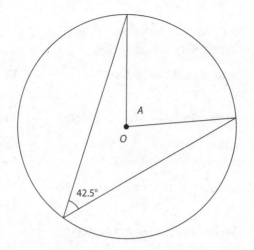

Mark your answer in the grid.

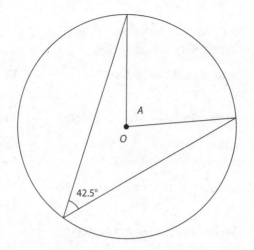

This is the end of the TASC Mathematics Pretest.

TASC Mathematics Pretest Answers

1. **4/13** Review 20. Conditional Probability and the Rules of Probability (pp. 205–208).

2. **D** Review 1. The Real Number System (pp. 145–147).

3. **C** Review 6. Creating Equations (pp. 158–160).

4. **D** Review 10. Linear, Quadratic, and Exponential Models (pp. 173–175).

5. **B** Review 17. Modeling with Geometry (pp. 197–198).

6. **C** Review 19. Making Inferences and Justifying Conclusions (pp. 203–205).

7. **C** Review 16. Geometric Measurement and Dimension (pp. 194–196).

8. **B** Review 8. Interpreting Functions (pp. 167–170).

9. **D** Review 11. Trigonometric Functions (pp. 176–178).

10. **A** Review 7. Reasoning with Equations and Inequalities (pp. 162–167).

11. $S = L - 290; S + L = 500$ Review 6. Creating Equations (pp. 158–160).

12. **B** Review 18. Interpreting Categorical and Quantitative Data (pp. 198–203).

13. **A and E** Review 1. The Real Number System (pp. 145–147).

14. **D** Review 4. Seeing Structure in Expressions (pp. 152–155).

15. **B** Review 5. Arithmetic with Polynomials and Rational Expressions (pp. 155–158).

16. **75** Review 13. Similarity, Right Triangles, and Trigonometry (pp. 184–186).

17. **6** Review 18. Interpreting Categorical and Quantitative Data (pp. 198–203).

18. **3** Review 8. Interpreting Functions (pp. 167–170).

19. **4** Review 8. Interpreting Functions (pp. 167–170).

20. **85** Review 14. Circles (pp. 187–190).

TASC Mathematics Test Review

The pages that follow briefly review each of the twenty standards listed in the Overview. To learn more about number and quantity, algebra, functions, geometry, and statistics and probability, find books on those topics in the library or look for instructional webinars online. An excellent, free source for math review of concepts and skills is available at www.khanacademy.org.

 ## The Real Number System

The real numbers are all those numbers that can be thought of as points along a number line. There is an infinite number of real numbers.

KEY TERMS: exponent, integer, irrational, radical, rational, root

Integers

The set of **integers** consists of the whole numbers (1, 2, 3 . . .), the negative whole numbers (–1, –2, –3 . . .), and zero.

Rational Numbers

A **rational number** may be expressed as a/b, where both a and b are integers, and $b \neq 0$. The sum or product of two rational numbers is always rational.

Irrational Numbers

An **irrational number** is a real number that cannot be expressed as a/b, where both a and b are integers, and $b \neq 0$. A repeating decimal is rational, but a decimal that does not repeat is irrational. Examples of such numbers include π and $\sqrt{2}$.

The sum of a rational number and an irrational number is irrational. The product of a rational number other than zero and an irrational number is also irrational.

Integer Exponents

For any number a where n is a positive integer, a with an exponent of n, or a^n, is equal to

$$\underbrace{a \times a \times a \ldots}_{n \text{ times}}$$

For example, $5^4 = 5 \times 5 \times 5 \times 5 = 625$

$$(-2)^3 = -2 \times -2 \times -2 = -8$$

For any number a where n is zero, a^n is equal to 1.

For example, $5^0 = 1$

$\qquad (-2)^0 = 1$

For any number a where n is a positive integer, $a^{-n} = \dfrac{1}{a^n}$.

For example, $5^{-4} = \dfrac{1}{625}$

$\qquad (-2)^{-3} = \dfrac{1}{-8}$

Roots and Radicals

The **radical** sign ($\sqrt{}$) is used to indicate square roots or nth roots. A **square root** is a number that when multiplied by itself results in a real, non-negative number, a square.

For example, $\sqrt{9} = 3$, because $3 \times 3 = 9$

You may indicate other kinds of roots other than square roots by placing a number in the radical sign.

For example, $\sqrt[4]{b}$ means the number that when multiplied by itself 4 times equals b.

$\qquad \sqrt[3]{125} = 5$, because $5 \times 5 \times 5 = 125$

Fractional Exponents

Exponents may be integers, or they may be other rational numbers, including fractions. Fractional exponents equate to roots.

For example, $4^2 = 16$

$\qquad 4^1 = 4$

$\qquad 4^0 = 1$

$\qquad 4^{\frac{1}{2}} = \sqrt{4} = 2$

$\qquad 4^{\frac{1}{3}} = \sqrt[3]{4}$

$\qquad 4^{\frac{1}{4}} = \sqrt[4]{4}$

Laws of Exponents

There are a few useful tricks to understand when it comes to dealing with exponents. Some were shown previously. Here are some others.

Laws of Exponents

LAW	EXAMPLE
$x^a x^b = x^{a+b}$	$2^3 2^4 = 2^{3+4} = 2^7$
$\dfrac{x^a}{y^b} = x^{a-b}$	$\dfrac{5^4}{5^2} = 5^{4-2} = 5^2$
$(x^a)^b = x^{ab}$	$(3^2)^3 = 3^{2 \times 3} = 3^6$
$(xy)^a = x^a y^a$	$(4 \times 1)^2 = 4^2 \times 1^2$
$\left(\dfrac{x}{y}\right)^a = \dfrac{x^a}{y^a}$	$\left(\dfrac{6}{3}\right)^2 = \dfrac{6^2}{3^2}$
$x^{-a} = \dfrac{1}{x^a}$	$2^{-4} = \dfrac{1}{2^4}$
$x^{\frac{a}{b}} = \sqrt[b]{x^a}$	$3^{\frac{1}{2}} = \sqrt[2]{3^1}$

CHALLENGE **The Real Number System**

Solve for each.

1. $\sqrt[3]{343}$

2. $5^2 + 5^3 + 5^0$

3. 30^{-2}

4. $8^{\frac{1}{3}}$

5. $\left(\dfrac{3}{5}\right)^3$

CHALLENGE ANSWERS

The Real Number System

1. 7 $7 \times 7 \times 7 = 343$.

2. 151   Solve each one, and then add them together.

3. $\dfrac{1}{900}$ 30^{-2} is the same as $\dfrac{1}{30}^2$.

4. 2 $8^{\frac{1}{3}}$ is the same as the cube root of 8, which is 2.

5. $\dfrac{27}{125}$ Cube the numerator. Then cube the denominator.

Quantities

The skills that the Common Core State Standards call "quantities" are modeling skills. At the high school level, they involve using units to guide the solution of problems. You need to choose units correctly in formulas and data displays, and you should understand levels of accuracy.

KEY TERMS: accuracy, convert, precision, unit

Accuracy and Precision

The **accuracy** of a measurement is the degree of closeness of that measurement to a quantity's actual value. The **precision** of a measurement is the degree to which repeated measurement yields the same results. Here is a common example that shows the difference. Imagine that you are aiming at a bull's eye. If your aim is accurate, you get within the same measurement of the center each time. If your aim is precise, your shots are grouped close together, no matter how many times you shoot.

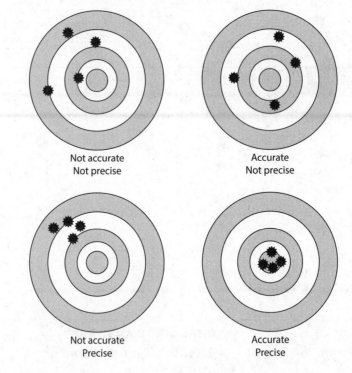

Not accurate
Not precise

Accurate
Not precise

Not accurate
Precise

Accurate
Precise

If you are weighing a bag of potatoes that is known to weigh 5 pounds, and your scale reads 3 pounds, the scale will not give you an accurate measurement. You may get a weight of 3 pounds every time you try. That means that your measurement is precise, but it is still not accurate. Your scale may need adjusting.

Unit Conversion

A variety of **units** are used to measure objects and substances. To measure length or distance, you may use meters, inches, miles, and so on. To measure temperature, you may use degrees Celsius or degrees Fahrenheit. To measure capacity, you may use cups, milliliters, gallons, and so on.

As you respond to word problems, make sure that you understand what units are being used. At times, problems may require you to make a **conversion** from one unit to another.

Jack drank a pint of milk at lunch and another pint at dinner. How many quarts of milk did Jack drink?

The square fence measures 6 yards on each side. How many feet of fencing is required?

In the first example, you need to convert pints to quarts—a smaller unit to a larger unit. If you know that 2 pints = 1 quart, this should be easy. In the second example, you must convert yards to feet—a larger unit to a smaller unit. By multiplying the number of yards (24) by 3 feet to the yard, you find that the number of feet of fencing will be 24 × 3, or 72 feet.

To convert from a smaller unit to a larger unit, divide. To convert from a larger unit to a smaller unit, multiply.

CHALLENGE   Quantities

Identify the units required to answer each problem. Then tell whether each situation represents accurate measurement, precise measurement, neither, or both.

1. Pete is studying Norway rats in a one-acre plot around a New York City museum. He wants to compare their lengths with those of country rats. He measures each rat he catches from nose to tail and records the lengths in centimeters. Because he is not tranquilizing the rats to measure them, he typically measures by sight against a metal grid in the trap. He records the measurement, marks the rat with a drop of dye so that he will not accidentally count it twice, and then releases the rat. The average Norway rat measures about 20 centimeters with a 20-centimeter tail. Pete's measurements range from 10 centimeters to 50 centimeters.

2. Kyra is putting a shed on her property. Zoning law is very specific; it states that her shed may be no closer than 5 feet to the property line. To ensure that she is not breaking the law, Kyra uses a metal measuring tape to stake out the boundaries for her shed. She measures five times, finding each time that the site she chose is 65.5 inches away from the property line. She checks her measuring tool by measuring herself against the tape and finds that she is exactly 5 feet 5 inches tall, just as the doctor told her at her last checkup. Satisfied, Kyra marks the edge with stakes.

CHALLENGE ANSWERS

Quantities

1. **centimeters, neither precise nor accurate**   The important unit is centimeters. Pete's measurements are neither highly accurate nor highly precise, because the rats are probably moving as he views them, and he measures each one only once. The range of his observations is well above and below the average rat size, making lack of accuracy a problem.

2. **feet, both precise and accurate**   The important unit is feet, because Kyra must compare her measurement to the rule regarding 5 feet. Kyra's measurements are probably both precise and accurate—she measures five times and gets the same measurement each time, and she compares the results from her measurement tool to one that she knows is accurate.

3 The Complex Number System

Beyond the real numbers lie the **imaginary numbers**, numbers such as the square root of −4. Since there is no real number that when multiplied by itself equals a negative number, the square root of −4 is not a real number, but it may exist as a concept. Mathematicians use imaginary numbers to create a whole new system of numbers, the **complex number system**. This allows certain problems that have no real solutions to have solutions, which sometimes comes in handy in engineering, economics, and the sciences.

KEY TERMS: complex, imaginary

Imaginary Numbers

The **imaginary unit** is represented by i in this equation: $i^2 = -1$. An **imaginary number** is any number that can be written as a real number times the imaginary unit.

For example, $8i$ is an imaginary number whose square is −64.

$10i$ is an imaginary number whose square is −100.

Complex Numbers

A **complex number** is a number that can be expressed in the form $a + bi$, where i is the imaginary unit. In this form, a is the real part of the complex number, and bi is the imaginary part of the complex number. The number may even be graphed on a coordinate plane where the x-axis represents real numbers and the y-axis represents imaginary numbers.

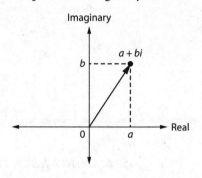

Computing with Complex Numbers

Complex numbers follow the same rules as real numbers when you add, subtract, and multiply them. You cannot add a real number to an imaginary number, so you handle the two parts of a complex number as though they were entirely separate.

Add complex numbers $2 + 3i$ and $4 + 5i$.

$2 + 3i + 4 + 5i =$

$(2 + 4) + (3i + 5i) =$

$6 + 8i$

Subtract complex number $2 + 3i$ from $4 + 5i$.

$(4 + 5i) - (2 + 3i) =$

$(4 - 2) + (5i - 3i) =$

$2 + 2i$

Multiply complex number $2 + 3i$ by $4 + 5i$.

$(2 + 3i)(4 + 5i)$

$= 2(4 + 5i) + 3i\,(4 + 5i)$ using the distributive property . . .

$= 8 + 10i + 12i + 15(i^2)$

$= 8 + 22i + 15(-1)$ because i^2 is equal to -1 . . .

$= -7 + 22i$

The Complex Number System

Solve.

1. What is the square of $6i$?

2. $(4 + 2i) + (3 + 2i)$

3. $(1 + 3i) + (8i)$

4. $5i \times 2i$

5. $(3 + 2i)(2 + 3i)$

CHALLENGE ANSWERS

The Complex Number System

1. −36   The square of any number ni is $-(n^2)$. Since $i^2 = -1$, and $6^2 = 36$, $(36)(-1) = -36$.

2. 7 + 4i   Add the real parts first and the imaginary parts second.

3. 1 + 11i $8i$ is the complex number $0 + 8i$.

4. −10 $5 \times 2 = 10$, and $i^2 = -1$.

5. 13i   Use the distributive property to get $3(2 + 3i) + 2i(2 + 3i) =$ $(6 + 9i) + (4i + 6i^2) = (6 - 6) + 13i = 13i$.

 ## Seeing Structure in Expressions

An algebraic expression may contain several parts, each with its own role in the expression.

KEY TERMS: coefficient, expression, factor, quadratic, simplify, terms, trinomial, variable

Variables, Terms, and Expressions

In algebra, letters called **variables** are used to represent numbers or unknown quantities. An algebraic **expression** is a group of numbers, variables, grouping symbols such as parentheses, and operation symbols. When an algebraic expression has several parts, the parts that are added or subtracted are called the **terms** of the expression.

For example, $x^2 + 6$ is an expression containing terms x^2 and 6.

$2(y + 3) - 4$ is an expression containing terms $2(y + 3)$ and −4.

$5 - x + 3x$ is an expression containing terms 5, −x, and 3x.

Coefficients

The numerical part of a term is the term's **coefficient**.

For example, in $7x$, the coefficient is 7.

In $4(x + 2)$, the coefficient is 4.

In $\frac{3x}{5}$, the coefficient is $\frac{3}{5}$.

In $-6x$, the coefficient is -6.

Like and Unlike Terms

Like terms have the same variables with the same exponents.

For example, $6x$ and $17x$ are like terms.

$2x^2$ and x^2 are like terms.

$5(x + 2)$ and $3(x - 1)$ are like terms.

But $6x$ and x^2 are unlike terms, because their exponents are different.

17 and $2x$ are unlike terms, because their variables are different.

$5x$ and $3y$ are unlike terms, because their variables are different.

Simplifying an Expression

The distributive property allows you to remove parentheses from an expression in order to simplify or solve it.

For example, $2(x + 4) = 2x + 2(4) = 2x + 8$

$3(x - 2) = 3x + 3(-2) = 3x - 6$

$(x + 2)(x - 1) = x^2 - 1x + 2x - 2 = x^2 + x - 2$

When you **simplify** an expression, you remove parentheses and combine like terms. You may have learned this as the FOIL method:

» **First:** Multiply the first term in each set of parentheses.
» **Outer:** Multiply the outer term in each set of parentheses.
» **Inner:** Multiply the inner term in each set of parentheses.
» **Last:** Multiply the last term in each set of parentheses.

Solving Quadratic Equations

A **quadratic expression** is in the form $ax^2 + bx + c$, where a, b, and c are real numbers, and $a \neq 0$. Such expressions may also be called **trinomials**, because they contain three distinct terms. Quadratic equations may be solved in several possible ways.

Factoring to Find the Zeros

1. Start with a quadratic equation; for example, $x^2 + 4x - 5 = 0$.
2. To factor the expression, try to think of two numbers whose sum is $b(4)$ and whose product is $c(-5)$.
3. Find the two distinct factors of the expression: $(x + 5)(x - 1)$.
4. Find the x values that make the expression equal to zero: $(-5 + 5)$ or $(1 - 1)$.
5. The solutions are -5 and 1.
6. Plug the solutions into the expression to check: $(-5)^2 + 4(-5) - 5 = 0$; $1^2 + 4(1) - 5 = 0$.

Completing the Square

1. Start with a quadratic equation; for example, $x^2 + 6x + 5 = 0$.
2. Move the third term to get the squared and x terms on the left side of the equation. In this case, you subtract 5 from both sides: $x^2 + 6x = -5$.
3. Determine $\frac{1}{2}$ the coefficient of the x term: $\frac{6}{2} = 3$. Square this. $3^2 = 9$.
4. Add the square to both sides of the equation: $x^2 + 6x + 9 = 4$.
5. You now have a perfect square trinomial on the left side of the equation. Express this as its factors: $(x + 3)(x + 3)$.
6. Now take the square root of both sides of the equation: $x + 3 = \pm 2$.
7. Solve for x: $x = 2 - 3 = -1$; $x = -2 - 3 = -5$.
8. Plug the solutions into the expression to check: $(-1)^2 + 6(-1) + 5 = 0$; $(-5)^2 + 6(-5) + 5 = 0$.

Using the Quadratic Formula

1. Start with a quadratic equation; for example, $x^2 + 2x - 8 = 0$.
2. Substitute the values into the quadratic formula:

$$x = \frac{-b \pm \sqrt{b^2 - 4ac}}{2a}$$

3. Solve: $x = \dfrac{-2 \pm \sqrt{2^2 - 4(1)(-8)}}{2(1)}$

$$= \frac{-2 \pm \sqrt{4 + 32}}{2}$$

$$= \frac{-2 \pm \sqrt{36}}{2}$$

$$= \frac{-2 \pm 6}{2}$$

$$= \frac{4}{2}, \text{ or } 2; -\frac{8}{2}, \text{ or } -4$$

4. Plug the solutions into the expression to check: $2^2 + 2(2) - 8 = 0$; $(-4)^2 + 2(-4) - 8 = 0$.

CHALLENGE Seeing Structure in Expressions

Solve for x.

1. $x + 15 = 2x$

2. $2x = 3 - x$

3. $x^2 + 2x - 3 = 0$

4. $0 = x^2 + 13x + 36$

5. $x^2 - 8x + 15 = 0$

CHALLENGE ANSWERS

Seeing Structure in Expressions

1. 15   Subtract x from both sides of the equation to solve.

2. 1   Add x to both sides to get $3x = 3$.

3. −3, 1   Factor: $(x + 3)(x - 1)$. Find the x that makes each factor equal to 0.

4. −9, −4   Factor: $(x + 9)(x + 4)$.

5. 3, 5   Try completing the square: $x^2 - 8x = -15$. $\dfrac{-8}{2} = -4$; $-4^2 = 16$.

$x^2 - 8x + 16 = 1$; $(x - 4)^2 = 1$; $x - 4 = \pm\sqrt{1}$; $x = 4 + 1$, $x = 4 - 1$.

5   Arithmetic with Polynomials and Rational Expressions

Arithmetic with expressions is similar to arithmetic with integers. The systems are closed under the operations of addition, subtraction, and multiplication. In other words, just as an integer plus an integer results in an integer, so a polynomial plus a polynomial results in a polynomial.

KEY TERMS: identity, polynomial, rational expression

Polynomials

A **polynomial** is an expression that contains variables, constants, and non-negative, whole number exponents.

For example, $2x$ is a polynomial, but $x^{\frac{1}{2}}$ is not.

$x^2 + 2x - 1$ is a polynomial, but $3x^2 - x^{-1} + 4$ is not.

Polynomials are written in descending powers of the variable, so that x^3 would precede x^2, which would precede x, which would precede any integer.

For example, $2x^2 + 15x - 3$ is in correct form.

$15x + 2x^2 - 3$ is not in correct form.

Adding Polynomials

To add polynomials, add the like terms of those polynomials.

$(4x^2 + 6x + 3) + (2x^2 + 5x - 1)$

$= 4x^2 + 2x^2 + 6x + 5x + 3 - 1$

$= 6x^2 + 11x + 2$

Subtracting Polynomials

To subtract polynomials, begin by removing the parentheses. Notice that this changes the sign of each term within the parentheses for the polynomial being subtracted.

$(5x^2 - 4x + 5) - (x^2 - 3x + 2)$

$= 5x^2 - 4x + 5 - x^2 + 3x - 2$

$= 5x^2 - x^2 - 4x + 3x + 5 - 2$

$= 4x^2 - x + 3$

Multiplying Polynomials

When you multiply terms with exponents, add the exponents.

For example, $(x^4)(x^3) = x^7$

Just as you do when you multiply integers, when you multiply polynomials, be sure to multiply every term in the first polynomial by every term in the second polynomial. It may help to stack the polynomials so you can be sure to do so.

$(x^2 + 3x + 2)(2x^2 - 3)$

Stack the polynomials:

$$
\begin{array}{r}
x^2 + 3x + 2 \\
2x^2 - 3 \\
\hline
-3x^2 - 9x - 6 \\
2x^4 + 6x^3 + 4x^2 \\
\hline
2x^4 + 6x^3 + x^2 - 9x - 6
\end{array}
$$

Polynomial Identities

A polynomial expression that is true for all values of x is a polynomial **identity**. Here are a few useful identities to learn.

$$(a + b)^2 = a^2 + 2ab + b^2$$

$$(a + b)(c + d) = ac + ad + bc + bd$$

$$a^2 - b^2 = (a + b)(a - b)$$

$$x^2 + (a + b)x + ab = (x + a)(x + b)$$

The Remainder Theorem

When you divide a polynomial $f(x)$ by $(x - c)$, the remainder r will be $f(c)$.

For example, $2x^2 - 3x - 2$ divided by $x - 3$

Calculate $f(3)$ using the 3 in $(x - 3)$ in place of x in the polynomial.

$2(3)^2 - 3(3) - 2 = 2(9) - 9 - 2 = 7$

The remainder in the division will be 7.

Try another: $x^2 - 3x - 4$ divided by $x - 4$

$(4)^2 - 3(4) - 4 = 16 - 12 - 4 = 0$

Here, the remainder is 0, so $(x - 4)$ is a factor of $x^2 - 3x - 4$.

Rational Expressions

A **rational expression** is an algebraic expression in the form a/b where a and b are polynomials and $b \neq 0$. As with any fraction, a rational expression is reduced to lowest terms when the numerator and denominator have no common factors other than 1.

For example, $\dfrac{ab - b^2}{2b}$ may be reduced by factoring out b: $\dfrac{\cancel{b}(a - b)}{2\cancel{b}} = \dfrac{(a - b)}{2}$.

Try another: $\dfrac{x^2 - 16}{x - 4} = \dfrac{(x + 4)\,\cancel{(x - 4)}}{\cancel{x - 4}} = x + 4$.

CHALLENGE Arithmetic with Polynomials and Rational Expressions

Solve.

1. $(2x^2 + 4x) + (5x - 4)$

2. $(6x^2 + 3x) - (2x^2 + 8x)$

3. $(x^2 + 6)(x^2 - 6)$

4. $\dfrac{x^2 + 2x - 3}{x + 3}$

CHALLENGE ANSWERS

Arithmetic with Polynomials and Rational Expressions

1. $2x^2 + 9x - 4$ Remember to add only the like terms.

2. $4x^2 - 5x$ Subtract like terms: $6x^2 - 2x^2 = 4x^2$. $3x - 8x = -5x$.

3. $x^4 - 36$ Multiplying every term in the first polynomial by every term in the second results in $x^4 + 6x^2 - 6x^2 - 36$.

4. $x - 1$ Factor the numerator: $(x + 3)(x - 1)$. Then divide out the common factor, $x - 1$.

 ## Creating Equations

You may use algebra to solve problems by creating and solving equations and inequalities.

KEY TERMS: formula, inequality, linear, viable

Equations in One Variable

You can translate verbal statements into algebraic expressions.

VERBAL EXPRESSION	ALGEBRAIC EXPRESSION
4 more than a number	$x + 4$
a number decreased by 8	$x - 8$
twice a number	$2x$
a number divided by 9	$\dfrac{x}{9}$
one-fifth of a number	$\dfrac{1}{5}x$ or $\dfrac{x}{5}$
3 more than twice a number	$2x + 3$
the difference of four times a number and 2	$4x - 2$

Moving beyond this, you can also use algebraic expressions to set up and solve verbal problems.

For example, John is 7 years younger than Mollie. If Mollie is 25, how old is John?

Let x = John's age.

$25 - 7 = x$

$x = 18$

John is 18 years old.

Inequalities in One Variable

The symbols < and > are used to show that one number or quantity is less than or greater than another. The symbol ≤ means "less than or equal to." The symbol ≥ means "greater than or equal to."

Creating and solving **inequalities** of this kind is similar to creating and solving equations.

For example, John has a collection of 198 coins. Mollie's collection is smaller than John's.

Let x = Mollie's collection.

$x < 198$

That is all we know. Mollie's collection may contain anywhere from 0 to 197 coins. The solution to an inequality is often a set of numbers. In this case, you know that Mollie's collection is not a negative number, because she cannot have a negative amount of coins. Replacing x with a negative number would not be **viable** in this case—it would not represent a practical answer.

Equations in Two Variables

Equations with more than one variable provide a means of comparing numbers or showing a relationship between two or more numbers.

For example, John has nickels and dimes in his collection totaling $2.00. If he has 25 nickels and dimes, how many of each does he have?

Use d to mean "dime" and n to mean "nickel." Then set up two equations.

$d + n = 25$ $\qquad$ $(0.10)d + (0.05)n = \$2.00$, or $10d + 5n = 200$

Stack the equations: $\qquad$ $d + n = 25$
$$10d + 5n = 200$$

Now multiply the terms in the first equation by any amount that allows you to cancel out one variable:

$$-10d - 10n = -250$$
$$\underline{10d + 5n = 200}$$
$$-5n = -50 \text{ or } 5n = 50$$

So $n = 10$. John has 10 nickels and $(25 - n) = 15$ dimes.

Graphing Equations in Two Variables

A **linear** equation is one that can be expressed in the form $ax + by = c$, where a, b, and c are real numbers. Equations of this kind are straight lines when they are graphed.

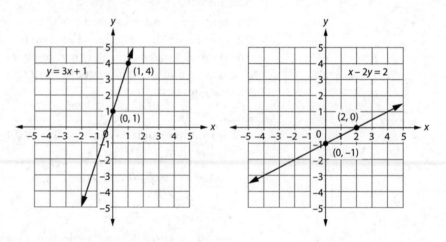

Formulas in Two or More Variables

Many scientific and mathematic **formulas** are represented in more than one variable. You can manipulate the formulas to highlight the quantity that is important to your problem.

For example, rate $= \dfrac{\text{distance}}{\text{time}}$, or $r = \dfrac{d}{t}$. To focus on time in this equation, you could rewrite the equation as $t = \dfrac{d}{r}$. The volume of a cylinder is $v = bh$. To focus on the height of the cylinder, you could rewrite the equation as $h = \dfrac{v}{b}$.

CHALLENGE **Creating Equations**

Rewrite each verbal statement as an algebraic expression or equation.

1. A number *x* is less than or equal to 5.

2. Francine is 22 years old, and her brother Jake is $\frac{1}{2}$ her age.

3. Kelly's salary is \$2 more per hour than Nate's. Graph the equation you wrote for item 3.

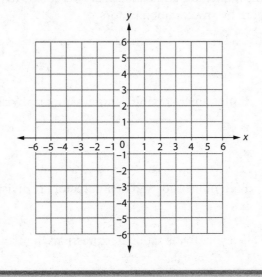

CHALLENGE ANSWERS
Creating Equations

1. $x \leq 5$ **or** $5 \geq x$ See "Inequalities in One Variable."

2. $J = \frac{F}{2}$ **or** $J = \frac{1}{2}F$ You may use any variable you like to stand for Francine's and Jake's ages.

3. $k = n + 2$ Let *x* = Nate's salary and *y* = Kelly's salary. Your graph will include points (0, 2), (1, 3), (2, 4), and so on.

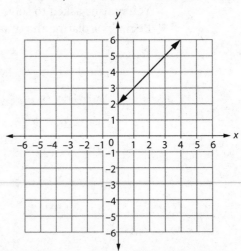

Reasoning with Equations and Inequalities

In addition to solving equations of all kinds, you may be expected to explain your reasoning.

KEY TERMS: extraneous solution, parabola, systems of equations

Rational Equations in One Variable

When you compute with rational expressions ($\frac{a}{b}$), you begin by factoring the numerator and denominator as completely as possible and dividing both by any common factors.

$$\frac{{}^1\cancel{3}}{5} \times \frac{-2}{\cancel{9}\,_3} = ?$$

Both numerator and denominator are divisible by 3, so the answer is $\frac{-2}{15}$.

$$\frac{4\cancel{x}}{\cancel{x}} = ?$$

Both numerator and denominator are divisible by x, so the answer is 4.

When you divide rational expressions, invert the divisor and multiply.

$$\frac{2}{5} \div \frac{4}{5} = ?$$

$$\frac{2}{5} \times \frac{5}{4} = \frac{2}{4} = \frac{1}{2}$$

$$\frac{9x}{2} \div \frac{3x}{4} = ?$$

$$\frac{9x}{2} \times \frac{4}{3x} = \frac{36x}{6x} = 6$$

Radical Equations in One Variable

You may be asked to solve for x when there are square roots in the equation. Begin by isolating the square root term on one side of the equation.

$\sqrt{x + 4} = 6$ Square each side.

$(\sqrt{x + 4})^2 = 6^2$

$x + 4 = 36$

$x = 32$

Anytime you square both sides of an equation, you run the risk of introducing an extraneous root and thus an **extraneous solution**. To make sure that you do not have an extraneous solution, always check your answer.

$2x = 4$

Imagine squaring both sides of the equation: $(2x)^2 = 16$

x may equal either 2 or −2, but only 2 works in the original equation!

Quadratic Equations

See pages 153–154 for information on solving quadratic equations. Occasionally, the solution to a quadratic equation may be a complex number. If a and b are real numbers, complex solutions to quadratic equations may be written $a \pm bi$.

Graphing Quadratic Equations

The solution to a quadratic equation forms a shape called a **parabola** when graphed. You can easily check your work by seeing where the parabola crosses the axes.

For example, graph this equation: $y = x^2 + 4x - 1$.

It helps to start with a function table.

x	y
−2	−5
−1	−4
0	−1
1	4
2	11

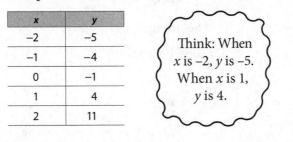

Think: When x is −2, y is −5. When x is 1, y is 4.

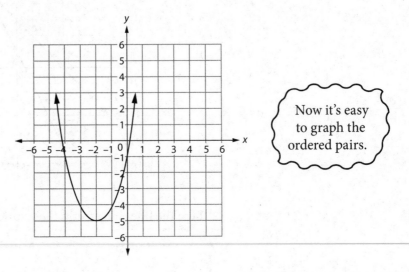

Now it's easy to graph the ordered pairs.

Solving Systems of Equations

When you must find a common solution to two or more equations, the equations are called a **system of equations**. The solution is an ordered pair or pairs.

$y = x + 3$

$y = 2x + 1$

Solve by substitution:

$x + 3 = 2x + 1$

$2 = x$

Plug 2 into the original equations in place of x: $y = 2 + 3$; $y = 4 + 1$.

Therefore, $y = 5$

Solution: $(2, 5)$

Or solve by addition or subtraction:

$$\begin{array}{r} y = x + 3 \\ - \underline{y = 2x + 1} \\ 0 = -x + 2 \end{array}$$

$x = 2$

Therefore, $y = 5$

Solution: $(2, 5)$

Or solve by graphing:

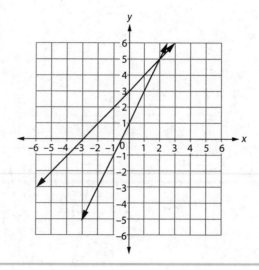

Where the lines intersect is the solution: $(2, 5)$.

Graphing Inequalities

The solution to an inequality typically appears on a graph as a half-plane.

$x \geq 2$

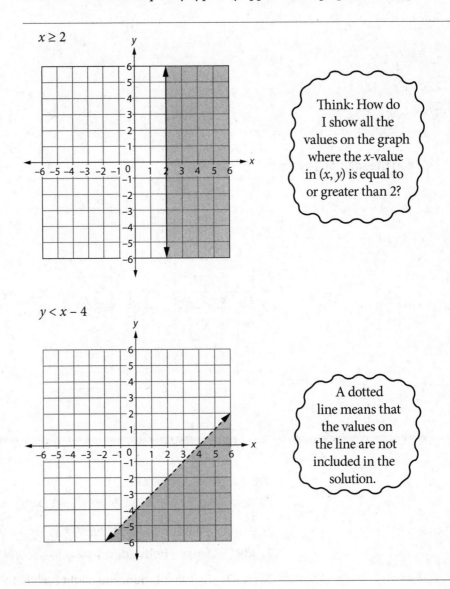

Think: How do I show all the values on the graph where the x-value in (x, y) is equal to or greater than 2?

$y < x - 4$

A dotted line means that the values on the line are not included in the solution.

| CHALLENGE | **Reasoning with Equations and Inequalities** |

Solve.

1. $\dfrac{x}{6} \div \dfrac{2x}{4} = ?$

2. $\sqrt{5 + x} = 12$

3. $y = -5x + 3$
   $y + 3 = x$

Graph the solution to item 3.

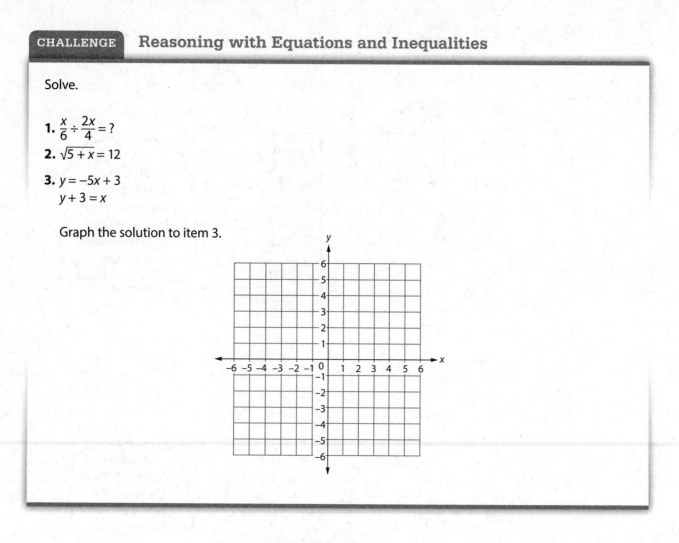

CHALLENGE ANSWERS

Reasoning with Equations and Inequalities

1. $\dfrac{1}{3}$ Multiplying by the inverse, $\dfrac{x}{6} \times \dfrac{4}{2x}$, yields $\dfrac{4x}{12x}$, or $\dfrac{1}{3}$.

2. 139   Square both sides: $5 + x = 144$, so $x = 139$.

3. (1, –2)   By substitution, you might find that $y = -5(y + 3) + 3$, or $y = -5y - 15 + 3$, so $6y = -12$, so $y = -2$ and $x = 1$. See the graph on the following page.

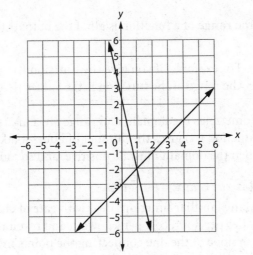

Interpreting Functions

You can use functions to explore relationships among numbers.

KEY TERMS: domain, exponential function, function, intercept, interval, logarithmic function, maximum, minimum, range, rate of change

Defining Functions

For any number x, you can input that number into a **function** and derive a value: $f(x)$. Ordered pairs form a function when for each value of x, there is one and only one value of y.

For example, suppose that $f(x) = x^2 + 2$.

For $f(2)$, the result is 6.

For $f(\frac{1}{2})$, the result is $2\frac{1}{4}$.

For $f(100)$, the result is 10,002.

The **domain** of a function is all the values you can input and get a valid answer. In the example shown, the domain is equal to the set of real numbers. Any number outside of the complex numbers can be input into $f(x) = x^2 + 2$.

However, suppose that $f(x) = \frac{1}{x}$.

In this case, the domain can be all the real numbers EXCEPT for zero, because there is no valid way to divide by zero.

In addition, suppose that $f(x) = \sqrt{x}$.

In this case, the domain must be greater than or equal to zero. You cannot find the square root of a negative number.

The **range** of a function is all of the outputs the function can produce.

For example, if you give the function $f(x) = x^2$, the values $x = \{1, 2, 3, \ldots\}$, the range of the function is the values $\{1, 4, 9, \ldots\}$.

Sometimes the domain and range are a matter of common sense. If function $f(x)$ gives the number of hours it takes to drive a certain distance x, then the domain must be positive, and so must the range.

Rate of Change Functions

Many familiar functions deal with **rate of change**. Some examples include miles per hour, cost per kilowatt, and revolutions per minute. On a graph, the slope of the line connecting the points in a rate of change function equals the average rate of change.

Here is the formula for average rate of change:

$$A(x) = \frac{\text{change in } y}{\text{change in } x} = \frac{f(b) - f(a)}{b - a}$$

where $x =$ the change in the input of function f, and $f(b) - f(a) =$ the change in the function f as the input changes from a to b.

Rate of change may be positive, or increasing, as when speed is increasing. It may be negative, or decreasing, as when temperature is dropping.

A linear function has a constant rate of change. In a linear function, as x values change in a constant way, so do y values.

Intercepts and Intervals

The **y-intercept** of a function is the point where its graph intersects with the y-axis—the point or points at which $x = 0$. The **x-intercept** of a function is the point where its graph intersects with the x-axis—the point or points at which $y = 0$.

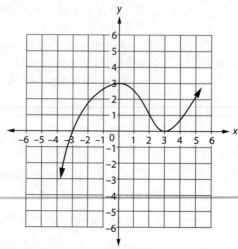

This graph of $f(x)$ has a y-intercept of 3 and two x-intercepts: -3 and 3.

In the graph, the function is both increasing and decreasing. If you look at a given **interval**, a set of values that you select, you may see a specific pattern to the function. Suppose you choose the interval from $x = 0$ to $x = 3$. The function is decreasing for that interval. The **maximum** (highest value) for that interval is (0, 3). The **minimum** (lowest value) for that interval is (3, 0).

Exponential Functions

Exponential functions change by a given proportion over a set interval. An example might be a culture of bacteria whose population triples every day. A typical exponential graph shows a line that starts very close to the x-axis, never quite reaching $y = 0$, and then shoots upward dramatically.

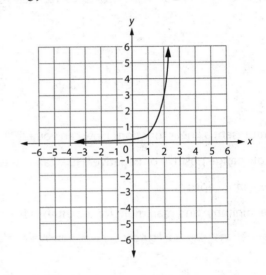

Logarithmic Functions

A logarithm is the inverse of an exponential number, so the graph of a **logarithmic function** is the inverse of the graph of the related exponential. In this example, the top line represents $f(x) = 2^x$. The lower line represents $f(x) = \log_2(x)$, the inverse.

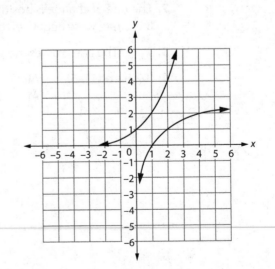

CHALLENGE | Interpreting Functions

Look at the graph. Then answer the questions.

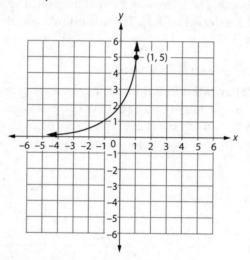

1. Does this represent a linear function? How can you tell?

2. Is the rate of change positive or negative? How can you tell?

3. What is the *y*-intercept?

4. What is the minimum and maximum for the interval from *x* = 0 to *x* = 1?

CHALLENGE ANSWERS

Interpreting Functions

1. No. It is not a straight line; the rate of change in *x* compared to *y* is not constant. A linear function may always be graphed as a straight line. This is more likely to show an exponential function.

2. The rate of change is positive, because the slope of the line increases. If the rate were negative, the line would slope downward.

3. **2**   The line crosses the *y*-axis at (0, 2).

4. **(0, 2) and (1, 5)**   At *x* = 0, the lowest point in the interval, *y* = 2. At *x* = 1, the highest point in the interval, *y* = 5.

Building Functions

You can construct a function to show the relationships between sets of numbers. In any function, each x value may output no more than one y value. Two x values may produce the same y value, as in $f(x) = x^2$, where x may be positive or negative—but no x value may produce more than one y value.

KEY TERMS: arithmetic sequence, common difference, common ratio, explicit function, Fibonacci sequence, geometric sequence, inverse function, recursive function

Explicit Functions

An **explicit function** is simply one in which one variable may be written directly in terms of the other variable.

For example, $y = 2x^2$

$f(x) = x - 3$

Recursive Functions

Recursion has to do with repetition. A **recursive function** is one that uses the function itself to define all applications of the function. The **Fibonacci sequence** is a common example.

$\text{Fib}(0) = 0$

$\text{Fib}(1) = 1$

For all other integers where $x > 1$, $\text{Fib}(x) = (\text{Fib}(x - 1) + \text{Fib}(x - 2))$.

Recursion is an especially important concept in computer programming. If you can define a function in terms of itself, you do not need to program endless specific examples.

Arithmetic and Geometric Sequences

Functions often result in sequences of numbers. An **arithmetic sequence** moves from one term to the next by adding a constant value called the **common difference**.

For example, 1, 3, 5, 7, 9, . . .   The common difference is 2.

5, 0, –5, –10, –15, . . .   The common difference is –5.

A **geometric sequence** moves from one term to the next by multiplying a constant value called the **common ratio**.

For example, 2, 4, 8, 16, 32, . . . The common ratio is 2.

$1, \dfrac{1}{3}, \dfrac{1}{9}, \dfrac{1}{27}, \dfrac{1}{81}, \ldots$ The common ratio is $\dfrac{1}{3}$.

From Problem to Function

There are very few situations involving numbers that cannot be expressed in terms of functions. Here are some simple examples of problems expressed as functions.

There are 12 inches in a foot. How many inches are there in x feet?

$f(x) = 12x$

A cell phone company charges $50 for a phone and $32 per month. What will the plan cost over the course of x months?

$f(x) = 32x + 50$

A population of bacteria doubles every 4 weeks. If you start with 100 bacteria, how many bacteria will there be in x weeks?

$f(x) = 100(2^{\frac{x}{4}})$

Inverse Functions

To find an **inverse function**, simply reverse the process in the original function.

For example, start with $f(x) = 2x + 1$.

The process: multiply by 2, add 1.

The inverse: subtract 1, divide by 2.

So the inverse function is $f^{-1}(x) = \dfrac{(x-1)}{2}$.

CHALLENGE **Building Functions**

Match each problem to the function that describes it. Use each function only once. Then tell whether each function represents an arithmetic or a geometric sequence.

1. Jerry can make $3 for each bushel of apples he picks.

a. $f(x) = x + 3$

2. Kyra fills her tank and then uses up 3 gallons of gas driving to the lake.

b. $f(x) = 3x$

3. Leo consistently earns $3 more than his brother on his paper route.

c. $f(x) = \dfrac{x}{3}$

4. Malik expects to sell about one-third of his inventory in any given month.

d. $f(x) = x - 3$

5. Which of the functions shown are inverses?

CHALLENGE ANSWERS

Building Functions

1. b, geometric   A function based on price per item is always one that involves multiplication.

2. d, arithmetic   If x is the number of gallons Kyra has, $x - 3$ is the amount after driving to the lake.

3. a, arithmetic   If his brother earns x, Leo earns $x + 3$.

4. c, geometric   If Malik's inventory is x, he expects to sell $\frac{x}{3}$.

5. a and d are inverses; b and c are inverses   An inverse function reverses the process in the original function.

 ## 10 Linear, Quadratic, and Exponential Models

You have seen that functions come in many versions. Knowing which situations call for which kinds of functions is a useful skill.

KEY TERMS: exponential function, linear function, logarithm, quadratic function

Three Kinds of Functions

The graph of a **linear function** is a straight line. The function increases or decreases at a constant rate. The graph of an **exponential function** has a horizontal line approaching zero and then moving rapidly upward. In this function, a constant change in x leads to a proportional change in y. The graph of a **quadratic function** is a parabola with an axis of symmetry parallel to the y-axis. The standard form for this function is $f(x) = ax^2 + bx + c$.

Logarithms

A **logarithm** is the inverse of an exponential number. If $a^n = b$, then $\log_a (b) = n$.

For example, $2^3 = 8$, so $\log_2 8 = 3$.

$4^2 = 16$, so $\log_4 16 = 2$.

$10^4 = 10{,}000$, so $\log_{10} 10{,}000 = 4$.

Telling Functions Apart

Suppose you are given a function table. How can you tell whether a function is linear, exponential, or quadratic?

For example,

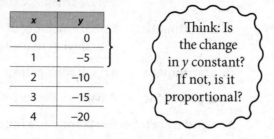

x	y
0	0
1	−5
2	−10
3	−15
4	−20

Think: Is the change in *y* constant? If not, is it proportional?

To determine what kind of function this is, first look at the change in *y*, as illustrated. Here, the change in *y* is constant. For every increase in *x*, *y* changes by −5. The function is linear.

Now try this:

x	y
1	4
2	6
3	6
4	4
5	0

The change in *y* is not constant. As *x* increases by 1, *y* increases by 2, then 0, then −2, then −4. Instead of looking at the change in *y*, look at the *change in the change* in *y*. From 2 to 0 is −2. From 0 to −2 is −2. From −2 to −4 is −2. The change in the change in *y* is constant, so the function is quadratic.

Finally, consider this:

x	y
1	30
2	90
3	270
4	810
5	2,430

The change in *y* is not constant. As *x* increases by 1, *y* increases by 60, then 180, then 540, then 1,620. However, the change is proportional. The change in *y* increases threefold for every increase in *x*. Because the change is in proportion, the function is exponential.

CHALLENGE **Linear, Quadratic, and Exponential Models**

Tell whether each function is linear, quadratic, or exponential.

1. $y = 5x$

2. The US population grows at 1.5 percent annually.

3.

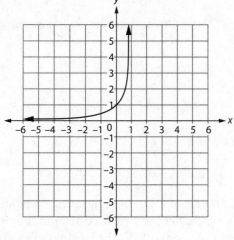

4.

x	y
2	15
3	29
4	43
5	57
6	71

5.

x	y
1	12
2	12
3	14
4	18
5	24

CHALLENGE ANSWERS
Linear, Quadratic, and Exponential Models

1. linear As x increases by 1, y increases by 5.

2. exponential The change is proportional, so the function is exponential.

3. exponential The graph skims the x-axis before ratcheting upward.

4. linear As x increases by 1, y increases by 14.

5. quadratic The change in the change in the y factors is constantly 2.

Trigonometric Functions

Trigonometry is the study of six special functions that involve relationships among the sides and angles of right triangles.

KEY TERMS: amplitude, arc, cosine, frequency, hypotenuse, periodic phenomena, Pythagorean theorem, radian measure, right triangle, sine, tangent, unit circle, wavelength

Angles on a Unit Circle

Any circle measures 360 degrees (360°). One full revolution of a ray around a circle covers 360°.

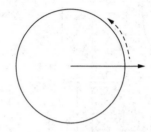

A **unit circle** is a circle with a radius of 1. On the diagram shown, four quadrants are labeled I through IV. Angles are measured around the circle counterclockwise from quadrant I to quadrant IV. The location of an angle in a given quadrant determines whether the points that define that angle have positive or negative values.

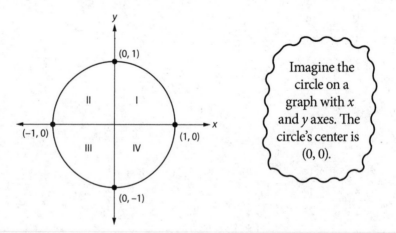

An **arc** of a circle is a portion of the circle's circumference. We usually call that arc s. The **radian measure** (θ) of a central angle of a circle equals the ratio of the length of arc s to the length of the radius. In a unit circle, the radius is 1, so $\frac{s}{r} = s$.

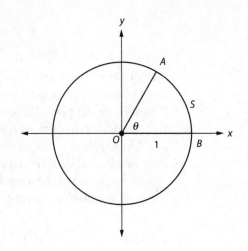

Right Triangles

A **right triangle** has one 90° angle. Here is a right triangle with central angle θ.

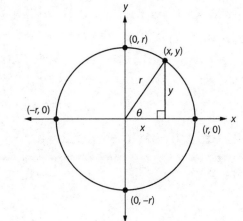

The longest side, the **hypotenuse**, has a length equal to the radius of the circle. The side adjacent to the central angle has a length of x, and the side opposite the central angle has a length of y.

For any right triangle, the **Pythagorean theorem** tells us that the sum of the lengths of the shorter sides squared equals the length of the hypotenuse squared. This is usually written $a^2 + b^2 = c^2$. In the case of the triangle pictured, we could say that $x^2 + y^2 = r^2$. This relationship is important to trigonometry.

Sine, Cosine, and Tangent

There are six trigonometric functions, but you will be responsible for only three. All trigonometric functions are simply ratios made from the numbers x, y, and r in a right triangle such as the one shown.

SINE	COSINE	TANGENT
$\sin \theta = \dfrac{\text{opposite}}{\text{hypotenuse}}$	$\cos \theta = \dfrac{\text{adjacent}}{\text{hypotenuse}}$	$\tan \theta = \dfrac{\text{opposite}}{\text{adjacent}}$

Using the diagram shown, then $\sin \theta = \dfrac{y}{r}$, $\cos \theta = \dfrac{x}{r}$, and $\tan \theta = \dfrac{y}{x}$.

Practical Uses of Trigonometry

Trigonometry is used to compute angles and lengths for navigational purposes and in engineering problems. Sines and cosines are also often used to model **periodic phenomena** such as temperature variations, wave frequency, sound velocity, and so on.

The graph of a sine or cosine has a wave pattern that repeats. The length of the interval between repetitions is called the **wavelength**. The height of the wave is called the **amplitude**. The **frequency** is the number of ups and downs (oscillations) a wave has in a given period of time.

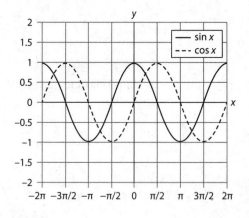

CHALLENGE **Trigonometric Functions**

Solve.

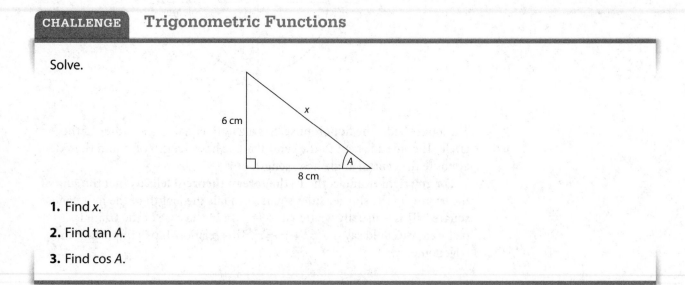

1. Find x.

2. Find $\tan A$.

3. Find $\cos A$.

CHALLENGE ANSWERS

Trigonometric Functions

1. 10 cm   Use the Pythagorean theorem: $6^2 + 8^2 = x^2$. $36 + 64 = 100$, so $x = 10$.

2. $\dfrac{3}{4}$ Tangent $= \dfrac{\text{opposite}}{\text{adjacent}} = \dfrac{6}{8} = \dfrac{3}{4}$.

3. $\dfrac{4}{5}$ Cosine $= \dfrac{\text{adjacent}}{\text{hypotenuse}} = \dfrac{8}{10} = \dfrac{4}{5}$.

12 Congruence

Angles with equal measures, line segments with equal lengths, and figures with equal sizes and shapes are said to be **congruent**. Many of the important theorems that define geometry involve congruence.

KEY TERMS: bisect, congruent, dilation, parallel, parallelogram, perpendicular, reflection, rigid motion, rotation, transformation, translation

Points, Lines, and Planes

Most geometric figures are composed of points, which may be represented by ordered pairs of numbers; lines, which are defined by two points and extend forever in two opposite directions; and planes, which represent flat surfaces and extend in all directions.

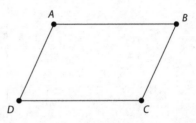

The shape shown is composed of line segments, sections of lines. Segment *AB* intersects with segment *BC* at point *B*. Segment *CD* intersects with segment *AD* at point *D*. Segments *AB* and *CD* never intersect. In fact, if you extended lines *AB* and *CD* forever, they would never intersect. Such lines are **parallel**. Because this shape is made up of two sets of parallel line segments, it is called a **parallelogram**.

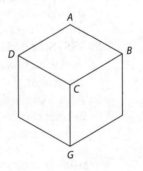

A parallelogram exists in one plane. The shape shown, a cube, exists in more than one plane. Each of its faces is in a different plane. The planes intersect at segments *AB*, *CD*, *CG*, and so on.

Each face of a cube is a square. Each square is made up of four line segments. Segments *AD* and *BC* are parallel, but segments *AB* and *BC* intersect to form a right angle. Such segments are called **perpendicular**.

Congruence

When two geometric figures share the same angle measurements and lengths of sides, they are **congruent**. You can tell by looking at the parallelogram previously shown that its opposite sides are congruent, and its opposite angles are congruent as well.

The measures of the interior angles of any triangle add up to 180°. That does not mean that all triangles are congruent.

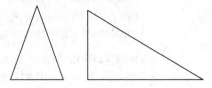

You can see at a glance that these triangles are not congruent. One has a right angle, and the other does not. One has a hypotenuse that is longer than any of the sides of the other triangle.

For triangles to be congruent, they must share angle measurements and side measurements.

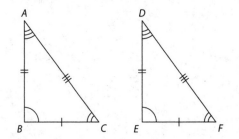

Here, triangle *ABC* is congruent to triangle *DEF*. Angle *A* is congruent to angle *D*, angle *C* is congruent to angle *F*, and angle *B* is congruent to angle *E*. Side *BC* is congruent to side *EF*, and so on.

There are three simple rules for congruent triangles.

1. **SAS (Side-Angle-Side):** If two sides and the angle between them in one triangle are congruent to the corresponding sides and angle of another triangle, the triangles are congruent.
2. **SSS (Side-Side-Side):** If three sides of one triangle are congruent to the corresponding three sides of another triangle, the triangles are congruent.
3. **ASA (Angle-Side-Angle):** If two angles and the side between them in one triangle are congruent to the corresponding angles and side of another triangle, the triangles are congruent.

Transformations

In a coordinate plane, any shape may be moved from one position to another. Such movement is called **transformation**. When a transformation maintains the shape's congruence, it is called **rigid motion**. Nothing in the movement of the shape changed its angle measurements or side lengths.

The following page shows the three kinds of transformations that involve rigid motion.

Translation

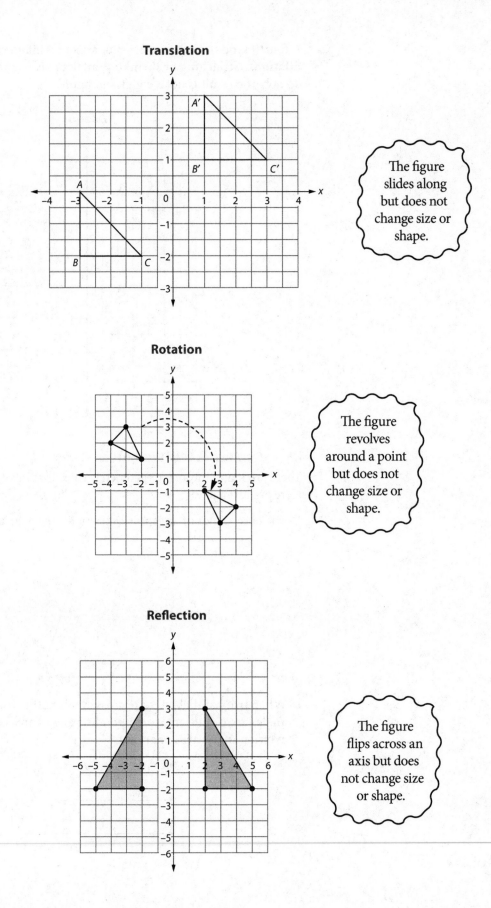

The figure slides along but does not change size or shape.

Rotation

The figure revolves around a point but does not change size or shape.

Reflection

The figure flips across an axis but does not change size or shape.

A fourth kind of transformation does not maintain rigid motion. In a **dilation**, a stretching or shrinking, angles may remain the same, but sides do not. The result is not a congruent figure.

Dilation

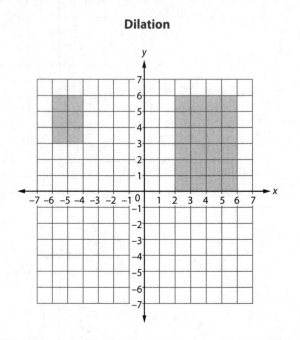

Important Aspects of Congruence

There are many important geometric rules that involve congruence. Here are just a few.

» The base angles of an isosceles triangle are congruent.

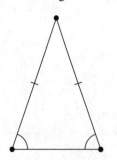

» When two parallel lines are crossed by another line, alternate interior angles are congruent, corresponding angles are congruent, and alternate exterior angles are congruent.

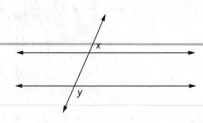

>> The diagonals of any parallelogram **bisect** each other (intersect at their midpoints). Rectangles are parallelograms with congruent diagonals.

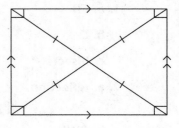

CHALLENGE Congruence

For each figure, complete each statement.

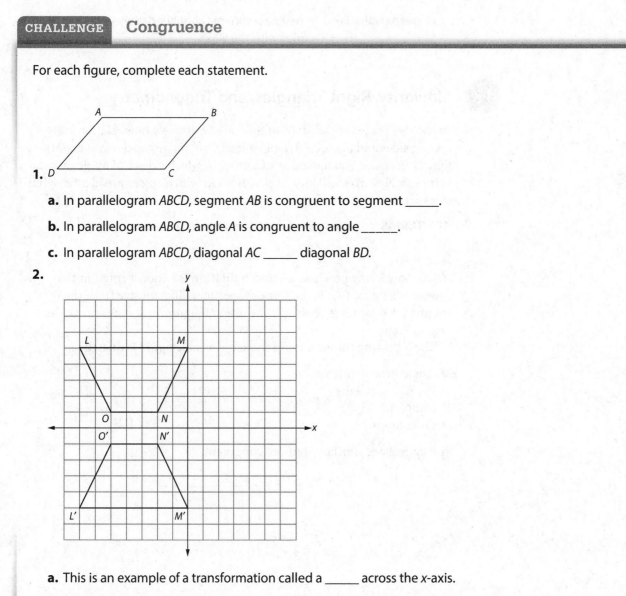

1.

a. In parallelogram *ABCD*, segment *AB* is congruent to segment _____.

b. In parallelogram *ABCD*, angle *A* is congruent to angle _____.

c. In parallelogram *ABCD*, diagonal *AC* _____ diagonal *BD*.

2.

a. This is an example of a transformation called a _____ across the *x*-axis.

b. In this example of rigid motion, segment *ON* above the *x*-axis is congruent to segment _____ below the *x*-axis.

c. Segments *LM* and *NO* are _____ to the *y*-axis.

CHALLENGE ANSWERS
Congruence

1. a. *CD*   Parallel segments are congruent in a parallelogram.

   b. *C*   Opposite angles are congruent in a parallelogram.

   c. bisects   The diagonals of any parallelogram bisect each other.

2. a. reflection   The clue is "across the *x*-axis": the second trapezoid is a mirror image of the first.

   b. *O'N'*   The segments are equal in length.

   c. perpendicular   If the line segments continued, they would form right angles with the *y*-axis.

13   Similarity, Right Triangles, and Trigonometry

In the two preceding sections of this review, you saw how relationships among sides and angles of triangles lead us to many conclusions about figures in space. You looked at situations in which sides and angles are identical. Now you will look at situations in which angles are identical, but sides are not.

KEY TERMS: complementary, dilation, scale factor, similar

Dilations

As you saw in the previous section, a **dilation** is a transformation that produces a figure that is the same shape but a different size from the original. A dilation may stretch the original figure, or it may shrink the original figure.

The following things remain the same when a figure is dilated:

» Angle measurements
» Parallel segments
» Midpoint
» Orientation

The figures are **similar**—but not congruent.

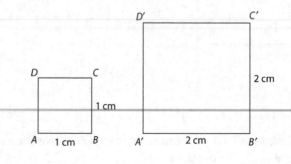

The **scale factor** of a dilation is the ratio of the figures' sizes. In the figure shown, the scale factor is 2. Each segment in figure $A'B'C'D'$ is twice the length of the segments in figure $ABCD$.

If the scale factor < 1, the dilation is a reduction, or shrinking. If the scale factor > 1, the dilation is an enlargement, or stretching. If the scale factor = 1, the dilation creates congruent figures.

On page 180 you learned three rules of congruence in triangles: SAS, SSS, and ASA. There is a fourth rule for similarity: AA. If any two angles of a triangle are equal in measurement to any two angles in a second triangle, the triangles are similar.

Complementary Angles

Two angles are **complementary** if the sum of their measurements is 90°. In a right triangle, then, the two angles that are not right angles are complementary.

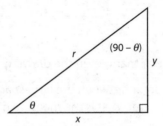

Sine and cosine then may be defined in terms of complementary angles.

$$\cos \theta = \frac{x}{r} = \sin (90 - \theta)$$

$$\sin \theta = \frac{y}{r} = \cos (90 - \theta)$$

In addition, because the sides of similar triangles are proportional and the angles are identical, the trigonometric ratios—sine, cosine, and tangent—of similar triangles are the same. For any right triangle with acute angle θ, the value of sin θ will be the same, and so will the values of cos θ and tan θ. You can see this easily with a 3-4-5 right triangle:

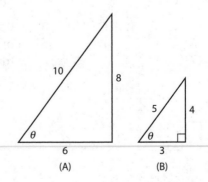

For triangle A, $\sin \theta = \frac{8}{10}$, and $\cos \theta = \frac{6}{10}$.

For triangle B, $\sin \theta = \frac{4}{5}$, and $\cos \theta = \frac{3}{5}$.

Since $\frac{8}{10} = \frac{4}{5}$ and $\frac{6}{10} = \frac{3}{5}$, the ratios are the same.

CHALLENGE **Similarity, Right Triangles, and Trigonometry**

Look at the drawing. Then answer the questions.

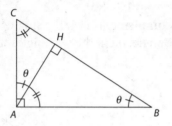

1. Name the three similar triangles in the drawing.

2. Suppose the scale factor between the largest and smallest triangles is 0.75. If side *CH* measures *x* cm, what is the measure of side *AC*?

3. Complete this equation: $\cos \theta = \frac{BH}{AB} = \frac{\square}{AC}$.

CHALLENGE ANSWERS
Similarity, Right Triangles, and Trigonometry

1. ***ABC, HAC, HBA***   It is useful to name the points in a logical order. In this case, start with the right angle and move to the smaller and then the larger of the two acute angles.

2. $\frac{x}{0.75}$ Side *CH* is the shortest side of the smallest triangle, and side *AC* is the shortest side of the largest triangle. If the scale factor is 0.75, each side in triangle *HAC* is 0.75 times the length of a side in triangle *ABC*.

3. ***AH***   Cosine = adjacent/hypotenuse. *AB* is the hypotenuse of *ABC*, and *BH* is the adjacent side to θ. In the similar triangle *HAC*, *AC* is the hypotenuse, and *AH* is the adjacent side to θ.

Circles

Circles have many interesting properties. Among them is the fact that all circles are similar.

KEY TERMS: central angle, chord, circumscribed angle, inscribed angle, intercepted arc, radian measure, radius, sector, supplementary, tangent, vertex

Relationships in a Circle

A line segment from the center of a circle to any point on the circle is a **radius**. A **central angle** is any angle formed by two intersecting radii. The **vertex** of the angle is the center of the circle. Remember that the measure in degrees of an entire circle is 360°. The measure in degrees of the central angle equals the measure in degrees of its **intercepted arc**, the arc shown here as ranging from A to B.

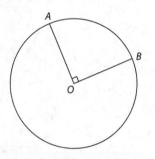

So if the measure of angle AOB is 90°, the measure of arc AB is 90° as well.

A **chord** is a line segment that joins any two points on a circle. A chord that runs through the center of the circle is a **diameter**. An **inscribed angle** is any angle formed by intersecting chords with its vertex on the circle. The measure of an inscribed angle is $\frac{1}{2}$ the measure of its intercepted arc.

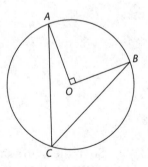

So if the measure of arc AB is 90°, the measure of angle ACB is 45°.

Inscribed angles on a diameter are always right angles.

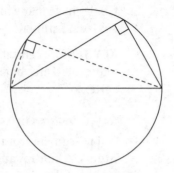

A line that intersects one point on a circle is said to be **tangent** to the circle. Any radius that intersects the circle at that same point intersects the tangent at right angles.

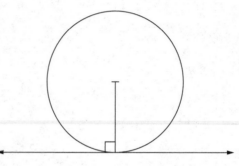

Any quadrilateral inscribed in a circle has opposite angles that are **supplementary** (their measurements add up to 180°). As with a circle, the angles of a quadrilateral add up to 360°.

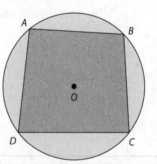

So in the figure shown, angles *ABC* and *CDA* are supplementary, and angles *BCD* and *DAB* are supplementary.

A **circumscribed angle** is one that has rays tangent to the circle.

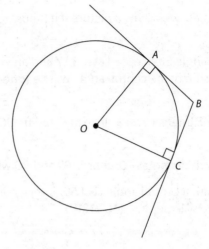

In this figure, a circumscribed angle and a central angle share an arc. Because you know that the sum of the angles of a quadrilateral = 360°, and you know that the angles formed by a tangent are right angles (90° + 90°), you know that the measure of angle *ABC* must equal to 180° minus the measure of the central angle.

Area of a Sector

A **sector** of a circle is the part of the interior intercepted by a central angle.

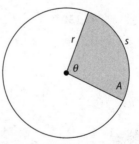

In Section 11, Trigonometric Functions, you learned that the **radian measure** of a central angle of a circle equals the ratio of the length of the intercepted arc to the length of the radius. This leads to several formulas:

» The arc length *s* intercepted on a circle with radius *r* by a central angle of θ radians may be expressed as $s = r\theta$.
» The area of a sector *A* of a circle with radius *r* and central angle of θ radians may be expressed as $A = \frac{1}{2}r^2\theta$.

| CHALLENGE | Circles |

Choose the correct answer. Draw a picture if it helps.

1. Given a central angle intercepted at arc *XY* and an inscribed angle intercepted at arc *XY*, the measure of the central angle will be **(one-half/twice)** that of the inscribed angle.

2. Given tangent *AB* intersecting a circle at *C*, radius *OC* will be **(parallel/perpendicular)** to *AB*.

3. Given a circle with diameter *PQ*, chords *PR* and *RQ* will form an angle of **(90°/180°)**.

4. Given a circle with a central angle *O* of 50° intersecting tangents *AB* and *BC* at points *A* and *C*, angle *ABC* will measure **(40°/130°)**.

CHALLENGE ANSWERS

Circles

1. twice An inscribed angle has a measure $\frac{1}{2}$ its arc or $\frac{1}{2}$ the measure of the central angle with that same arc.

2. perpendicular A tangent intersects the radius at right angles.

3. 90° Inscribed angles on a diameter are right angles.

4. 130° The figure formed is a quadrilateral with angles measuring 50° (the central angle), 90° (the first tangent intersection), 90° (the second tangent intersection), and *x*. Since a quadrilateral has angles that add up to 360°, the answer must be 130°.

15 Expressing Geometric Properties with Equations

You can use what you know about geometric figures to derive equations that will allow you to find measurements and prove theorems.

KEY TERMS: directrix, distance formula, focus, parabola

Equation of a Circle

The equation of a circle with center (h, k) and radius r is $(x - h)^2 + (y - k)^2 = r^2$. You can see this more clearly by starting with a unit circle and thinking about the Pythagorean theorem.

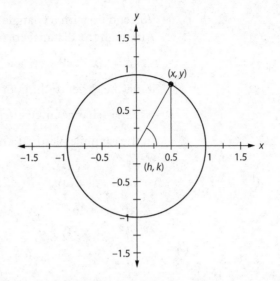

The Pythagorean theorem tells you that in any triangle with sides a, b, and c, $a^2 + b^2 = c^2$. In the triangle shown, side c (the hypotenuse) is the radius of the circle, r. Side b runs parallel to the y-axis from h to x, so its length equals $(x - h)$. Side c runs along the x-axis from k to y, so its length equals $(y - k)$. Plugging these new lengths into the Pythagorean formula gives you:

$$a^2 + b^2 = c^2$$
$$(x - h)^2 + (y - k)^2 = r^2$$

Distance Formula

You can use the Pythagorean theorem to find the length of any segment in the coordinate plane. When the theorem is used this way, the process is called the **distance formula**.

For example, find the distance from (0, 2) to (3, 6).

Begin by drawing lines to make a right triangle, as shown by the dotted lines in the figure.

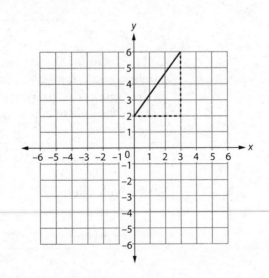

You end up with a triangle with vertices at (0, 2), (3, 6), and (3, 2). Although the distance formula is usually written

$$d = \sqrt{(x_2 - x)^2 + (y_2 - y_1)^2}$$

it may be easier to think of it as

$$d^2 = (\text{change in } x)^2 + (\text{change in } y)^2$$

In the example pictured, the change in x is $3 - 0 = 3$. The change in y is $6 - 2 = 4$.

$$d^2 = (3)^2 + (4)^2$$

$$d^2 = 9 + 16$$

$$d^2 = 25$$

$$d = 5$$

So the distance from (0, 2) to (3, 6) is 5.

You can use this distance formula to compute the perimeter of any polygon as well as the area of any triangle or a rectangle in a coordinate plane.

Equation of a Parabola

Imagine a line parallel to the x-axis. Call that line the **directrix**. Then picture a point somewhere not on that line. Call that point the **focus**. A **parabola** is the set of points in that plane that are the same distance from both the directrix and the focus. Although parabolas may face in any direction, you will primarily deal with parabolas that face upward or downward.

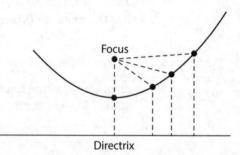

Focus

Directrix

Call the focus (a, b) and the directrix $y = c$. Then pick any point on the parabola and call it (x, y). Because the distance from the focus to (x, y) must be the same as the distance from the directrix to (x, y), you can use the distance formula to equate the distances and solve for y.

$$\sqrt{(x - a)^2 + (y - b)^2} = |y - c|$$

Square both sides.

$$(x - a)^2 + (y - b)^2 = (y - c)^2$$

Expanding and simplifying leaves you with this equation, which is true for all parabolas:

$$(x - a)^2 + b^2 - c^2 = 2(b - c)y$$

Equations of Parallel and Perpendicular Lines

The slopes of <u>parallel</u> lines are identical.

For example, $y = 3x + 4$

$y = 3x - 1$

$y = 3x + 20$

The slopes (coefficients of x) are all 3, so the lines are parallel.

The slopes of <u>perpendicular</u> lines are opposite reciprocals.

For example, $y = \frac{1}{2}x$

$y = -2x$

The slopes are reciprocals: $\frac{1}{2}$ and $\frac{2}{1}$. They are also opposite: positive and negative. The lines must be perpendicular.

Try another example: $y = 5x + 3$

$y = -\frac{1}{5}x - 2$

Again, the slopes are negative reciprocals, so the lines must be perpendicular.

CHALLENGE Expressing Geometric Properties with Equations

Answer each question.

1. What is the equation of a circle with center (0, 0) and radius of 3?

2. Does this equation name a parabola or a circle: $8x^2 + 8y^2 = 200$?

3. What is the length on the coordinate plane of a segment that runs from (1, 2) to (5, 4)?

4. Are these lines perpendicular, parallel, or neither: $y = \frac{1}{3}x$, $y = 3x + 4$?

CHALLENGE ANSWERS

Expressing Geometric Properties with Equations

1. $x^2 + y^2 = 9$ The equation of a circle is $(x - h)^2 + (y - k)^2 = r^2$. If h and k are both equal to zero, this can be simplified to $x^2 + y^2 = r^2$.

2. a circle   Dividing both sides by 8 gives you $x^2 + y^2 = 25$. The equation names a circle with a radius of 5.

3. $2\sqrt{5}$ The distance formula states that $d = \sqrt{(x_2 - x_1)^2 + (y_2 - y_1)^2}$. The change in x is 4, and the change in y is 2. Squaring those and adding them gives you 16 + 4, or 20. If $d^2 = 20$, $d = \sqrt{20}$, or $2\sqrt{5}$.

4. neither   The slopes are not identical, nor are they opposite reciprocals. They are reciprocals ($\frac{1}{3}$ and 3), but to be opposite, one of them would need to be negative.

16 Geometric Measurement and Dimension

You may explore the relationships between two-dimensional and three-dimensional figures using measurement or visualization.

KEY TERMS: area, Cavalieri's principle, circumference, dissection, volume

Connecting Two and Three Dimensions

You should be able to visualize the shapes formed when you cut through a given three-dimensional figure. For example, if you cut this cylinder horizontally, the resulting two-dimensional shape is a circle. If you cut it vertically, the resulting two-dimensional shape is a rectangle.

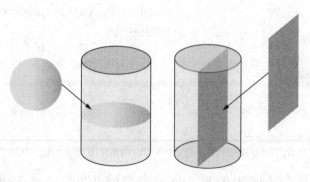

You should also be able to visualize the three-dimensional figure formed when you rotate a given two-dimensional shape. For example, rotating the following triangle in three-dimensions around the x-axis gives you a cone with the x-axis as its axis of symmetry.

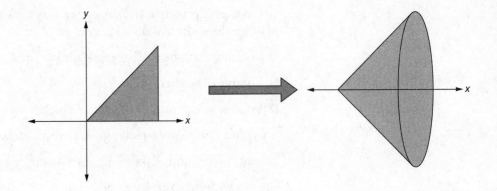

Circumference and Area of a Circle

Circumference is the distance around a circle. **Area** is the inside space of any two-dimensional shape, measured in square units.

» Circumference of a circle = $2\pi r$
» Area of a circle = πr^2

Given a unit circle then with radius 1, $C = 2\pi$ and $A = \pi$.

A common way to prove the area of a circle is through **dissection**, taking apart one figure to form a different, known figure. You can perform dissection on any plane figure.

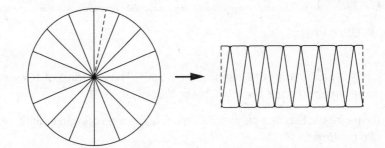

If you rearrange the parts of a circle to form a parallelogram whose base is $\frac{1}{2}$ the circumference of the circle (or πr) and whose side is r, it should be easy to see that the area of the parallelogram is $\pi r \times r$, or πr^2.

Volume of a Solid Figure

The **volume** of a solid figure is the amount of space inside it, measured in cubic units.

Cavalieri's principle states that given two regions in space between parallel planes, if every plane parallel to those two planes intersects both regions in cross-sections of equal area, then the two regions have equal volume. If you think of a cylinder as endless circles, all with the same area, you can easily derive the formula for the volume of a cylinder.

» Volume of a cylinder = base × height = $\pi r^2 h$

In other words, when you find the volume of a cylinder, you are multiplying the area of the circle that forms the base of the cylinder times the height of the cylinder.

Cavalieri's principle and dissection may also be used to find the volumes of other three-dimensional figures:

» Volume of a cone $= \frac{1}{3}(\text{base} \times \text{height}) = \frac{1}{3}\pi r^2 h$

» Volume of a sphere $= \frac{4}{3}\pi r^3$

» Volume of a pyramid $= \frac{1}{4}(\text{base} \times \text{height})$

A pyramid may have a rectangular base or a triangular base. Either way, the formula is the same. Essentially, the volume of a pyramid is $\frac{1}{3}$ the volume of a prism with the same base and height.

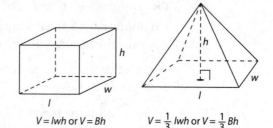

$V = lwh$ or $V = Bh$ $V = \frac{1}{3}lwh$ or $V = \frac{1}{3}Bh$

CHALLENGE   **Geometric Measurement and Dimension**

Solve. Use 3.14 as pi.

1. Circle *O* has a radius of 5 centimeters. Circle *P* has a radius of 10 centimeters. Is the circumference of circle *P* twice that of circle *O*?

2. To the nearest square centimeter, what is the area of a circle with a diameter of 6 centimeters?

3. Which has the greater volume: a cone with a radius of 8 centimeters and a height of 12 centimeters or a sphere with a radius of 8 centimeters?

CHALLENGE ANSWERS

Geometric Measurement and Dimension

1. yes   The circumference of circle *O* is 10π, and that of circle *P* is 20π.

2. 28 cm²   If the diameter is 6 cm, the radius is 3 cm. $\pi 3^2 = 9\pi = 28.26$.

3. the sphere   The volume of the cone is $\frac{1}{3}(\pi 8^2)12$, and the volume of the sphere is $\frac{4}{3}(\pi 8^3)$. Simplified, the volume of the cone is about 804 cm³, and that of the sphere is about 2,144 cm³.

17 Modeling with Geometry

Geometric figures and their measurements can help you solve real-life problems.

KEY TERM: density

Matching Shapes to Objects

Suppose you were asked to calculate the volume of a baby. It's an odd request, but it is possible to figure out if you think about the baby in terms of geometric figures. Perhaps the baby's head is a sphere. Her torso, arms, and legs might be a series of cylinders. Thinking about real-life objects in geometric terms can be useful when it comes to solving design problems. Architects do it when they determine how large a museum room should be to allow a given number of viewers to view art easily. Engineers do it when they consider how small a compact car can be and still seat four people comfortably. And those are only examples of thinking about *people* in geometric terms! For a grocery store, designers consider how many boxes (prisms) can fit on a shelf of a given size or how many oranges (spheres) can be displayed at once in a given bin. Because the Common Core State Standards try to provide real-life applications of the skills and concepts you are learning, you can expect to see real-life applications on the TASC test.

Concepts of Density

The **density** of any material is its mass per unit volume. The ratio of mass to volume can be expressed as $\text{density} = \dfrac{\text{mass}}{\text{volume}}$.

For example, the density of water at sea level at a temperature of 4°C (39.2°F) is $\dfrac{1 \text{ gram}}{\text{cm}^3}$.

In some cases, you can use area instead of volume to determine density, because the material (a sheet of paper, an acre of land) is essentially two-dimensional. In the case of population density, for example, the ratio may be expressed as $\text{population density} = \dfrac{\text{population}}{\text{unit area}}$.

For example, Hong Kong has 7 million people in an area of only around 1,100 square kilometers.

Hong Kong's population density then is $\dfrac{7,000,000}{1,100}$, or around 6,364 people per square kilometer.

CHALLENGE | Modeling with Geometry

Solve. Use 3.14 as pi.

1. Hector wants to know the volume of his head. Deciding that his head is basically spherical, he measures the circumference around the widest part of his head as 22 inches. To the nearest tenth, what is the volume of his head in cubic inches?

2. Which city has the greatest population density?

CITY	AREA IN KM²	POPULATION (2010)
Miami	2,891	4,919,000
Denver	1,292	1,985,000
New Orleans	512	1,009,000
Las Vegas	741	1,314,000

CHALLENGE ANSWERS
Modeling with Geometry

1. 179.6 in³   Start by finding the radius of Hector's head, working backward from the circumference. $C = 2\pi r$, so Hector's head's radius $= \dfrac{C}{2\pi}$, or about 3.5. Now use that radius to determine the volume: $V = \dfrac{4}{3}(\pi r^3) \approx \dfrac{4}{3}(134.7) \approx 179.6$ in³.

2. New Orleans   Divide population by area to find density. Miami's density is around 1,701 people per km². Denver's is around 1,536; New Orleans's is around 1,971; and Las Vegas's is around 1,773.

 Interpreting Categorical and Quantitative Data

Statistics are used to collect and analyze data. Using statistics allows you to group, compare and contrast, and report information. Often, that information is reported in the form of a graph.

KEY TERMS: box plot, conditional relative frequency, correlation, dot plot, histogram, joint relative frequency, marginal relative frequency, mean, median, normal distribution, outlier, quartile, range, relative frequency, scatter plot, standard deviation

Representing Data

A **dot plot** is a simple statistical chart that helps show at a glance the distribution of data. A **histogram** is more elaborate and often shows the frequency of observations over time. A **box plot** shows groups of data through their **quartiles**, dividing each data set into four equal groups.

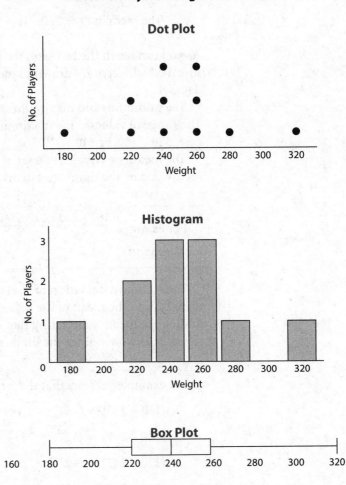

Football Players' Weights in Pounds

Median, Range, Mean, and Standard Deviation

The box plot shown is based on medians. The **median** of a set of data is the middle number, or the number that separates the upper values of data from the lower values of data.

To find the median, you begin by arranging the data in numerical order.

For example, 180, 220, 220, 240, 240, 240, 260, 260, 260, 280, 320.

Because there are 11 values, the median is the sixth value.

$Q_2 = 240$

To complete a box plot, you also need the medians of the top half of the values and the bottom half of the values, leaving out Q_2.

For example, 180, 220, 220, 240, 240 represents the bottom half.

The median $Q_1 = 220$.

260, 260, 260, 280, 320 represents the top half.

The median Q_3 = 260.

As you can see in the box plot, the boxed section goes from Q_1 to Q_3. Then so-called whiskers are drawn to the minimum and maximum values in the data set.

The minimum and maximum values of the set shown are 180 and 320. The **range** of values is the maximum minus the minimum value; in this case, 320 – 180, or 140.

The **mean**, or average, of a set of data is the sum of the values in the data set divided by the number of items in the data set.

For example, $\dfrac{180 + 220 + 220 + 240 + 240 + 240 + 260 + 260 + 260 + 280 + 320}{11} \approx$

247.27

The **standard deviation** of a set of data shows how much variation there is from the mean of the data. You calculate the standard deviation by finding the mean, subtracting that mean from each value, and squaring the result. Then you average the differences and take the square root of that.

For example, let's say that the mean is 247.

$(180 - 247)^2 = (-67)^2 = 4,489$

$(220 - 247)^2 = (-27)^2 = 729$

$(220 - 247)^2 = (-27)^2 = 729$

$(240 - 247)^2 = (-7)^2 = 49$

$(240 - 247)^2 = (-7)^2 = 49$

$(240 - 247)^2 = (-7)^2 = 49$

$(260 - 247)^2 = (13)^2 = 169$

$(260 - 247)^2 = (13)^2 = 169$

$(260 - 247)^2 = (13)^2 = 169$

$(280 - 247)^2 = (33)^2 = 1,089$

$(320 - 247)^2 = (73)^2 = 5,329$

Now average those values and take the square root.

$\sqrt{\frac{13,019}{11}} \approx \sqrt{1,184} \approx 34.4$

In this population of football players, most players have a weight within 34.4 pounds of the mean. If a player were to deviate from the mean by two or three times the standard deviation (68.8 pounds or more), he might be considered an **outlier**, outside the **normal distribution** of data.

Outliers may affect the shape of the data. If the mean and median of a data set are identical, the data, when graphed, is symmetric. If the mean is less than the median, the data may skew left. If the median is less than the mean, the data may skew right.

Two-Way Frequency Tables

You can construct tables in a matrix format to show the frequency distribution of two variables. Such tables show totals in two places plus a grand total in the lower right corner.

Suppose you wanted to compare certain qualities of the members of the 11-man football team.

	FROM TEXAS	NOT FROM TEXAS	TOTAL
Played in high school	6	3	9
Did not play in high school	1	1	2
Total	7	4	11

Such a table may show **relative frequency**, the ratio of the value of a subtotal to the value of the total. To find the relative frequency, you divide each value by the grand total, 11.

	FROM TEXAS	NOT FROM TEXAS	TOTAL
Played in high school	0.55	0.27	0.82
Did not play in high school	0.09	0.09	0.18
Total	0.64	0.36	1

The **joint relative frequency** of a player's being from Texas and having played in high school is $\frac{6}{11}$, or about 0.55. The joint relative frequency of a player's not being from Texas and not having played in high school is much smaller—$\frac{1}{11}$, or around 0.09.

The **marginal relative frequency** of a player's being from Texas is found in the Total row at the bottom—$\frac{7}{11}$, or around 0.64. The marginal relative frequency of a player's not having played in high school is found in the Total column on the right—$\frac{2}{11}$, or around 0.18.

To find **conditional relative frequency**, you divide the joint relative frequency by the marginal relative frequency. You may use conditional relative frequency to find conditional probability.

For example, find the probability that a player who's from Texas did not play football in high school.

Start with the total for players who are from Texas. That marginal relative frequency is 0.64. Out of those players, only 0.09 (9%) did not play in high school. The conditional relative frequency then is $\frac{0.09}{0.64} \approx 0.14$. Given players on this team who are from Texas, there is a probability of 14% that they did not play football in high school.

Scatter Plots

You can represent two variables on a type of graph called a scatter plot. Going back to the data about the weight of football players, you could create a scatter plot that compares the players by weight in pounds and height in inches.

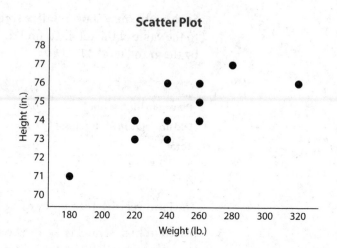

Although it is not perfectly consistent, you can see that there is a **correlation** (relationship) between players' heights and weights. In general, the taller the player, the heavier he is. If you were to draw a line to show the trend, or direction, of the data, it would move upward diagonally from left to right. You could draw conclusions from the slope of the line about how closely height and weight are correlated.

Correlation and Causation

Just because two sets of data are correlated does not mean that one caused the other. For example, being heavy does not make you tall. Height is caused by a variety of factors, including genetics and overall health. Be careful not to assume that data set *A* causes data set *B* merely because you see a trend in the data.

CHALLENGE Interpreting Categorical and Quantitative Data

Use the grade list and table to answer the questions.

Grades: 92, 84, 96, 86, 84

	ENGLISH MAJORS	NOT ENGLISH MAJORS	TOTAL
A Average	5	1	6
Not A Average	12	14	26
Total	17	15	32

1. The grade list shows Ana's grades on five assignments in her English class. What is Ana's median grade? What is her average grade?

2. The two-way table shows statistics for the 32 students in Ana's freshman English class. What is the joint relative frequency for an English major having an A average? What is the probability **(conditional relative frequency)** that a student who is not an English major has an A average?

CHALLENGE ANSWERS

Interpreting Categorical and Quantitative Data

1. **86, 88.4** The median is the central value, and the average is the values added and divided by 5.

2. $\frac{5}{32}$**, or 0.16; 6%** Find the joint relative frequency by dividing the number of English majors with an A average (5) by the total number of students (32). Find the conditional relative frequency by dividing the joint relative frequency of a student who is not an English major having an A average ($\frac{1}{32}$, or 0.03) by the marginal relative frequency of students who are not English majors ($\frac{5}{32}$, or 0.47).

 19 # Making Inferences and Justifying Conclusions

Statistics are used to make predictions or inferences about populations. It's important to have enough data and to determine whether differences in data are meaningful.

KEY TERMS: confidence level, margin of error, model, random sample, significant

Random Sample

If you wanted to find the average height of students in a high school, you could measure all the students, add those measurements, and divide by the total number of students. If you wanted to find the average height of high school students in Vermont, that method would not be very efficient. Instead, you could measure a **random sample** of students and make a prediction based on what you found.

For a sample to be random, every item or person in that sample must have an equal chance of being picked. In the example shown, choosing every student with the last name *Smith* might seem random, but it would leave out students with different ethnic heritages. You might do better to pick students by ID numbers, birth dates, or some other attribute unrelated to their backgrounds.

Models and Simulations

You can start an experiment with a **model** in mind. For example, in an experiment involving tossing a coin, the model gives you the set of possible outcomes (heads, tails) and the probability of each response (0.5, or 50%). If you are looking at the heights of students, you might start with statistics from an earlier time and make a prediction about how heights may have changed with improved nutrition.

You then might conduct a **simulation** and compare your results to your predictions. Your coin-tossing simulation might involve tossing a coin 10 times. Your height-measuring simulation might involve testing a random sample. Today large simulations can be done on computers or graphic calculators without ever tossing a coin or measuring a student.

Margin of Error

When you use a random sample, you are using a subset to draw conclusions about a much larger population. Since your sample is not complete, the data you receive may vary from the expected data. How much variation is OK? That depends on how close you want to be.

The **margin of error** in an experiment or survey is the range of values within which results accurately measure what they are supposed to measure. These factors affect the margin of error:

» Confidence level
» Sample size
» Proportion in the sample

The **confidence level** is something you decide. Often, experimenters choose a 95% confidence level. That means that out of 100 attempts or measurements or surveys, they expect that 95 will return accurate results. The sample size matters. You might toss a coin 10 times and get heads 8 times. That does not mean that the probability of tossing a head is 80%. It means that your sample size is too small. You might need to toss the coin 100 times to even out at 50%.

The proportion in a sample makes a difference in the margin of error as well. In the coin toss, you expect to find $\frac{50}{100}$ heads in 100 tosses. In your student height experiment, you might predict that $\frac{1}{100}$ students will be over 6 feet tall. An estimate of $\frac{50}{100}$ is subject to more variability than an estimate of $\frac{1}{100}$ is.

You may find margin of error by using a formula, using a preexisting table, or using an online calculator.

Significance

If a result is **significant**, it is likely to be caused by something other than random chance. You measure significance using p-values, which represent the probability that random chance cannot explain the result. Usually, a p-value of 0.05 (5%) or less is considered statistically significant.

CHALLENGE Making Inferences and Justifying Conclusions

Choose the word or phrase in parentheses that makes the sentence true.

1. In an experiment involving tossing a number cube, the model would probably indicate that the chances of tossing a 2 were $(\frac{1}{6} / \frac{2}{6})$.

2. If you tossed a number cube 10 times and got three 5s, two 2s, four 6s, and one 1, you might want to adjust your **(margin of error/sample size)**.

3. Results with a p-value of $p < 0.01$ would probably be considered **(significant/insignificant)**.

CHALLENGE ANSWERS

Making Inferences and Justifying Conclusions

1. $\frac{1}{6}$ If the cube is fair, each result has a 1 in 6 chance with each toss.

2. **sample size**   Results that far from expected values could result from a sample size that is too small.

3. **significant**   A p-value of 5% or less is usually considered significant.

 20 ## Conditional Probability and the Rules of Probability

Sometimes you look at more than one event at a time, as you did in the two-way frequency tables in Section 18. **Conditional probability** is the likelihood that given event B, event A will occur, or vice versa.

KEY TERMS: addition rule, complement, conditional probability, event, independent, intersection, sample space, subset, union

Sample Space and Subsets

In a random experiment, the **sample space** is the set S that includes all possible outcomes.

For example, throwing a number cube yields the sample space
$S = \{1, 2, 3, 4, 5, 6\}$.

Tossing a coin yields the sample space $S = \{H, T\}$.

Within a given sample space are **subsets** known as *events*. An **event** is a set of outcomes of the experiment. Given two events, A and B, there are a variety of possible relationships.

» The **union** of events A and B is the event that takes place only if A occurs *or* B occurs.
» The **intersection** of events A and B is the event that takes place only if A occurs *and* B occurs.
» The **complement** of event A is all outcomes that are *not* the event. The event plus its complement equals all possible outcomes.

For example, toss a number cube. The sample space is
$S = \{1, 2, 3, 4, 5, 6\}$.

Let A be the event "an odd number" and B be the event "divisible by 3."

$A = \{1, 3, 5\}$ and $B = \{3, 6\}$.

The union of A and $B = \{1, 3, 5, 6\}$.

The intersection of A and $B = \{3\}$.

The complement of $A = \{2, 4, 6\}$ and the complement of $B = \{1, 2, 4, 5\}$.

Independent Events

An **independent** event is not affected by previous events. Rolling a number cube and getting a 4 does not mean that the next time you roll a number cube, you will get a 1, or a 2, or any specific number. The events are unrelated. Every time you roll, you have a 1 in 6 chance of rolling a 4.

To calculate the probability of two or more independent events, multiply the probabilities of each.

For example, given a number cube, what is the probability of rolling three 4s in a row?

$$\frac{1}{6} \times \frac{1}{6} \times \frac{1}{6} = \frac{1}{216}$$

Given a coin, what is the probability of tossing heads five times in a row?

$0.5 \times 0.5 \times 0.5 \times 0.5 \times 0.5 = 0.03125$

The probability of achieving a series of independent events decreases rapidly as the series increases.

A good way to think about independent events is to consider the conditional probability of A and B this way: The conditional probability of A given B is the same as the probability of A. The conditional probability of B given A is the same as the probability of B.

Addition Rules

Sometimes two events are mutually exclusive. If one occurs, the other cannot. In such a case, to find the probability of event A or B, add the probabilities of each event:

$P(A \text{ or } B) = P(A) + P(B)$

For example, given a number cube, what is the probability of rolling a 2 *or* a 4?

$P(2) = \dfrac{1}{6}$

$P(4) = \dfrac{1}{6}$

$P(2 \text{ or } 4) = \dfrac{1}{6} + \dfrac{1}{6} = \dfrac{2}{6} = \dfrac{1}{3}$

You have a 1 in 3 chance of rolling a 2 or a 4.

Sometimes two events are non-mutually exclusive. It is possible to have both events occur at once. You can chart events like this on a two-way table. (See page 201.) When two events are non-mutually exclusive, find the probability of event A or B by subtracting the overlap of the two events from the sum of the probability of each event:

$P(A \text{ or } B) = P(A) + P(B) - P(A \text{ and } B)$

For example, return to the table of football players on page 201. There are 11 players in all. Of those, 7 are from Texas, and 4 are not. In addition, 9 played ball in high school, and 2, including 1 Texan, did not. If you choose a player at random, what is the probability of choosing someone from Texas *or* someone who played ball in high school?

$P(\text{Texas or HS}) = P(\text{Texas}) + P(\text{HS}) - P(\text{Texas and HS})$

$= \dfrac{7}{11} + \dfrac{9}{11} - \left(\dfrac{6}{11}\right)$

$= \dfrac{16}{11} - \dfrac{6}{11} = \dfrac{10}{11}$

Conditional Probability and the Rules of Probability

Read the problem. Then answer each question.

There are 52 cards in a standard deck of cards in four equal suits from 2 through Jack, Queen, King, and Ace. The suits are clubs, spades, hearts, and diamonds.

1. Let A = clubs and B = 10s. What is the intersection of A and B?

2. If you put the card back and reshuffle each time you draw, what is the probability of drawing three 2s in a row?

3. You pick one card from the deck at random. What is the probability that the card will be a heart **or** a spade?

4. You pick one card from the deck at random. What is the probability that the card will be a Jack **or** a diamond?

CHALLENGE ANSWERS

Conditional Probability and the Rules of Probability

1. **{10 of clubs}** In this intersection, both A (clubs) **and** B (10s) must occur.

2. $\dfrac{1}{2,197}$ The odds of drawing a 2 are $\dfrac{4}{52}$, because there are four 2s in the deck. In lowest terms, that is $\dfrac{1}{13}$. Because the events are independent when you put the card back and reshuffle, you can multiply to find the probability: $\dfrac{1}{13} \times \dfrac{1}{13} \times \dfrac{1}{13} = \dfrac{1}{2,197}$.

3. $\dfrac{1}{2}$ These are mutually exclusive events—a card cannot be both a heart and a spade. Therefore, use the first addition rule. P(hearts) + P(spades) = $\dfrac{13}{52} + \dfrac{13}{52} + \dfrac{26}{52} = \dfrac{1}{2}$.

4. $\dfrac{4}{13}$ These are non-mutually exclusive events, because one card is both a Jack and a diamond. Use the second addition rule. P(Jacks) + P(diamonds) – P(Jacks and diamonds) = $\dfrac{4}{52} + \dfrac{13}{52} - \dfrac{1}{52} = \dfrac{16}{52} = \dfrac{4}{13}$.

TASC Mathematics Practice Test

---
52 questions, 105 minutes

The following test is designed to simulate a real TASC Mathematics Test section in terms of question formats, number, and degree of difficulty. To get a good idea of how you will do on the real exam, take this test under actual exam conditions. Complete the test in one session and follow the given time limit. Answers and explanations begin on page 228.

Part 1: Calculator Allowed

1. Voltage = current × resistance. Voltage is measured in volts, current is measured in amperes, and resistance is measured in ohms. What is the resistance in ohms if the voltage is 3 volts and the current is 1.5 amperes?

   Ⓐ 4.5 ohm
   Ⓑ 3 ohm
   Ⓒ 2 ohm
   Ⓓ 1.5 ohm

2. Solve for x: $\log_2 64 = x$.

   Ⓐ 3
   Ⓑ 4
   Ⓒ 5
   Ⓓ 6

3. There are 52 cards in a standard deck of cards in four equal suits from 2 through Jack, Queen, King, and Ace. The suits are clubs, spades, hearts, and diamonds. If you pick a card at random, put it back, and reshuffle each time you draw, what is the probability of drawing four Aces in a row?

   Ⓐ $\frac{1}{52}$

   Ⓑ $\frac{1}{2,197}$

   Ⓒ $\frac{1}{2,704}$

   Ⓓ $\frac{1}{28,561}$

4. Which number is equivalent to $216^{\frac{1}{3}}$?

(A) 6

(B) 36

(C) 72

(D) 612

5. Drag and drop to put the cities in order from greatest to least population density.

CITY	AREA IN KM²	POPULATION (2010)
Jakarta, Indonesia	1,360	14,250,000
Beijing, China	748	8,614,000
Delhi, India	1,295	14,300,000
Ho Chi Minh City, Vietnam	518	4,900,000

Jakarta

Beijing

Delhi

Ho Chi Minh City

①

②

③

④

6. Which number is equivalent to $\sqrt[4]{81}$?

(A) 3

(B) 9

(C) 20.25

(D) 36

7. Greta ran 5 kilometers in the Dryden Lake Festival 5K Race. How many meters did she run?

(A) 5

(B) 50

(C) 500

(D) 5,000

8. Use the distance formula to find the perimeter of *ABC*. Think:

$$d^2 = (\text{change in } x)^2 + (\text{change in } y)^2$$

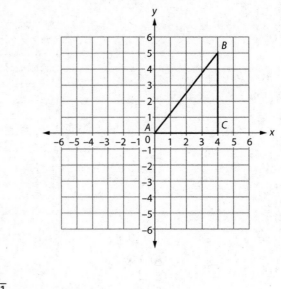

Ⓐ 15
Ⓑ $\sqrt{41}$
Ⓒ $9 + \sqrt{41}$
Ⓓ 50

9. Density = $\dfrac{\text{mass}}{\text{volume}}$. Gasoline has a density of about 0.66 grams per cubic centimeter. To the nearest kilogram, what is the mass of a container of gasoline that measures 30 centimeters by 30 centimeters by 30 centimeters deep?

Ⓐ 136
Ⓑ 59
Ⓒ 40
Ⓓ 18

10. Solve: $4^2 + 4^3 + 4^0$

Ⓐ 1,024
Ⓑ 84
Ⓒ 81
Ⓓ 0

11. What is the scale factor of this dilation?

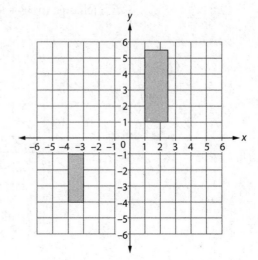

Ⓐ 1.5
Ⓑ 2
Ⓒ 3
Ⓓ 4.5

12. Which is another way to write $x^4 + y^4$?
Ⓐ $(x + y)^2 + (x + y)^2$
Ⓑ $x^5 + y^3$
Ⓒ $(x + y)^4$
Ⓓ $(x^2)^2 + (y^2)^2$

13. Which names the function for this arithmetic sequence?

2, −13, −28, −43, . . .

Ⓐ $f(x) = x − 5$
Ⓑ $f(x) = x + 11$
Ⓒ $f(x) = x − 11$
Ⓓ $f(x) = x − 15$

14. In this drawing, the measure of angle $\theta = 55°$. What is the measure of arc s?

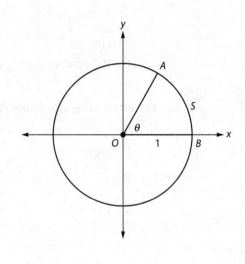

(A) 27.5°
(B) 55°
(C) 73.5°
(D) 110°

15. For a grocery display, Matt constructed a pyramid with a square base measuring 3 feet on each side. If the pyramid was 5 feet high, what was the volume of Matt's pyramid?

(A) 5 ft³
(B) 15 ft³
(C) 45 ft³
(D) 60 ft³

16. To calculate the standard deviation of a set of values, first find the mean of the values. Then subtract that number from each value, and square the result. Then average those differences and take the square root of that.

Jasmine measured five seedlings and got these results. Find the standard deviation for the values in the table.

PLANT 1	PLANT 2	PLANT 3	PLANT 4	PLANT 5
18 cm	12 cm	15 cm	15 cm	20 cm

(A) 16
(B) 8
(C) $\sqrt{7.6}$
(D) 6

17. Quadrilateral *ABCD* is inscribed in circle *O*. If angle *ABC* measures 90°, what is the measure of angle *BCD*?

(A) 45°

(B) 90°

(C) 135°

(D) The answer cannot be found with the information given.

18. Which is another name for 50^{-2}?

(A) $\dfrac{1}{2,500}$

(B) $\dfrac{2}{50}$

(C) 25

(D) −2,500

19. Find all of the possible values for *x*: $2x^2 - 3x = 5$

(A) −2.5

(B) −2

(C) −1

(D) 1

(E) 1.5

(F) 2.5

20. Ellen sliced a cylinder of icebox cookie dough to make cookies. In the package, the dough measured 12 inches long by 2 inches in diameter. As they bake, the cookies expand by about 10 percent. What is the least distance by which Ellen can separate the cookies on the cookie sheet to avoid overlap?

(A) $\dfrac{1}{4}$ inch

(B) $\dfrac{1}{2}$ inch

(C) 1 inch

(D) 2 inches

21. The function $f(x)$ is shown on the graph. Find $f(-2)$.

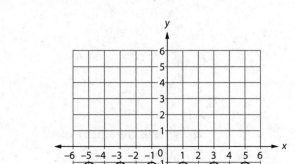

(A) -5

(B) -2

(C) 2

(D) 4

22. Find an equivalent expression: $(5x^2 + x) - (2x^2 + x)$

(A) $7x^2 + 2x$

(B) $10x^4 - x^2$

(C) $3x^2 + 2x$

(D) $3x^2$

23. Flora discovered that this year, she is $\frac{1}{2}$ the age of her mother minus $\frac{1}{2}$ her own age. How could Flora express this algebraically?

(A) $F = \frac{M}{2} - \frac{F}{2}$

(B) $F = \frac{M + F}{2}$

(C) $\frac{F}{2} = \frac{M - F}{2}$

(D) $F = \frac{M}{2} - 2F$

24. If $f(x) = 3x + 4$, what is the inverse function?

Ⓐ $f^{-1}(x) = 4x + 3$

Ⓑ $f^{-1}(x) = 3x - 4$

Ⓒ $f^{-1}(x) = (\frac{1}{3}x) - 4$

Ⓓ $f^{-1}(x) = \frac{(x - 4)}{3}$

25. What is the square of $4i$?

Ⓐ $4i^2$

Ⓑ -4

Ⓒ -16

Ⓓ $-2i$

26. This box plot shows the sales of water heaters over one year at Hefty Water and Heating.

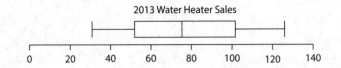

2013 Water Heater Sales

What is the median number of water heaters sold in 2013?

Ⓐ 50

Ⓑ 75

Ⓒ 100

Ⓓ 125

27. The function $m(g)$ tells the number of miles driven using g gallons of gas. What is a reasonable domain for that function?

Ⓐ only positive integers

Ⓑ all real numbers

Ⓒ real numbers except for zero

Ⓓ all rational numbers

28. Drag and drop two numerals to create a number equivalent to $\left(\frac{2}{3}\right)^3$.

| 2 | | 3 | | 8 | | 9 | | 27 |

29. Nathan wrote the letters of his first and last name on separate cards:

NATHAN GOLD

Then he placed the cards face down in two piles, one for his first name, and one for his last name. If Nathan picks a card at random from each pile, what is the probability that he will choose an N and a G?

Ⓐ $\frac{1}{3}$

Ⓑ $\frac{1}{4}$

Ⓒ $\frac{1}{10}$

Ⓓ $\frac{1}{12}$

30. Which system of equations corresponds to this graph?

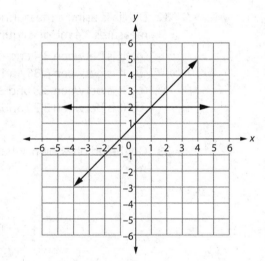

Ⓐ $y = x + 2$; $y = x + 1$
Ⓑ $x = 2$; $y = x - 1$
Ⓒ $y = 2x$; $y = x + 2$
Ⓓ $y = 2$; $y = x + 1$

31. The diagram shows an arc on circle *O* with central angle *θ*.

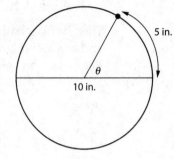

What is the measure of *θ*?

(A) 1 radian
(B) 2 radians
(C) *π* radians
(D) 5 radians

32. Dahlia is using a measuring device with divisions of 0.1 mL. If she measures 3.4 mL of a liquid, what is true of the amount of liquid?

(A) It is between 3.4 and 3.45 mL.
(B) It is between 3.35 and 3.45 mL.
(C) It is between 3.3 and 3.4 mL.
(D) It is between 3.25 and 3.35 mL.

33. On the graph shown, what is the maximum for the interval *x* = 1 to *x* = 2?

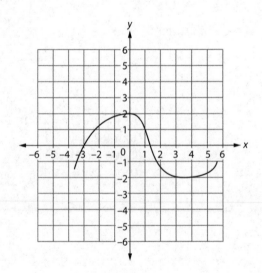

(A) (0, 1)
(B) (1, 1)
(C) (0, 2)
(D) (2, 0)

34. Which two lines would be perpendicular to a line whose equation is $y = 2x - 3$?

Ⓐ $y = -\frac{1}{2}x + 7$

Ⓑ $y = 2x + 3$

Ⓒ $-y = 2x - 3$

Ⓓ $y = \frac{(x-3)}{2}$

Ⓔ $y = -2x + 5$

Ⓕ $y = -\frac{1}{2}x + 6$

35. Which of these describes two independent events?

Ⓐ Joan picks two cards in a row from the magician's hand.
Ⓑ Joan rolls two number cubes, one in each hand.
Ⓒ Joan picks two coins, one after the other, from a pile of coins.
Ⓓ Joan pulls two socks from her drawer.

36. Imagine that this square rotates 360° around the y-axis. What three-dimensional figure will it form?

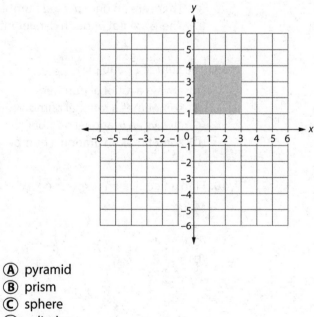

Ⓐ pyramid
Ⓑ prism
Ⓒ sphere
Ⓓ cylinder

37. Drag and drop on equivalent expression: $(3 + 4i) + (7 + i) =$ ☐

| $28i + 3i$ |

| $15i$ |

| $10 + 4i$ |

| $10 + 5i$ |

38. The human resources department at Widgets, Inc., prepared this scatter plot to show income relative to years of experience on the job.

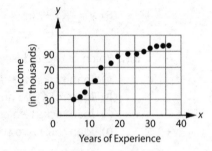

What trend do the data show?

Ⓐ There is a positive correlation between experience and pay.
Ⓑ There is a negative correlation between experience and pay.
Ⓒ There are an unexpected number of outliers in the data.
Ⓓ There are not enough data points to draw a conclusion.

39. The sum of $\frac{3}{16}$ and pi is _____.

Ⓐ always a rational number
Ⓑ sometimes a rational number
Ⓒ always an irrational number
Ⓓ sometimes an irrational number

40. Find an equivalent expression: $(x^2 + 2x)(x^2 - 2x)$

Ⓐ x^4
Ⓑ $2x^2 - 4x$
Ⓒ $x^4 - 4x^2$
Ⓓ $x^4 + 2x^3 - 2x^2$

Part 2: No Calculator Allowed

41. Solve for x: $\sqrt{6 + x} = 14$

Mark your answer in the grid.

42. If the moon's circumference is 6,784 miles, what is its radius? Use 3.14 as pi, and solve to the nearest mile.

Mark your answer in the grid.

43. Find the next *y*-value in this exponential function.

x	y
−1	0.25
0	1
1	4
2	16
3	64
4	?

Mark your answer in the grid.

44. If $f(x) = x^2 - 1$, what is $f(x)$ when $x = 12$?

Mark your answer in the grid.

45. Find the <u>positive</u> value of *x* that solves this quadratic equation.

$$8x^2 + 2x - 3 = 0$$

Mark your answer in the grid.

46. Two parallel lines are crossed by a transversal. What is the measure of angles $x + y$?

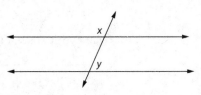

Mark your answer in the grid.

47. Steve has 10 US coins in his pocket. Half of the coins are dimes, and the value of all 10 coins is $0.95. How many nickels does Steve have?

Mark your answer in the grid.

48. What is the whole number between 2 and 9 that when added to this data set would result in a perfectly symmetrical data set?

2   5   6   6   8   8   9

Mark your answer in the grid.

49. *AB* is a diameter of circle *O*. If angle *x* measures 52°, what is the measure of angle *y*?

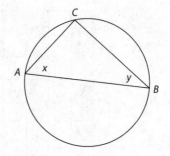

Mark your answer in the grid.

50. What fraction is equivalent to 4^{-3}?

Mark your answer in the grid.

51. In fractional terms, what is the probability of tossing a nickel, a dime, and a quarter and getting heads on all three?

Mark your answer in the grid.

52. A geometric sequence moves from one term to the next by multiplying a constant value called the common ratio. If the common ratio in a sequence is $\frac{1}{2}$, what number follows 75 in that sequence?

Mark your answer in the grid.

This is the end of the TASC Mathematics Practice Test.

TASC Mathematics Practice Test
Explanatory Answers

1. C If voltage = current × resistance, resistance = voltage ÷ current. $3 \div 1.5 = 2$.

2. D $\text{Log}_2 64 = x$ means that 2 is raised to some power to achieve 64. $2^6 = 64$, so the answer is 6.

3. D The probability of these independent events is the product of their probabilities. The probability of drawing 1 Ace is $\frac{4}{52}$, so the probability of drawing 4 Aces, assuming you put the cards back each time, is $\frac{4}{52} \times \frac{4}{52} \times \frac{4}{52} \times \frac{4}{52} = \frac{256}{7,311,616}$, or $\frac{1}{28,561}$. Another way to think of this is that the odds of choosing each Ace in a suit is $\frac{1}{13}$, and $\frac{1}{13}$ four times is $\frac{1}{28,561}$.

4. A An exponent of $\frac{1}{3}$ is the same as the cube root. The cube root of 216 is 6.

5. 1. Beijing, 2. Delhi, 3. Jakarta, 4. Ho Chi Minh City Population density is determined by dividing population by area. In this case, the greatest density is that of Beijing, with around 11,516 people per square kilometer, followed by Delhi with around 11,042, Jakarta with around 10,478, and Ho Chi Minh City with around 9,459.

6. A Which number multiplied by itself four times equals 81? The answer is 3.

7. D One kilometer equals 1,000 meters.

8. C The perimeter is the distance around the figure. You already know the lengths of two of the legs: segment BC is 5 units long, and segment A is 4 units long. To find the length of AB, use the distance formula. The change in x is from 4 to 0, or 4 units. The change in y is from 5 to 0, or 5 units. $4^2 + 5^2 = d^2$, so $16 + 25 = d^2$, making d equal to $\sqrt{41}$. The entire perimeter then is $5 + 4 + \sqrt{41}$, or choice C.

9. D Calculate the volume: $30 \times 30 \times 30 = 27,000 \text{ cm}^3$. If density $= \frac{\text{mass}}{\text{volume}}$, then mass = (density)(volume). $27,000 \times 0.66 = 17,820$ grams, or around 18 kilograms.

10. C Calculate each one, and then add: $16 + 64 + 1 = 81$.

11. A The small rectangle measures 1 by 3 units. The large rectangle measures 1.5 by 4.5 units. The scale factor is 1.5—each length in the small rectangle is multiplied by 1.5 to form the large rectangle.

12. D If necessary, plug in real numbers as x and y to prove that only choice D names the same number as $x^4 + y^4$.

13. D To check, test the function on the sequence: $2 - 15 = -13$, $-13 - 15 = -28$, $-28 - 15 = -43$.

14. B The arc contained by a central angle has the same measure as the central angle.

15. B The base is 3×3, or 9 feet. The height is 5 feet. The formula for volume of a pyramid is $\frac{1}{3}bh$. In this case, $\frac{1}{3}(9 \times 5) = 15$.

16. C Follow the steps. Find the mean: $(18 + 12 + 15 + 15 + 20) \div 5 = 16$. Subtract the mean from each value: $18 - 16 = 2$. $12 - 16 = -4$. $15 - 16 = -1$. $15 - 16 = -1$. $20 - 16 = 4$. Square the results: 4, 16, 1, 1, 16. Now average those values: $4 + 16 + 1 + 1 + 16 = 38$. Divide 38 by $5 = 7.6$. Finally, take the square root of that: $\sqrt{7.6}$.

17. B Draw a picture if it helps. You should be able to figure out that if one angle of a quadrilateral is equal to 90°, and the opposite angle must also be 90° because the quadrilateral is inscribed in a circle, all the angles must equal 90°.

18. A Any number n^{-2} is equivalent to $\frac{1}{n^2}$.

19. C and F Put the equation in a form where the right side is 0: $2x^2 - 3x - 5 = 0$. Factor: $(2x - 5)(x + 1) = 0$. Find the numbers that make that equation true: $2x - 5 = 0$, so $x = 2.5$. $x + 1 = 0$, so $x = -1$.

20. A The cylinder shape is irrelevant, except to help you recognize that the cookies will be circular. If the cookies' diameter is 2 inches, and they expand by 10 percent, each cookie may end up with a diameter of 2.2 inches. Two cookies will expand toward each other by 0.1 inches apiece, or 0.2 inches in all. You will be safe if the cookies are 0.25 inches apart.

21. **B** At the point on the graph where $x = -2$, $y = -2$.

22. **D** Subtract like terms. $5x^2 - 2x^2 = 3x^2$, and $x - x = 0$.

23. **A** Let F be Flora's age and M be her mother's age. Flora's age is half her mother's age $\left(\dfrac{M}{2}\right)$ minus half her own age $\left(\dfrac{F}{2}\right)$. Only choice A shows that relationship. For example, Flora may be 18, and her mother may be 54. Plugging those numbers into the other equations should show you that they are incorrect choices.

24. **D** To find the inverse of the equation, picture y as a replacement for $f(x)$ and then switch x and y:

$y = 3x + 4$

$x = 3y + 4$

Then solve for y:

$\dfrac{x}{3} = y + 4$

$\dfrac{(x - 4)}{3} = y$, so $y = \dfrac{(x - 4)}{3}$

Finally, replace y with the inverse notation: $f^{-1}(x)$.

25. **C** The square of any number ni is $-(n^2)$.

26. **B** The median appears as the central line in the box on a box plot. Here it equals around 75.

27. **A** You cannot drive negative miles using negative gallons of gas, so it makes sense that the domain should be all positive integers.

28. **C** Cube the numerator and then the denominator. The result is $\dfrac{8}{27}$.

29. **D** These are independent events. The first may result in 2N, 2A, T, or H. The second may result in G, O, L, or D. The odds of choosing an N are $\dfrac{2}{6}$, or $\dfrac{1}{3}$. The odds of choosing a G are $\dfrac{1}{4}$. Multiplying those odds yields $\dfrac{1}{12}$.

30. **D** You should see at a glance that $y = 2$ for the horizontal line, so only choice D is possible. To check the second equation, pick any point on that line and see whether $y = x + 1$. It is true for (0, 1), (2, 3), and so on.

31. **A** The definition of a radian is the angle made by taking the radius of a circle, in this case 5 inches, and wrapping it around the circumference of the circle. In any circle where the radius equals the measure of the arc formed by a central angle, that central angle measures 1 radian.

32. **B** For a measuring instrument calibrated at 0.1 mL intervals, the expected level of error would be ± 0.05 mL.

33. **B** Look for the highest point within that interval. The interval ranges from (1, 1) to (2, 0).

34. **A** For the lines to be perpendicular, the x-coefficients must be inverse reciprocals. The inverse reciprocal of 2 is $-\dfrac{1}{2}$.

35. **B** In choices A, C, and D, removing one object means that the second pick is dependent on the first, because the first has eliminated choices from the second. Only choice B offers truly independent choices, because the result of the first roll has nothing to do with the result of the second.

36. **D** Imagine that you staple the left side of a paper square along the y-axis and spin it freely otherwise around that axis. Rotating it all the way around would form a cylinder the height of the square with a radius the width of the square.

37. **10 + 5i** Add like elements first: $3 + 7 = 10$, and $4i + (1)i = 5i$.

38. **A** There is a positive correlation: If you drew a line through the data so that equal numbers of points were above and below the line, the line would travel upward, showing that more experience correlates with more pay. There are few outliers on the graph (choice C), and the data points here seem to point to a clear conclusion (choice D).

39. **C** A rational number plus an irrational number is always an irrational number. Pi is an example of an irrational number, because it cannot be written as a simple fraction.

40. C Think of the four separate values as a, b, c, and d. Multiply ac, ad, bc, and bd, and add all four products, as here: $(x^2 + 2x)(x^2 - 2x) = (x^2)(x^2) - 2x^3 + 2x^3 - 4x^2$, or $x^4 - 4x^2$.

41. 190 Get rid of the square root sign by squaring each side. $6 + x = 196$, so $x = 190$.

42. 1080 If you know the moon's circumference, you can work backward to find its radius by using the formula for circumference: $C = 2\pi r$. $6{,}784 = 6.28r$, so $r = 6{,}784 \div 6.28 = 1{,}080.2547$, or 1,080 miles to the nearest mile.

43. 256 Look for the pattern. For every increase by 1 in the x-values, the y-values increase fourfold. Therefore, the missing value should be 64×4, or 256.

44. 143 Substitute 12 as x: $12^2 - 1 = 144 - 1 = 143$.

45. $\frac{1}{2}$ or 0.5 Factoring that original equation gives you $(4x + 3)(2x - 1) = 0$. Make each of the parenthetical statements equal to zero: $(4x + 3) = 0$, so $4x = -3$, so $x = -0.75$. $(2x - 1) = 0$, so $2x = 1$, so $x = \frac{1}{2}$ or 0.5. You are asked for the positive value only.

46. 180 The transversal crosses both parallel lines to form angles x and y on each. Since the angles are complementary, they must add up to 180°.

47. 4 You may guess-and-check, or you may use algebra. Because you know that half the coins, 5 coins, are dimes, you may subtract that $0.50 and think of the total as $0.45, not $0.95. It should be clear that none of the remaining coins can be pennies or half dollars, so write an equation involving quarters and nickels: $Q + N = 5$ coins in all; $25Q + 5N = 45$. You may not need to go farther and substitute, but if you wish to do so, rewrite the second equation as $25(5 - N) + 5N = 45$. Factor out 5: $5(5 - N) + N = 9$. $25 - 4N = 9$. $4N = 16$. $N = 4$. Check against the original problem: 5 dimes + 4 nickels + 1 quarter = 10 coins. $5(0.10) + 4(0.05) + 1(0.25) = 0.95$.

48. 4 For the data set to be exactly symmetrical, the mean must be equal to the median. In the given data set, the median is 6 and the mean is about 6.286. Adding 4 to the data set gives you a median of 6 and a mean of 6.

49. 38 Because one angle is formed by two chords with endpoints on the diameter, that angle must measure 90°. The sum of the angles in a triangle is 180°. Therefore, $180 - (52 + 90) =$ the measure of angle y. Angle y measures 38°.

50. $\frac{1}{64}$ Any number n^{-3} is equivalent to $\frac{1}{n^3}$.

51. $\frac{1}{8}$ The probability of heads on the nickel is $\frac{1}{2}$, heads on the dime is $\frac{1}{2}$, and heads on the quarter is $\frac{1}{2}$. To find the probability of all three, multiply those probabilities.

52. 37.5 The sequence is geometric, with each value half that of the one before. If $x = 75$, the next number in the sequence is half that, or 37.5.

The TASC
Social Studies Test

HOW TO USE THIS CHAPTER

>> Read the Overview to learn what the TASC Social Studies Test covers.

>> Take the TASC Social Studies Pretest to preview your social studies knowledge and skills.

>> Study the TASC Social Studies Test Review to refresh your knowledge of TASC test social studies topics.

>> Take the TASC Social Studies Practice Test to sharpen your skills and get ready for test day.

Overview

Unlike earlier high-school equivalency tests, the TASC test requires you to know some basic social studies content. It is not just a reading test, although you may be asked to read passages related to history, government, and economics.

The TASC Social Studies Test is based on several national sets of social studies standards, which you may review online:

>> National Standards for History: US and World History
http://www.nchs.ucla.edu/history-standards/us-history-content-standards
http://www.nchs.ucla.edu/history-standards/world-history-content
-standards

>> National Standards for Civics and Government
http://new.civiced.org/resources/publications/resource-materials
/national-standards-for-civics-and-government

>> Voluntary National Content Standards in Economics
www.councilforeconed.org/resource/voluntary-national-content
-standards-in-economics/

>> National Geography Standards
http://education.nationalgeographic.com/education/standards
/national-geography-standards/?ar_a=1

The core ideas for high-school social studies are as follows:

US HISTORY

1. Explain the political conflict that led to the American Revolution.
2. Describe the causes, effects, and course of westward expansion and the major political issues of the early nineteenth century.
3. Describe the causes, major events, and outcome of the Civil War. Explain the causes, effects, and course of Reconstruction in the former Confederacy.
4. Discuss how the United States became a major industrial nation in the late nineteenth century.
5. Analyze and explain how the United States became a world power in the early twentieth century.
6. Explain the causes and effects of the Great Depression. Discuss the US role in World War II.
7. Discuss the social, economic, and cultural issues facing ordinary Americans after World War II ended. Discuss the US role in the Cold War.
8. Understand and discuss the major political, social, and cultural issues facing the United States at the start of the twenty-first century.

WORLD HISTORY

9. Define *civilization* and describe and locate the earliest human civilizations.
10. Analyze and describe classical Greece and Rome, early Chinese and Indian civilizations, and the major religions of the ancient world.
11. Describe the early patterns of migration, the settlement of Western Europe during the Dark Ages, the establishment of European nation-states and empires, and the founding of Islam in the Middle East.
12. Analyze and describe the causes and effects of the Renaissance, the Reformation, and the Scientific Revolution, identifying key people, ideas, and achievements.
13. Identify the causes and patterns of European colonization in Asia, the Americas, and Africa, and explain the effects of colonization on both sides.
14. Discuss the Age of Revolution in Europe, beginning with the Glorious Revolution and ending with the Bolshevik Revolution. Analyze the influence of the Enlightenment on the Age of Revolution.
15. Discuss and describe major world crises and achievements from 1900 to 1945 in Europe, China, India, and the Arab world. Analyze and describe the two world wars.
16. Analyze the changing relationships among nations from the end of World War II to the present day, including the causes and effects of the Cold War and the rise of global terrorism.

CIVICS AND GOVERNMENT

17. Define *politics*, *civic life*, and *government*.
18. Explain the foundations of the American political system.

19. Connect the form of the US government to the purposes and principles of American democracy.
20. Explain and analyze the US role in world affairs.
21. Describe the role a US citizen plays in the American democracy.

ECONOMICS

22. Explain and apply basic economic principles such as the law of supply and demand.
23. Explain and apply the concepts of microeconomics—the economic decisions made by individuals.
24. Explain and apply the concepts of macroeconomics—the workings of an economy as a whole.
25. Describe the role the government plays in the national economy.
26. Analyze the connection between international trade and foreign policy.

GEOGRAPHY

27. Describe the physical and human characteristics of places.
28. Explain how humans modify the physical environment and how physical systems affect human systems.
29. Understand human migration and the characteristics of human settlements.
30. Read and interpret maps.
31. Define *ecosystem* and explain how the elements of an ecosystem work together.

You can expect to see questions on the TASC test in any and all of these areas. The new standards for social studies focus on asking you to think critically about history and about political, civic, and economic issues of the real world today—taking into account how these areas are connected to one another. For example:

1. Analyze cause-and-effect relationships in US and world historical events.
2. Read and interpret historical documents, taking into account the author or source.
3. Compare and contrast multiple perspectives on events.
4. Analyze and interpret economic, geographical, and historical data.
5. Use mathematics and computational thinking.
6. Construct arguments and explanations based on evidence.
7. Obtain, evaluate, and communicate information.

These practices of critical thinking apply to all social studies areas. They are based on the National Standards for History: Historical Thinking Standards at www.nchs.ucla.edu/history-standards/historical-thinking-standards /overview.

To perform well on the TASC test, you should recognize the connection between social studies and "real life." You should understand how historians and economists think and work to solve problems. You may be asked to read historical documents and excerpts, interpret photographs and political cartoons, and apply your analysis of historical events to issues facing people in the present day.

TASC Social Studies Pretest

Use the items that follow to preview your knowledge of social studies concepts and skills. Answers appear on page 241.

Read the excerpt. Then answer questions 1–3.

Fourscore and seven years ago, our fathers brought forth on this continent a new nation, conceived in liberty and dedicated to the proposition that all men are created equal.

Now we are engaged in a great civil war, testing whether that nation, or any nation so conceived and so dedicated, can long endure. We are met on a great battlefield of that war. We have come to dedicate a portion of that field as a final resting-place for those who here gave their lives that that nation might live. It is altogether fitting and proper that we should do this.

But in a larger sense we cannot dedicate, we cannot consecrate, we cannot hallow this ground. The brave men, living and dead, who struggled here have consecrated it far above our poor power to add or detract. The world will little note nor long remember what we say here, but it can never forget what they did here. It is for us the living, rather, to be dedicated here to the unfinished work which they who fought here have thus far so nobly advanced. It is for us here to be dedicated to the great task remaining before us—that from these honored dead we take increased devotion to that cause for which they gave the last full measure of devotion—that we here highly resolve that these dead shall not have died in vain—that this nation, under God, shall have a new birth of freedom—and that government of the people, by the people, for the people, shall not perish from the earth.

—*Abraham Lincoln, 1863*

1. In the first sentence of the speech, President Lincoln quotes from

Ⓐ the Declaration of Independence
Ⓑ the United States Constitution
Ⓒ the Federalist Papers
Ⓓ the Emancipation Proclamation

2. President Lincoln gave this speech after the Battle of Gettysburg, which took place in July of 1863. Why was the Battle of Gettysburg considered the turning point of the Civil War?

Ⓐ It ended Confederate attempts to invade the North.
Ⓑ It was a major victory for the Union army.
Ⓒ It led directly to the Confederate surrender at Vicksburg.
Ⓓ It gave the Union control of the Mississippi River.

3. What kind of government does President Lincoln describe in the final paragraph of the speech?

Ⓐ a democracy
Ⓑ an oligarchy
Ⓒ a monarchy
Ⓓ a dictatorship

4. Until Americans realized that the climate of the Great Plains was ideal for growing wheat, they referred to the region as the Great American Desert. Why was this nickname appropriate?

Ⓐ because it was the least populated region of the United States
Ⓑ because of its extremely high temperatures
Ⓒ because of its low rainfall and lack of trees
Ⓓ because wild animals would not live in the region

Look at the chart. Then answer questions 5–8.

This chart shows the checks and balances of power in the three-branch federal government designed by the founders of the United States.

Checks and Balances of Power in the United States Federal Government

	LEGISLATIVE BRANCH	EXECUTIVE BRANCH	JUDICIAL BRANCH
Legislative branch power over . . .		Can impeach president Can override veto of legislation Can refuse permission to declare war Must approve international treaties	Confirms or rejects presidential nominees for high-court justice Can impeach federal justices
Executive branch power over . . .	Can veto legislation Can call special sessions		Nominates high-court justices
Judicial branch power over . . .	Can declare legislation unconstitutional	Can declare legislation unconstitutional Presides over impeachment proceedings	

5. Which of these is the source of this design for a government based on the separation of powers?

Ⓐ the French Enlightenment

Ⓑ the Magna Carta

Ⓒ the Roman Republic

Ⓓ the English Revolution

6. Why were the founders of the United States hesitant to create a strong chief executive?

Ⓐ They wanted the judicial branch to hold most of the federal power.

Ⓑ They feared that a single all-powerful leader was not compatible with democratic government.

Ⓒ They felt that the United States was too large a nation to be effectively governed by one individual.

Ⓓ They thought that the states would never be able to agree on who the executive should be.

7. In 1972, a Senate committee investigating criminal activity in the White House asked President Richard Nixon to submit tape-recorded Oval Office conversations as evidence. President Nixon refused on the grounds of executive privilege and appealed his case to the Supreme Court. The Court decided that Nixon must submit the tapes. Drag and drop the words that correctly complete the sentence.

This is an example of the [_____] checking the power of the [_____].

| executive branch | legislative branch | judicial branch |

8. The chart shown previously is called "Checks and Balances of Power in the United States Federal Government." Which of these best defines a *federal* government?

Ⓐ one in which there are three branches of power and responsibility

Ⓑ one in which power is shared by the nation and its member states

Ⓒ one in which the people elect leaders and representatives to speak for them

Ⓓ one in which the people have a say in how they are governed

Read the excerpt. Then answer questions 9–12.

From the *Constitution of the United States*

Amendment XVIII. After one year from the ratification of this article, the manufacture, sale, or transportation of intoxicating liquors . . . for beverage purposes is strictly prohibited. (August 26, 1920)

Amendment XXI. The eighteenth article of amendment to the Constitution of the United States is hereby repealed. (February 6, 1933)

9. The Eighteenth Amendment, known as Prohibition, was repealed following intensive lobbying by the hotel industry, women's groups, and others. Which principle of American democracy is illustrated by the repeal of Prohibition?

   Ⓐ freedom of the press
   Ⓑ freedom of individual choice
   Ⓒ the right to petition the government
   Ⓓ universal equality under the law

10. The repeal of Prohibition meant that alcoholic beverages could once again be legally bought and sold. What was the <u>main</u> economic reason why the federal government favored repeal?

    Ⓐ The government would gain revenue from sales taxes on alcoholic beverages.
    Ⓑ The government would stop spending money on investigating alcohol smuggling.
    Ⓒ The government could cut back on the number of police in all major cities.
    Ⓓ The government could put people back to work in the bottling and restaurant industries.

11. Which of the following were major results of Prohibition? Choose all that apply.

    Ⓐ the formation of citizens' groups to lobby for repeal of the amendment
    Ⓑ an increase in the power of organized crime in many major cities
    Ⓒ a willingness among ordinary Americans to break the law as a matter of routine
    Ⓓ the crash of the stock market at the end of the 1920s
    Ⓔ the rise of National Socialism in Europe
    Ⓕ increased spending on consumer goods

12. Prohibition was repealed during the Great Depression. Which of these defines an economic depression?

Ⓐ Wages, prices, and employment all rise.
Ⓑ Wages, prices, and employment all fall.
Ⓒ Wages and employment fall while prices rise.
Ⓓ Wages and prices fall while employment rises.

13. What advantage did the Confederacy have over the Union at the beginning of the Civil War?

Ⓐ It was geographically larger and had a larger population.
Ⓑ It had more heavy industry, more factories, and more railroads.
Ⓒ It had smarter and more experienced military commanders.
Ⓓ It had close economic and political ties to the American West.

14. In the 1970s, the cartel of oil-producing countries called OPEC significantly increased the price of crude oil. Why did nations of the world continue to purchase the crude oil at the higher price?

Ⓐ because they felt that the higher prices were reasonable
Ⓑ because they could not produce oil for themselves
Ⓒ because they were politically allied to the OPEC nations
Ⓓ because they planned to start using more nuclear power

15. When the OPEC countries cut their exports of crude oil in the 1970s, many Americans found themselves waiting in long lines at gas stations. This behavior is an example of

Ⓐ inflation
Ⓑ competition
Ⓒ the law of supply and demand
Ⓓ a comparison of costs with benefits

16. What was the main economic purpose of federal New Deal programs like the Civilian Conservation Corps, the Civil Works Administration, and the Works Progress Administration?

Ⓐ to cut prices
Ⓑ to cut unemployment
Ⓒ to raise wages
Ⓓ to raise revenue

Look at the maps. Then answer questions 17–20.

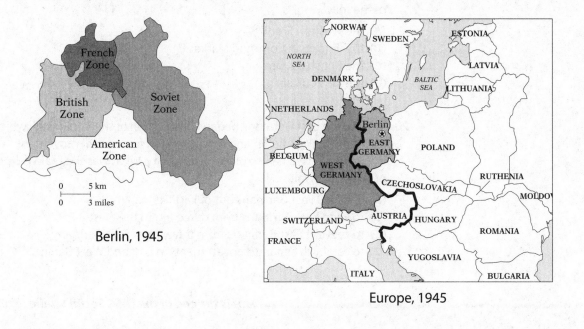

Berlin, 1945

Europe, 1945

17. Up to the time of World War II, Germany (previously Prussia) had been the greatest military power in Europe for nearly 300 years. Which geographical factor is <u>most likely</u> responsible for this long-standing German emphasis on military power? Write your answer in the box.

18. Why was the defense of West Berlin a special challenge for the United States and its allies during the Cold War?

Ⓐ Berlin was located within East Germany.
Ⓑ Berlin is not on the coast.
Ⓒ Berlin has no major rivers.
Ⓓ Berlin is in northern Europe.

19. The heavy north-south black line on the map of Europe represents which of the following?

Ⓐ the Western Front
Ⓑ the European Common Market
Ⓒ the British Empire
Ⓓ the Iron Curtain

20. In 1961, the East Germans began construction of the Berlin Wall, which surrounded West Berlin and strictly limited freedom of movement between the two halves of the divided city. What was the <u>main</u> purpose of the Berlin Wall?

Ⓐ to keep West Germans out of East Germany
Ⓑ to keep East Germans from defecting to the West
Ⓒ to prevent East Berliners from traveling in East Germany
Ⓓ to establish separate governments in East and West Berlin

This is the end of the TASC Social Studies Pretest.

TASC Social Studies Pretest Answers

1. **A** Review 3. Describe the Causes, Major Events, and Outcome of the Civil War, and Explain the Causes, the Course, and the Effects of Reconstruction in the Former Confederacy (pp. 246–248).

2. **A** Review 3. Describe the Causes, Major Events, and Outcome of the Civil War, and Explain the Causes, the Course, and the Effects of Reconstruction in the Former Confederacy (pp. 246–248).

3. **A** Review 17. Define *Civic Life*, *Politics*, and *Government* (pp. 271–272).

4. **C** Review 27. Describe the Physical and Human Characteristics of Places (pp. 287–289).

5. **A** Review 18. Explain the Foundations of the American Political System (pp. 272–273).

6. **B** Review 18. Explain the Foundations of the American Political System (pp. 272–273).

7. **Judicial branch, executive branch** Review 18. Explain the Foundations of the American Political System (pp. 272–273).

8. **B** Review 18. Explain the Foundations of the American Political System (pp. 272–273).

9. **C** Review 19. Connect the Form of the US Government to the Purposes and Principles of American Democracy (pp. 274–277).

10. **A** Review 19. Connect the Form of the US Government to the Purposes and Principles of American Democracy (pp 274–277).

11. **A, B, and C** Review 6. Explain the Causes and Effects of the Great Depression, and Discuss the US Role in World War II (pp. 250–251).

12. **B** Review 22. Explain and Apply Basic Economic Principles Such as the Law of Supply and Demand (pp. 281–282).

13. **C** Review 3. Describe the Causes, Major Events, and Outcome of the Civil War, and Explain the Causes, the Course, and the Effects of Reconstruction in the Former Confederacy (pp. 246–248).

14. **B** Review 24. Explain and Apply the Concept of Macroeconomics—the Workings of an Economy as a Whole (pp. 283–284).

15. **C** Review 22. Explain and Apply Basic Economic Principles Such as the Law of Supply and Demand (pp. 281–282).

16. **B** Review 6. Explain the Causes and Effects of the Great Depression, and Discuss the US Role in World War II (pp. 250–251).

17. **Possible answer: Germany is surrounded on all sides by other nations and thus is vulnerable to attack.** Review 28. Explain How Humans Modify the Physical Environment and How Physical Systems Affect Human Systems (pp. 289–290).

18. **A** Review 16. Analyze the Changing Relationships Among Nations from the End of World War II to the Present Day, Including the Causes and Effects of the Cold War and the Rise of Global Terrorism (pp. 268–271).

19. **D** Review 16. Analyze the Changing Relationships Among Nations from the End of World War II to the Present Day, Including the Causes and Effects of the Cold War and the Rise of Global Terrorism (pp. 268–271).

20. **B** Review 16. Analyze the Changing Relationships Among Nations from the End of World War II to the Present Day, Including the Causes and Effects of the Cold War and the Rise of Global Terrorism (pp. 268–271).

TASC Social Studies Test Review

The pages that follow briefly review the five core subjects of social studies. To learn more about each core area, look online or in the library. Note that in social studies, the five core subjects are interlinked. To understand history, you have to consider geography, economics, and government. Geography and government policy both affect economic choices. To understand why governments work the way they do, it helps to understand their origins in history. As you work through the Review section of this book, you will find that all five of these core areas overlap one another.

United States History

 Explain the Political Conflict That Led to the American Revolution

KEY TERMS: colonies, Parliament, representation, revolution

The United States of America came into being on July 4, 1776, when the Declaration of Independence was officially adopted. There were two main causes for the colonies' determination to break away from Great Britain. First, westward colonial expansion had led to the French and Indian War (1756–1763). Second, Britain made a series of hasty postwar decisions that denied Americans their full rights as British subjects.

The Establishment of the British Colonies

Great Britain claimed thirteen **colonies** along the Atlantic coast of North America between 1584 and 1732. By the mid-1700s, the colonists represented a variety of cultures—British, Irish, Dutch, Welsh, Swedish, and German, plus the Africans brought west in the slave trade and the Native Americans. The early immigrants had many different motives: to escape political or religious oppression, to pursue economic opportunity, to escape debt or other personal troubles, and to seek adventure.

Due to geographical distance, the British **Parliament** delegated its supervision of everyday colonial business and affairs to the individual colonial governors and legislatures. Some of the governors were British, appointed by the king; others were American, locally elected. This system accustomed Americans to having a great deal of say in their own government.

The French and Indian War

The American population soon outgrew the original settlements; westward expansion was the obvious solution. However, the land to the west was not just there for the British colonists to take; both the French and the Native Americans also laid claim to it.

In 1756, rival French and British claims to the Ohio River Valley led to full-scale war. Since the colonies had no armies of their own, Britain and France both sent troops across the Atlantic. Colonial volunteers and Native Americans supplemented these trained fighting forces on both sides; George Washington, then in his twenties, was among the American officers. Fighting in the colonies ended with a British victory in 1761. The 1763 Treaty of Paris granted Britain possession of Canada and all French holdings east of the Mississippi River (except New Orleans).

During and after the war, a rift developed between Britain and its colonies. There were several reasons for this. First, the experienced British troops had snubbed the raw American volunteers, who naturally resented this British arrogance. Second, Britain felt that since the war had been fought partly for the Americans' benefit, the colonies should help pay the war debt. Third, the colonists had fought bravely and well, thus acquiring pride and confidence in themselves. Fourth, fighting side by side against a common enemy established new bonds among men from different colonies and helped forge a common American identify.

The Road to Revolution

The basic issue at stake between Britain and the colonies was **representation** in government—having some say in the laws under which one had to live. This principle of the British political system dated all the way back to the Magna Carta, signed by King John in 1215.

To solve the problem of the war debt, Parliament began enforcing colonial trade regulations it had largely ignored for decades. This hurt the Americans economically, but also made them angry because there were no American members of the British Parliament. Americans argued that as long as they were not represented in Parliament, they did not have to obey its laws. Parliament argued that the colonists, like all subjects in distant parts of the British empire, were "virtually represented" and thus did have to obey.

The Stamp Act of 1765 proved to be the last straw. This was a new tax on all paper and stamps throughout the colonies—a true tax, not a trade regulation. The colonists argued that as British subjects, they could not be taxed without their own consent. All colonies responded violently to the Stamp Act, and it was soon repealed. Boycotts of many British imports followed. A boycott on British tea led to the Boston Tea Party—this large-scale destruction of valuable property led Parliament to pass the so-called Intolerable Acts, largely aimed at Massachusetts but affecting all the colonies in principle. This led to the forming of the First Continental Congress and a series of formal and informal protests against Britain and Parliament. In 1775, British soldiers and the colonial militia exchanged gunfire at Concord and Lexington. The Revolutionary War had begun. The Second Continental Congress formally declared independence from Great Britain in 1776, and after seven years of fighting, British troops surrendered at Yorktown in 1783.

For a discussion of the American government, its founding principles, and its Constitution, see the Civics and Government section of this Review.

Describe the Causes, Effects, and Course of Westward Expansion and the Major Political Issues of the Early Nineteenth Century

KEY TERMS: abolition, Forty-Niner, manifest destiny, reservation, temperance, wagon train

As the US population grew, people pushed westward, settled new territories, formed local governments, and applied for statehood. In 1845, magazine editor John O'Sullivan wrote that it was America's "**manifest destiny** to overspread and to possess the whole of the continent which Providence has given us for the development of the great experiment of liberty."

The Northwest Ordinance (1787) created the Northwest Territory in the Great Lakes region. In 1803, the Louisiana Purchase doubled the size of the United States. The government began offering land grants to Americans willing to settle the West; between 1815 and 1819, the first "Great Migration" saw the building of major roads and large numbers of people moving westward.

Complications

Westward expansion was complicated by two issues: the territorial claims of various Native American tribes, and African chattel slavery. The US government treated the Native Americans as a hostile foreign population, continually making and then breaking treaties with the Native Americans according to whatever best served US interests at a given time. The early nineteenth century saw many all-out battles between Native Americans and US troops. Although various Native American tribes won some key victories, the US military had too great an advantage in both numbers and weapons. In the end, the Native Americans were all forced onto **reservations** on land that Americans did not want to settle, such as the barren lands of the Oklahoma Territory.

American officials agreed on the Native American question but argued fiercely about the expansion of slavery. The Northwest Ordinance of 1787 had banned slavery in new territories, but slaveholding states wanted it to spread so that their voting bloc in Congress would be larger. Free states opposed the expansion of slavery because they did not want slave states outvoting them on every political issue. The divide was regional, with all slaveholding states being in the South and all free states in the North and West.

The slaveholding South maintained the advantage during a series of political compromises. The Missouri Compromise of 1820 allowed the expansion of slavery in the new state of Missouri and in areas to the south of it. The Compromise of 1850 allowed California to enter the United States as a free state, but only in exchange for the passage of a new, extremely harsh Fugitive Slave Act.

Settling the West

Between 1830 and 1850, the United States gained control of the Oregon Territory and won the Southwest in a successful war against Mexico. People flowed westward in a steady stream to settle the new territory. When gold was discovered at Sutter's Mill, California, thousands of young people, nicknamed **Forty-Niners** because the year was 1849, headed west in search of their fortunes—hence the boom in the California population that led to its application for statehood. In addition to prospectors and miners, entrepreneurs also went west and made fortunes. Levi Strauss, the maker of durable workman's denim trousers called "blue jeans," is only one example.

Pioneers had to be tough and enduring to settle the American West. **Wagon trains** would leave Independence, Missouri, in May and travel as swiftly as possible to cross the mountains before the heavy snowfalls that began in October. Covered wagons offered little protection against stifling summer heat and downpours. Illness was frequent and spread quickly. Pregnant women had to give birth out in the open, as there were no hospitals along the trail; many women died of complications from the birth. Apart from replenishing the stock of fresh water, and shooting game to cook and eat, it was not possible to restock any supplies during the journey.

Agitation for Women's Rights

During this era, American women had very few civil or political rights. Married women, their personal belongings, and any wages they earned belonged legally to their husbands. Women could not vote, get a college education, work in most professions, or even attend most public events without a male escort. Women rebelled against this situation, rallying around three political causes: **temperance**, the **abolition** of slavery, and equality. In the 1820s, the temperance movement—the crusade against the sale and consumption of alcoholic beverages—offered large numbers of women leading roles in a public organization for the first time. Society accepted women's active participation in the temperance movement because drunkenness affected the welfare of the family and was thus clearly a women's issue. Women also spoke out publicly on the question of the abolition of slavery (again, this was a moral issue and therefore considered an appropriate topic for women).

In 1848, women's rights activists meeting at Seneca Falls, New York, produced a Declaration of Sentiments arguing forcefully for the equality of women. Its authors echoed language from the Declaration of Independence, pointing out that American women were unrepresented in their own government, just as the colonists had been before the Revolutionary War. By the time of the Civil War, many states had passed laws that granted women certain important civil and legal rights.

Describe the Causes, Major Events, and Outcome of the Civil War, and Explain the Causes, the Course, and the Effects of Reconstruction in the Former Confederacy

KEY TERMS: abolition, Black Codes, Confederacy, Emancipation Proclamation, freedmen, Reconstruction, secede, sectionalism, Three-Fifths Compromise

Background and Causes

The Civil War (1861–1865) was a conflict on many levels—between economic and social systems, geographic regions, political parties, and points of view. The seeds of the war were sown in 1776, when Southern delegates to the Second Continental Congress insisted on deleting a reference to slavery as "cruel war against human nature" from the Declaration of Independence. Northern delegates gave in on the issue because independence from Britain was the primary goal; they believed that the issue of slavery could be resolved later.

Southerners justified slavery on economic and racist grounds. They argued that the Southern cotton crop was crucial to the national economy and that paying wages to a large labor force would cost too much money. They also convinced themselves and continued to teach every generation of their children that Africans were an inferior race fit only for slavery. Abolitionists replied that slaveholding was wrong because liberty was a basic human right. They could also point out that many slaves were in fact the same race as their owners, because free Southern white men fathered thousands of children by African slave women. In addition, abolitionists pointed out that slaveholders had no right to blame slaves for being poor and ignorant when the slaveholders were the ones who denied them wages and education.

In 1787, Congress outlawed the expansion of slavery into the territories. However, the ban was not enforced; both Missouri and Texas entered the Union as slaveholding states. In the US Constitution of 1787, the rules for counting the population to determine how many representatives a state could send to Congress were based on a **Three-Fifths Compromise**: all free persons were counted, as well as three-fifths of "all other persons" (i.e., enslaved people who were not allowed to play any role in the political process). This created an illogical situation in which white Southerners ended up with more than their due share of representatives. The Fugitive Slave Act of 1850 ushered in an era of violent **sectionalism**, in which the Southern region became increasingly divided from the North and West.

At first, Southerners appeared to be gaining the upper hand in the debate. The Kansas-Nebraska Act (1854) allowed the residents of Kansas and Nebraska to decide for themselves whether to become slave states or free states. In 1855, Missouri "Border Ruffians" stormed into Kansas Territory and illegally voted a pro-slavery legislature into office. In 1857, the US Supreme Court case *Dred Scott v. Sandford* declared that the US government had no power to protect runaway slaves or to ban slavery.

The Dred Scott decision and the harsh Fugitive Slave Act began to turn the tide of public opinion in favor of **abolition**. In 1852, Harriet Beecher Stowe's novel *Uncle Tom's Cabin* opened many Northern eyes to the realities of slavery, outselling every book except the Bible in the years leading up to the war. Abolitionist John Brown and his supporters tried unsuccessfully to start an armed slave uprising in Harpers Ferry, Virginia. And in Illinois, a self-educated lawyer named Abraham Lincoln decided to run for national office.

The Election of 1860

Lincoln was the candidate of the Republican Party, formed a few years earlier by men determined to end the spread of slavery. Voting was divided along regional lines, with Lincoln winning a narrow victory. Southern states, certain that Lincoln would insist on abolishing slavery, responded to his election by **seceding** from the United States and forming a new country called the Confederate States of America, or the **Confederacy**.

The Civil War

The Southerners went to war to defend their economic and social system; they felt that the federal government had no right to dictate to the South. The Northern motives for the war were to restore the Union and to end the spread of slavery.

The Union had the advantage in geographical size, population, wealth, and the factories and heavy industry that could supply the troops. The Confederacy had only one advantage—greatly superior military commanders who won an early series of victories that made the South overconfident. The turning point of the war came when the Confederates lost the Battle of Gettysburg in Pennsylvania in 1863 and, on the same day, surrendered to Union forces surrounding Vicksburg, Mississippi. The war dragged on for two more years, finally ending in the spring of 1865.

An entire generation died on the battlefield or from wounds, disease, or starvation. Many Southern towns and cities were in ruins. Railroad lines had to be rebuilt and mail service reestablished. Slaves freed by the **Emancipation Proclamation** suddenly found themselves unemployed and homeless. The defeated white South cherished a bitter hatred toward the North—an emotion that found immediate expression in the tragic assassination of President Lincoln by emotionally unstable Southern sympathizer John Wilkes Booth. Perhaps most daunting of all, the South would have to rebuild its entire society to function and prosper without slave labor.

Reconstruction

After the Union victory, the Republican majority in Congress was eager to reform the old Confederacy along the lines of the North, where all adult men had the right to vote and no one owned another person as property. However, two obstacles stood in the way: President Andrew Johnson and the old guard of the Confederacy.

Congress began the era of **Reconstruction** by swiftly granting African Americans a number of basic civil and political rights. However, laws could not wipe out deep-seated prejudice, bitterness in defeat, and racism. Johnson had supported the Union during the war, but he blocked congressional attempts to extend African-American rights. For their part, Southern whites were forced to accept the Thirteenth Amendment, which outlawed slavery, but they refused to accept the idea that African Americans were equal to whites. They used terrorist tactics to intimidate the **freedmen**, defeating Reconstruction reforms on the state level and replacing them with the notorious **Black Codes** that re-created the climate of racial apartheid that had existed before the war. It would take a century to enforce the three Civil Rights Amendments that were passed between 1865 and 1870.

4 Discuss How the United States Became a Major Industrial Nation in the Late Nineteenth Century

KEY TERMS: Bessemer process, cotton gin, labor union, Progressive Party, transcontinental railroad

First Industrial Revolution

The United States underwent two Industrial Revolutions. The first began in 1793, with the invention of the **cotton gin**. This machine could process as much cotton in one day as 1,000 slaves; Southern planters found that it multiplied their profits tenfold. The invention of the steamboat, which could sail upstream against the current, made it possible to move huge boatloads of cotton north; this made possible a thriving New England textile industry.

The first wave of the US national transportation system included canals, paved roads, and the **transcontinental railroad**, completed in 1869. The purpose of a national system of transportation was to link the agricultural and industrial regions so that both would benefit as sellers expanded into new territories and found new markets for their goods. For example, the railway boom made possible the cattle boom of the 1870s. Railroads took the cattle north to the slaughterhouses of Chicago. As profits grew, so did the sizes of towns and the movement of settlers.

There were no safety or wage regulations to protect factory workers until after the Civil War. Owners set wages as low as they could, demanded a 60- to 85-hour workweek, and shrugged off unsafe working conditions because the constant flood of new immigrants meant that dissatisfied or injured workers could easily be replaced. Factories exposed workers to high levels of industrial pollution. Machinery was dangerous to operate at the best of times—more so when workers were always exhausted from the long hours. **Labor unions** and federal regulations to protect the workers finally arrived with the Second Industrial Revolution.

Second Industrial Revolution

This second revolution took place during the post–Civil War era. Instant long-distance communication (telegraph, telephone), a machine that could produce a perfectly printed letter (typewriter), and cheap, steady lamplight with the flick of a switch (the electric lightbulb) made great changes in the way people lived and worked. Before electricity, most people rose and went to bed with the sun; when electricity was perfected, people could work or enjoy themselves in brightly lit rooms all through the night if they wanted to.

The **Bessemer process**, which made possible the easy and cheap conversion of iron ore into steel, led to a rise in steel production and became the most important factor in the success of the Second Industrial Revolution. Men at the head of heavy industries and large-scale construction companies made fortunes, and American cities became forests of skyscrapers, suspension bridges, and elevated train lines. With the rise of the reform-minded **Progressive Party** and the creation of labor unions, workers were also in a position to enjoy some of the profits of their labor.

5 Analyze and Explain How the United States Became a World Power in the Early Twentieth Century

KEY TERMS: great power, League of Nations, peace conference, protectorate

At the start of the twentieth century, the United States was a wealthy and strong nation, but not a world power. Occupied with internal issues such as the Civil War, Reconstruction, industrialization, and westward expansion, the United States had taken very little active interest in world affairs. In 1900, Western Europe dominated world politics and the world economy. Great Britain, France, Austria-Hungary, Russia, and the recently unified Germany were the **great powers** of the world.

Colonization

The United States had several motives for acquiring colonies. The first was to gain trade partners on favorable terms—partners that could supply natural resources the United States could not, such as sugar, rubber, and coffee. The second was to establish naval bases. The third was simply to prove to the world that the United States was a great power—a force other nations would have to reckon with. Between 1898 and 1903, the United States annexed Hawaii, Guam, Puerto Rico, and the Philippines; made Cuba a **protectorate**; and took control of the construction of the Panama Canal. The United States would retain control of this important trade route for most of the twentieth century.

World War I

World War I—called at the time the "Great War"—marked the United States' first major entry into world affairs. The war began in 1914 as a territorial conflict among European nations, with the Central Powers (Austria and Germany) on one side and the Entente, or Allied, Powers (Britain, Russia, and France) on the other. By 1916, the United States was supplying money and arms to the Allied Powers; US troops joined the fight in late 1917, and the Central Powers surrendered in November 1918.

Despite its late entry into the war, the United States was treated as an equal partner at the **peace conference**, marking the first time in history that a non-European nation had played a major role in the peace settlements of a European war. The United States had played a small but crucial role on the battlefield and ended the war in a much stronger military and economic position than the European nations, which had suffered much greater losses. Ironically, President Woodrow Wilson's dream of the **League of Nations**—an international organization to settle differences over a conference table, taking up arms only as a last resort—was realized without American participation.

For further details on World War I, see the World History section of this Review.

6 Explain the Causes and Effects of the Great Depression, and Discuss the US Role in World War II

KEY TERMS: crash, depression, drought, Dust Bowl, dust storms, Hooverville, New Deal, margin buying, Okie, stock market

The Great Depression

The Great Depression began with the **crash** of the **stock market** in October 1929. Although the United States had weathered several financial panics since the 1790s, this **depression** was nicknamed "great" because it was the worst, longest-lasting economic crisis in US history.

The simple cause of the stock market crash was the practice of **margin buying**, which had become common during the 1920s. Speculators would borrow money and buy stock, and then keep an eye on its value and sell it as soon as its price went up. The large number of speculators meant that share prices were constantly fluctuating, usually upward. This meant a booming market built on an insubstantial foundation of unpaid debt. When buyers lost confidence in the market and began selling their shares, prices dropped and debts fell due. Banks failed because people could not repay their loans. When a bank failed, everyone who had an account with that bank lost all his or her money; there was no mechanism in place to protect account holders from loss. Across the nation, businesses closed and workers were laid off. Landlords evicted tenants who could not pay rent. Millions could not make their mortgage payments and so lost their houses. All social and economic classes were affected.

The failure of businesses and banks coincided with many months of **drought** in the Great Plains, turning the 50-million-acre breadbasket into the **Dust Bowl**. The topsoil in this region was a thin layer over hard, dry dirt. With no rain to keep it moist and anchored in place, the thin topsoil blew away during **dust storms**, and the crops failed. Thousands of small farmers lost everything they had. These **Okies** (nicknamed for the state of Oklahoma, although they were from several neighboring states as well) migrated westward, hoping for a fresh start in the favorable climate of California. All they found there was hostility, prejudice, and starvation wages.

Many Americans blamed the Depression on President Herbert Hoover, who had failed to predict it and seemed not only unable, but unwilling, to resolve it. People who had lost their homes built shantytowns called **Hoovervilles** in ironic tribute to the president. In the 1932 presidential election, Hoover lost in a landslide to Franklin Delano Roosevelt.

Roosevelt immediately took action to address the financial crisis. His **New Deal** programs created millions of jobs and restored the nation's banks to a sound financial footing. During Roosevelt's first term, unemployment dropped by about 8 percent. Unsurprisingly, he was reelected in 1936 in the greatest landslide in a hundred years.

World War II

It took World War II to bring the United States out of the Depression and back to prosperity. The military draft and the change to a war production economy combined to put millions of Americans back to work. The United States officially entered the war in December 1941, after Japan attacked the American naval base at Pearl Harbor, Hawaii. America was faced with a two-front war; it joined Britain's battle against Nazi Germany in Western Europe, and it sent troops to the Pacific to fight the Japanese. The United States was a formidable ally against Germany because of its almost unlimited manpower and its ability to produce an endless flow of military supplies and weapons.

The war in Europe ended in the spring of 1945; Japan held out until the United States dropped atomic bombs on Hiroshima and Nagasaki at the end of August 1945. At the peace conference at Potsdam, Germany, it was clear that the United States and the Soviet Union were the only great powers left in the world. The munitions industry had completely reinvigorated the American economy, American casualties had been minor compared to European losses, and the United States itself was far from the combat zones and physically undamaged. Britain, France, and the other European nations recovered, but would never again be more than second-rate powers.

For further details on World War II, see the World History section of this Review.

7 Discuss the Social, Economic, and Cultural Issues Facing Ordinary Americans After World War II Ended, and Discuss the US Role in the Cold War

KEY TERMS: Civil Rights Movement, Cold War, nonviolent protest, segregation, sit-ins, suburbs, superpower, women's movement

The Cold War

The late 1940s ushered in a new era of **Cold War** between the two **superpowers**: the United States and the Soviet Union. With their opposing political systems and economic policies, these World War II allies quickly became enemies; throughout the Cold War, each tried to contain the other's sphere of influence. The war was called "cold" because the two enemies did not actually fire on one another—but from the Asian point of view, the term *cold war* is a misnomer. When civil wars erupted in Korea and Vietnam, the Soviets backed one side and the United States the other. The Korean War ended in a stalemate, and the Vietnam War in a Communist victory. Apart from these two "hot wars," the Cold War was largely a standoff between the two powers, punctuated by frequent uprisings in Eastern European nations trying to shake off Soviet control. In 1989, the United States claimed a Cold War victory when Communism collapsed of its own accord, having proved impossible to sustain economically.

For further details on the Cold War, see the World History section of this Review.

The Civil Rights Movement

On the home front, the **Civil Rights Movement** took root after the war. Americans eager to claim the leadership of the "free world" against Communist foes began to realize that the legal **segregation** of African Americans in the South seriously undermined that claim. Furthermore, African Americans who had fought for freedom overseas were no longer willing to accept legal restrictions when they returned home. Black students across the South staged a series of **sit-ins** that ended segregation in many public places. President Harry S Truman ordered the integration of the US military. Martin Luther King, Jr., a clergyman from Georgia, organized and led **nonviolent protests** throughout the South, in which protesters exercised their First Amendment rights to "peaceably assemble" and thus won public opinion over to their side against white Southern police officers, who responded with violence. By 1964 the Civil Rights Act had been signed into law, ending segregation in law and in fact.

Postwar America

Americans enjoyed an era of prosperity and plenty after the hard times of the Great Depression. The GI Bill of Rights gave veterans the chance to get a college education, buy a house or a farm, attend training school for a particular profession, or start a business. This enabled many to marry, start families, and move to the newly built **suburbs**. People were buying cars, television sets, and other consumer goods.

The Women's Movement

During World War II, many women had gone to work in traditionally male jobs (including military service) and proved very capable. Victory in the war brought the men home and sent many working women back to the home. This situation did not last, however, because women were no longer content with the old assumption that they should have no ambitions beyond marriage and children. By the 1960s, more and more women were getting college educations and competing for skilled professional jobs. A proposed Equal Rights Amendment to the Constitution failed to pass, but American women made great strides toward social and legal equality during the last decades of the twentieth century.

Understand and Discuss the Major Political and Social Issues Facing the United States at the Start of the Twenty-First Century

KEY TERMS: hacking, Internet, terrorists

Technology

At the turn of the twenty-first century, a technological revolution swiftly changed the way Americans communicate. The advent of e-mail, cell phones, personal computers, online social networks, and portable **Internet** access made sweeping changes to society, both at home and on the job. Financial security and personal privacy became major social and legal concerns due to a rise in **hacking**, the practice of illegally breaking into electronic data systems.

Immigration

A great wave of Latin American immigration to the United States began in the late twentieth century and continued into the twenty-first century. For the first time, American culture began changing to meet the needs of the immigrants, rather than expecting the immigrants to assimilate. One result was a nativist backlash among some groups of non-Hispanic Americans. Immigration had a huge impact on the US economy, as many immigrants (not only Latin Americans) entered the United States illegally and worked without proper documentation.

Religion

In the early twenty-first century, religious faith became an increasingly divisive political issue, with many Republicans advocating a more Christian society and many Democrats advocating a society that treats all faiths equally, or that is secular. Christians pointed to the First Amendment phrase "Congress shall make no law . . . prohibiting the free exercise [of religion]." Non-Christians pointed to the phrase "Congress shall make no law respecting an establishment of religion." Many Americans were unwilling to compromise on this issue. Controversies over abortion rights and the right to legal same-sex marriage were closely linked to religious issues.

Foreign Affairs

Saudi **terrorists** attacked the United States in 2001, leading to a violent breach in US–Arab relations. US troops attacked the fundamentalist Islamic group Al Qaeda and its local allies in Afghanistan, and in 2003 US forces invaded Iraq and toppled its government. After an occupation marked by violence, the United States withdrew from Iraq in 2011. Fighting continued against Al Qaeda forces in Afghanistan and in other Arab countries.

China, India, Israel, North Korea, and Pakistan all possess strategic nuclear weapons. Mutual hostility between India and Pakistan, between North and South Korea, and between Israel and its Arab neighbors is of particular concern to US leaders because tension might escalate into nuclear warfare at any time.

| CHALLENGE | United States History |

Briefly explain the importance of each item in the history of the United States. Write one or two sentences.

1. Black Codes

_____

_____

_____

2. the Declaration of Sentiments

_____

_____

_____

3. the Dust Bowl

_____

_____

_____

4. sit-ins

_____

_____

_____

5. the Stamp Act

_____

_____

_____

CHALLENGE ANSWERS
United States History

Your answers should be similar to the following:

1. Black Codes were a series of laws passed in the former Confederate states after the Civil War. These laws overturned Republican reforms and deprived African Americans of most of the civil rights they had gained.

2. The Declaration of Sentiments (1848) used language from the Declaration of Independence to argue that American women were being deprived of important civil, legal, and political rights. The Declaration helped lead to the passage of reform legislation.

3. The Dust Bowl was a nickname given to the Great Plains during the Great Depression, when the area suffered from an extended period of drought and severe dust storms.

4. Sit-ins were peaceful protests staged by young African Americans and other Civil Rights supporters from the late 1950s to the late 1960s. These sit-ins pressured public places like restaurants to change their segregationist policies.

5. The British Parliament passed the Stamp Act in 1763. It taxed paper goods throughout the colonies, leading to widespread violent protests. The Stamp Act increased colonial hostility toward Britain and thus helped cause the American Revolution.

World History

 ## Define *Civilization*, and Describe and Locate the Earliest Human Civilizations

KEY TERMS: Bronze Age, civilization, temperate

Human Civilization

A **civilization** is more than a group of people; it represents the next step toward social organization. In a civilization, people organize governments and social classes, establish writing systems, build cities, create works of art, study science and mathematics, and invent new ways of doing things.

To sustain human life, two things are required: a **temperate** climate and ready sources of food and fresh water. Under the right conditions, this leads to a surplus of food and thus an increase in health, life span, and income. With extra resources and more spare time, people turn to pursuits beyond the hunting and gathering of food—they create civilizations. All the early human civilizations have left written records, scientific discoveries, beautiful art objects, and works of architecture that go well beyond simple shelters from the weather.

The Fertile Crescent

Human beings began to organize themselves into civilizations around 3500 BCE (before the Common Era). The Fertile Crescent (present-day Iraq, Syria, and Egypt) was home to the early civilizations. This period of human civilization is called the **Bronze Age** for the copper-tin alloy people discovered around 3000 BCE. Bronze produced stronger, sturdier tools and weapons than copper did alone.

Mesopotamia (present-day Iraq) gave the world its first written language, its first organized religion, the basics of modern mathematics, the wheel (used first for making pottery, then for transportation), and the first literary epic (*The Descent of Inanna*). The first city-states were created in southern Mesopotamia by a people called the Sumerians. Archaeologists have unearthed many luxury objects at Sumerian sites, including musical instruments, game boards, and jewelry. These artifacts support the conclusion that a wealthy class of Sumerians existed: only the wealthy can purchase luxury items. The objects' fine quality shows that the Sumerians were skilled artisans. The use of metal in a region where no metal existed proves that the Sumerians traded with other civilizations (probably in the Indus Valley in present-day Pakistan).

The Babylonian Empire came into being around 2000 BCE. Babylonians could plot the fixed stars, follow the course of the sun, and predict lunar eclipses. Their mathematicians were the first to use the number 60 as a base for measuring circles, spheres, and time; we use that system today. Babylonian law codes, such as the Code of Hammurabi, show that in ancient times, people valued the concept of abstract justice and believed in punishing criminals. Another great civilization arose at the same time in the Nile River Valley in Egypt. The Great Pyramids of Egypt prove that the Egyptians were able not only to design monumental buildings, but also to plan and carry out their construction—a remarkable engineering feat in an era with no technology beyond the wheel and the lever. Less is known about the Indus Valley civilization in present-day Pakistan because historians have not yet been able to decipher its written records. However, this civilization did leave behind planned cities with impressive works of architecture and sophisticated drainage systems.

10 Analyze and Describe Classical Greece and Rome, the Early Chinese and Indian Civilizations, and the Major Religions of the Ancient World

KEY TERMS: Buddhism, Christianity, democracy, Hinduism, Judaism, patrician, philosophy, plebeian, Silk Road

China

China has existed as a culturally unified entity since at least 1000 BCE; aspects of Chinese culture that may date back even further include the domestication of silkworms, the production of ceramic and jade objects, and the use of chopsticks. The classical Chinese written language, originating well before 1000 BCE, served as an important unifying force in ancient Chinese kingdoms; although different dialects were spoken in different regions, written Chinese was the same everywhere.

The early Chinese settlements were located along the rivers—the highways of the ancient world. China was isolated from the Fertile Crescent not only by distance, but by obstacles such as deserts and mountain ranges. There is no evidence that ancient China and the ancient Near East had any knowledge of one another.

K'ung-Fu-tzu, known in the West as Confucius, became as influential in Chinese thought and culture as Jesus would later become in the West. Born into the minor nobility in the sixth century BCE, Confucius became a teacher and a scholar. Confucius supported the established order of society, in which everyone had a place. If each person knew and kept his place, did his duty, and respected tradition, society would function smoothly. By the same token, personal integrity would guarantee a wise and just use of authority.

Under the Han dynasty (206 BCE–220 CE) China achieved a free-market economy, the invention of paper, a universal law code, and a merit-based bureaucracy. This period also saw the establishment of the **Silk Road**, a major overland trade route from Luoyang in the east all the way to Constantinople and Alexandria in the west. Horses from Iran, luxury objects from Rome, silks from China, spices and cotton from India, and stories and ideas from all cultures were traded along the Silk Road.

India

Geography played a major role in the isolation of ancient India. The Himalayas, which include some of the world's tallest mountains, blocked access from the north; the other two sides of the triangular peninsula border on the Indian Ocean. This unique geographical location ensured that India could be invaded only from the northwest, through present-day Pakistan.

The Aryans, Eastern Europeans who invaded and settled in Persia and the Indus Valley around 1500 BCE, had a lasting influence on Indian culture. Historians believe that **Hinduism** is a mix of Indian and Aryan ideas and beliefs. Hinduism links a religious belief in sacrifice with a caste system based on duty to others; it continues to hold sway over present-day India.

Siddhartha Gautama, born into the nobility in 563 BCE, is known to history as the Buddha (the title means "Enlightened One"). The Buddha taught that since all suffering and conflict in the world came from frustrated ambition, passion, or egotism, the elimination of these emotions would lead to contentment and spiritual peace. **Buddhism** also opposed the caste system. Ironically, Buddhism had its greatest influence in China, not India.

Greece

The beginning of an identifiable Greek culture goes back to 2000 BCE and the arrival of the Achaeans from the present-day Balkan region of southeastern Europe. The peninsular and island culture of Greece meant a close relationship with the sea; trading was done by boat, and the Greek navy became the strongest and best of the era. The Greek idea of abstract **philosophy**—that people could use their reasoning powers to understand the workings of the universe—is Greece's most important contribution to the development of Western culture. During the Greek Classical Age (roughly 750–400 BCE), the Greeks created the basis of Western art, architecture, literature, science, philosophy, and government.

At a time when the world was ruled by the principle of the divine right of emperors, some of the Greek city-states featured a new form of government called **democracy**. This was not democracy as understood today; neither slaves nor free women had many legal rights or freedoms, and only men in positions of power (about 10 percent of the total population) could vote. Still, the government did give some of its citizens some say in the laws they had to live by. This principle of government by the consent of the governed would eventually hold sway throughout the Western world.

The northern Greek kingdom of Macedonia took over the Greek civilization under Philip II and his son and successor Alexander the Great. During the fourth century BCE, Alexander's wars of conquest spread Greek culture, language, and customs all the way from the Danube River in the west to the Indus River in the east.

Rome

The Roman Empire (500 BCE–476 CE) was the largest and most impressive political achievement of the ancient world. With the aid of its bureaucracy and army, Rome brought all the Western civilizations together into a unified whole that allowed each individual culture to flourish. The phrase "Western Civilization" refers to the Greco-Roman heritage—the history, culture, and understanding of the world common to all Western nations that were part of the Roman Empire or influenced by it.

The key to the Roman Empire's success and longevity was tolerance. Roman rulers allowed diversity to flourish, requiring only three things: obedience to the Roman law code, payment of taxes, and loyalty to the Roman state. Worship of the Roman gods was mandatory, but the people might also worship any other gods they pleased.

Romans adopted elements of mythology, religion, and culture from the Greeks and the Etruscans (an earlier Italian people). Rome's most important original achievements were in law, government, and engineering. Latin, the Roman language, would be the common language of all educated Westerners for well over 1,000 years after the empire fell. Rome began as a monarchy, but in 509 BCE a republic was established. Both **patricians** (aristocrats) and **plebeians** (commoners) were represented in the Senate, and the plebeians' representatives had veto power over those of the patricians. By 100 BCE the republic had become a dictatorship, but the institution of the Senate endured.

Christianity

Christianity came into existence under the Roman Empire as a new sect of **Judaism**, the ancient religion of the Hebrews. Judaism was revolutionary for two things: its followers worshipped only one god instead of many, and its moral code (the Ten Commandments) applied to all people, from monarchs to slaves. This defied the common ancient belief that monarchs were divine and not to be questioned.

Christians and Jews worship the same god, but Christians believe that Jesus of Nazareth was the son of God, the Messiah or Christ (both words mean "anointed one") whose appearance on earth was foretold in the Hebrew Bible. After Jesus's execution, his most influential follower, Paul, preached his message of universal love and eternal salvation through the eastern half of the Roman Empire. To make Christianity appeal to his culturally Greek audience, Paul blended Hebrew beliefs with elements of Hellenistic culture and religion, such as the abstract philosophy of the Trinity. Christianity spread rapidly across the Roman Empire and would hold sway throughout Western Europe until the present day.

By the fourth century CE, the Roman Empire had become too large to govern effectively from one city; it split into two halves, with the eastern half eventually breaking away altogether as the Byzantine Empire, governed from Constantinople (founded 330 CE). Disagreements over dogma split the Christian religion; Rome became the seat of Roman Catholicism, while Constantinople became the seat of Eastern Orthodoxy. Rome was culturally Latin, while Constantinople was culturally Greek—another reason for the division. Finally, the Roman Empire was mired in economic troubles and faced serious threats of invasion from the north.

11 Describe the Early Patterns of Migration, the Settlement of Western Europe During the Dark Ages, the Establishment of European Nation-States and Empires, and the Founding of Islam in the Middle East

KEY TERMS: barbarians, Dark Ages, feudalism, Islam, lord, Magna Carta, medieval, migration, steppes, vassal

Westward Migration

From the 6th millennium BCE, people had inhabited the **steppes** of Central Asia—bleak grasslands bordered by the Ural Mountains and the Gobi Desert. Small tribes of people roamed the harsh terrain, following the herds on which they depended for milk and meat. By mastering horses and learning to work with iron—they were the first people to make wheels with spokes—the Central Asian tribes became formidable bands of warriors. They spearheaded a great westward **migration** that ended in the settlement of Europe.

The Settlement of Europe

Peoples from Central Asia migrated into Europe in waves. The Goths established a stronghold around present-day Poland and Hungary; the Huns drove them out between 100 CE and 300 CE. The Goths moved south, defeating the Roman army at Adrianople and achieving official

Roman recognition of a Goth state in 382 CE. By 550–600 CE, the Slavs had become the dominant culture in southeastern Europe. In the West, the Germanic tribe of the Franks divided, with the West Franks eventually becoming the French and the East Franks eventually becoming the Germans. The West Franks dominated a mixed culture that included Roman Gauls, Bretons, Belges, Vikings, and a mix of others; the East Franks absorbed Slav elements into their culture. At the same time, the Sueves, Burgundians, and Anglo-Saxons established themselves in present-day Spain, France, and Britain.

The culture of these nomadic migrants was primitive compared to Greco-Roman classical civilization, which is why the Romans referred to all the Northern peoples as "**barbarians**." Instead of emphasizing intellectual and artistic achievement or creating sophisticated governments and law codes, the Northern tribes concentrated on pillage and plunder. The **Dark Ages** were an era of conflict, with the various peoples continually struggling for supremacy.

The period 750–1054 was a time of continual raids on France, Britain, and Eastern Europe by Viking tribes from Scandinavia. In the same period, Vikings traveling through what is now Russia founded the cities of Kiev and Novgorod; the local Muscovy princes would later absorb these states into the expanding Russian empire. After the Christian conversion of Vladimir I in 988, Kiev became culturally more Slavic and Byzantine. To meet the threat of the Viking invaders, the local Slavs began reorganizing themselves along Viking-style political lines; this led to greater social organization and thence to true civilization rather than tribal culture.

Feudalism

The feudal system developed during this early **medieval** era—not only in Europe, but also in India, China, and Japan. The social contract between classes was based on an oath of loyalty, which people of this era considered legally binding. The monarch provided warriors with vast land grants and noble titles in exchange for their loyal military service. The warrior thus became the **lord** of a large estate—the ruler of his own small feudal realm, in which he protected and housed his **vassals** in exchange for their military service, loyalty, and obedience. The "lord" of the estate might even be a lady; very few medieval women were warriors (there were rare exceptions even to this rule, such as Joan of Arc), but some women achieved positions of great power through marriage or widowhood.

The monarch and the lords worked out an uneasy balance of power. The monarch wanted to control the realm and command the obedience of all his subjects, but the lords held so much independent power on their estates that they might easily defy the monarch, even though they agreed that the monarch ruled by divine right. The **Magna Carta** is an example of what could happen when the lords united against the monarch. King John of England had such a disgraceful record of bad administration and unwise rule that in 1215, his barons forced him to sign the Magna Carta, which specifically stated that even the monarch was not above the law, and laid the foundations for the parliamentary system that England would eventually adopt.

The Middle East

Islam, the religion that would eventually unify the entire Near East, was founded in the early seventh century in Arabia. Muslims worship the same god as Jews and Christians; Allah is simply the Arabic name for him. Muslims regard Jesus as a great prophet, but secondary to Islam's founder Muhammad. Islam is based on the Five Pillars: faith, prayer, alms, fasting, and pilgrimage to Mecca.

By the end of the tenth century, Islam had taken firm hold on a sizable region of the world. Muhammad was not only the founder of a major world religion; he was also an extraordinary political leader who unified all the Arab tribes under one central government for the first time in their history. Muslim armies conquered an empire that was highly diverse, embracing Turkish, Persian, and North African cultural and artistic traditions. The Muslims even penetrated Europe as far as northern Spain; they would remain in power on the Iberian Peninsula for the better part of 800 years.

Africa

The major African civilizations of the first millennium included Nubia, Axum, and the kingdom of Ghana, in addition to Egypt. Foreign invasion, religious conversion, and international trade are the major themes of these civilizations.

12 Analyze and Describe the Causes and Effects of the Renaissance, the Reformation, and the Scientific Revolution, Identifying Key People, Ideas, and Achievements

KEY TERMS: Enlightenment, Industrial Revolution, *philosophe*, Protestantism, Reformation, Renaissance, Scientific Revolution

The Renaissance

Two important factors made the **Renaissance**, a cultural movement that began in Italy around 1350, a great turning point in Western history. One was a resurgence of interest in classical philosophy, literature, and art. The second was the questioning of Church teachings, which was encouraged by a sharp rise in literacy—the effect of the development of movable type and the printing press. The Koreans invented movable type; it was modified in Germany and ended up having a much greater effect in the West than in Korea and China. With books readily available, people could read on their own instead of simply trusting what the learned authorities told them.

The Reformation

The religious movement called the **Reformation** began in 1517, when the founding of the Lutheran Church ended the thousand-year supremacy of Catholicism. By 1600, thousands of Europeans—particularly Northern Europeans—were worshipping in Lutheran, Calvinist, and Anglican churches. The success of **Protestantism** (so named because its believers *protested* against Catholic doctrine) had multiple causes: a growing opinion among some Christians that the Catholic Church was neither all-powerful nor morally above reproach, a rise in secular political power, and the perfection of the printing process. People could now read the Bible (and all other books) for themselves; they no longer had to accept the Church's interpretation of Scripture.

The Scientific Revolution

The **Scientific Revolution** was a time of great progress in human understanding of the laws of the universe. This era changed not only *what* people thought, but more important, *how* they thought. The discoveries of the Scientific Revolution (such as the moons of Jupiter and the paths of the planets around the sun) were the product of practical experimentation rather than abstract philosophy—conclusions were based on what scientists perceived with their five senses.

The Enlightenment

The *philosophes* (the French word for *philosophers*) of the eighteenth-century **Enlightenment** applied this scientific process of critical thinking to social and political problems. They argued that all people were born free and equal, and that individuals should be able to make their way in the world as reasonable beings with a right to decide how and where they wished to live. Their works encouraged people to believe that they did not have to accept existing conditions and that they could create new institutions to their own liking. In the end, Enlightenment teachings led directly to major revolutions in British North America and in France.

The Industrial Revolution

Later on in the eighteenth and nineteenth centuries, the **Industrial Revolution** demonstrated a third way of using the process of observation and experimentation: by applying it to the mechanical challenges of manufacturing and agriculture. New machines appeared with bewildering rapidity, permanently altering the pace of human life and shifting the Western economy from a basis in agriculture to a basis in mass production and consumption. People who had been artisans or rural laborers migrated to big cities to become factory workers.

The Near East

During this period, much of the Near East was controlled by Ottoman Turkish rulers based in Constantinople. Under the Ottomans, the Islamic world reached a zenith of cultural, literary, and artistic achievement—but soon lagged behind the West, partly due to its inability or refusal to embrace new scientific methods. While Europeans devised their first printing press in 1455, the Arab peoples did not acquire this technology until 1727. At a time when a pendulum clock was an ordinary household object in Europe, it was a curiosity and a rare luxury in India. Beginning around the mid-1700s, the Ottoman Empire steadily lost power and influence; the Islamic world would not play a significant power role in international politics again until the 1970s.

13 Identify the Causes and Patterns of European Colonization in Asia, the Americas, and Africa, and Explain the Effects of Colonization on Both Sides

KEY TERMS: colonization, natural resources

At the end of the 1400s, European monarchs began sponsoring voyages of exploration beyond the world they knew. Their purposes were fourfold: trade, conquest and expansion, religious conversion, and curiosity.

Trade

The **natural resources** of the colonized regions—Asia, Africa, and the Americas—included such non-European items as rice, coffee, sugar, rubber, silk, cotton, gold, diamonds, and spices. West Africa was also the source of slave labor throughout the eighteenth century. **Colonization** meant that Europeans could set their own prices for what they bought from the colonies and what they sold to them.

Conquest and Expansion

A larger population meant more revenue for the crown in taxes, more income for the churches in tithes, and more soldiers in the army. Therefore, three of the most powerful branches of society—the court, the clergy, and the military—were united in the desire to explore the seas and lands beyond Europe in the hope of establishing colonies, which would make them richer and stronger than their neighbors.

Religious Conversion

The third motive, religious conversion, was a product of the universal Christian belief that it was a Christian's duty to convert non-Christians and thus save their souls. Any church is stronger with more believers; therefore, the European churches eagerly sent missionaries to Asia, Africa, and the Americas.

Curiosity

The last motive, and a very powerful one, was the universal human sense of adventure and curiosity—the drive to find out things that has characterized human beings since the beginning of civilization and is responsible for all scientific discovery and technological achievement.

Empire Building

Nations become empires in two ways—either by swallowing up adjoining land and thus expanding their borders, or by seizing colonies some distance away. Rome, China, India, Russia, and the United States are examples of the first type of empire (the United States would acquire a few offshore colonies at the turn of the twentieth century). Spain, France, Prussia (later Germany), and Britain are examples of the second. Between them, Spain and Portugal colonized all of Central and South America and Mexico, plus nearly one-third of the present-day United States. France colonized

Canada, the Great Lakes region, and the Louisiana Territory, which it later sold to the United States. France and Britain fought to control India; in 1850, Britain won the fight and would govern India until after World War II. Britain also sent settlers to colonize Australia and New Zealand. The European powers colonized the entire continent of Africa (except Ethiopia and Liberia), and all the Southeast Asian kingdoms except Siam (present-day Thailand). These colonies could not match the military might of the invaders, so they had to accept foreign rule. The age of colonization ended with World War II for two reasons: the European powers could no longer afford to maintain colonies, and the people living in the colonized countries began to rebel against foreign rule.

 ## Discuss the Age of Revolution in Europe, Beginning with the Glorious Revolution and Ending with the Bolshevik Revolution, and Analyze the Influence of the Enlightenment on the Age of Revolution

KEY TERMS: aristocracy, Bolshevik, conservatism, constitutional monarchy, dictatorship, French Revolution, Glorious Revolution, liberalism, Marxism, nationalism, socialism

Revolution

Between 1689 and 1789, the West saw three major political revolutions—one in England, one in America, and one in France. These three revolutions demonstrated a turning of the tide in the West; they ushered in an era of steady progress toward representative government that would continue into the nineteenth century.

The Glorious Revolution

In Great Britain, fifty years of violent conflict between Parliament and the absolutist monarchy led to the **Glorious Revolution**. In 1649, following defeat in battle, Charles I was captured by Parliamentary forces and executed for treason; after a brief military dictatorship under Oliver Cromwell, Charles's son Charles II was crowned in 1660. When Charles II died and his unpopular Catholic brother James became king, Parliament rebelled, inviting James's Protestant daughter Mary and her husband William of Orange (in Holland) to rule jointly. James II fled to France and the Glorious Revolution was won without a shot being fired. The English Bill of Rights, passed by Parliament in 1689, ushered in a new era of individual rights and **constitutional monarchy**.

The French Revolution

The American Revolution of 1776–1783 created the world's first lasting government whose founding principle (if not reality) was the equality of all the people. The **French Revolution** of 1789 saw the commoners rebelling against an absolute monarch and an overprivileged **aristocracy**.

Unable to devise a viable republican government to replace the monarchy, France became a military **dictatorship** under Napoleon Bonaparte. His attempt to conquer all of Europe united all the other nations against France and ended in his defeat and exile. The French monarchy was restored, but with constitutional limits on the monarch's power.

Many new political forces came into being in the nineteenth century—**liberalism**, **socialism**, **nationalism**, **conservatism**, and **Marxism**. The following table helps explain what each term means.

Political Philosophies of the Nineteenth Century

POLITICAL PHILOSOPHY	DEFINITION/DESCRIPTION
conservatism—the philosophy of those who looked back toward the era of absolute monarchy	Hereditary monarchy is the best form of government.
	Those of aristocratic birth should hold government office because they know best how to run the country.
	A hereditary monarch and well-born ministers of state will keep their end of the social contract—they will act in the best interests of their people.
	The social and political arrangements created by history are the best ones; tampering with them is perilous.
	A free press is dangerous; the government is the best judge of what should be published.
liberalism—the philosophy of those who looked ahead toward an age of constitutional government, legal rights, and free enterprise	A limited monarchy with a freely elected legislative assembly and a written constitution is the best form of government.
	Voting rights should be limited to property owners because they are generally better-educated and have a greater stake in the government.
	Educated, qualified people of merit, regardless of their birth, should hold government office.
	Citizens should have individual rights such as private property and freedom of speech.
socialism—the belief that government control of the economy can reduce or eradicate social injustice	The good of the whole people is more important than the rights of the individual.
	What benefits one citizen benefits all citizens; therefore all citizens should cooperate with and help one another.
	The government should control business and industry and regulate wages and prices to promote economic and social justice and equality.
Marxism—the philosophy developed by Karl Marx and Friedrich Engels; states that the working class should take power through an international revolution	Social classes are inherently enemies, opposed to one another's interests.
	The worker is a far more valuable member of society than the owner because the worker produces goods while the owner produces nothing.
	Workers, not owners or managers, should enjoy the greatest share of the profits of their labor.
	Workers should themselves run the industries in which they work.
nationalism—pride in one's ethnic, cultural, and linguistic heritage and support for the interests of the nation in world affairs	A nation should be composed of people who share the same linguistic, ethnic, and cultural heritage.
	People who do not share that heritage may not be considered part of the nation.
	Generally, it is a unifying force in a culturally homogenous nation such as France.
	Generally, it is a divisive, explosive force in a multiethnic empire such as Austria-Hungary.

Examples of constitutional governments in Great Britain, France, and the United States led to loud calls for written constitutions in many European nations. One wave of European revolutions took place in 1830 and another in 1848. In those revolutions, the forces of liberalism, which supported representative government, scored some victories—although conservative governments were still in power in several countries at the end of the century. One of the most conservative was the Austro-Hungarian Empire, which included a diverse mix of Germans, Czechs, Hungarians, Croats, and Italians. Nationalism—pride in one's culture and language—made all these groups chafe at living in an empire instead of being independent. The growing strength of nationalism was a major factor in the unification of Italy in 1861 and of Germany in 1871. Nationalism in Ireland made the Irish restive under British rule and led to some reforms in Britain's Irish policy.

Nationalism also contributed to the decline and fall of the Ottoman Empire. Throughout the nineteenth century the Ottomans steadily lost territory and influence, until the empire was eliminated altogether after World War I. Other contributing factors included European aggression and the Ottomans' failure to match European military and technological progress. By the outbreak of World War I, Greece and almost all the Balkan states had won their independence from the Ottoman Empire. In 1923 the empire was transformed into Turkey, a secular Islamic republic. In Russia, a rebellion in 1905 did not succeed in overthrowing the czar, but it did lay the groundwork for the **Bolshevik** Revolution of 1917 (see the next section).

15 Discuss and Describe Major World Crises and Achievements from 1900 to 1945 in Europe, China, India, and the Arab World, and Analyze and Describe the Two World Wars

KEY TERMS: balance of power, Bolshevik Revolution, Great War, fascist, League of Nations, reparations, totalitarian

The Great War

World War I (called the **Great War** at the time, because no one anticipated World War II) happened primarily for two reasons. The first was nationalism: nationalist agitation among Serbs and other Slavs in Austria's Balkan provinces threatened the power of the Austro-Hungarian Empire, and German nationalism had led to a major buildup of the German military during the 1910s. The second reason for going to war was maintaining the European **balance of power**. The unification of Germany had created a large, strong, powerful nation-state whose ambitions caused grave concern to Britain, Russia, and especially France. Those three countries formed a defensive alliance. Germany allied itself with Austria-Hungary. When a Serb nationalist assassinated an Austrian archduke at Sarajevo in 1914, Austria declared war on Serbia, Russia mobilized to defend the Serbs, and the alliances went into action. Soon Britain, France, and Russia (the "Allies") were at war with Germany, Austria, and the Ottoman Empire (the "Central Powers").

The Bolshevik Revolution

The war wrecked the European economy; Russian farmers and workers were hit especially hard. Czar Nicholas II was unable to take control and improve matters. Resentment against the czar led to a popular uprising in 1917, and as a result Nicholas abdicated. After a chaotic power struggle, control of the government passed to the leftist Bolshevik Party (*Bolshevik* is Russian for "majority") led by V. I. Lenin. Lenin signed a peace treaty with Germany, withdrew Russian troops from World War I, and began to convert the newly renamed Soviet Union into a communist dictatorship. Britain and France, dismayed by the abrupt withdrawal of a powerful ally, were heartened when the United States joined the war. The tide turned in the Allies' favor, and Germany agreed to an armistice on November 11, 1918.

At the peace conference, the Allied leaders did three things to restore the balance of power in Europe. First, they partially redrew the map of Europe along nationalist lines, creating new states, expanding others, and breaking up the Austro-Hungarian Empire. Second, after making Germany accept responsibility for the war, they reduced Germany's strength by ordering the Germans to maintain the German Rhineland as a demilitarized zone, to pay enormous **reparations**, and to reduce the size of the German army and navy. Third, the Allied leaders created the **League of Nations** as an international forum for resolving conflicts and maintaining peace.

The Rise of Fascism

During the 1920s and 1930s, **fascist** governments arose in Italy, Germany, Spain, and Eastern Europe; by 1937, Japan was also under strict military rule, and Communist forces were on the rise in China. Fascism was a political doctrine that promoted extreme nationalism as a way of achieving national unity and eliminating domestic social and economic strife. In this it differed from Communism, which in theory offered a new social order run by the working class, and fascists and Communists despised each other. In day-to-day practice, however, fascism and Communism often amounted to the same thing—absolute dictatorship of a police state, with only one political party that tolerated no opposition. This system of total government control over individuals' lives was termed **totalitarianism**. Social and political conditions of the period gave rise to these dictatorships. The first was the rise of mass political parties. The second was dissension among liberals in government and parliaments, and their helplessness to respond effectively when a massive economic depression struck in the 1930s. The third was the large class of World War I veterans who made an enthusiastic audience for nationalist rhetoric.

World War II

World War II was a war of German aggression—a war fought partly to change the defeat of World War I into a victory and partly to take over Europe as Napoleon had temporarily succeeded in doing at the beginning of the nineteenth century. World War II began in the late 1930s with the German takeover of Austria, Czechoslovakia, and Poland. f by German conquest of the Netherlands, Belgium, and Fra attempted assault on Great Britain. After failing to cor

Germany launched an invasion of the Soviet Union. Germany and its ally Italy (the "Axis" powers) maintained control of the war until late 1942. Their well-planned invasions succeeded more or less by surprise, the German troops were extremely effective, and Germany and Italy eventually controlled almost all of Europe and a sizable chunk of North Africa.

In the Pacific, Japan had invaded the Manchurian region of China and was seeking further conquests. It joined Germany and Italy in the Axis alliance, and when Japan attacked the United States at Pearl Harbor in Hawaii in 1941, Germany also declared war on the United States. Great Britain, the United States, and the Soviet Union then joined in a great alliance to defeat Germany, and their numerical and economic strength eventually turned the tide. Additionally, the distant American factories were well out of danger of being bombed or captured, so the Allied source of tanks and munitions never dried up.

The war is accurately called a "world war" because of the extent of the fighting outside of Europe. After more than three years of fighting in the Pacific, Japan finally conceded defeat after it was attacked with nuclear weapons in 1945.

16 Analyze the Changing Relationships Among Nations from the End of World War II to the Present Day, Including the Causes and Effects of the Cold War and the Rise of Global Terrorism

KEY TERMS: Arab Spring, Berlin Wall, Communist, European Union, Iron Curtain, OPEC, Prague Spring, space race

The End of European Dominance

At the start of the twentieth century, Europe was the world's most powerful region, controlling many parts of Asia and most of Africa. After 1945, the former European powers had no resources to spare for their colonial empires; all their energies and resources were concentrated on rebuilding. The postwar era therefore saw a wave of independence throughout all of Africa. It was not gained easily, peacefully, or overnight, and in some African nations it led to an era of harsh military rule, corruption, and violent social and political unrest. India also finally broke free from British rule and was divided into two separate states: a Hindu India and an Islamic Pakistan. Millions of Indian Muslims immediately crossed the border into Pakistan, while Pakistani Hindus fled to India.

The Soviet Union

By 1945, the Soviet Union held total political sway over all of Eastern Europe. Puppet **Communist** governments under the control of Moscow existed in all these small Slavic nations except Yugoslavia, ruled by the fiercely independent Marshall Tito. Germany was divided into two nations, democratic West Germany and Communist East Germany. A political border nicknamed the "**Iron Curtain**" would exist between Western and Eastern Europe from the late 1940s until 1989. In the divided city of Berlin, the Iron Curtain became an actual concrete wall in 1961; the **Berlin Wall** would be the most powerful symbol of the Cold War. The Soviet Union did not hesitate to use brute force in suppressing popular uprisings and attempts at reform such as the **Prague Spring** of 1968.

Soviet Communism proved economically unfeasible, despite major Soviet victories in the "**space race**" with the United States. Each superpower tried to outdo the other in exploring the universe beyond Earth. After the death of dictator Joseph Stalin and a lengthy period of economic stagnation, a gradual thaw in Soviet policy eventually led to the end of the Cold War, successful political uprisings, and the coming of democratic government to Eastern Europe. The Berlin Wall was demolished in 1989, and the Soviet Union broke up into independent republics in 1991.

China Today

Communist one-party rule was established in China in 1949 after a civil war. After several decades of isolation, a certain amount of market free enterprise was reintroduced, and Communist China began rising to world prominence and power. However, the country continues to suffer grave social problems. Chinese citizens do not have unrestricted access to outside information sources, the press is censored, and political dissidence is not tolerated. Tens of thousands of workers earn extremely low wages turning out cheap, low-quality clothing, household items, small appliances, and other export items, which the United States and other nations continue to import because the prices are so low.

The European Union

During the late 1950s, Western European nations began to profit from the experience of their wartime alliance; they realized they were stronger united than they were on their own. A European Economic Community was created, and this led to the formation of the **European Union** in 1991. EU nations are entirely independent and self-governing, but they share common foreign and security policies, and they cooperate on matters of domestic policy and affairs of international justice. They have had a common currency, the euro, since 1999.

The Arab World

A massive demand for oil in the post–World War II era led to an enormous economic change in the Middle East. As the source of most of the world's oil, the region leapt into a position of international consequence and great prosperity almost overnight. In 1960, five of the Arab nations created a cartel called the **Organization of Petroleum-Exporting Countries** (OPEC) with the purpose of regulating oil prices and controlling the supply of oil to the rest of the world. Today, OPEC has twelve member nations including four in Africa and two in South America.

Most Middle Eastern nations are either military dictatorships or monarchies; the press is heavily censored in these countries. In many of these countries, Islamic leaders constantly pressure their governments to enforce Islamic values and practices. Arab nations were outraged at the creation of the state of Israel in the late 1940s, and the situation was worsened when Israel began a long-term occupation of territories with Arab populations during the "Six-Day War" in 1967. In 2011 a series of popular uprisings in Arab countries (dubbed the "**Arab Spring**") raised hopes for the creation of democratic governments, but they also opened new conflicts between pro-Western liberals and Islamists.

CHALLENGE World History

Fill in the blank with a word or phrase that makes each sentence true.

1. The earliest human civilizations occurred in a region called _____ because its climate was ideal for good harvests.

2. The Romans referred to Northern tribes like the Goths and Huns as _____ because Northern tribal culture was based on plunder and pillage, not on building cities, writing law codes, and creating works of art.

3. _____ is a medieval system that bound together people of different social classes with oaths of loyalty and mutual responsibilities and duties.

4. _____—pride in one's ethnic, linguistic, and cultural heritage—was one of the major forces that drove political change in Europe in the nineteenth and early twentieth centuries.

5. The _____ Party seized power in Russia during the 1917 Revolution.

CHALLENGE ANSWERS
World History

1. the Fertile Crescent: This region was home to the Sumerian, Babylonian, and Egyptian civilizations.

2. barbarians: In classical Greek and Roman usage, the word *barbarian* meant "foreigner"; the Greeks thought that non-Greek languages sounded like "bar-bar" or the sounds made by someone who stammers.

3. Feudalism: Feudalism was an early form of the social contract in which persons received privileges and power in exchange for duties and responsibilities such as providing military service in wartime.

4. **Nationalism:** Patriotism is pride in one's country of citizenship, but nationalism is pride in one's identity as a member of a cultural and ethnic group and support for that group's interests. Nationalism is a force for unity in a homogenous country like France, but it has been a force for rebellion in multinational states like the Austro-Hungarian Empire.

5. **Bolshevik or Communist:** During the Russian Revolution, the terms *Bolshevik* and *Communist* were equivalent.

Civics and Government

 Define *Civic Life, Politics,* and *Government*

KEY TERMS: civic life, government, politics

Civic Life

The words *civics, civil, civility, city, citizen,* and *civilization* all come from the same root—all have to do with obeying the rules that govern society. These rules are needed because no human society of any size can function smoothly unless everyone agrees to obey the same code of behavior. This is why there are laws, governments, and social customs. Your **civic life** is the life you lead in public, where your behavior is governed not only by your individual choices but by obedience to rules.

For example, you must appear in court when summoned. You must serve as a juror unless the court grants you an exemption. You must obey traffic laws. You must apply for a passport for foreign travel. You must obey laws that restrict the freedom to purchase alcohol and tobacco products. You may not endanger society. You may not commit libel or slander. You must behave properly in public places, according to social customs and written rules (such as sitting in your assigned seat in the theater or stadium, and obeying "No Smoking" signs). You must obey certain rules in your school or workplace, such as dress codes. The press has freedom to publish only opinions and true facts—it does not have the freedom to publish deliberate lies.

Politics

Police, metropolis, polite, and *politics* all come from the same Greek root. These words all deal with concepts of human communities and the rules governing behavior. **Politics** is the process of debate, persuasion, and voting that people use to decide two things: who will represent them in the government and which laws will be passed.

Government

A **government** is an institution with two purposes: to serve and protect its citizens, and to make and enforce laws. The following table shows the most common forms of government in world history.

Forms of Government

FORM OF GOVERNMENT	DESCRIPTION	TITLE OF RULER
dictatorship	One individual rules; he or she has absolute power to make and execute the laws. There may be a legislative body, but it has no powers. Dictators usually seize and hold power by military force. There is only one political party.	dictator
hereditary monarchy	The head of the royal family has the power to make and execute the laws. • An absolute monarch has the same authority as a dictator. • A constitutional monarch shares authority with an elected legislative body. When a hereditary monarch dies, power goes to the next family member in line.	emperor, king/queen, pharaoh, czar, kaiser
republic	One elected executive heads the government and shares authority with a legislative body of elected representatives. There are multiple political parties. The elected executive serves for a set term of years; he or she is replaced by another elected executive, in a peaceful transfer of power.	president, premier, prime minster
democracy	The citizens serve as their own representatives and play an active role in making and enforcing the laws.	

18 Explain the Foundations of the American Political System

KEY TERMS: amendment, lobby, separation of powers

The American political system is based on several sources. These include the Roman Republic, the Magna Carta, the British parliamentary system, and the ideas of the European Enlightenment. The following table shows which aspects of the American political system came from each of these sources.

Sources of the American Political System

Roman Republic	A legislative body called the Senate, which makes the laws and advises the head of the government
	Elected officials who represented different segments of the population
Magna Carta	The concept that everyone is equal under the laws of the land, and that no one will be denied justice
	The concept that the executive is not above the law
	The concept that people are entitled to some say in how they are governed
	The idea that accused criminals are presumed innocent until proven guilty
	The custom of a speedy trial by a jury of one's peers
British Parliament	A bicameral legislature with an upper and lower house, with the members of the lower house being directly and freely elected by the people
Enlightenment	The idea that all people are born free and equal
	The idea that people should be able to rise in the world according to merit, not birth
	The notion of **separation of powers** within the government

The basic ideas behind the American political system include the following:

A. The law applies equally to all citizens, from the President of the United States on down. All have equal rights; none has special privileges.

This concept was in place from the founding of the country, but it has only gradually become reality; many people argue that the ideal has still not been achieved. Women, African Americans, and Native Americans all had to fight for ordinary civil and political rights. Even today, many would argue that there is one justice system for the rich and another for the poor. Rich people are usually educated, and they know their legal and Constitutional rights; poor people are often uneducated about their rights and are thus more vulnerable to intimidation and unfair treatment by the police and the courts. The justice system has attempted to even the balance with such rulings as *Miranda v. Arizona*, which states that anyone being arrested must be informed of his rights to remain silent and consult an attorney.

B. Citizens may voice their concerns freely and may criticize the existing administration without fear of retaliation.

The Declaration of Independence states that all governments "derive their just powers from the consent of the governed." This means that the government must meet the needs of the people.

This works in practice because the First Amendment guarantees American citizens the right to criticize their government and to "petition for a redress of grievances"—in other words, to try to get the government to change unpopular laws. Citizens can write to or call their representatives, join associations that **lobby** for change, take part in demonstrations, and of course vote against candidates who don't agree with their views.

In 1787, this idea was truly revolutionary. At that time in most parts of the world, criticizing one's government was very dangerous. The least that might happen was censorship of written work; people who spoke out might also be imprisoned, exiled, or even executed for what was considered treason.

C. The political system can be changed to meet changing times.

The Constitution has been amended several times. **Amendment** to the Constitution is a slow process by design so that any changes to the fundamental laws of the land can only happen after everyone has been given plenty of time for consideration. Altering the national Constitution is a serious business and is treated seriously.

Constitutional amendments have addressed many individual rights and freedoms. For example, they outlawed slavery; extended voting rights to major segments of the population; guaranteed freedom of speech, religion, and of the press; and made certain changes to the electoral process.

Connect the Form of the US Government to the Purposes and Principles of American Democracy

KEY TERMS: all men are created equal, associations, balance, Bill of Rights, checks and balances, citizens, Congress, Constitution, equality, executive, federal republic, impeach, judicial, legislative, liberty, Preamble, press, political parties, republic, representatives, veto, voting rights

In 1776, Thomas Jefferson put into words the great central principle on which the American government is based:

> We hold these truths to be self-evident: that **all men are created equal**, that they are endowed by their creator with certain unalienable rights, that among these are life, liberty, and the pursuit of happiness.

A belief in **liberty** and **equality** is the most important aspect of the American identity. The United States is a nation of immigrants whose people do not share a common cultural heritage, religious faith, or ethnic identity. Instead, they have the common experience of citizenship in a nation founded on the ideals of equality under the law and liberty for all.

Of course, these were only ideals when the nation was founded—as the authors of the Constitution knew very well. In practice, virtually the entire African population south of Pennsylvania was enslaved, with no civil rights whatsoever. In legal terms, free women were almost as badly off; they could not vote, they had few legal rights, and they were denied many freedoms available to men. Men who did not own a certain amount of property could not vote. Native Americans were not citizens; they were considered foreigners and enemies and were continually pushed farther and farther from their ancestral lands. It is remarkable that Americans were faithful enough to the ideals of equality and freedom that over time, they protested against all these inequities—eventually resolving most of them in large part.

Expansion of Voting Rights in the United States

1770	1790	1810	1830	1850	1870	1890	1910	1930	1950	1970

1776 The British colonies declare independence and the individual states begin to write constitutions. Eligibility to vote varies by state, but free men (including Africans) who own a certain amount of property may vote. This is less than 40 percent of the adult population.

1809 Maryland amends its constitution to make voting a whites-only privilege. Other Southern states follow suit.

early 1800s State constitutions begin eliminating the requirement of property ownership.

1868, 1870 The Fourteenth and Fifteenth Amendments grant voting rights to African-American men ages 21 and over.

1924 Native Americans are granted full citizenship, including voting rights.

1920 The Nineteenth Amendment grants voting rights to women ages 21 and over. Four of the Western states had already granted women this right.

1971 The Twenty-Sixth Amendment lowers the voting age from 21 to 18.

1964 The Twenty-Fourth Amendment outlaws the poll tax (an illegal charge for voting, established throughout the South by the Black Codes of the Reconstruction era). This amendment removes that obstacle for tens of thousands of low-income Southerners.

In 1787, during weeks of debate, the authors of the **Constitution** designed a government that would uphold the principles of liberty and equality for which the Continental Army had fought a revolution. Every aspect of this government is designed to **balance** the interests of all the conflicting groups that make up the nation.

The Constitution begins with a **Preamble** that states the purposes of the American government:

> We the people of the United States, in order to form a more perfect union, insure domestic tranquility, provide for the common defense, promote the general welfare, and secure the blessings of liberty to ourselves and our posterity, do ordain and establish this Constitution for the United States of America.

The Constitution describes a **republic**—a government in which the citizens elect **representatives** to make and enforce the laws. The United States is a **federal republic**—one in which the national government shares its authority with the state governments. The following is a brief look at the Constitution:

The United States Constitution

Article I	Describes the legislative branch with two houses, a Senate and a House of Representatives. • Senators are chosen by state legislatures; there are two for each state. • Representatives are popularly elected; there is one for every 30,000 people in a state (excluding Native Americans and originally counting each slave as three-fifths of one person). Gives the rules by which the legislature will conduct business and pass laws.
Article II	Describes the executive branch, which will be headed by a president. In a system known as the electoral college, voters will choose electors who will in turn cast their votes for president. Sets forth the duties and powers of the president.
Article III	Describes the judicial branch, which will consist of a Supreme Court with nine justices who will serve for life, during good behavior.
Article IV	Describes the powers and rights of the states.
Article V	Describes the process by which the Constitution can be amended.
Article VI	States that the Constitution is the supreme law of the land and that no religious test will be administered as a qualification for office.
Article VII	States that the Constitution will become law when nine states have ratified it.

As the following chart shows, the Constitution describes a government of three branches—**legislative**, **executive**, and **judicial**.

Branches of the US Government

Legislative branch	US Congress: • Senate • House of Representatives	Makes the laws
Executive branch	White House: • President of the United States • Cabinet departments	Carries out the laws
Judicial branch	Supreme Court	Enforces the laws Determines how to apply the laws

The framers of the Constitution based their work on the writings of the Baron de Montesquieu, a French *philosophe* of the Enlightenment who had first suggested such a system in his book *The Spirit of the Laws*. Montesquieu argued that each branch of the government should provide a check on the powers of the other two, to prevent any one arm of the government from gaining too much power. The framers of the Constitution agreed with this view, creating multiple **checks and balances** in the system:

» The president can **veto** any law passed by Congress and has the sole power to nominate Supreme Court justices.

» Congress can override the president's veto, but it must do so by a two-thirds majority vote in both houses. The Senate must approve presidential nominees to the Supreme Court. Congress can **impeach** a president or a Supreme Court justice for serious misconduct in office.

» The Supreme Court can declare a law unconstitutional. If a president is impeached, the chief justice presides over the proceedings.

Other important checks and balances are built into the US government:

» The **press**, whose freedom to publish is guaranteed in the First Amendment, reports on the activities of the three branches of government, thus keeping the citizens informed. The press can also use its voice to support or oppose government officials and candidates for office.

» The **citizens** have the power to vote leaders into and out of office, to call for the repeal of established laws, and to urge the passage of new laws.

» The **political parties** serve as checks on one another so that no one party can be too powerful for too long. Each party acts as a watchdog on the others, quickly informing the public of mistakes, corruption, or inaccurate statements.

» The **associations** provide powerful voices for citizens who support a particular issue—for example, the American Medical Association (AMA) represents the interests of the medical profession, while the American Civil Liberties Union (ACLU) focuses on the constitutional rights of the individual.

>> **Congress** is designed to balance several interests. It has two chambers—a House of Representatives and a Senate. Each can check the power of the other:
- All states are represented equally in the Senate—so no one region can overpower the others and large states cannot ignore the interests of small states.
- States are represented in the House according to the total population—so small states cannot ignore the interests of larger ones.

>> Both the House and the Senate must vote Yes on a bill before it can become a law.

State governments are designed along the same lines as the federal government. Each state has a governor and a lieutenant-governor, who serve as the executives. Each state has a legislature and a state supreme court. Major cities have a mayor, a deputy mayor, and a city council. All the same checks and balances of the federal system also exist in the state and city governments. The great rule of American government is that to pass laws, opposing interests must be balanced—lawmakers must try to represent as many citizens as possible.

Although the Constitution was ratified, many political leaders objected to it because it said almost nothing about the rights of individual citizens. In response, the First Congress of the United States submitted twelve constitutional amendments to the states. Ten of these were ratified in 1791 and are collectively known as the **Bill of Rights**.

The Bill of Rights

First Amendment	Guarantees freedom of religion, freedom of speech, freedom of the press, freedom to peaceably assemble, and the right to petition the government for redress of grievances
Second Amendment	States that the people have the right to bear arms because a well-regulated militia is necessary to the security of the state
Third Amendment	Guarantees that private citizens cannot be forced to house soldiers in peacetime and can only be forced to house them in wartime by the passage of laws to that effect
Fourth Amendment	Protects the people against unreasonable search and seizure of personal property Requires probable cause for the issue of a search warrant
Fifth Amendment	Protects an accused criminal from self-incrimination, outlaws double jeopardy, requires a grand jury indictment for trial, and requires due process of law
Sixth Amendment	Guarantees a speedy and public trial by jury, requires that an accused criminal must be told the charges against him and be confronted with the evidence, and guarantees him the right to present his own case and to legal representation
Seventh Amendment	Requires a trial by jury in any case where the disputed value of property exceeds $20
Eighth Amendment	Bans excessive bail and cruel or unusual punishment
Ninth Amendment	States that listing certain rights in the Constitution does not imply that the people do not have other rights as well
Tenth Amendment	States that any powers not delegated to the national government are reserved to the states, or to the people

Explain and Analyze the US Role in World Affairs

KEY TERMS: communications revolution, isolation, natural resources, world affairs

The United States took very little interest in **world affairs** until the twentieth century. This changed with the US entry into World War I. Since that time, the United States has been a major world power. Geography, science, and economics have all played a role in the US status among the nations of the world.

Geography and World Affairs

Three geographical factors enabled the United States to maintain independence from world affairs for so long and to keep it powerful: its **isolation**, its abundance of natural resources, and its vast size.

The United States was geographically far from Europe during the days of European empires. Once it had broken away from Britain and established its own military strength, it was not geographically vulnerable to invasion. On its north and south borders, the United States has friendly neighbors, neither of which is a significant military power. On the east and west lie the Atlantic and Pacific Oceans.

Before the days of air attacks, the vast size of the United States protected it from any conventional attempt at a takeover. No army or navy could be strong enough to attack on both coasts at once—and even if such attacks succeeded, the interior was so vast that it could not easily be conquered. America is so rich in **natural resources** that the United States could grow or manufacture almost everything it needed. This gave the nation the upper hand in foreign trade.

Science and World Affairs

The United States led the world in the Second Industrial Revolution—the one that produced the elevator, the typewriter, the telephone, and the electric lightbulb. Emerging from World War II as the richest nation, the United States had great success with scientific and technological advances and took the lead in the **communications revolution** at the end of the twentieth century. For the past century, the US military has been among not only the world's largest but also the best-equipped.

Economics and World Affairs

The United States has been a wealthy country since its beginnings, with a much higher standard of living than exists in many parts of the world. Wealthy nations are desirable allies and bad enemies. They can pick and choose their battles and their trading partners.

For a detailed discussion of US involvement in foreign affairs, see the US History section of this Review.

(21) Describe the Role a US Citizen Plays in American Democracy

KEY TERM: citizen

A US **citizen** may do any or all of the following to participate in the American democracy:

» Vote: In the twentieth century, voter turnout in major presidential elections hovered between 50 and 60 percent of the eligible adult population.
» Run for office: All government officials are also citizens.
» Follow the news: Keep informed—and keep others informed—via word of mouth, the press, and the Internet.
» Join an organization: Lobby the government by supporting or joining a powerful association such as the American Civil Liberties Union (ACLU).
» Speak out: Sign a petition, call or write to your representatives, publish newspaper articles or books, or take part in a peaceful demonstration.
» Serve on a jury: The legal system of the United States requires the participation of citizens. A panel of jurors represents the entire community; jurors listen to evidence on both sides and give a fair and unprejudiced verdict.
» Volunteer for a political campaign: Most people who work for political candidates are not paid. Some people volunteer their time because they strongly identify with the positions of a particular candidate. Others have their own political ambitions and want to get a taste of what such a career might be like. Volunteers do a great deal of essential work in political campaigns: making and receiving phone calls, processing donations, speaking to crowds, answering questions, providing transportation, polling potential voters, and so on.

CHALLENGE　　Civics and Government

Answer the questions that follow. Write one or two sentences for each.

1. What determines the number of congressional representatives for each state?

_____

_____

_____

2. Explain the difference between a dictatorship and a monarchy.

_____

_____

_____

3. What is the purpose of the Bill of Rights?

_____

_____

_____

4. What is the US government's responsibility to the citizens?

_____

_____

_____

5. How has geography enabled the United States to play a leading role in world affairs?

_____

_____

_____

CHALLENGE ANSWERS

Civics and Government

Your answers should be similar to the following:

1. The state's total population determines its number of representatives in the House of Representatives. All states have two representatives in the Senate.

2. A dictator is a person who seizes absolute power and holds it with the support of the military. A monarch is a member of a ruling family who inherits his or her title.

3. The Bill of Rights guarantees certain individual rights and privileges of citizens that are not addressed in the main body of the Constitution.

4. The government's responsibility is to serve and protect the citizens, and to make and enforce the laws. It must try to balance all interests fairly and equally.

5. Geographical isolation and enormous size have protected the United States from invasion. The climate and the presence of many natural resources have led to abundance and wealth.

Economics

 Explain and Apply Basic Economic Principles Such as the Law of Supply and Demand

KEY TERMS: barter, cost, cost-benefit analysis, demand, economics, interest, mortgage, supply, trade

The term *economics* refers to the continuous exchange of goods, services, and resources necessary in any society of human beings. Far back in prehistory, the first social human beings developed the system of **barter** and **trade** that eventually became known as economics.

Here are some of the basic principles of economics.

A. Everything you want to acquire has a cost.

The most basic principle of economics is that you can't get something for nothing; everything has a **cost**. You have to give something up to get something. Cost may not be a matter of money or of money alone. It may be computed in money, time, effort, or a combination of those things. Likewise, the things you want may not be material things. They may be intangibles like academic success or excellence in a particular sport.

For example, suppose you have set your heart on becoming a ballet dancer. Classes, ballet shoes and dancewear, transportation to and from ballet school, and medical care for dance-related injuries all cost money. Dance itself takes tremendous physical and mental effort, and dancers have to practice every day. Young dancers have to fit in their training outside of school hours, which means sacrificing other activities like sports. Dancers also risk serious injuries and the possibility of frequent unemployment. Time, money, risk, and effort are all part of the cost of a career in ballet.

B. A cost-benefit analysis can help you decide whether to pay the cost of what you want.

To make the best economic choices, you need to conduct a **cost-benefit analysis**. This means weighing the cost (what you have to give up) against the benefits (what you will gain). If you want to become a dancer, you have to weigh time, money, effort, physical discomforts, and constant risk of injury (all part of the cost) against the joy of performing, audience applause and cheers, and possible fame and fortune (all part of the benefits).

C. Something that is rare has a higher cost. Something that is abundant has a lower cost.

This principle is also known as the law of **supply** and **demand**. When there is a large supply of an item, supply can satisfy demand, and the price stays low. When the item becomes scarce, demand becomes greater than the available supply, and the price goes up.

You have probably experienced the law of supply and demand when buying airplane tickets. If you book well in advance before most seats are sold, the price is low. If you wait until the last minute, when most seats are gone, the price is much higher. You may also have taken part in live or online auctions. When many people want a particular item, bidding drives up the price. When only a few people want that item, bidding is over quickly at a low price.

D. You can borrow money to buy something, but you must pay back more than the actual sum you borrow.

For a very expensive purchase such as a house, you can arrange to borrow money from a bank. The bank pays the seller in full at the time of purchase, and you repay the bank an agreed amount per month, most often over a period of thirty years. The sum of money you borrow is called a **mortgage**. The monthly mortgage payments include **interest** charges based on the total number of years of the loan. The interest represents the cost of borrowing. Early repayment means you pay less overall, because you save the interest charges. The mathematical equation for calculating interest is $R \times P \times T = I$ (Rate × Principle × Time = Interest). Other expensive purchases that people routinely take out loans for include cars and college educations.

 ## Explain and Apply the Concept of Microeconomics— the Economic Decisions Made by Individuals

KEY TERMS: balanced budget, bankruptcy, boycott, budget, cost-benefit analysis, debt, microeconomics

Microeconomics

Microeconomics refers to the economic decisions individuals make. Household budgets are an example of microeconomics. You must **budget** for your necessary expenses every month: rent or mortgage payment, groceries, utility bills, gasoline and parking or a monthly transit pass, insurance payments, and so on. You can conduct a **cost-benefit analysis** to decide how best to spend any money that is left over.

Balanced Budget

A **balanced budget** is one in which your income is equal to or greater than your expenses. If you spend more than your income, you will end up in **debt**. As explained in the previous section, debtors must pay back not only the principal they owe, but also any interest that has accrued over time. Because the total amount owed continues to grow over time, many people soon find that their debts grow so large they cannot repay them. In extreme cases of debt, individuals can declare **bankruptcy**.

Boycott

A **boycott** is a refusal to buy certain products. The decision to boycott is made at the individual level, but a large number of individuals have to participate for the boycott to be effective. When people don't purchase a product, the law of supply and demand takes effect, and the seller loses profits. People normally boycott products for political reasons rather than high prices. The loss in sales pressures the seller to change his or her policies. For example, concern over unsafe factory working conditions and poverty-level wages in Bangladesh and elsewhere has prompted many Americans to stop buying clothing made in these countries.

24 Explain and Apply the Concept of Macroeconomics—the Workings of an Economy as a Whole

KEY TERMS: deficit, depression, inflation, labor union, macroeconomics, prices, profit, recession, strike, unemployment, wages

An economic system is one of the key elements of human civilizations. For a large human society to function smoothly, people have to agree on a system of government, a law code, and a system of exchange.

Wages, prices, and unemployment are all part of a national economy. **Wages** refers to the money workers earn. **Prices** refers to the cost, in money, of consumer goods and services. **Unemployment** refers to the percentage of workers who are looking for work but do not have a job.

When wages go up, spending goes up. This means an increased demand for goods, so prices go up, too. In this situation, unemployment is usually low. The economy is strong. When wages stay the same or fall, spending goes down. The economy is weak.

The following are three types of bad economic conditions, with their definitions:

Bad Economic Conditions

depression: an economic crash	Wages, prices, and employment fall far and fast.
recession: an economic slowdown	Wages, prices, and employment fall slowly and gradually.
inflation: a rise in the cost of living	Prices rise while wages and employment stay the same or fall.

Small businesses and larger companies and corporations form the major part of a market-based economy. Companies earn money by selling goods or services. They spend money to pay wages and to purchase supplies and equipment or goods for resale. The purpose of these operations is to earn more money than the company spends. The excess earnings are called **profit**. The company can save profits; distribute them to owners, workers, or both; or invest them in ways that expand or improve the business. Companies can also borrow money for investment by issuing stocks or bonds. A company may spend more than it earns in profit. The excess spending is called a loss, or a **deficit**. If a company fails to earn a profit, it can wind up in bankruptcy and it may go out of business.

Negotiations between business owners and workers play an important part in the economy. Because there are hundreds or thousands of workers for every individual owner, the workers have the power of their numbers. This is why workers began to form **labor unions** whose members agree to act together to obtain better wages, working conditions, and so on. The **strike** is a strong weapon for workers because when they walk off the job, the factories stop running and the owner earns no profits. Owners have tried to replace striking workers, only to realize this is a highly unpopular move with the general public and that it is difficult to replace skilled workers. Therefore, they usually negotiate with the striking workers until the two sides can come to terms. Major labor strikes began in the United States in the late nineteenth century and they continue to this day.

 ## Describe the Role the Government Plays in the National Economy

KEY TERMS: bond, income tax, revenue, sales tax

Like any large organization, the government has income (called **revenue**) and expenses. Revenue comes mainly from two sources: payment of taxes and the sale of bonds. **Income tax** is a percentage of individual or business income paid to the government. **Sales tax** is a small percentage added to the price of an item or a service.

A **bond** (sometimes called a savings bond or a war bond) is, in effect, a loan. You pay the government the price of the bond—say, ten dollars. In exchange, you receive a piece of paper marked with that amount, as well as a year and series number. You can cash in your bond at any time; the longer you hold it, the more it will be worth, because the government will pay you interest based on the length of time you've held the bond. Suppose you are given a ten-dollar bond as a birthday gift for your first child. When your child graduates from college and needs some cash to put down a security deposit on an apartment, that bond may be worth more than one hundred dollars.

The government uses these sources of revenue to meet its expenses. These include financing the armed forces and paying the salaries of all government workers all the way up to the president of the United States. The federal government also funds education at all levels; runs programs such as Medicare, Medicaid, and Social Security; regulates commerce and enforces safety standards; provides funding for the arts and scientific research; maintains national parks and nature preserves; and helps fund and maintain a national transportation system. State taxes pay for services such as the state police force and bridge and highway maintenance. Local city taxes pay for services such as public schools, garbage collection, the library system, and municipal parks.

The US government manages the national economy by setting tax rates and interest rates and sometimes by passing laws. For example, individuals are required to pay a small percentage of their earnings into Social Security, a government program that provides income to Americans over the age of sixty-seven. In effect, the government ensures by law that all working Americans must save money for their retirement.

State governments also depend on taxes for their revenue. Each state determines what taxes it will assess. For example, Pennsylvania does not charge sales tax on clothing, Delaware does not charge tax on restaurant meals, and Vermont does not charge state income tax.

In a socialist economy, the government owns all business and industry and fixes prices artificially. In a capitalist economy, business and industry are in private hands, and a free market of competition sets wages and prices. A mixed economy is a combination of these two systems. Because Alexander Hamilton, the first secretary of the treasury, believed that capitalism was the soundest economic system, the United States developed as a largely capitalist economy. Most other Western nations have mixed economies.

The US government has repeatedly been called on to arbitrate major labor strikes in business and industry—particularly in industries that affect the entire nation, such as the national transportation system. Before the Progressives came into power in the early 1900s, most strikes were settled on terms favorable to the owners. Beginning with the presidency of Theodore Roosevelt, the workers began to gain a share of power.

 ## Analyze the Connection Between International Trade and Foreign Policy

KEY TERMS: colonization, embargo, export, import, natural resources, surplus, trade

A **trade** is an exchange—something you don't need for something you want. In international trade, people and businesses **export** (sell to foreigners) the goods they don't need and **import** (buy from foreigners) the goods they want.

Geography is closely connected to international trade. A nation's geographic location determines its climate and its **natural resources**. Nations must trade to obtain the natural resources they cannot provide for themselves. Often a nation will have **surplus** natural resources it can trade away. For example, Great Britain's climate is perfect for raising sheep—but all wrong for growing tea. The sheep can supply all the wool the British need for their own clothing and textiles, with plenty left over to trade away for the tea they cannot produce.

It is easy to see the connection between international trade and foreign policy. Economics can drive foreign policy, and foreign policy can dictate economic choices. **Colonization** is one example of how economics can drive foreign policy. When a country acquires a colony, the country controls the trade relationship. The colony must buy whatever the country wants to export, and sell the country whatever it wants to import, at the country's prices. These facts helped shape a foreign policy of aggressive European colonization from about 1500 to 1945, when colonies in Asia, Africa, and the Americas provided a number of commodities and resources Europeans could not produce for themselves—coffee, tea, sugar, cotton, spices, potatoes, copper, tin, and many more.

Trading with other independent nations is different from trading with a colony because the bargaining power between the two is more equal. If a nation is your country's enemy, it may refuse to trade with your country—or it may demand unreasonably high prices for its goods. If an enemy nation is rich in a commodity your country wants to import, your country is under economic pressure to improve political relations with that nation. If nations can become allies, they are much more likely to come to a trade agreement that will please both sides. But sometimes a nation may decide that the best way to obtain natural resources from a neighboring country is through a war of conquest.

A nation that has a political dispute with another country may sometimes employ a tactic called an **embargo** to apply pressure against its opponent. When your country establishes an embargo against another country, your country does not export to that country and your country do not import that country's goods. This means finding alternatives to whatever goods that country produces. An example of this occurred during the US Civil War, when for political reasons Britain decided to break off trade relations with the Confederacy. Instead of importing American cotton, Britain imported cotton from India until after the war ended and the Confederacy rejoined the Union.

For further comments on international trade and foreign policy in history, see the US and World History sections of this Review.

CHALLENGE Economics

Choose the word or phrase that makes each sentence true.

1. A bond is worth more with each year after its purchase because it earns **(income, interest)**.

2. A continuing fall in the value of the dollar is called **(inflation, recession)**.

3. A nation exports its **(deficit, surplus)** goods in exchange for what it cannot produce for itself.

4. The risk of a serious head injury is part of the **(benefits, cost)** of playing football.

5. An item will be less expensive if the **(demand, supply)** is very high.

CHALLENGE ANSWERS

Economics

1. interest: Interest is the money due to a lender on a loan in addition to the principal amount borrowed. It represents the cost of borrowing.

2. inflation: When prices rise steadily, a dollar buys less than it did previously.

3. surplus: Surplus goods are extra goods beyond what the nation needs for its own people.

4. cost: Remember, the cost is not necessarily money only. Cost includes time, effort, and risk as well as money.

5. supply: When there is a lot of an item available, its value is less.

Geography

 ### Describe the Physical and Human Characteristics of Places

KEY TERMS: historical atlas, map, place, region

The terms **place** and **region** refer to a location on Earth. A place is an individual location—a single country, town, or city. A region is a group of locations—the collective identity of several adjoining countries, states, or provinces. Places and regions may or may not be settled by human beings.

Physical Characteristics

Physical characteristics include the climate, type of soil, crops that grow, natural resources, amount and type of precipitation, direction and strength of the winds, presence or absence of large bodies of water, and species of wild plants and animals.

Human Characteristics

Each place or region is unique because of what people have made of the physical environment they settled in. A place's human characteristics include answers to the following questions:

» What is the cultural, ethnic, and linguistic makeup of the population?
» Is it a rural or urban population or a mix of both?
» What do people do to earn a living?
» What do people do for recreation or relaxation?
» Is the landscape largely natural or completely built up with cities and suburbs?
» What kind of transportation do people rely on?
» What do people produce that makes this place famous (e.g., New York City is famous for its theaters, Detroit for its cars, and New Orleans for its music)?

Different types of **maps** can show many physical and human characteristics of places and regions. Take for instance an ordinary map of the United States:

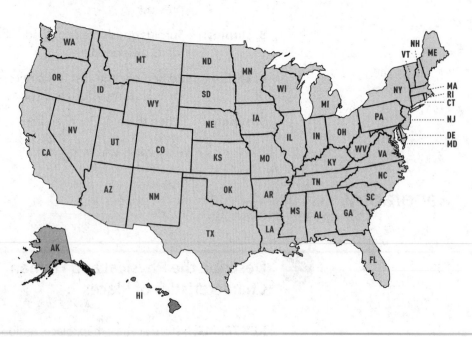

This map shows a particular human characteristic—how Americans decided to divide up their country into specific states for political purposes. You might take the same map and shade it to show the different regions: Northeast, Midwest, Southeast, Southwest, and Northwest. You might shade the map in different colors to show where different major crops are grown—such as wheat, corn, potatoes, and oranges. You might shade the map to show average temperature, rainfall, or elevation above sea level. You might shade the map to show the proportion of Democratic and Republican voters in each state.

A **historical atlas** is a book of special kinds of maps that display the physical and human characteristics of places and regions at times in the past. The maps in a historical atlas of the American Revolutionary War, for example, might show the boundaries of the then-existing British colonies, the location of major battles, the deployment of British and American military forces, the routes followed by the armies, and so on.

28 Explain How Humans Modify the Physical Environment and How Physical Systems Affect Human Systems

KEY TERMS: environment, global warming, green movement, organic

The Physical Environment

The natural **environment** of a place includes various factors: the climate, type of soil, temperature, elevation above sea level, topography, and so on. Except for those who live in very small groups in a primitive style, human beings have significantly altered every natural environment in which they have settled.

When people find a hospitable climate with a ready source of fresh water, they build shelters for themselves and their animals. They turn over the soil and sow crops. They may fell whole forests to clear land for farming or building. They create systems for irrigation and waste disposal. They build walls and fences to mark property borders.

Large human civilizations go beyond these steps. They build bridges, roads, and cities. Since the beginning of the industrial age, people have been building factories, mines, and railroads. All these human activities alter an environment.

Just as human society changes an environment, the environment affects the choices people make. The climate people live in affects the clothing they wear, the crops they grow, the animals they can raise for food, and the kinds of transportation they use. For example, the Italian peninsula is mountainous with dry, rocky soil. Together with the mild temperatures of the Mediterranean region, this makes the perfect environment for growing grapes. These geographical factors have made Italy a major producer and exporter of wine since the days of ancient Rome.

Geography and Trade

Geographical factors foster networks of economic interdependence. Rivers, canals, and roads link regions and allow them to trade with one another. The impressive system of Roman roads linked all parts of the Roman Empire, fostering a lively mercantile economy. In medieval times, the Silk Road was a major trade route linking Asia and Europe. The Mississippi River linked the northern and southern regions of the United States, so the cotton grown in the South could feed the textile mills in the North and profit both regions.

Geography and Conflict

Geography has always been a major factor in war. Nations develop a foreign policy based in part on how easily they can defend their borders. For example, Germany (formerly Prussia) is in the middle of Europe and has no natural border defenses, such as a high mountain range or an ocean. Its central location meant that it could be invaded from almost any side. Geographical vulnerability made Prussia develop the strongest and most intimidating army in Europe.

Geographical factors can dictate success or failure in war. Distance is one important factor—this was especially true before the invention of airplanes. The farther an army marches from its sources of supply, the greater the risk of defeat. This is why Napoleon's 1812 invasion of Russia ended in a humiliating retreat; the French army had gone too far from its supply lines. Other geographical factors contributed to the Russian victory. An invading army normally lived off the land, foraging for food while on the march, but the barren Russian plains provided little food for French soldiers or horses. The Russian winter was too severe for the French, who came from a milder climate. These factors made disease, frostbite, and starvation as dangerous to Napoleon's army as the Russian guns.

The Environment and Industrialization

Human activity did not seriously affect the environment until the early nineteenth century, when large-scale industrialization and the use of fossil fuels began. Industrialization resulted in widespread pollution of air, land, and water on a massive scale. The problem has only grown worse over time; as the twenty-first century begins, it has resulted in **global warming**. Average temperatures have risen all over the Earth. In response to this serious concern, governments have instituted mandatory recycling programs, planted millions of trees, and worked to cut back on pollution and fuel emissions. However, not all nations participate in these protective measures; some fear damage to their economies if they have to convert factories to cleaner, more environmentally responsible methods of production and waste disposal.

Individuals have responded to global warming in a variety of ways, creating a "**green movement**." People recycle used products to reduce the amount of waste. They plant gardens in cities, on vacant land, and on rooftops. Farmers have changed their farming methods to make better use of the soil. Some farmers forgo the use of manufactured pesticides to raise **organic** crops. It remains to be seen whether the great damage done to the climate can or will be reversed.

29 Understand Human Migration and the Characteristics of Human Settlements

KEY TERMS: migration

Geography and Migration

Migration is a mass movement of people away from one place and toward another. The basic reason for human migration is to find a better situation. In primitive times, people migrated in search of food or warmer temperatures. When civilization began, new factors came into play: people sought better economic opportunities and greater political or religious liberty. People have also migrated in large numbers in the wake of major wars, to escape the devastation of battle and find safer and more peaceful surroundings.

Major examples of human migration in world and US history include the following:

Human Migrations

DATE	WHO WENT WHERE	REASON
c. 38,000–14,000 BCE	Asians crossed a land bridge from Siberia to Alaska and eventually settled all habitable areas in the Americas.	Search for food and better climate
c. 100–500 CE	Migratory peoples from the steppes of Central Asia traveled west and south and eventually settled most of Europe.	Search for food and plunder
c. 1700–1800	Africans were kidnapped and taken westward to work as slaves in the Americas.	Taken by force for economic reasons
mid-1800s	Americans migrated westward to settle the North American continent between Canada and Mexico.	Economic opportunity
	Northern Europeans migrated to the United States.	Economic opportunity Escape from oppression
	Native Americans were forced to leave their lands.	Moved by force for political and economic reasons
about 1900–1940	Southern and Eastern Europeans migrated to the United States.	Economic opportunity Escape from oppression and war
since 1945	Latin Americans migrate north to the United States. North Africans migrate north to Europe. Eastern Europeans migrate to Western Europe. Asians migrate across the Pacific to the United States.	Economic opportunity Escape from oppression and war

The earliest human civilizations arose in the Fertile Crescent, where the abundant fresh water and the warm climate made for a surplus of food. Over the centuries, human beings migrated from this area, eventually settling all the regions of the world that are suitable for human habitation. The least-populated areas are the ones where climate does not provide what human beings need. Large desert regions like the Sahara, frozen tundra like much of eastern Russia and northern Canada, and barren plains like much of central Australia are very sparsely populated.

Geography and Culture

Peoples who lived near one another in similar environments developed similar languages and cultures. This makes sense because culture is shaped in part by the environment and because the people who lived nearby were usually the only people one got to know; travel was difficult, risky, and slow. Before the nineteenth century, most people lived their entire lives without ever leaving a fairly small area around their home town or city.

For this reason, whole regions of the world tend to have identifiable cultures. Eastern Europe, for example, is culturally and linguistically Slavic. South America is linguistically Spanish and Portuguese and also maintains elements of the early native cultures—Inca, Maya, and Aztec.

Cultural exchanges took place when large groups of people traveled over a great distance. This happened during major migrations or during medieval wars such as the Crusades, when thousands of Western Europeans traveled to the Middle East. An era of global cultural exchange developed with the Age of Exploration beginning in the late 1400s.

 ## Read and Interpret Maps

KEY TERMS: climate map, degrees, equator, globe, latitude, longitude, map, minutes, political map, topographical map

Maps and globes are used to show the spatial organization of people, places, and environments on Earth's surface. A **globe** is the most accurate representation because it is the same spherical shape as Earth. However, even the largest globe is scaled down so far in size from the actual Earth that it cannot show much detail. Flat maps distort the actual curvature of the land, but a close-up **map** of a small area can show much more detail than a globe.

You can locate any place on Earth by plotting its **latitude** and **longitude**. When you look at a globe, you will see a crisscross grid of latitude and longitude lines. A location's latitude gives its distance north or south of the **equator**. A location's longitude is an angular measure giving its east-west position on the Earth. Latitude and longitude are measured in **degrees** (°) and **minutes** ('). For example, in April 1912 the ocean liner *Titanic* struck an iceberg in the North Atlantic at 41° 46′ N, 50° 14′ W. The ship's radio operators included the latitude and longitude in their distress calls, enabling other ships to come to the rescue and help save several hundred lives.

Maps come in many varieties. A **political map** shows the names and borders of countries, provinces or states, cities, and towns. A **topographical map** shows comparative elevation above sea level. A **climate map** can show which areas receive the most and least annual rainfall and which have the coldest and hottest temperatures.

31 Define *Ecosystem* and Explain How the Elements of an Ecosystem Work Together

KEY TERMS: climate, ecosystem, precipitation

Over the millennia, physical processes have shaped and reshaped Earth's surface. Today's continents did not always exist in their current form. Over time, landmasses break away from one another or collide with one another, forming new landmasses. Forces inside Earth cause mountain ranges to rise up, but over time wind and water wear the rocks away. As a result, Earth has a highly varied landscape. Different locations have different landforms and different climates, and they are inhabited by different groups of plants and animals.

The **climate** of a region encompasses many things: the prevailing winds, temperatures, and the amount and type of **precipitation**, averaged over time. Climate is affected by geographical factors such as the proximity of mountains or large bodies of fresh or salt water. Climate can change when any of these factors change.

The term *ecosystem* refers to the ongoing interaction between the land, the climate, and living organisms in a particular location. All the factors work together in a certain way to create a natural system that sustains the organisms that live there. For example, in a forest in a temperate region of North America, trees produce nuts and fruits as part of their reproductive cycle. Small animals and birds survive by eating the nuts and fruits. Wolves and hawks survive by preying on the smaller animals and birds. Other animals survive by eating the insects that live in the soil and on the trees. The remains of dead plants and animals supply nutrients to the soil that nourish plants and trees. The whole system works together to sustain one generation of living things after another.

Human beings are the greatest cause of change in ecosystems. Human beings have cleared massive forests and rainforests, turned diverse ecosystems into farms growing a single crop, built artificial asphalt-and-steel environments such as major cities, pumped or dumped a great variety of poisons into the air and water, and preyed on many forms of wildlife to extinction or near-extinction. On the positive side, human beings are capable of recognizing the dangers in an industrial society and working to offset them.

CHALLENGE | Geography

Define each term.

1. climate

_____

_____

2. ecosystem

_____

_____

3. globe

_____

_____

4. latitude

_____

_____

5. migration

_____

_____

CHALLENGE ANSWERS

Geography

Your answers should closely match the following:

1. The climate of a particular place is the combination of temperatures, winds, and precipitation levels of that place, averaged over time.

2. An ecosystem is the interaction of all the natural elements of a particular location: the land, living organisms, and climate.

3. A globe is a spherical representation of Earth—literally, a spherical world map.

4. Latitude is the measure of how far north or south of the Equator a given place is.

5. Migration is mass human movement away from a place in search of a better place.

TASC Social Studies Practice Test

47 questions, 75 minutes

The following test is designed to simulate a real TASC Social Studies Test section in terms of question formats, number, and degree of difficulty. To get a good idea of how you will do on the real exam, take this test under actual exam conditions. Complete the test in one session and follow the given time limit. Answers and explanations begin on page 310.

1. What is the main reason that Great Britain has not been successfully invaded since the Norman Conquest of 1066?

   Ⓐ Britain is an island nation.
   Ⓑ Britain does not have an extensive seacoast.
   Ⓒ Britain's capital city is not on the ocean.
   Ⓓ Britain is northwest of continental Europe.

2. During the 1960s and 1970s, the United Farm Workers repeatedly called for Americans to boycott grapes, lettuce, and other produce grown by companies that did not treat migrant workers fairly. How does a boycott put economic pressure on company owners?

   Ⓐ Workers go on strike, bringing operations to a halt.
   Ⓑ Workers put in too much overtime, cutting into profits.
   Ⓒ People buy up the product quickly, driving up the price.
   Ⓓ People refuse to buy the product, driving down the price.

3. In the United States, people vote by secret ballot. What is the main reason for a secret ballot?

   Ⓐ to prevent voter fraud
   Ⓑ to allow for write-in voting
   Ⓒ to allow voters to change their minds
   Ⓓ to protect voters from political pressure

4. In 1498, Portuguese explorer Vasco da Gama became the first European to reach India by sea. Da Gama returned to Europe with a cargo of Indian pepper, which he sold for sixty times the price it cost him. This is an example of

   Ⓐ the law of supply and demand
   Ⓑ inflation
   Ⓒ deficit spending
   Ⓓ revenue sharing

5. Which of the following provided a new, much shorter shipping route between Asia and Europe when it opened in 1869?

Ⓐ the Canal du Midi
Ⓑ the Erie Canal
Ⓒ the Panama Canal
Ⓓ the Suez Canal

Look at the photograph. Then answer questions 6–9.

LBJ Library photo by Frank Wolfe

6. How are the people in this photograph participating in the American political system? Write your answer in the box.

7. The Twenty-Sixth Amendment to the Constitution, adopted in 1971, lowered the voting age to eighteen. How did this change the role of young people in American democracy?

Ⓐ It gave them a voice in selecting the lawmakers who governed them.
Ⓑ It required them to fight for their country if drafted.
Ⓒ It made them responsible for major foreign-policy decisions.
Ⓓ It allowed them to avoid responsibility for the mistakes of their government.

8. In 1964, soon after North Vietnamese torpedo boats in the Gulf of Tonkin exchanged fire with United States destroyers, Congress passed the Tonkin Gulf Resolution, allowing President Lyndon Johnson to take "all necessary measures . . . to prevent further aggression." In effect, Congress was giving up its constitutional right to

Ⓐ override a presidential veto
Ⓑ represent the citizens
Ⓒ declare war
Ⓓ make law

9. Congress repealed the Tonkin Gulf Resolution in 1970 after Americans learned that President Richard Nixon had used it to justify the bombing of neutral Cambodia. Drag and drop the words that correctly complete the sentence.

This repeal is an example of the ⬚⬚⬚⬚⬚ checking the power of the ⬚⬚⬚⬚ .

| executive branch | legislative branch | judicial branch |

10. World War II ended in 1945. In 1947, Jackie Robinson became the first African-American player in the modern history of major-league baseball. In 1948, President Harry S Truman ordered full integration of the United States armed forces. Which aspect of World War II served as a spark to the postwar Civil Rights Movement?

Ⓐ the founding of the United Nations
Ⓑ the passage of the GI Bill of Rights
Ⓒ the entry of thousands of women into the workforce
Ⓓ the military service of African-American soldiers

11. In the late nineteenth century, why did many American factory owners insist on the "open shop" principle in hiring workers?

Ⓐ to save money on wages
Ⓑ to show support for labor unions
Ⓒ to bar African Americans from applying for work
Ⓓ to bar recent immigrants from applying for work

Read the excerpt. Then answer questions 12–15.

From *Declaration of the Rights of Man and of the Citizen*

(enacted by the French National Assembly during the French Revolution)

Articles

1. Men are born and remain free and equal in rights. Social distinctions may be founded only upon the general good.
2. The aim of all political association is the preservation of the natural and imprescriptible rights of man. These rights are liberty, property, security, and resistance to oppression.
5. Law can only prohibit such actions as are hurtful to society. Nothing may be prevented which is not forbidden by law, and no one may be forced to anything not provided for by law.
6. Law is the expression of the general will. Every citizen has a right to participate personally, or through his representative, in its foundation. It must be the same for all, whether it protects or punishes.
7. No person shall be accused, arrested, or imprisoned except in the cases and according to the forms prescribed by law.
10. No one shall be disquieted on account of his opinions, including his religious views, provided their manifestation does not disturb the public order established by law.
11. The free communication of ideas and opinions is one of the most precious of the rights of man. Every citizen may, accordingly, speak, write, and print with freedom, but shall be responsible for such abuses of his freedom as shall be defined by law.

—August 26, 1789

12. What was the <u>main</u> way in which ideas of the Enlightenment helped bring about the French Revolution? Use the document above to support your ideas. Write your answer in the box.

13. Which founding document of the United States had the greatest influence on the Declaration of the Rights of Man and of the Citizen?

Ⓐ the Federalist Papers
Ⓑ the Bill of Rights
Ⓒ the Articles of Confederation
Ⓓ the Declaration of Independence

14. Before the Revolution, France had a powerless legislative body called the Estates-General. Members represented the three estates, or ranks, of French citizens. Drag each group to its proper place in the table.

Rank	First Estate	Second Estate	Third Estate
Members			

common people	clergy	hereditary nobility

15. In prerevolutionary France, members of the First and Second Estates were exempt from taxes. The Third Estate carried the entire tax burden. Why did many members of the First Estate support the Third Estate's calls for reform?

Ⓐ Their religious convictions made them support reform.
Ⓑ They were intimidated by the military.
Ⓒ Their economic situation was no better than that of the commoners.
Ⓓ They felt that they had to vote with the aristocracy.

16. Why is a strike an effective way for workers to achieve improvements in wages and working conditions?

Ⓐ because a strike throws hundreds of people out of work
Ⓑ because a strike enables business owners to hire new workers
Ⓒ because a strike makes people sympathize with business owners
Ⓓ because a strike shuts down a business and harms the owner financially

Study the map. Then answer questions 17–20.

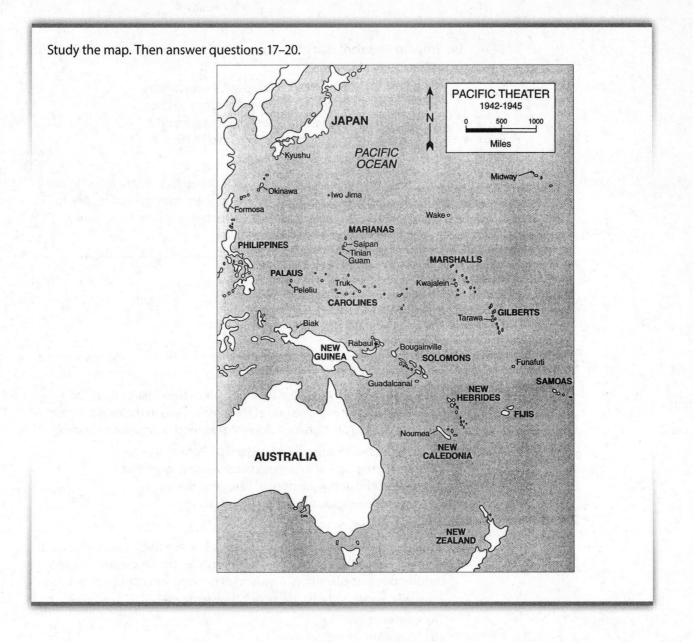

17. During World War II, the United States Marines worked their way north toward Japan, taking over one Pacific island at a time. How did the United States use the geography to its own advantage?

Ⓐ The United States gained valuable natural resources on the islands.
Ⓑ The United States needed the islands to house prisoners of war.
Ⓒ The United States used the small islands for supply bases.
Ⓓ The United States tested the atomic bomb on the islands.

18. Which factor helped bring about Japan's defeat in the war?

Ⓐ its great distance from its allies
Ⓑ its lack of natural energy resources
Ⓒ the repeated failure of its rice crop
Ⓓ its vulnerability to invasion from the sea

19. Why did President Harry S Truman decide to use atomic weapons against Japan in 1945?

(A) to free the Philippines from Japanese occupation

(B) to prevent Japan from invading the United States

(C) to bring about an immediate Japanese surrender

(D) to convince the Germans to surrender in Europe

20. Under the Tokugawa shogunate, Japan closed its borders, refusing all but the most minimal contact with foreigners from the early 1600s to the mid-1800s. What geographical factor best explains how this was possible? Write your answer in the box.

21. In the early Middle Ages, Constantinople was the capital city of the Byzantine Empire and also one of the largest cities in the world. Which factor helps explain Constantinople's tremendous economic success?

(A) Its artists were strongly influenced by Persian styles.

(B) Its diverse population represented a variety of cultures.

(C) It is located at the juncture of Europe and Asia.

(D) It was the headquarters of a powerful army.

22. After World War II, national governments in Western Europe took over and ran many major businesses, such as banks, power companies, and automobile manufacturers. This kind of government control of industry is usually associated with the political system called

(A) conservatism

(B) liberalism

(C) socialism

(D) capitalism

23. In the "Great Migration" that began around 1915 and continued through the 1920s, hundreds of thousands of African Americans moved from the South to the Northeast and Midwest. Why did they migrate? Choose two major reasons.

(A) to find well-paying industrial jobs

(B) to attend college

(C) to enlist in the military

(D) to become farmers in rural areas

(E) to escape harsh segregation laws

(F) to relocate to states with lower taxes

Look at the engraving. Then answer questions 24–26.

Engraving by Paul Revere

24. In his engraving of the Boston Massacre of 1770, how did artist Paul Revere misuse the principle of a free press?

Ⓐ He depicted an event at which he was not actually present.

Ⓑ He made up an event that did not actually take place.

Ⓒ He drew a biased and inaccurate picture of what really happened.

Ⓓ He himself staged the event to make it come out a certain way.

25. Several British soldiers ("redcoats") were arrested after the Boston Massacre. Outspoken patriot John Adams agreed to defend them—a decision that was very unpopular among his fellow Bostonians. Which basic democratic principle was involved in Adams's decision?

Ⓐ the redcoats' right to a fair trial by jury

Ⓑ the redcoats' right to be tried by a military court

Ⓒ the redcoats' right to be tried in their own country

Ⓓ the redcoats' right to immunity from prosecution

26. At the time of the Boston Massacre, the colonists were boycotting many British goods, such as tea, to avoid paying the taxes on these goods. Why did Britain continue to assess taxes on the goods it exported to the colonies?

Ⓐ to lower unemployment in the British Empire

Ⓑ to raise revenue for the British treasury

Ⓒ to prevent a rise in prices

Ⓓ to encourage consumer spending

Study the political cartoon. Then answer questions 27–29.

Cartoon by Alexander Anderson

27. The political cartoon refers to the Embargo Act of 1807, signed into law by President Thomas Jefferson. Which of these best describes an embargo?

Ⓐ a tax on imports into the United States
Ⓑ a ban on exports to specified countries
Ⓒ a law establishing free trade among the states
Ⓓ a law establishing international free trade

28. Why was the Embargo Act of 1807 so unpopular?

Ⓐ It reduced the profits of American manufacturers and farmers.
Ⓑ It set the states against each other in economic competition.
Ⓒ It allowed the slave trade to continue unchecked.
Ⓓ It encouraged people to buy American-made products.

29. President Jefferson originally hoped the Embargo Act would eliminate contact between United States and British ships on the high seas. He wanted to avoid this contact because the British navy practiced impressment. Impressment means that the British

Ⓐ held up American ships and stole their cargoes
Ⓑ fired on American ships and killed most of their crews
Ⓒ kidnapped American sailors and forced them into military service
Ⓓ bribed American captains to sell their cargoes at low prices

Read the excerpt. Then answer questions 30–33.

From Farewell Address to the Nation

Until the latest of our world conflicts, the United States had no armaments industry. American makers of plowshares could, with time and as required, make swords as well. But now we can no longer risk emergency improvisation of national defense; we have been compelled to create a permanent armaments industry of vast proportions. Added to this, three and a half million men and women are directly engaged in the defense establishment. We annually spend on military security more than the net income of all United States corporations. . . .

In the councils of government, we must guard against the acquisition of unwarranted influence, whether sought or unsought, by the military-industrial complex. The potential for the disastrous rise of misplaced power exists and will persist.

We must never let the weight of this combination endanger our liberties or democratic processes. We should take nothing for granted. Only an alert and knowledgeable citizenry can compel the proper meshing of the huge industrial and military machinery of defense with our peaceful methods and goals, so that security and liberty may prosper together.

—*President Dwight D. Eisenhower, 1961*

30. What was the main reason for the "permanent armaments industry" and the "defense establishment" to which President Eisenhower refers?

(A) World War II
(B) the Cold War
(C) the Korean War
(D) the Vietnam War

31. At the time of President Eisenhower's speech, the most powerful enemy of the United States was the Soviet Union. What were two key reasons for this?

(A) The two countries had been political enemies for many decades.
(B) The two countries had fought on opposite sides during World War II.
(C) The two countries both wanted to take control of Western Europe.
(D) The two countries lived according to opposing economic and political principles.
(E) The two countries hoped to influence leaders in the Far East.
(F) The two countries had conflicting interests in the postwar world.

32. In 1962 the United States and the Soviet Union came to the brink of nuclear war in the Cuban missile crisis. Which factor made Cuba an important strategic ally for the Soviet Union?

- (A) its location
- (B) its size
- (C) its climate
- (D) its culture

33. President Eisenhower states that citizens must guard against the possible "unwarranted influence" of the military-industrial complex on government. How can citizens do this?

- (A) by keeping informed about governmental affairs
- (B) by voting against increases in defense spending
- (C) by trying to overthrow the government
- (D) by refusing to serve in the military when drafted

34. When World War II broke out in Europe, what made many Americans think that the United States could safely stay out of the conflict?

- (A) They knew that America's army had always been the strongest in the world.
- (B) They were told that United States scientists were building an atomic bomb.
- (C) They believed that the Atlantic Ocean was wide enough to offer protection.
- (D) They thought that Britain and France would win the war quickly and easily.

35. The United States Congress has two houses, the Senate and the House of Representatives. In the Senate, all states are represented equally. In the House, the states are represented according to their population. Why did the authors of the Constitution design this type of legislature?

- (A) to balance the interests of the states and the people
- (B) to give large states more power than small ones
- (C) to make sure that the people could outvote the states
- (D) to make sure that no state could block legislation

36. During the Ming dynasty, China sent ships on a tour of the Eastern Hemisphere. The ships returned with edible plants never seen before in China, including pineapples, potatoes, and tomatoes. Which of these best explains why these new crops led to good annual harvests?

- (A) The new crops grew better in China's cold climate than in their native hot climate.
- (B) Chinese farmers rotated the new and old crops, allowing the soil to rest and recuperate.
- (C) The new crops added variety to the Chinese diet and cuisine.
- (D) The new crops had come from many different countries and cultures.

Read the list in the box. Then answer questions 37–39.

>> To find a water route to the Pacific Ocean
>> To establish friendly relations with Indian tribes
>> To gather samples of plants and animals
>> To map the territory
>> To keep detailed notes of the journey

37. To whom did President Thomas Jefferson give the list of tasks shown?
- Ⓐ the Donner party
- Ⓑ the Forty-Niners
- Ⓒ the Union Pacific Railroad
- Ⓓ the Lewis and Clark expedition

38. What economic motive did the United States government have for seeking a water route across the continent?
- Ⓐ A water route would permit safe and efficient transport of goods by boat.
- Ⓑ A water route would enable people to settle the country more quickly.
- Ⓒ A water route would reduce the possibility of encountering hostile Native American tribes.
- Ⓓ A water route would remove obstacles to immigration.

39. What was the greatest potential hazard faced by the people who undertook the tasks?
- Ⓐ They might have to fight off unfriendly Native American tribes.
- Ⓑ They might have to defend themselves against French troops.
- Ⓒ They would have to navigate treacherous ocean currents.
- Ⓓ They would have to travel through barren desert territory.

40. Britain expended financial, human, and military resources to conquer and govern its colonies. In return, Britain gained new markets for its exports and bought the colonies' natural resources at good prices. Britain's decision to conquer colonies like India and Egypt is an example of
- Ⓐ cost-benefit analysis
- Ⓑ deficit spending
- Ⓒ balancing a budget
- Ⓓ microeconomics

Study the political cartoon. Then answer questions 41–43.

FREE TRADE WOULD MAKE GOODS CHEAPER, BUT IT WOULD LOWER THE AMERICAN WORKMAN'S WAGES SO MUCH THAT HE WOULD BE UNABLE TO PURCHASE THEM.

THE GOOSE THAT LAYS THE GOLDEN EGGS
Democratic Politician (to Workingman)—"Kill the Goose and get all your Eggs at once."

Cartoon by Bernhard Gillam

41. The label *PROTECTION* on the goose in the cartoon refers to a tariff. What does a tariff do? Drag the correct words to complete the sentence.

It adds a tax to ☐ , ☐ their prices.

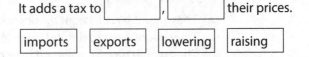

imports   exports   lowering   raising

42. Why would workers be inclined to support tariffs?

(A) Tariffs increase demand for American-made goods.
(B) Tariffs lower prices on American-made goods.
(C) Tariffs promote free trade among all nations.
(D) Tariffs create hostile relations with other nations.

43. Why would free trade lower the American worker's wage, as the cartoon suggests?

(A) Free trade would encourage Americans to spend more and save less.
(B) Free trade would raise wages in other nations.
(C) Free trade would lower the demand for American-made goods.
(D) Free trade would reduce American exports to other nations.

44. Article I, Section 3 of the United States Constitution states that senators will serve six-year terms, with an election year scheduled every two years. Senators are divided into three groups as evenly as possible, so that only one-third of the seats are up for election in any given year. What is the reason for this rule?

 Ⓐ It ensures that the majority of the Senate will always be experienced legislators.
 Ⓑ It prevents any individual senator from serving more than one term.
 Ⓒ It eliminates the possibility of political corruption within the Senate.
 Ⓓ It discourages voter bias in favor of incumbent candidates for the Senate.

45. The Winter Olympic Games, in which athletes compete in skating, skiing, hockey, bobsled, and other winter sports, are held every four years. Nations all over the world bid for the right to hold the Winter Olympics. For a nation to succeed in its bid, which geographical feature must be present, and why? Write your answer in the box.

46. Cities of the world aggressively bid against one another for the privilege of hosting the Winter and Summer Olympic Games, in spite of the high cost in money, time, effort, and disruption of normal routines. What is the main benefit a city expects to gain from hosting the Olympics?

 Ⓐ an influx of new residents, as people who come to see the Games will move to the city permanently
 Ⓑ new public facilities and buildings that can be used for other purposes after the Games are over
 Ⓒ an enhanced reputation as a great international center of culture and the arts
 Ⓓ cash profits from meals, souvenirs, and lodging purchased by Olympic spectators

47. Philadelphia was the site of the First and Second Continental Congresses and the original capital city of the United States. Which two of the following made Philadelphia the logical choice to host the national government?

 Ⓐ its central location in the colonies
 Ⓑ its year-round temperate climate
 Ⓒ its large, ethnically varied population
 Ⓓ its booming local economy
 Ⓔ its role as the colonies' largest city and busiest port
 Ⓕ its reputation as a city amenable to southerners

This is the end of the TASC Social Studies Practice Test.

TASC Social Studies Practice Test Explanatory Answers

1. A Until the invention of the airplane in the twentieth century, armies carried on wars in Europe by marching over the border into enemy territory. In this era of land wars, islands like Britain could be attacked only by sea. The English Channel to the south and the North Sea to the east constituted a safety zone between Britain and any potential European attacker.

2. D When you boycott a product, you refuse to buy it. If a large number of people boycott a product, demand goes down; when the demand goes down, the price goes down.

3. D In the early years of American politics, ballots were not secret; each candidate had a ballot of a different color, which made it easy for political bosses to keep track of who voted for whom. If you did not vote for the right candidate, you might be attacked or your business destroyed. Secret ballots removed any possibility of political pressure on individual voters.

4. A Pepper was plentiful and therefore cheap in India—but Europeans could not produce it for themselves. They had to import it. Since the supply was small, the demand and therefore the price was high.

5. D The Suez Canal provided a direct waterway across Egypt from the Mediterranean Sea to the Red Sea. This meant that European ships bound for Asia no longer had to sail all the way around Africa.

6. Possible answer: They are peacefully assembling in protest. Citizens who protest government policy are speaking freely, assembling peaceably, and petitioning the government for a redress of their grievances—all First Amendment rights. They are expressing direct popular opposition to a government policy in the hope that the government will take their opinions into account.

7. A When the Vietnam War began, men as young as eighteen could be drafted and sent overseas into combat. Young people argued that if they were old enough to be sent to their death at age eighteen, they were old enough to vote for the leaders who decided on such actions. The right to vote is a basic principle of democratic government.

8. C The Tonkin Gulf Resolution was so broadly phrased that a president could easily interpret it to mean he could order an attack without waiting for Congress to declare war—if he thought the attack would lead swiftly to surrender and peace.

9. legislative branch, executive branch Congress is the legislative branch of the government. The legislature repealed its resolution to check the power of the president, who is the head of the executive branch.

10. D African-American soldiers helped fight for freedom and liberty in Europe. When they returned home, many were willing to challenge the restrictions of legal racial segregation.

11. A A closed shop is one that will hire only union workers; an open shop will hire nonunion workers. Since union workers earn more money and receive greater benefits, factory owners generally prefer an open shop.

12. Possible answer: The Enlightenment emphasized that people are born free and equal, and that all have rights. One basic idea of the Enlightenment was that people are born equal, and therefore it is wrong to give them social and economic privileges on the basis of birth. People should have the right to rise in the world according to merit, not birth.

13. B The ten amendments in the Bill of Rights contain language very similar to several articles in the Declaration of the Rights of Man—freedom of religion, freedom of speech, freedom from imprisonment without cause, and so on.

14. clergy, hereditary nobility, common people We often refer to the fourth estate, meaning the press, but these three strata were the estates of the realm from the time of medieval Europe.

15. C The majority of the French clergy were poor; they supported reform because in spite of the tax exemption, they suffered as much as the Third Estate from food shortages, high prices, and so on.

16. D The workers' strike is an effective weapon because it shuts down the operation of a business. Business owners want to settle strikes quickly so that they can once again begin to make profits.

17. C During war, fighting forces need bases stocked with supplies, hospitals, and so on. The farther a military force gets from its sources of supply, the greater its chances of losing important battles. Therefore, it is important to establish bases near the fighting.

18. B Japan had to import all the oil it needed to fuel its ships and planes and to power its factories. The United States cut the supply lines between Japan in the north and its fuel sources in the south.

19. C Only an extreme measure like an atomic bomb would convince the Japanese to surrender immediately and thus avoid the need for an invasion of Japan that would likely cost the lives of thousands of United States soldiers and sailors.

20. Possible answer: Japan is an isolated nation. All islands, by definition, are physically isolated; no one can interfere with their control over their own borders except by a full-scale attack. Japan did not open its borders until it was forced to do so by the "gunboat diplomacy" of the Western powers, especially the United States.

21. C Constantinople is on the Black Sea, just across the Bosphorus Strait from the Asian mainland. This location made the city a natural place for westbound Asian merchants and eastbound European merchants to meet, trade, buy, and sell.

22. C Following the end of World War II, Western European voters elected many social democratic governments. These governments took control of many important industries, promising to manage them to the benefit of their workers and of the nation as a whole. This kind of government control of industry is usually associated with the political system called socialism. Many economic policies from that era remain in effect in Western Europe today.

23. A and E The main reason for the Great Migration was economic. The advent of World War I created thousands of factory and industrial jobs in the United States. Many African Americans also wanted to escape the legal segregation they faced in the South, but they encountered de facto segregation when they reached the Northeast and Midwest.

24. C The Boston Massacre was actually a small-scale street fight in which a few idle colonists were taunting and bullying a few British soldiers ("redcoats") on sentry duty. Tension erupted into violence when the colonists began throwing stones and the redcoats fired a few shots. Revere's engraving distorts the facts to make the redcoats look like brutal aggressors firing without cause on defenseless civilians.

25. A The right to a fair trial by a jury of one's peers has been a basic principle of the British justice system since the Magna Carta was signed in 1215. The colonists followed the British tradition of making this right a central principle of their government.

26. B The British treasury needed revenue from taxes to pay off continuing war debts and other obligations.

27. B An embargo is a ban on trade. The Embargo Act of 1807, banning trade with Britain and France, stopped most United States exports.

28. A Unable to export their cash crops or their products, the farmers, traders, and manufacturers saw their profits drop to about one-fifth of the pre-1807 levels.

29. C Impressment—forcing crew members of merchant ships into military service—was a common practice in the early nineteenth century. In that era, many British navy officers still considered American sailors to be mere rebels against Great Britain.

30. B World War II and the Korean War were long over by 1961, and only a very small number of "military advisors" were serving in Vietnam. The Cold War and the great buildup of nuclear weapons was responsible for the drastic increase in United States defense spending.

31. D and F The United States was a democratic republic with a largely capitalist economy, while the Soviet Union was a one-party dictatorship with a Communist economy. The countries had different, incompatible visions for the postwar world.

32. A Cuba is only 90 miles off the United States coast and was therefore ideally positioned as a Soviet military base.

33. A Eisenhower spoke of an "alert and knowledgeable citizenry," meaning it was up to the citizens to keep themselves informed about governmental affairs. People should not just accept that there was a great need for high defense spending; they should keep aware of what was going on in the world so that they could exercise the constitutional right to oppose their own government if it proposed an unjustified war.

34. C Before World War II and especially before the advent of long-range bomber aircraft, Americans believed that the United States could safely ignore problems elsewhere in the world because of the protection afforded by the Atlantic and Pacific Oceans.

35. A The composition of the Senate and the House was designed as another feature of a system of checks and balances. The people are represented proportionally in the House, while the states are represented equally in the Senate.

36. B Crops draw certain minerals and nutrients from the soil. When farmers grow the same crops year after year, the soil runs out of those minerals; a poor harvest is the result. A new crop planted in the same soil will thrive because it draws on the minerals that the soil has been able to store up. This is why farmers rotate their crops.

37. D The Lewis and Clark expedition set out from St. Louis to explore the newly acquired Louisiana Territory and the lands that lay between it and the Pacific Ocean.

38. A Until the invention of the railroad and later the automobile, a water route was the quickest, safest, and most efficient way to transport quantities of goods.

39. A The United States formally acquired the Louisiana Territory six months after Lewis and Clark set out. There were no French troops in the territory at that time, but there were numerous Native American tribes, some of whom might be hostile. Luckily for Lewis and Clark, the presence of the Native American guide Sacagawea in the expedition party guaranteed friendly relations between the explorers and the Native Americans they met along the way. Since the explorers traveled along rivers in fertile country, the expedition was not likely to run out of provisions. Also, their route did not involve any navigation on the ocean.

40. A Cost-benefit analysis means weighing what something will cost you against what you will gain. Britain decided that the economic benefits of acquiring a colonial empire were greater than the cost.

41. imports, raising A tariff is a tax or duty imposed on imported goods. The tariff makes the price of the imported good higher.

42. A Tariffs would encourage Americans to buy American-made goods rather than imports, because the American-made goods would have lower prices. The high demand for products from American factories would give American workers job security.

43. C Free trade means trade without import duties or tariffs. Without those tariffs, imported goods might cost the same or less than American-made goods. That would cause the demand for American-made goods to drop, meaning that fewer workers would be needed to produce them.

44. A Because the Senate's power of making laws is so important to the nation, the authors of the Constitution ensured that at all times, two-thirds of the senators would have legislative experience. They also hoped that the senators would benefit from working with many of the same colleagues for a longer amount of time than if all their terms expired at once.

45. Possible answer: mountains, because they are needed for certain winter sports Downhill skiing and ski-jumping events can be held only where there are mountains present. These events cannot be staged indoors.

46. D The main benefit to a city holding a major international event is in money. The city hopes that the enormous expense of holding the Games will pay off because people will come from all over the world and they will all spend money. The city also hopes to be featured as an attractive destination for tourists, thus adding long-term gains in the money those tourists will spend on their visits.

47. A and E It made sense to choose a central location as a gathering place for leaders from all the colonies and later all the states. This meant that each person would have to travel the least possible distance in an era when long-distance travel was slow, uncomfortable, and risky. In addition, Philadelphia was already a well-established city—the largest and busiest in the colonies.

The TASC Science Test

6

HOW TO USE THIS CHAPTER

» Read the Overview to learn what the TASC Science Test covers.

» Take the TASC Science Pretest to preview your science knowledge and skills.

» Study the TASC Science Test Review to refresh your knowledge of TASC test science topics.

» Take the TASC Science Practice Test to sharpen your skills and get ready for test day.

Overview

Unlike earlier high school equivalency tests, the TASC test requires you to know some basic science content. It is not just a reading test, although you may be asked to read science-related passages.

The TASC Science Test is based on the Next Generation Science Standards, which you may review at:

www.nextgenscience.org/next-generation-science-standards.

The twelve disciplinary core ideas for high school science are as follows:

Physical Sciences

1. Matter and Its Interactions
2. Motion and Stability: Forces and Interactions
3. Energy
4. Waves and Their Applications in Technologies for Information Transfer

Life Sciences

5. From Molecules to Organisms: Structures and Processes
6. Ecosystems: Interactions, Energy, and Dynamics
7. Heredity: Inheritance and Variation of Traits
8. Biological Evolution: Unity and Diversity

Earth and Space Sciences

9. Earth's Place in the Universe
10. Earth's Systems
11. Earth and Human Activity

Engineering

12. Engineering Design

You can expect to see questions on the TASC test in any and all of these areas. On the TASC test, engineering practices will be integrated across the other content areas, as described.

The Next Generation Science Standards focus on science as it is practiced and experienced in the real world. The Standards ask you to think the way a scientist thinks, using these "practices of science and engineering":

1. Asking questions (for science) and defining problems (for engineering)
2. Developing and using models
3. Planning and carrying out investigations
4. Analyzing and interpreting data
5. Using mathematics and computational thinking
6. Constructing explanations (for science) and designing solutions (for engineering)
7. Engaging in argument from evidence
8. Obtaining, evaluating, and communicating information

To perform well on the TASC test, you should recognize the connection between science and "real life." You should understand how scientists think and work to solve problems. You may be asked to read scientific materials, interpret graphics, and apply scientific understanding to real-life problems.

TASC Science Pretest

Use the items that follow to preview your knowledge of science concepts and skills.
Answers appear on page 324.

Use the following information to help answer questions 1–3.

Helium is a stable element that will not react or burn with oxygen
in air, and the low density of helium gas allows it to float easily.
That is why helium gas is used to safely fill balloons. A balloon
filled with hydrogen will float in air just like a balloon filled with
helium. However, a balloon filled with hydrogen is dangerous
because hydrogen can burn in oxygen. The reaction of the burning of
hydrogen is as follows:

$$2H_2(g) + O_2(g) \rightarrow 2H_2O(l) + heat$$

---

1. This reaction can be classified as which type?

   (A) endothermic
   (B) exothermic
   (C) nuclear fission
   (D) decomposition

2. Gases with a lighter molecular weight will travel faster than gases with a
   heavier molecular weight. A container with a mixture of hydrogen gas,
   helium gas, and oxygen gas in equal amounts has a hole poked in it,
   allowing the gases to escape. Drag the tiles to make the sentence true.

   After 3 minutes there will be less ⬜ in the container than either
   ⬜ or ⬜ .

   | helium | hydrogen | oxygen |

3. When hydrogen gas reacts with oxygen gas, the potential energy
   diagram for the reaction will look <u>most</u> like which of these?

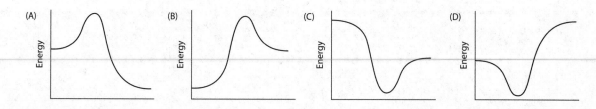

Use the following information to help answer questions 4 and 5.

There is evidence that the continents have moved over time. It is believed that at one point in Earth's history, all of the current continents were one landmass called Pangaea. Here is a map showing what Pangaea is believed to have looked like:

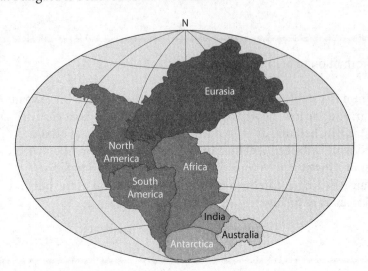

Today the arrangement of the continents looks like this:

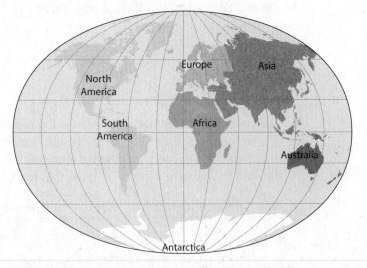

Based upon current models of the movement of the continents, it is estimated that if Christopher Columbus were to sail today to the Americas as he did in 1492, his ship would have to sail approximately 155 feet farther to reach land.

4. This movement of the continents is <u>best</u> related to which cause?

   Ⓐ weathering at Earth's surface
   Ⓑ the diversity of life on Earth
   Ⓒ the increase in the number of humans present on Earth over time
   Ⓓ plate tectonics and convection within Earth

5. Which of these is associated with the movement of two continents away from each other?

   Ⓐ the formation of hurricanes
   Ⓑ the formation of an ocean ridge
   Ⓒ the formation of fjords
   Ⓓ the formation of a V-shaped valley

6. In the past it was believed that our sun and other stars were balls of fire. Today, however, scientists have confirmed that the sun is not fueled by combustion. Instead, the sun is known to be fueled by a nuclear reaction. The nuclear reaction that takes place within the sun is <u>best</u> described as

   Ⓐ a series of reactions in which chemical bonds are broken to release energy
   Ⓑ energy production via convection that takes place on the sun's surface
   Ⓒ the burning of fossil fuels within the sun
   Ⓓ a series of fusion reactions that take place within the sun

7. The photoelectric effect and the double slit experiment are two methods for demonstrating the dual nature of light. They prove that light can act like <u>both</u>

   Ⓐ a wave and a particle
   Ⓑ a fusion reaction and a fission reaction
   Ⓒ matter and antimatter
   Ⓓ protons and neutrons

8. Ernest Rutherford's gold foil experiment proved that atoms are mostly empty space. His experiment also helped determine that the mass of an atom is highly concentrated in the nucleus of the atom. Which particle accounts for the least part of the mass of an atom?

   Ⓐ nucleon
   Ⓑ proton
   Ⓒ neutron
   Ⓓ electron

Use the following information to help answer questions 9 and 10.

In 1945 an atomic bomb was dropped on Hiroshima, Japan. The bomb worked via the bombardment of a uranium-235 nucleus with a neutron to set off a chain reaction. Each step of the chain reaction gave off more and more energy.

9. This type of nuclear reaction is classified as what kind of reaction?
   Ⓐ fusion
   Ⓑ endothermic
   Ⓒ fission
   Ⓓ reversible

10. Despite its potential benefits, nuclear energy is regarded as controversial. Which of these is a potential benefit from a nuclear reaction?
    Ⓐ radioactive waste
    Ⓑ clean energy production that does not produce greenhouse gases
    Ⓒ exposure to radiation
    Ⓓ possible nuclear meltdowns

Use the following information to help answer questions 11 and 12.

Populations of white moths and black moths live in a forest that is located near a factory. The factory releases airborne black soot that eventually covers the trees in the area. As a result, the trees become darker in color.

11. This set of events could result in
    Ⓐ a decrease in the white moth population
    Ⓑ a decrease in the black moth population
    Ⓒ a decrease in respiratory problems among people living nearby
    Ⓓ an increase in the number of trees growing in the area

12. Which of these would help prevent pollution from entering the air? Choose all that apply.
    Ⓐ using solar power to power the factory
    Ⓑ using wind power to power the factory
    Ⓒ driving hybrid vehicles
    Ⓓ using fossil fuels to power the factory
    Ⓔ installing filters on smokestacks
    Ⓕ digging ponds for wastewater

Use the following information to help answer questions 13–15.

Fritz Haber was awarded the 1918 Nobel Prize in Chemistry for his work in creating the Haber process, a process by which ammonia is made. The reaction for the Haber process is as follows:

$$3H_2(g) + N_2(g) \longleftrightarrow 2NH_3(l) + heat$$

13. Which of these would <u>not</u> drive the reaction to make more ammonia?
  Ⓐ heating the reactants
  Ⓑ reacting the gases at a low pressure
  Ⓒ using a catalyst
  Ⓓ using higher concentrations of reactants

14. For the hydrogen and nitrogen to react, there must be
  Ⓐ contact between the hydrogen and nitrogen atoms
  Ⓑ a sufficient amount of ammonia present to form the hydrogen and nitrogen
  Ⓒ effective collisions between the hydrogen and nitrogen gases so as to cause a rearrangement of atoms
  Ⓓ smaller amounts of hydrogen and nitrogen present

15. If 12 grams of hydrogen gas are completely reacted with 56 grams of nitrogen gas to make ammonia, what is the total amount of ammonia that can be generated?
  Ⓐ 4.67 grams
  Ⓑ 0.214 grams
  Ⓒ 44 grams
  Ⓓ 68 grams

16. Survival of the fittest <u>best</u> describes
  Ⓐ mitosis
  Ⓑ mutations
  Ⓒ natural selection
  Ⓓ recessive traits

Use the following information to help answer questions 17–18.

The picture represents an ecosystem.

17. Drag all four tiles to their correct places on the chart.

Producers	First-Order Consumers	Second-Order Consumers

| Wolf | Grass | Rabbit | Squirrel |

18. The wolves in the ecosystem hunt for rabbits, which eat the plants present in the ecosystem. This is an example of

- Ⓐ cannibalism
- Ⓑ a food web
- Ⓒ a food chain
- Ⓓ photosynthesis

Use the following information to help answer questions 19–20.

An object at rest on a frictionless table has a number of forces applied to it. The table shows each force and the acceleration resulting from each force.

FORCE APPLIED (in newtons, N)	RESULTING ACCELERATION (in m/s^2)
5	1
12.5	2.5
20	4

19. What is the mass of this object?

Ⓐ 1 kilogram
Ⓑ 5 kilograms
Ⓒ 12.5 kilograms
Ⓓ 20 kilograms

20. The object is picked up and held above the table. It is then dropped and falls to the table. Which two statements are true about the velocity and acceleration of the object while it is moving through the air?

Ⓐ The velocity will increase.
Ⓑ The velocity will stay the same.
Ⓒ The velocity will decrease.
Ⓓ The acceleration will increase.
Ⓔ The acceleration will stay the same.
Ⓕ The acceleration will decrease.

This is the end of the TASC Science Pretest.

TASC Science Pretest Answers

1. **B** Review 3. Energy (pp. 336–338).
2. **hydrogen, oxygen, helium; or hydrogen, helium, oxygen** Review 1. Matter and Its Interactions (pp. 324–333).
3. **D** Review 10. Earth's Systems (pp. 359–367).
4. **D** Review 10. Earth's Systems (pp. 359–367).
5. **B** Review 10. Earth's Systems (pp. 359–367).
6. **D** Review 1. Matter and Its Interactions (pp. 359–367).
7. **A** Review 1. Matter and Its Interactions (pp. 324–333).
8. **D** Review 1. Matter and Its Interactions (pp. 324–333).
9. **C** Review 1. Matter and Its Interactions (pp. 324–333).
10. **B** Review 11. Earth and Human Activity (pp. 368–370).
11. **A** Review 11. Earth and Human Activity (pp. 363–370).
12. **A, B, C, and E** Review 11. Earth and Human Activity (pp. 368–370).
13. **B** Review 1. Matter and Its Interactions (pp. 324–333).
14. **C** Review 1. Matter and Its Interactions (pp. 324–333).
15. **D** Review 1. Matter and Its Interactions (pp. 324–333).
16. **C** Review 8. Biological Evolution: Unity and Diversity (pp. 353–355).
17. **producers: grass; first-order consumers: rabbit, squirrel; second-order consumers: wolf** Review 6. Ecosystems: Interactions, Energy, and Dynamics (pp. 344–349).
18. **C** Review 6. Ecosystems: Interactions, Energy, and Dynamics (pp. 344–349).
19. **B** Review 2. Motion and Stability: Forces and Interactions (pp. 333–336).
20. **A and E** Review 2. Motion and Stability: Forces and Interactions (pp. 333–336).

TASC Science Test Review

The pages that follow briefly review each of the twelve disciplinary core ideas listed in the Overview. To learn more about each core area, look online or in the library.

Physical Sciences

 Matter and Its Interactions

KEY TERMS: activation energy, atom, bond, bonding, electron, element, endothermic reaction, exothermic reaction, fission, fusion, ion, matter, molecule, neutron, nucleosynthesis, nucleus, periodic table, proton, radioactive decay, reactivity, transmutation

Atoms

All substances are made of **matter**; that is, all substances have mass and volume (space that they occupy). The most basic unit of matter is the **atom**. The atom is made up of three subatomic particles: **protons**, **neutrons**, and **electrons**. Protons carry a positive electrical charge, while electrons carry a negative charge. Neutrons do not carry any charge. The protons and neutrons (nucleons) are located in the **nucleus** of the atom, while the electrons are located around the nucleus in orbits called principal energy levels. Because the protons are the only charged particles in the nucleus, they give the nucleus a positive charge.

Carbon atom

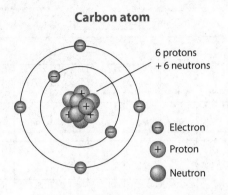

The diagram shows the atomic structure for a carbon atom. The atom can be identified as carbon because it has six protons. This and other information about atoms and the substances they compose can be found in the **periodic table**.

Periodic Table

The periodic table shows the different **elements** (substances that contain only one kind of atom) organized into *periods* (horizontal rows numbered 1 through 7) and *groups* (vertical rows numbered 1 through 18). Each element is identified by its chemical symbol. The table also gives some information about each element. The elements are listed in order of their atomic number; that is, the number of protons in the nucleus of that kind of atom. The location of the different elements in the periodic table can also be used to predict some of the properties of those elements. For example, hydrogen (in the upper left corner of the table) and the elements in the upper right corner of the table are nonmetals. The elements in the middle and on the left side of the table (except for hydrogen) are metals. Along a heavy black line running through the middle of the table are the semimetals or metalloids.

Periodic Table of the Elements

KEY

Atomic Mass → 12.011 −4 ← Selected Oxidation States
+2
Symbol → **C** +4
Atomic Number → **6**
Electron Configuration → 2-4

Relative atomic masses are based on $^{12}C = 12.000$

Note: Mass numbers in parentheses are mass numbers of the most stable or common isotope.

1																	18
1 H Hydrogen																	2 He Helium
	2											13	14	15	16	17	
3 Li Lithium	4 Be Beryllium											5 B Boron	6 C Carbon	7 N Nitrogen	8 O Oxygen	9 F Fluorine	10 Ne Neon
11 Na Sodium	12 Mg Magnesium	3	4	5	6	7	8	9	10	11	12	13 Al Aluminum	14 Si Silicon	15 P Phosphorus	16 S Sulfur	17 Cl Chlorine	18 Ar Argon
19 K Potassium	20 Ca Calcium	21 Sc Scandium	22 Ti Titanium	23 V Vanadium	24 Cr Chromium	25 Mn Manganese	26 Fe Iron	27 Co Cobalt	28 Ni Nickel	29 Cu Copper	30 Zn Zinc	31 Ga Gallium	32 Ge Germanium	33 As Arsenic	34 Se Selenium	35 Br Bromine	36 Kr Krypton
37 Rb Rubidium	38 Sr Strontium	39 Y Yttrium	40 Zr Zirconium	41 Nb Niobium	42 Mo Molybdenum	43 Tc Technetium	44 Ru Ruthenium	45 Rh Rhodium	46 Pd Palladium	47 Ag Silver	48 Cd Cadmium	49 In Indium	50 Sn Tin	51 Sb Antimony	52 Te Tellurium	53 I Iodine	54 Xe Xenon
55 Cs Cesium	56 Ba Barium	57–71 La Lanthanum	72 Hf Hafnium	73 Ta Tantalum	74 W Tungsten	75 Re Rhenium	76 Os Osmium	77 Ir Iridium	78 Pt Platinum	79 Au Gold	80 Hg Mercury	81 Tl Thallium	82 Pb Lead	83 Bi Bismuth	84 Po Polonium	85 At Astatine	86 Rn Radon
87 Fr Francium	88 Ra Radium	89–103 Ac Actinium	104 Rf Rutherfordium	105 Db Dubnium	106 Sg Seaborgium	107 Bh Bohrium	108 Hs Hassium	109 Mt Meitnerium	110 DS Darmstadtium	111 Rg Roentgenium	112 Cn Copernicium	113 Uut Ununtrium	114 Uuq Ununquadium	115 Uup Ununpentium	116 Uuh Ununhexium	117 Uus Ununseptium	118 Uuo Ununoctium

58 Ce Cerium	59 Pr Praseodymium	60 Nd Neodymium	61 Pm Promethium	62 Sm Samarium	63 Eu Europium	64 Gd Gadolinium	65 Tb Terbium	66 Dy Dysprosium	67 Ho Holmium	68 Er Erbium	69 Tm Thulium	70 Yb Ytterbium	71 Lu Lutetium
90 Th Thorium	91 Pa Protactinium	92 U Uranium	93 Np Neptunium	94 Pu Plutonium	95 Am Americium	96 Cm Curium	97 Bk Berkelium	98 Cf Californium	99 Es Einsteinium	100 Fm Fermium	101 Md Mendelevium	102 No Nobelium	103 Lr Lawrencium

Another important piece of information given by the periodic table is the number of electrons in the outermost principal energy level (PEL) of each element. These electrons are most important when it comes to **reactivity** and bonding. The following table shows the number of electrons in the outermost PEL for elements in certain groups. Note the predictable pattern for these electrons:

Group number	1	2	13	14	15	16	17
Number of electrons in the outermost PEL	1	2	3	4	5	6	7

This pattern helps determine the **bonds** that can form between atoms to make **molecules**. Notice that group 18 (the noble gases) is missing from the table. That is because in these elements, the outermost PEL has 8 electrons. With that number, the PEL is considered to be "full," and the atom has no need to gain, lose, or share electrons with other atoms to achieve stability. So these particular gases are stable and will not react with other elements. Helium is an exception to this rule; although it has only 2 electrons in its outermost PEL, the PEL is full. Therefore, helium will not react with other elements.

Bonding

An atom is most stable when it has 8 electrons in the outermost PEL. Atoms are said to "desire" this condition and will gain or lose electrons or even share electrons to achieve this goal. This process is called **bonding**. A simple rule to remember is that similar atoms will share electrons. For example, nonmetals will share electrons with other nonmetals. Water is a good example: hydrogen and oxygen are both nonmetals and will share electrons so that each has a full outermost PEL. Oxygen in group 16 has 6 electrons in its outermost PEL. It needs 2 more to achieve stability. Hydrogen, in group 1, has just 1 electron in its outermost PEL. It needs 1 more to achieve stability. Thus, two hydrogen atoms will each share 1 electron with one oxygen atom. The oxygen atom will then have 6 plus 2, or 8, electrons in its outermost PEL, filling it completely. Each hydrogen atom will have 1 plus 1, or 2, electrons in its outermost PEL, filling it completely. This bonding process is shown in the diagram:

Bonding in a Water (H$_2$O) Molecule

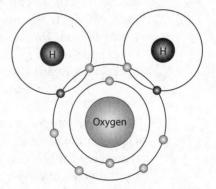

The other type of bonding involves the gain and loss of electrons between two atoms. These bonds occur when one atom is a metal and the other is a nonmetal. A perfect example is table salt, or sodium chloride. When these two atoms bond, the sodium atom (a metal) loses an electron to the chlorine atom (a nonmetal). Each atom then has the full 8 electrons in the outermost PEL. However, in each one the number of negatively charged electrons no longer balances the number of positively charged protons. So each atom is now an **ion** with an electrical charge. The bond forms as a result of the opposite charges attracting each other. This bonding process is shown in the diagram:

Bonding in Table Salt (NaCl) Molecules

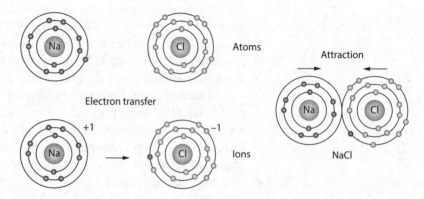

States of Matter

Matter exists in three states: solid, liquid, and gas. Each state of matter has different properties. In solids, indicated in chemistry notation by (s), the atoms or molecules are in a fixed position and are packed tightly. In liquids, indicated by (l), the atoms or molecules are touching, but they are not in a fixed position. That is what allows the liquid molecules to "roll over" each other and flow. In gases, indicated by (g), atoms or molecules are spaced far apart and have little to no attraction for each other.

Strengths of Materials

The different types of bonds between atoms have different strengths. Determining bond strength is a relatively easy task provided you have some data about the physical properties of the substances involved. Two of the most important properties to consider are the melting and boiling points of a substance. In general, the higher the melting or boiling point, the stronger the bonds between the atoms and molecules and the more energy it will take to break those bonds. For example, water has a boiling point of 100°C, while ethanol (drinking alcohol) has a boiling point of 78.4°C. The forces holding the water molecules together are stronger than those holding the alcohol molecules together. For another example, iron has a melting point of 1,538°C, while sodium chloride has a melting point of 801°C. Thus iron has stronger bonds than salt. That is the reason iron, not salt, is used to construct the frames of buildings!

There is a general rule regarding which substances have a higher melting point than others. In general, a compound made up of all nonmetallic elements (such as wax, $C_{20}H_{42}$) will have a low melting point. A compound containing a metal such as iron or potassium chloride will have a much higher melting point, indicating stronger bonds between the molecules. Substances that contain a semimetal or metalloid (such as the silicon in sand, SiO_2) will have a high melting point. The melting point of sand is over 1,700°C.

Chemical Energy

When atoms bond together, they possess a special type of energy called chemical energy. Energy is needed to break chemical bonds, causing substances to boil or melt. Energy is also needed to initiate chemical reactions, causing the chemicals to react. However, sometimes more energy is absorbed by a reaction than is released, and sometimes more energy is released than was absorbed. Here are two examples. When ammonium nitrate is dissolved in water, the reaction absorbs energy and will feel cold. This is called an **endothermic reaction**. For this type of reaction, the heat energy (or thermal energy) is written on the left side of the equation:

$$\text{Energy} + NH_4NO_3(s) + H_2O(l) \longrightarrow NH_4 + (aq) + NO_3 - (aq)$$

By contrast, when methane gas is burned, more energy is released than is absorbed. This excess energy is given off and will feel hot. This is called an **exothermic reaction**, and the heat energy is written on the right side of the equation:

$$CH_4(g) + O_2(g) \longrightarrow H_2O(l) + CO_2(g) + \text{Energy}$$

In the first reaction, because more energy was added than was released, the excess energy will be stored in the chemical bonds of the products of the reaction, $NH_4 + (aq) + NO_3 - (aq)$. In the second reaction, because more energy was released than was absorbed, there must have been more energy stored in the chemical bonds of the reactants, $CH_4(g) + O_2(g)$. These two types of reactions can be visually compared with the two following diagrams:

Exothermic and Endothermic Chemical Reactions

Also note that not just any amount of energy is needed to start a reaction. Instead, the reaction needs a minimal amount of energy, called the **activation energy**.

Reaction Rates

Other factors to consider when initiating a reaction are the conditions in which the reaction is occurring. Just because two molecules collide does not mean that they will react. For a reaction to take place, the molecules must collide effectively and with enough energy to react. One way to get molecules to collide more often and more effectively is to raise the temperature of the reaction. The added kinetic energy of each molecule will make the molecules hit each other harder and more frequently. This will cause them to react more often, speeding up the reaction. Using higher concentrations of reactants will also speed up a reaction by increasing the odds of the reactants hitting each other.

Other factors to consider in speeding up a reaction include pressure, surface area, and the use of catalysts. Increasing the pressure on gases (and gases only) causes the gas molecules to pack together more tightly and to collide more often. This speeds up a reaction. Using reactants that are powdered rather than in a single block will cause them to react faster because the small pieces have more surface area exposed and available to react. Finally, a catalyst will speed up a reaction. The most common catalysts are the enzymes in the human body. These are made up of protein and help speed up reactions. For example, digestive enzymes are catalysts that break down food quickly so that energy is rapidly available.

Chemical Equilibrium

Some reactions are reversible. In this type of reaction, as the reactants form products, some of the products react with each other to re-form the reactants. A reversible reaction can be counterproductive. One example is the Haber process, a reaction that is used to make ammonia:

$$3H_2(g) + N_2(g) \longleftrightarrow 2NH_3(l) + Heat$$

Note the double arrow in this reaction. This indicates that the reaction can be reversed. There are a number of ways to make sure that this reaction makes the desired product, ammonia. First, the amount of reactants must be kept high; that is, more hydrogen gas and nitrogen gas must be added to ensure that more ammonia is made. Second, as soon as the ammonia is made, it must be removed or drained from the reaction vessel. Third, the ammonia must be kept cold because heat is a product, too. Keeping the reaction cold removes the heat that reverses the reaction and causes the ammonia to break down.

Conservation of Mass

In chemical reactions there is conservation of mass. That is, the number of atoms of each element that go into the reaction must be the same as the number that come out. In the Haber process reaction previously noted, the 3 in front of the hydrogen gas means that there are three molecules of hydrogen gas. Because there is no number in front of the nitrogen gas, you can assume that the number of molecules is 1. Finally, the 2 in front of the ammonia indicates that two molecules of ammonia were made. The following diagram shows the reaction:

Haber Process Reaction

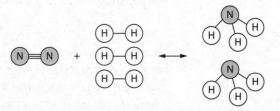

Note that there are two atoms of nitrogen to the left of the arrow (the reactant side) and two to the right of the arrow (the product side). Likewise, there are six hydrogen atoms to the left of the arrow and six to the right. Because the number of atoms of each element on either side of the arrow is the same, there is conservation of mass and the equation is said to be balanced. Suppose that the equation were written without the molecule numbers, simply as:

$$H_2(g) + N_2(g) \longleftrightarrow NH_3(l) + \text{Heat}$$

The equation would be wrong because it now indicates that two hydrogen atoms enter the reaction and three exit. It also now indicates that two nitrogen atoms enter the reaction and just one exits. Both are impossibilities. The molecule numbers are needed to balance a chemical reaction.

Nuclear Decay and Radioactivity

In a chemical reaction there is conservation of mass and atoms, but there are other reactions in which atoms can break down. For an atom to break down, there must be a change in the nucleus, or a **transmutation** (or sometimes **nucleosynthesis**). An example of a transmutation is the nuclear decay of radium-226 (Ra-226):

$$^{226}_{88}\text{Ra} \longrightarrow {}^{222}_{86}\text{Rn} + {}^{4}_{2}\text{He}$$

This shows a **radioactive decay** that releases an alpha particle. In this case, a radium nucleus decayed into a helium nucleus (alpha particle) and a radon nucleus. Another example is when Pb-214 decays naturally:

$$^{214}_{82}\text{Pb} \longrightarrow {}^{214}_{83}\text{Bi} + {}^{0}_{-1}\text{e}$$

The radioactive decay in this example releases a beta particle, $^{0}_{-1}\text{e}$. Finally, some nuclear decays emit gamma rays. In this case the element does not change. Instead, just the energy content of the nucleus changes as the high-energy gamma ray is emitted:

$$^{99}_{43}\text{Tc} \longrightarrow {}^{99}_{43}\text{Tc} + \gamma$$

The rate at which a substance decays due to radioactive emissions is called the half-life of the substance. Literally, the half-life is the time it takes for half of the mass of a sample to decay.

Besides undergoing a natural decay and transmutation, elements can be bombarded with another particle to cause a **fission** (splitting) reaction.

One example is the atomic bomb and the splitting of a uranium nucleus by bombarding it with a neutron:

$$^{235}_{92}U + {^1_0}n \longrightarrow {^{141}_{56}}Ba + {^{92}_{36}}Kr + 3{^1_0}n + energy$$

Note that this reaction is exothermic. The released energy is what makes the bomb so destructive. If properly controlled, a fission reaction can be used in a nuclear reactor to produce energy with no greenhouse gas emission. Another nuclear reaction that you witness every day is a **fusion** reaction. You have also been exposed to its radiation (in the form of light) and heat. This is the reaction that occurs within the stars and sun. Inside the sun is a fusion reaction that takes the simplest nuclei of hydrogen and fuses them together to make helium:

$$4{^1_1}H \longrightarrow {^4_2}He + 2{^0_1}e + energy$$

The newly formed nuclei can join with other nuclei to form other elements. In fact, the stars are the "factories" that create the elements that you know of on the periodic table. Once again, take note of the energy released in this exothermic reaction. This energy can be calculated using Einstein's famous equation $E = mc^2$.

CHALLENGE Matter and Its Interactions

1. The number of positively charged particles in the nucleus of the atom is also the **(atomic mass/atomic number)** of the atom.

2. Sodium (Na) is a **(metal/nonmetal/semimetal)**.

3. When energy is released from a reaction, the reaction is said to be **(balanced/ endothermic/exothermic)**.

4. The rate at which a reaction takes place can be increased by **(an increase/ a decrease)** in temperature.

5. A substance with a low melting and boiling point has **(stronger/weaker)** forces holding the atoms and molecules together.

CHALLENGE ANSWERS
Matter and Its Interactions

1. **atomic number:** The number of positively charged particles in the nucleus of the atom is also the atomic number of the atom. This number can be found on the periodic table.

2. **metal:** Sodium (Na) is a metal, as metals are located on the right side and middle of the periodic table. One exception is hydrogen (H), which is a nonmetal.

3. **exothermic:** When energy is released from a reaction, the reaction is said to be exothermic. When energy is absorbed by a reaction, it is said to be endothermic.

4. **increase:** The rate at which a reaction takes place can be increased by an increase in temperature, because an increase in temperature makes the reactants collide more often and with more energy to react.

5. **weaker:** A substance with low melting and boiling points has weaker forces holding the atoms and molecules together.

2 Motion and Stability: Forces and Interactions

KEY TERMS: acceleration, electric field, force, friction, gravity, magnetic field, momentum, velocity

Gravitational Forces

All objects exert a certain **force** on each other. This force is called the gravitational force, or **gravity**. In terms of gravity, an object with a greater mass will have a greater pull than an object with less mass. An apple falling to the ground will pull on Earth, but the pull of Earth on the apple will be much, much greater. This is the English physicist Isaac Newton's universal law of gravitation:

$$F_g = \frac{Gm_1 m_2}{r^2}$$

Note that this equation for the force of gravity (F_g) takes into the account the masses of the two objects (m_1 and m_2) and a gravitational constant (G), and it takes into account the distance between the two objects (r) to the second power (r^2). In regard to the distance between the two objects, as the objects are moved farther away from each other, the force will become exponentially less. For example, if the two objects are 2 meters apart, then 2^2 means that the force is divided by the number 4. But if the same two objects are 3 meters apart, then 3^2 means that the force is divided by the number 9. Dividing by 9 makes the force much less than does dividing by 4.

Electrostatic Forces

The French scientist Charles-Augustin de Coulomb made a similar connection between charged particles. Two objects of the same charge will repel each other, but two objects with opposite charges will attract each other. The force of the repulsion or attraction can be determined using the following formula:

$$F = k\frac{q_1 q_2}{r^2}$$

Note how this equation looks similar to the equation for determining the force of gravity. Because you are measuring the force due to electrostatic charge, you are concerned not with the masses of the objects, but rather with the charges of the objects.

Magnetism

Magnets with their two poles can repel or attract the poles of other magnets. Like electrostatic charges, same poles will repel each other and opposite poles will attract each other. This is because of the (invisible) **magnetic field** lines that exist about the poles of a magnet:

Magnetic Field Lines

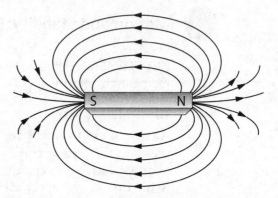

Note how the field lines move away from the north pole of the magnet and toward the south pole of the magnet. Because of the iron in the inner core of Earth, a similar magnetic field exists around the planet. That is why Earth also has a north magnetic pole and a south magnetic pole. A similar situation exists for positive and negative charges in an **electric field** where the lines go away from the positive charge and toward the negative charge:

Electric Field Lines

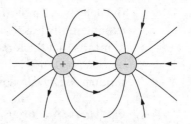

A magnetic field can also be created using electricity. When electric wire is wrapped around a piece of metal, the metal will be magnetized when the electricity is turned on. A device of this kind is called an electromagnet. Electromagnets have many uses. A junkyard uses an electromagnet to lift heavy metallic items. A doorbell uses electromagnets to produce amplified sounds and the movement of the clapper. Likewise, when a magnet is passed through a coil of wire, the wire will start to generate an electric current. That is how a power plant generates electricity. As long as the magnetic field around the wire keeps changing, a current will be produced.

Newton's Laws of Motion

Isaac Newton also developed three laws governing the physics of motion. According to Newton's first law of motion, an object in motion will stay in motion, while an object at rest will stay at rest. However, this will change if a force is applied to the object in motion or at rest. For example, a car rolling down a hill will continue to roll. But if it rolls into a brick wall, it will come to an abrupt stop. Likewise, a car that is parked on the street is not in motion and will stay at rest. But if a truck comes crashing into it, the car will move as a result of the crash.

Newton's second law of motion describes what happens to the **acceleration** of an object when a force (a push or a pull) is applied to that object. For example, when an object at rest is struck by a moving object, it accelerates from zero **velocity** (speed and direction) to a new velocity. This law of motion is expressed by the equation $F = ma$, where F is the force (measured in newtons, N), m is the mass (measured in kilograms, kg), and a is the acceleration (in meters per seconds squared, m/s^2). An object falling due to the force of gravity near Earth's surface will have an acceleration of 9.81 m/s^2. Because force and acceleration have a direct relationship, the more force applied to an object, the greater the acceleration.

A force that counteracts acceleration is **friction**. If you slide a book across a tabletop, the book will quickly come to a stop. The reason it stops is the frictional force produced by the rubbing of the book's surface against the tabletop. Frictional force works in the opposite direction to that of a moving object and slows down its motion.

Newton's third law of motion states that when one object exerts a force on a second object, the second object exerts an opposite and equal force on the first object. An example is an ice skater who pushes against the boards at an ice rink. As the ice skater pushes against the boards, the boards push back causing the ice skater to bounce off of the boards.

Momentum

Every moving object has a certain velocity, that is, a speed and direction. If you know the velocity and mass of the object, you can calculate its **momentum**. The momentum of a moving object is the quantity of its motion. Momentum is calculated as $p = mv$ where p is the momentum of the object (in units of kg•m/s), m is the mass of the object (in kilograms, kg), and v is the velocity of the object (in meters per second, m/s). Remember that momentum depends on both mass and velocity. For example, a baseball weighing 145 grams and moving at a velocity of 40 meters per second (90 mph) will not have as much momentum as a truck weighing 5,600,000 grams and moving at a velocity of 20 meters per second.

An important property of momentum is that it is conserved. That is, when two objects collide, the sum of the momentum that they possessed before the collision will be equal to the sum of the momentum that they possess after the collision. This property is demonstrated when two billiards balls collide and then separate, when two cars hit each other head-on, or when a rifle produces kickback after a bullet is fired.

CHALLENGE   Motion and Stability: Forces and Interactions

Choose the word or phrase that makes each sentence true.

1. When the force on an object increases, the acceleration of the object will **(decrease/increase)**.

2. Magnetic field lines go **(away from/toward)** a negatively charged particle.

3. Momentum is calculated by multiplying mass by **(acceleration/velocity)**.

4. Opposite charges, like opposite poles on a magnet, will **(attract/repel)** each other.

5. Mass, energy, and momentum are always **(conserved/destroyed)** when a reaction or process takes place.

CHALLENGE ANSWERS
Motion and Stability: Forces and Interactions

1. **increase:** According to the equation $F=ma$, when the force on an object increases, the acceleration of the object will increase.

2. **toward:** Magnetic field lines go toward a negatively charged particle, just as they go toward the south pole of a magnet.

3. **velocity:** Momentum is calculated by multiplying mass by velocity. Force is calculated by multiplying mass by acceleration.

4. **attract:** Opposite charges, like opposite poles on a magnet, will attract each other. Like charges and poles will repel each other.

5. **conserved:** Mass, energy, and momentum are always conserved when a reaction or process takes place. That is, they cannot be created or destroyed.

 Energy

KEY TERMS: energy, heat, kinetic energy, mechanical energy, potential energy, temperature

Mechanical Energy: Kinetic and Potential Energy

Energy is the ability to do work. Scientists take careful note of the transfer of energy from one system to another and the conversion of one form of energy to another. Two forms of energy that are regularly encountered are **kinetic energy** and **potential energy**. Kinetic energy is the energy that an object has while it is in motion. Potential energy, by contrast, is the energy an object has stored within it. Because kinetic energy involves motion, the velocity and mass of the object are needed to calculate kinetic energy. The equation for this calculation is $KE = mv^2$. Potential energy is the energy stored within an object. For example, when an object is lifted above a surface, it has the potential to fall back down. Potential energy therefore depends upon the height (h) that the object is above the surface. The equation for potential energy is $PE = mgh$ where g is the acceleration due to gravity, 9.81 m/s².

Mechanical energy is the term used to define the sum of the kinetic energy and potential energy that an object has while moving. A book falling to the ground has both kinetic energy (because it is moving) and potential energy (because it has not yet hit the ground). The swinging pendulum of a clock is another example. At the high points of its swing, the pendulum has the most kinetic energy and at the middle (low) point of its swing, it has the least kinetic energy. As the pendulum swings, one form of energy is converted to the other, and back again. The total amount of energy is conserved; no energy is lost. The total mechanical energy remains the same because mechanical energy is the sum of kinetic and potential energies.

Conservation of Energy

Energy is always conserved. That is, energy cannot be created or destroyed. It can only be converted from one form to another. Say that a block is held 2.5 meters above the ground. If you let go of the block, it starts to fall. This block, which was once at rest, now has a velocity. What does that show? The potential energy of the block is converted to kinetic energy as the block falls through the air. Conservation of energy is a basic principle that underlies many everyday devices that people use and take for granted. For example, a battery turns chemical energy into electrical energy; a toaster turns electrical energy into heat energy; a lightbulb turns electrical energy into light energy. The potential energy of the chemical bonds in a fuel can be converted to heat and light energy. The potential energy of a book held above the ground can be converted to kinetic energy when dropped and eventually into sound energy when the book hits the ground.

Heat and Temperature

Energy always flows from a higher concentration to a lower concentration. Consider thermal energy (**heat**) and its flow. If the two blocks shown (assume the same mass and material) at two different temperatures are put together, what will the final temperature be?

Assuming that no energy can enter or escape the system, the final temperature will be 60°C. Heat will flow from the higher temperature to lower temperature. That is why various kinds of insulation are used in homes to prevent the heat inside from flowing out into the cold air outside.

Do not confuse heat and temperature. Heat is thermal energy. **Temperature**, by contrast, is a measure of the motion of molecules. Strictly speaking, temperature is defined as the average kinetic energy of molecules.

CHALLENGE	Energy

Choose the word or phrase that makes each sentence true.

1. Stored energy is called (**kinetic/potential**) energy.

2. mv^2 is used to calculate (**kinetic/potential/nuclear**) energy.

3. A battery converts (**chemical/electrical**) energy to (**chemical/electrical**) energy.

4. Insulation in a home prevents (**heat/coldness**) from entering or exiting the home.

5. Average kinetic energy is the definition of (**heat/temperature**).

CHALLENGE ANSWERS
Energy

1. **potential:** Stored energy is called potential energy, while kinetic energy is energy in motion.

2. **kinetic:** mv^2 is used to calculate kinetic energy. $PE = mgh$ and $E = mc^2$ are used to calculate potential and nuclear energy, respectively.

3. **chemical, electrical:** A battery converts chemical energy to electrical energy. The energy stored in the chemical bonds in a battery is what the battery uses to produce electricity.

4. **heat:** Insulation in a home prevents heat from entering or exiting a home. Keep in mind that heat always flows from a higher temperature to a lower temperature.

5. **temperature:** Average kinetic energy is the definition of temperature; temperature measures the motion of molecules.

 ## Waves and Their Applications in Technologies for Information Transfer

KEY TERMS: diffraction, electromagnetic radiation, frequency, interference, photoelectric effect, photons, wave, wavelength, wave-particle duality of light

Electromagnetic Radiation

Electromagnetic radiation is a form of energy that travels through space as a **wave**. One kind of electromagnetic radiation is light. The kind of light that humans can see is called visible light. There are also other types of light, such as infrared light and ultraviolet light, that humans cannot see. Besides light, there are also many other kinds of radiation.

When radiation travels through a vacuum, it moves at the speed of light, 3×10^8 meters per second, and is represented by the letter v. All radiation has both a **frequency** (f) and a **wavelength** (λ, or lambda). The frequency is the number of wave cycles in a given time unit. The wavelength is the distance between two successive crests or other similar points in a wave. The speed, frequency, and wavelength of radiation are related according to the equation $v = f\lambda$. Because the speed of light remains constant (for our purposes here), frequency and wavelength are inversely proportional to each other. That is, as one increases in value, the other must decrease in value so that v stays constant. Note that this equation does not apply only to light in a vacuum. It also holds true for sound, for seismic waves traveling through the ground after an earthquake, and for light traveling through a medium like water or glass. Waves may change some of their properties when they travel through another medium. For example, a sound you hear in air will not be the same sound you hear in water. But one thing common to all waves is that they transfer energy along them as they travel.

Besides light, other kinds of waves include radio waves, microwaves, x-rays, gamma rays, UV rays, and infrared waves. Each of these types of waves has its own specific range of wavelengths. The following diagram shows these types of waves. Note that the types of radiation on the left have a longer wavelength (on top) and a shorter frequency (powers of ten below). From left to right, the wavelengths decrease and frequencies increase. That confirms the inverse relationship.

The Frequency and Wavelengths of Radiation

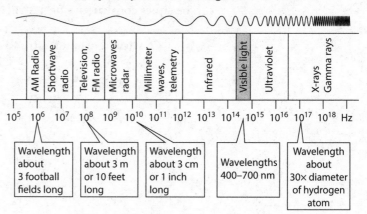

Uses of Radiation

Some forms of radiation are useful in medicine and dentistry. X-rays and gamma rays are useful in imaging parts of the body and detecting medical problems. However, long-term exposure to both types of radiation can be harmful to human tissue and DNA, and both need to be used with caution. Doctors use them sparingly, and medical technicians make sure to avoid exposing themselves to large amounts of radiation.

Other types of radiation with longer wavelengths are used to provide wireless telephone and computer connections. For example, radiation emitted by a router allows anyone within a certain range to surf the Web without interruption. Radiation from a remote control device allows you to change a television channel without moving from your chair. Radio transmission is a form of radiation. The transmitter has the ability to turn sound energy from human voices into waves that can be transmitted through the air. A radio can then interpret the various frequencies and amplitudes of the wave to turn the wave back into sound. These are much weaker forms of radiation and do not pose a risk to the health of living organisms.

Electromagnetic radiation is used today in many devices to transmit information in digital form. For example, in a fax (facsimile) machine, a picture can be scanned into a digital image that is then converted into what is called a bitmap. The bitmap is then transferred over a phone line to another fax machine that converts it into a printable picture. No matter what device is used to transmit information digitally, the same process is followed: information is first converted into an electromagnetic signal and then transferred either wirelessly, through a wire, through a fiber-optic cable, or even through a media storage device. A system that connects many devices to allow a number of people to access the information transmitted or stored is called a network. Networks can be configured in a number of ways to suit the needs of those who need to access information.

Wave-Particle Dual Nature of Light

Light acts as a wave, but it can also act as if it were made up of particles. This dual nature is called the **wave-particle duality of light**. Evidence that light acts as a wave is that light waves interfere with each other. The **interference** can be either constructive or destructive, as shown in the diagram:

Constructive and Destructive Interference of Light Waves

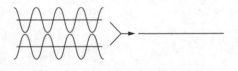

The top diagram shows constructive interference; the waves are said to be in phase with each other, creating a new wave with greater height (called amplitude) when combined. The bottom diagram shows destructive interference; the waves are said to be out of phase with each other, and they cancel each other out.

Another evidence for light acting as a wave is called **diffraction**. When light passes through two slits in a solid barrier, the light waves will be diffracted, or bent. This will cause a pattern of constructive and destructive patterns to appear on a screen beyond the barrier. You can produce this effect at home using a flashlight and a piece of cardboard in a dark room. You might also have seen it on the wall in a dark room when light was passing between two closely spaced blinds.

DNA is the molecule that codes for **amino acid** sequences. Amino acids are the building blocks of proteins, the molecules that make up muscles, the heart and other **organs**, eyes, hormones, enzymes, antibodies, and skin. A certain sequence of nucleotides in DNA tells your body how to put the amino acids into chains of a certain order. Once the amino acids are in a certain order, different types of tissues and organs can form. The endless number of possible sequences of amino acids is what gives organs and **organ systems** incredible diversity in structure and function. This is why a heart is different from a kidney and why each serves a different purpose from the other and from other substances in the body, such as enzymes and antibodies.

Homeostasis

Organ systems show a wide range of diversity, yet they all function together. For example, the mouth, stomach, esophagus, and intestines are very different in structure and function, but they work together for digestion. Other examples are the heart, veins, arteries, and capillaries working together to circulate blood, while the nose, lungs, trachea, bronchioles, and alveoli work together to draw oxygen into the body and expel carbon dioxide. All of these systems working together help keep the body in a normal, healthy state. This helps the body maintain **homeostasis**.

Homeostasis (literally meaning "similar standing") is the state in which an organism's body functions are properly regulated so that those functions remain stable. For example, when you exercise, carbon dioxide builds up in the blood. To counter this, your breathing rate increases to expel excess carbon dioxide, and your heart pumps faster and harder to move more oxygen to the cells. When you eat a meal, your levels of insulin increase to counter the higher levels of glucose entering the bloodstream. Even plants have feedback mechanisms that help them maintain homeostasis. Plants open or close the stomata on the leaves to adjust the amount of gas and water vapor exchange occurring at the leaf. They do this in response to changes in moisture and air temperature. This helps the plants maintain homeostasis.

Levels of Organization

Every organism is a living system with numerous components arranged in several levels of organization. The highest level is organ systems such as the respiratory system and circulatory system. These systems are made up of numerous organs functioning together to perform functions such as respiration or circulation. The organs themselves are composed of various **tissues** such as the muscle and valves within the heart. Each tissue is made up of cells, the basic units of life. Within cells there are **organelles** that perform different functions. Some organelles include the cell membrane that controls what enters and exits the cell, the nucleus that is the cell's "command center" and holds the DNA, mitochondria that are responsible for energy production, ribosomes that assist in protein synthesis, and vacuoles for storage. Each of these organelles is in turn composed of large molecules that are formed from atoms, the basic unit of matter. These levels of organization can be summarized as follows:

Atoms → Molecules → Organelles → Cells → Tissues →
Organs → Organ Systems → Organisms

| CHALLENGE | From Molecules to Organisms: Structures and Processes |

Choose the word or phrase that makes each sentence true.

1. Proteins are made up of (**DNA/fats/amino acids**).

2. Inside a cell there are (**tissues/organs/organelles**).

3. Regulatory mechanisms in living organisms help them remain (**stable/unstable**) and maintain homeostasis.

4. The basic unit of life is the (**atom/cell**); the basic unit of matter is the (**atom/cell**).

5. DNA is located in a cell's (**mitochondria/vacuoles/nucleus**).

<u>CHALLENGE ANSWERS</u>

From Molecules to Organisms: Structures and Processes

1. **DNA:** DNA provides the code for amino acid sequences.

2. **organelles:** Inside a cell there are organelles, each with its own function to help the cell carry out its life processes.

3. **stable:** Feedback mechanisms in living organisms help them remain stable and maintain homeostasis.

4. **cell, atom:** The basic unit of life is the cell; the basic unit of matter is the atom.

5. **nucleus:** DNA is located in a cell's nucleus, an organelle that serves as the "command center" for the cell.

 Ecosystems: Interactions, Energy, and Dynamics

KEY TERMS: aerobically, anaerobically, autotrophs, carrying capacity, cellular respiration, ecosystem, equilibrium, food chain, food web, heterotrophs, photosynthesis

Earth's Early Atmosphere

How and when did life first arise on Earth? Many scientists think that the key lies in Earth's early atmosphere. When life first appeared on Earth approximately 3.5 billion years ago, the atmosphere was quite different from what it is today. It is thought that Earth's early atmosphere was composed of carbon dioxide, ammonia, methane, and water. (By contrast, today's atmosphere is 21 percent oxygen and 78 percent nitrogen.) Scientists have re-created the early atmosphere in the laboratory and have subjected that mix of carbon dioxide, ammonia, methane, and water to simulated lightning strikes (electron beams) and sunlight (ultraviolet light). In these experiments, those four basic molecules of life began to form larger molecules, the very same macromolecules needed to form cells. It is believed that early Earth was covered in these organic macromolecules. Scientists call this the "hot thin soup" concept.

Autotrophs and Heterotrophs

It is thought that over time, the macromolecules on early Earth's surface reacted and combined with each other, and this process eventually gave rise to living cells. These first cells were probably able to survive by consuming the organic molecules that were present in the hot thin soup. Because these cells fed on those available materials, they are termed **heterotrophs**. And given the nature of Earth's early atmosphere, it is also believed that these first heterotrophs were capable of **anaerobic** function; that is, they could function without the use of oxygen gas, O_2. These first heterotrophs were also able to produce carbon dioxide, which is thought to have sparked the evolution of **autotrophs**, organisms that can produce their own food. Autotrophs (such as plants and algae) consumed the carbon dioxide produced by the early heterotrophs and produced oxygen gas, which the early heterotrophs were not equipped to use. Some early heterotrophs evolved so that they could use the oxygen-rich atmosphere generated by the autotrophs. Those that did not died off.

The autotrophs were able to produce food for themselves because they could capture the sun's energy and use it in the process called **photosynthesis**. In photosynthesis, carbon dioxide and water are combined with energy from the sun to produce oxygen gas and glucose, a simple sugar that provides energy. The chemical formula for photosynthesis is:

$$\text{Sunlight} + 6CO_2 + 6H_2O \rightarrow 6O_2 + C_6H_{12}O_6$$

In the sugar produced by photosynthesis, it is the bonds between the carbon, hydrogen, and oxygen atoms that store energy for later use. The sunlight energy that entered the leaves of the plant is now chemical energy, which is stored in the glucose molecules. Glucose can be converted to starch and stored in the plant.

Respiration

Animals consume plants to obtain the simple sugars and complex starches that are stored within the plants. In an animal's digestive system, the starches are broken down into the simple sugar glucose. This glucose enters cells where it is broken down in an **aerobic** process (with the use of oxygen gas). This process is called **cellular respiration**. The reaction for cellular respiration should look familiar; it is the opposite of photosynthesis:

$$6O_2 \text{ and } C_6H_{12}O_6 \rightarrow 6CO_2 + 6H_2O + \text{Heat Energy}$$

Notice how the sunlight that was once a reactant in photosynthesis is now heat energy, one of the products of cellular respiration. During cellular respiration one other molecule is produced, adenosine triphosphate, or ATP. This molecule stores energy in cells and is a ready source of energy as needed. Keep in mind that an animal can go weeks without food, days without water, but only minutes without oxygen. Why? Animals constantly need oxygen to react with glucose to make ATP and energy. Without the oxygen, energy production stops and the animal dies.

Energy Flow in an Ecosystem

An **ecosystem** is a community of organisms interacting with each other within a particular environment. In an ecosystem, autotrophs are the only organisms that produce their own food. Their ability to convert solar energy into food is the key to survival for all organisms in the ecosystem. Organisms that cannot produce their own food must consume the autotrophs to obtain energy. As one organism consumes another, energy is transferred from the prey to the predator. These transfers of energy can be diagrammed in a **food chain**. For example, if a rabbit eats grasses and is then eaten by a wolf, the food chain would look like this:

Sunlight → Grasses and Other Plants → Rabbit → Wolf

Of course, these are not the only organisms that consume each other. A fuller diagram showing the transfer of energy among multiple organisms is called a **food web**. Here is an example:

A Food Web

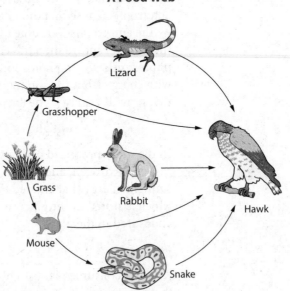

While there is conservation of mass at all times in this system, as each organism is consumed, some energy is lost to the surrounding ecosystem. This can be summarized in an energy pyramid:

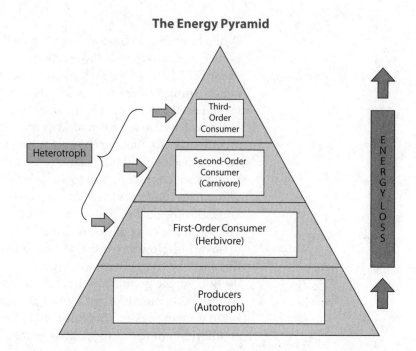

The Energy Pyramid

Humans, as third-order or tertiary consumers, are at the top of the energy pyramid. Besides having easy access to food, humans have also developed advanced technology and medicine. That is why the human population has risen dramatically over time. There was a time when disease and hunger kept human populations in check. In 1800 it was estimated that only about one billion people inhabited Earth. Today, however, when people live longer and healthier lives, there are an estimated 7.5 billion people on Earth. Now a new question must be addressed: what is Earth's **carrying capacity**? That is, how many people can Earth accommodate? No one knows, but when the Earth can no longer support more humans, the human population will once again be in check and stop growing.

Human Impact

The increase in the human population raises concerns about reducing the territories of other animal species, pushing them into competition for territory and food and possibly extinction. Even the building of a dam to meet the needs of humans can impact hundreds of species that live along a river. In addition to threatening other species, humans themselves face limits on the amount of natural resources available on planet Earth. In the future, renewable energy will have to be a way of life. Other factors to consider are pollution, waste, and the spread of new diseases among people living in close contact with one another. The introduction of an invasive species by humans can also be threatening to other species. For example, rats may be transported by ship to an island where there are no predators to keep the rat population in check. The invasive rats can impose much stress on the island species by competing for food and territory.

Population Equilibrium

While humans can have an impact on wildlife and their habitat, natural occurrences can impact those ecosystems as well. Normally, the populations of species in an ecosystem remain stable. This is called populations at **equilibrium**. While the populations might change slightly with the seasons, for the most part, they stay the same year after year. However, a natural cause such as disease can suddenly impact one species, producing effects on other species that depend on the first species for food. For example, if a certain species of rabbit died off from disease, the local wolves and hawks might find it harder to find food, causing their populations to decline. Other natural factors that can reduce wildlife populations include flooding and lightning strikes that start wildfires.

To beat the odds of survival, many animal species produce large numbers of offspring. However, if the population of the species becomes too large, there will be competition for resources, and the population will start to decline. As the population declines, competition will decrease and there will be less competition for resources. That will allow the population to begin growing again. This constant flux within a range is called population equilibrium, in which the relative number of organisms remains constant over time.

One other way of beating the odds is for groups of adults to share the job of raising offspring. For example, in a pride of lions, there might be two male lions that protect the territory, while a larger number of females raise the offspring and hunt for food. A clan of hyenas will work together to hunt and raise offspring. Meerkats will work together to raise their young and keep an eye out for predators. Humans have made efforts to help animal populations thrive. Law enforcement agents work to prevent poaching and illegal hunting. Conservation experts work to preserve natural habitats and also operate rehabilitation and release programs for animals that have been injured or abandoned.

CHALLENGE **Ecosystems: Interactions, Energy, and Dynamics**

Choose the word or phrase that makes each sentence true.

1. A population that has reached equilibrium is (**declining/remaining stable/ increasing**).

2. The biggest users of Earth's natural resources are (**plants/wildlife/humans**).

3. A food (**energy pyramid/web/chain**) illustrates the various levels of energy in an ecosystem.

4. The use of oxygen and glucose to produce energy is called (**respiration/photosynthesis**).

5. Photosynthesis will occur in (**an autotroph/a heterotroph**).

CHALLENGE ANSWERS

Ecosystems: Interactions, Energy, and Dynamics

1. **remaining stable:** A population that has reached equilibrium is relatively stable in number. The number may change if conditions in the ecosystem change.

2. **humans:** The biggest users of Earth's natural resources are humans. This is why clean, renewable energy sources are needed.

3. **energy pyramid:** A food energy pyramid illustrates the various levels of energy in an ecosystem. The most energy is contained in the producers; the least energy is contained in the tertiary consumers.

4. **respiration:** The use of oxygen and glucose to produce energy is called respiration. The opposite of this process is photosynthesis.

5. **autotroph:** Photosynthesis will occur in an autotroph. Examples of autotrophs are plants and algae.

7 Heredity: Inheritance and Variation of Traits

KEY TERMS: chromosome, gene, meiosis, mitosis, mutation, Punnett square, trait

Mitosis

The cells in the body of an organism continually grow and divide. This allows the organism to grow in size and in ability. Growth also allows for sexual maturity and the ability to pass on **traits**, or characteristics, to offspring. The process of cell division is called **mitosis**.

To function properly, cells need a large surface-area-to-volume ratio. That is, they need to be small in volume. To maintain this small volume, cells will divide from the larger parent cells into identical "daughter cells." But before a cell divides, it must make a copy of its DNA so that each daughter cell has an exact copy of the DNA present. Having an exact copy of the DNA will ensure that the two new cells will function the same way as the parent cell. Although many steps are involved in mitosis, the goals always remain the same: to reduce the volume of the cell and make sure that the genetic code being passed on in the DNA is identical from parent to daughter. The DNA is contained within structures called **chromosomes** within the nucleus. The chromosomes are replicated (copied) during mitosis. This is illustrated in the following diagram:

Mitosis

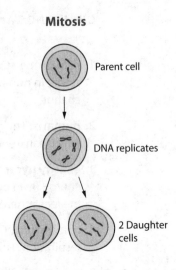

Parent cell

DNA replicates

2 Daughter cells

Notice that the two daughter cells have exactly the same DNA makeup as the parent cell.

Meiosis

A special kind of cell division is **meiosis**. This type of cell division produces the sex cells called eggs and sperm. These cells are needed for sexual reproduction. Unlike mitosis, which produces two new cells, meiosis produces four sex cells. Each of these four sex cells has exactly half as many chromosomes as the parent cell. When a sex cell from a male (with half the number of needed chromosomes) is combined with a sex cell from a female (with half the number of needed chromosomes), the offspring will then have the correct number of chromosomes. This can be seen in the diagram:

Meiosis

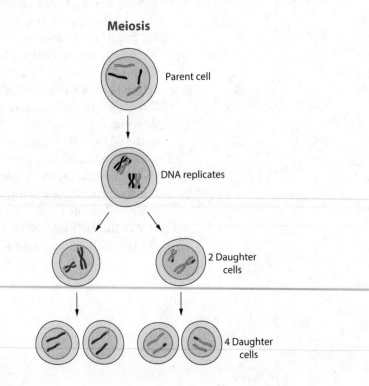

Parent cell

DNA replicates

2 Daughter cells

4 Daughter cells

Genetic Variation

One important benefit of meiosis is that it assists sexual reproduction in creating diversity among species members. Diversity is crucial for ensuring that no disease or environmental factor wipes out an entire population or species. Meiosis produces sex cells with half-sets of chromosomes. The chromosomes contain **genes**, segments of DNA that contain codes for various traits. When the sex cells from two parents are combined, the resulting chromosome mix distributes the traits to the offspring in varied ways. That is how diversity is maintained.

This process can be mapped using a device called a **Punnett square**. Say for example that a mother has brown eyes and a father has blue eyes. Will the children of this couple have blue eyes or brown eyes? A Punnett square will give the answer. In a Punnett square, the genes for traits are indicated with abbreviations. The gene for brown eyes happens to be genetically dominant over the gene for blue eyes. That is, if there is a gene of each kind present, the organism will have brown eyes, not blue. In a Punnett square, a dominant gene is shown with an uppercase letter, so the gene for brown eyes is shown with an uppercase B. The gene for blue eyes is genetically recessive (i.e., not dominant), so it is shown with a lowercase b.

Each parent has two genes for eye color. Suppose that the mother's two genes are B and b. She will have brown eyes because the brown gene is dominant. Suppose that the father has blue eyes. Because the blue gene is recessive, both of his genes must code for blue eyes, b and b. Now set up the Punnett square. The mother's eye-color genes are shown in the left column. The father's eye-color genes are shown at the top. The other unshaded boxes show how the parents' genes might combine in possible offspring.

Punnett Square

	b	b
B	Bb	Bb
b	bb	bb

Of the four unshaded boxes, two contain the dominant B gene that produces brown eyes. This means that the offspring have a 50 percent chance of having brown eyes. The two remaining unshaded boxes do not have the dominant B gene, meaning that the offspring have a 50 percent chance of not having brown eyes and instead will have blue eyes. This is how diversity is created in a species population.

Mutations

Occasionally in cell division the DNA of a parent cell is not copied exactly. This break in the DNA sequence is called a **mutation**. Some mutations may be beneficial to an organism, but most are not and may lead to life-threatening disorders. Mutations may also be due to environmental factors. For example, constant exposure to a harmful chemical can impact the DNA of a cell. When the defective cell divides and reproduces, more cells carry the mutation and can develop cancer.

CHALLENGE Heredity: Inheritance and Variation of Traits

Choose the word or phrase that makes each sentence true.

1. Mitosis produces daughter cells with **(half as many/the same number of)** chromosomes as the parent cell.

2. Sex cells are produced via **(mitosis/meiosis)**.

3. A change in the DNA of a cell is called **(a mutation/an evolution)**.

4. Genetic variation leads to a population of **(diverse/unicellular)** organisms in an ecosystem.

5. When an organism carries both a dominant and a recessive gene for a particular trait, the **(dominant/recessive)** gene is the one that will be expressed in the organism.

CHALLENGE ANSWERS

Heredity: Inheritance and Variation of Traits

1. **the same number of:** Mitosis produces daughter cells with the same number of chromosomes as the parent cell because the daughter cells are exactly like the parent cell.

2. **meiosis:** Sex cells are produced via meiosis. In this case each of the four daughter cells will have half as many chromosomes as the parent cell.

3. **a mutation:** A change in the DNA of a cell is called a mutation. Most of the time, this process will have a negative impact on the cell and organism.

4. **diverse:** Genetic variation leads to a population of diverse organisms in an ecosystem. This helps ensure the survival of the population so that no single factor can eliminate the species.

5. **dominant:** When an organism carries both a dominant and a recessive gene for a particular trait, the dominant gene is the one that will be expressed in the organism.

8 Biological Evolution: Unity and Diversity

KEY TERMS: adapted, competition, evolution, extinction, natural selection

Common Ancestry

DNA, which carries the genetic code, has been vital in helping scientists determine how different species are related. By analyzing the nucleotide sequences through a process called gel electrophoresis, scientists can compare the DNA of different individuals and, based on such comparisons, determine which species share a common ancestor.

An evolutionary tree is one way of showing **evolution** from a common ancestor. A sample common evolutionary tree for apes and humans is shown. The points along the diagonal line where the links between species intersect indicate a common ancestor. The nearer the point of intersection, the more closely related are the two species. Note the percent correlation between the DNA of the species shown in the tree.

An Evolutionary Tree

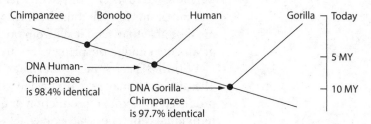

Related species will often have similar anatomical structures. The similarity may often be visible even when the species are not very closely related. The following diagram shows the similarity between the limbs of several related vertebrate species.

Limb Structures of Related Species

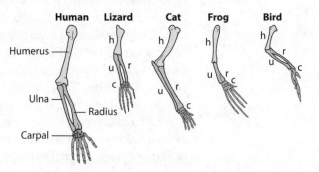

Related species will also have similar embryos. The following diagram shows the embryos of several related vertebrate species. Can you tell which one is the human embryo? The order from left to right is fish, salamander, turtle, chicken, rabbit, and human.

Embryos of Related Species

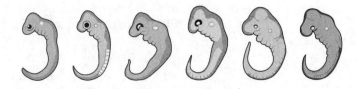

Natural Selection

Over time, species have evolved from common ancestors to populate Earth with all of the different kinds of organisms alive today. How does the process of evolution operate? The English scientist Charles Darwin identified **natural selection** as the mechanism underlying evolution. Natural selection is sometimes called "survival of the fittest," but the process is actually rather more complex. All species engage in **competition** for food and other resources. Those that can compete effectively are able to survive and reproduce; those that cannot may face **extinction**; that is, the species may die out. To compete effectively, an organism must be well adapted to its environment; that is, it must be able to find shelter and nutritious food, it must be able to survive in the local climate, and it must be able to defend itself from predators either by fleeing, hiding, or producing enough offspring to ensure the species' survival.

Within a species, individuals may differ physically from each other. The difference may perhaps be due to the varying combinations of genes produced by sexual reproduction or even to a gene mutation. Most individual differences have no effect on survival. However, a particular trait may make an individual better **adapted** to some change in the environment, that is, better able to thrive under the new conditions. That individual will be more likely to survive than others of the same species. For example, the new trait may enable an individual to cope with a climate that is becoming colder. An individual with a better chance of surviving has a better chance of producing offspring, who may also carry the new trait. Over time, the number of individuals with the new trait is likely to increase, and over a longer period, as further changes take place and differences between individuals increase, eventually a wholly new species may evolve.

How exactly does this mechanism work? Perhaps there is an environmental change such as an increase in the acidity of the water in lakes and streams. Some individual organisms in the water may be better able to tolerate more acid and are able to survive and pass on their genes to offspring. Over time, they may give rise to new species; organisms that cannot tolerate more acid may go extinct. Or perhaps a new species of predator enters an environment. Individual organisms that are better able to defend themselves, perhaps because their coloration makes them better camouflaged, have a better chance of surviving and passing on their genes. Over time, they may give rise to new species. Organisms that cannot defend against the new predator may go extinct.

CHALLENGE Biological Evolution: Unity and Diversity

Choose the word or phrase that makes each sentence true.

1. The DNA nucleotide sequence of organisms can be compared by using **(a microscope/gel electrophoresis/a family tree)**.

2. Examining the structures and DNA of organisms helps determine whether they have a(n) **(common ancestry/ability to mutate)**.

3. The overhunting of a species can lead to **(extinction/overpopulation)** of that species.

4. Some individuals of a species may be better able to adapt to environmental changes than others and thus have a better chance of **(survival/perishing)**.

5. Based on the diagram, species A and B are more **(closely/distantly)** related than species A and C.

CHALLENGE ANSWERS

Biological Evolution: Unity and Diversity

1. **gel electrophoresis:** The DNA nucleotide sequence of organisms can be compared by using gel electrophoresis. If the patterns of fragments match, then the DNA sequences are the same.

2. **common ancestry:** Examining the structures and DNA of organisms helps determine whether they have a common ancestry.

3. **extinction:** The overhunting of a species can lead to extinction of that species. This is just another way in which humans have had a negative impact upon Earth's natural resources.

4. **survival:** Some individuals of a species may be better able to adapt to environmental changes than others and thus have a better chance of survival. Because they are well adapted enough to survive, they have a better chance of passing their genes on to their offspring.

5. **closely:** In the diagram, species A and B are more closely related because they derive from a more recent common ancestor.

Earth and Space Sciences

 ## Earth's Place in the Universe

KEY TERMS: Big Bang theory, blue shift, elliptical orbit, light spectra, red shift

Nuclear Reactions

What is the source of the heat and light emitted by the sun? Within the sun and other stars, many simple hydrogen nuclei are continuously being fused together to form helium and heavier elements. This process is called nuclear fusion. The fusion of the nuclei releases energy in the form of heat and light.

At a certain point in the life span of a star, the hydrogen fuel for nuclear fusion becomes depleted. When that happens, a number of processes can occur that cause a stellar explosion. All of the elements formed within the star are ejected out into space. The explosion is called a supernova. Scientists believe that supernovas are the source of all known elements, including those that compose Earth and all living things.

Light Spectra

How do scientists know that the sun is composed mainly of hydrogen and helium? The answer lies in examining the **light spectra** (or spectral lines) obtained from the light of the sun. Each element has its own distinct pattern of the movements of electrons among the principal energy levels within the atom. As a result, when light from a sample of energized atoms of a particular element passes through a gradient, it produces a distinct set of lines. The pattern of spectral lines is different for every element. The spectral lines for hydrogen and helium are shown.

Spectral Lines for Hydrogen and Helium

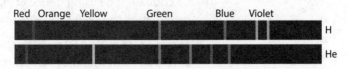

Light from the sun and other stars produces a combination of these two sets of spectral lines. From this, scientists conclude that stars are composed mainly of hydrogen and helium.

The heat within the sun causes the hydrogen and helium atoms to move in vast convection currents. Sometimes magnetic disturbances disrupt those currents. That causes some areas on the sun's surface to be cooler than others. When viewed through a telescope (using a solar filter for safety), those cooler areas appear as dark spots. These sunspots tend to grow and wane in eleven-year cycles. The resulting variation in radiation emissions causes changes in space "weather" and Earth's climate, as well. And just as some spots on the sun are cooler than others, other spots are hotter and emit more radiation. Those hotter areas are called solar flares.

The Big Bang Theory

The universe is now thought to have originated at a time billions of years ago when all the matter and energy that exists was concentrated together at one single tiny point. The matter was extremely hot, and it burst outward into space in a huge explosion. This idea is known informally as the **Big Bang theory**. As the matter flowed outward, over time it coalesced into simple atoms, elements, and finally stars and galaxies.

What is the evidence for the Big Bang? Again, spectral lines provide the key. Light from objects that are moving away from Earth produces spectral lines that are shifted slightly toward the red side of the spectrum. This is called the **red shift**. Light from most galaxies shows a red shift, meaning that the galaxies are continuously moving farther away. Scientists think that their movement is a result of the Big Bang. Galaxies are moving farther and farther apart from each other, and the universe is constantly expanding.

The diagram shows spectral lines that are red-shifted. They come from light from a galaxy that is moving farther away from us. The spectral lines are shifted slightly toward the red, or right, side of the spectrum. Also shown are spectral lines that have a **blue shift**. Blue-shifted spectra mean that the object producing the light is moving toward us. The spectral lines are shifted slightly toward the violet, or left, side of the spectrum. The light with blue-shifted spectral lines is from galaxies that are moving away from the point of origin of the universe, but happen also to be moving toward Earth.

Red-Shifted and Blue-Shifted Spectral Lines

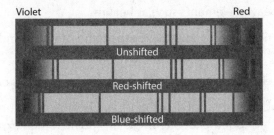

Orbital Motions

In planetary systems like our solar system, the planets orbit around a massive star at the center. Each planet travels at its own speed and at its own distance from the central star. The German astronomer Johann Kepler determined in the early 1600s that the planets in our solar system move in slightly **elliptical orbits**. The orbits are not perfectly circular. Kepler also determined that there is a relationship between a planet's distance from the sun and the speed at which it travels. If two planets of the same mass orbit at different distances from a star, the one that is closer to the star will travel faster than the one that is farther away.

The English physicist Isaac Newton determined that it is the force of gravity that keeps the planets in orbit around the sun and moons in orbit around the planets. Every object with mass exerts a gravitational force of attraction on other objects. Earth and its moon exert gravitational forces on each other. But Earth and the moon do not crash into each other. Instead, the moon stays in orbit because of its constant forward motion. The moon's motion counteracts the force of Earth's gravity. The moon comes no closer to Earth, but at the same time Earth's gravity keeps the moon revolving around Earth rather than traveling off into space.

Forces in the Earth–Moon System

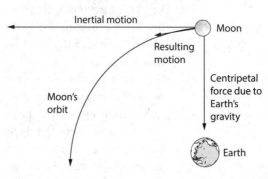

CHALLENGE   Earth's Place in the Universe

Choose the word or phrase that makes each sentence true.

1. In the sun and other stars, hydrogen nuclei undergo nuclear **(fusion/fission)** to make heavier elements such as helium.

2. The evidence that the universe is expanding can be found in the **(red/blue)** shift of light spectra from distant galaxies.

3. Earth travels around the sun in **(an elliptical/a circular)** orbit.

4. Scientists believe that all of the mass and energy of the universe was once concentrated together at one single tiny point. It then exploded. This is the **(hot thin soup/Big Bang)** theory.

5. If two planets of the same mass are orbiting a star at different distances, the planet that is closer to the star will travel **(faster/more slowly)** than the planet that is farther from the star.

CHALLENGE ANSWERS
Earth's Place in the Universe

1. **fusion:** In the sun and other stars, hydrogen nuclei undergo nuclear fusion to make heavier elements such as helium.

2. **red:** The evidence that the universe is expanding can be found in the red shift of the light spectra from distant galaxies. The red shift indicates that the galaxies are moving farther and farther apart from each other.

3. **an elliptical:** Earth travels around the sun in an elliptical orbit.

4. **Big Bang:** According to the Big Bang theory, all of the mass and energy in the universe was once concentrated together at one single tiny point. It then exploded. The universe has been expanding ever since.

5. **faster:** If two planets of the same mass are orbiting a star at different distances, the planet that is closer to the star will travel faster than the planet that is farther from the star.

10 Earth's Systems

KEY TERMS: carbon cycle, climate, convection, fossil fuels, greenhouse gases, hydrologic cycle, igneous rock, mantle, metamorphic rock, orogeny, Pangaea, plate tectonics, plateau, rock cycle, sedimentary rock, U-shaped valleys, V-shaped valleys, volcano, weather, weathering

Determining Earth's Age

Using radiometric dating, chemists and geologists have estimated that Earth and the rest of the solar system are approximately 4.6 billion years old. The oldest rocks on Earth today are approximately 4.4 billion years old. By contrast, the oldest life-forms on Earth are thought to have arisen about 3.7 billion years ago. In other words, it took about 1 billion years for life to first form on Earth.

Traces of meteorites that have struck Earth over time also offer clues to the age of the planet. The oldest meteorites and meteor craters on Earth have been measured to be about 4.5 billion years old. Meteorites continue to strike Earth, providing scientists with data about conditions in the early solar system. Space missions to the moon have provided evidence that the moon is slightly younger than Earth. Mars is thought to be about 4.5 billion years old.

Plate Tectonics

Great changes have taken place on Earth's surface over the life span of the planet. It is believed that at one time all of the continents were fused together in a single huge landmass that scientists call **Pangaea**. The following page shows a diagram of Pangaea:

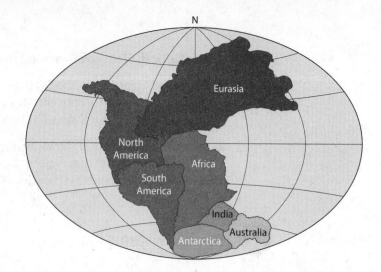

Compare the map of Pangaea to the following modern-day map of the globe. The evidence for Pangaea is that the continents look somewhat like pieces of a puzzle that could be fitted together.

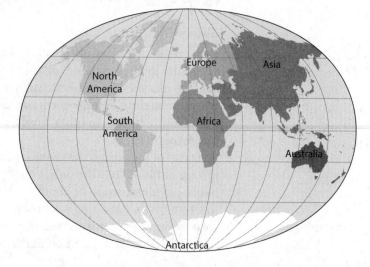

Note how perfectly the east coast of South America fits with the west coast of Africa. Fossils from the same species of land animals have been found on both coasts. Those animals could have lived in both places only if those two landmasses were once joined together.

If all of the world's landmasses were once joined together, what moved them apart? Deep within Earth is a mass of fluid molten rock in a layer called the **mantle**. The intense heat at that depth produces **convection** currents in the molten rock. Continent-sized pieces of Earth's crust called plates "float" on the surface of the mantle because they are less dense than the molten rock below. The motion of the molten rock causes the plates to move very slowly across Earth's surface. For example, the European and North American plates are moving farther apart by approximately 1.5 inches a year. This process is shown in the following diagram:

Plates "Floating" on Earth's Mantle

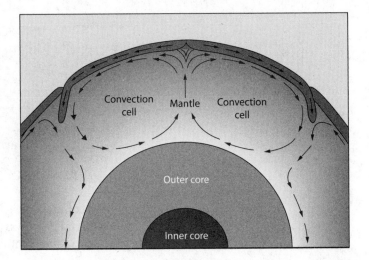

Assuming that the rate of movement has been constant, it is estimated that the various pieces of Pangaea began to separate from each other approximately 175 million years ago. The movement of the plates is called continental drift or **plate tectonics**.

The motion of the plates produces a number of natural phenomena. If two plates that are moving past each other become locked together, tension builds up over time. Eventually, the deadlock breaks and the two plates thrust past each other. The resulting release of energy is what people call an earthquake. If two plates are moving away from each other, molten rock from below can rise up through the gap. This often happens beneath an ocean. The ocean water cools the molten rock, forming a long underwater ridge as shown in the following diagram:

Plate Tectonics Forming an Underwater Ridge

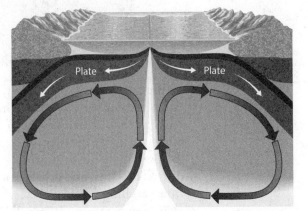

When two plates collide head-on, the crust at the point of collision can be thrust upward, creating mountains. This mountain-building process is called **orogeny**.

Plate Tectonics Forming a Mountain Range

Often when two plates collide, one is forced down beneath the other. The plate material that is forced downward becomes heated by the convection currents in the mantle and melts into molten rock, as shown in this diagram:

A Plate Collision Zone

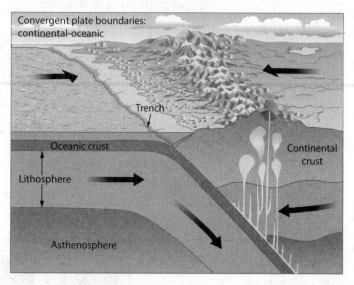

The molten rock formed in this way often forces its way back up to Earth's surface in a **volcano**. The molten rock (called magma as long as it remains below Earth's surface) forces a tube up through the crust. Pressure builds up inside the tube, and eventually the volcano erupts, releasing lava (magma above Earth's surface) along with gases and clouds of dust and debris. This dust and debris can form a massive cloud that blocks sunlight from reaching Earth's surface. This can actually have a cooling effect on global temperatures. When the lava cools, it can form a mountain peak around the volcano crater.

A Volcano

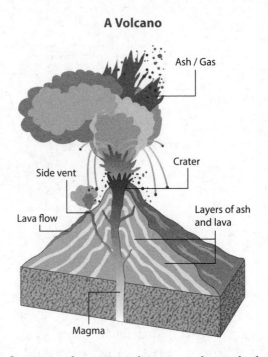

Ash / Gas

Crater

Side vent

Lava flow

Layers of ash
and lava

Magma

Sometimes a flat piece of continental crust can be pushed up between continental plates to form a **plateau**, a piece of land with a flat terrain.

Weathering

Other features on Earth are shaped by water and ice. This process is called **weathering**. Erosion caused by running water forms **V-shaped valleys**. Slow-moving glaciers, by contrast, cut through rocks to form **U-shaped valleys**. Water also alters surface features through hurricanes and tsunamis (large ocean waves created by undersea earthquakes). Both can seriously erode or even destroy coastal areas.

Hydrologic Cycle

Water circulates through the atmosphere and Earth's surface in the **hydrologic cycle**. Water evaporates from Earth's oceans and condenses into clouds. Winds move the clouds around the atmosphere, sometimes carrying the clouds long distances. Eventually the water precipitates back out of the clouds as rain, sleet, snow, or hail. When the water reaches Earth's surface, it flows downward in streams and rivers, or it seeps, or percolates, down into the ground. Finally, the water evaporates, starting the cycle over again.

The Hydrologic Cycle

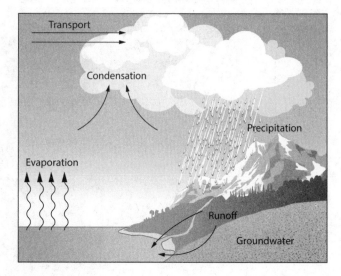

Rock Cycle

The rock in Earth's crust also passes through a cycle of destruction and renewal. **Igneous rock** is formed when magma flows up to Earth's surface and cools. **Sedimentary rock** is formed when small bits of material such as sand and gravel are compacted together beneath the surface. Heat from below and pressure from the weight of rocks above can turn sedimentary rocks into a different kind of rock called **metamorphic rock**. All three types of rock can be broken down into fragments or sediment by erosion and weathering. For example, water can enter crevices in rock and expand upon freezing, causing the rock to crack. Eventually, over long spans of time, heat and pressure causes the rock fragments to fuse or melt, starting the cycle over again. The diagram illustrates the **rock cycle**.

The Rock Cycle

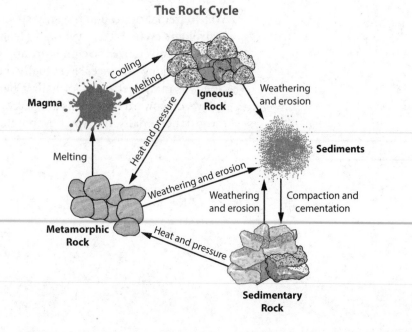

Carbon Cycle

The element carbon, which is the basis for all life on Earth, also passes through a regular cycle. In the **carbon cycle**, respiration by animals and plants (at times) releases carbon dioxide into the atmosphere. Human beings also release carbon dioxide from factories and automobiles. The carbon dioxide in the atmosphere is then used by plants in the process of photosynthesis. The carbon in plants (and in the animals that eat plants) may become "trapped" in the bodies of dead organisms. Those organisms decay over time into carbon-rich organic compounds that are the basis for the fossil fuels such as coal and petroleum that people now use every day. The diagram illustrates the carbon cycle.

The Carbon Cycle

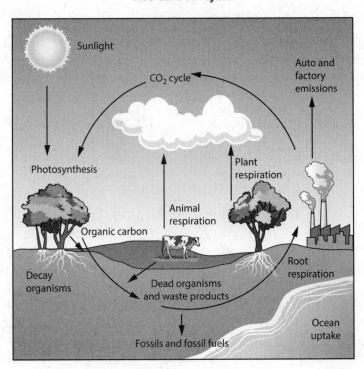

Climate and Seasons

Climate on Earth varies by location. Regions close to the Equator receive the most sunlight year-round and have the highest average temperature. Regions close to the poles receive the least amount of sunlight and have the lowest average temperatures. Locations on Earth also have seasons, or regular changes in average temperature at certain times of the year. The seasons are due to the fact that Earth is tilted slightly on its axis of rotation. As a result, different regions regularly receive different amounts of sunlight as Earth orbits the sun. There is evidence that Earth's tilt has been different at different times in history, creating seasons that are different from those of today. The following diagram shows the seasons in Earth's Northern and Southern Hemispheres as Earth revolves around the sun.

Earth's Seasons

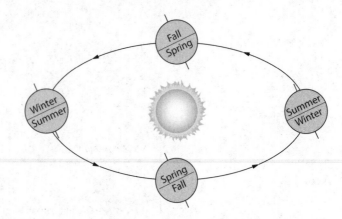

Climate is also greatly affected by Earth's surface features. High mountains have a cold climate, and they can also block flows of moist air, creating deserts in their "rain shadow." In coastal areas, the climate is moderated by the temperature of the nearby water. Warm or cold ocean currents can create warm or cold climates on nearby landmasses. (Great Britain, for example, which lies very far north, has a moderate climate because it is bathed by the warm Gulf Stream ocean current that originates in the tropics.) Winds flowing off the ocean onto land areas can create a rainy climate.

Climate refers to average conditions over the long term. **Weather**, by contrast, refers to conditions that change from day to day. Changes in weather can be caused by the winds that circulate through the atmosphere, by differences in atmospheric pressure, and other factors.

Human Impact

In recent times, human activities have begun to have an impact on Earth's climate. In particular, the burning of **fossil fuels** such as coal, petroleum, and natural gas has released huge quantities of so-called **greenhouse gases**, mainly carbon dioxide, into the atmosphere. These gases tend to trap heat that would otherwise radiate out into space, and the result has been a slight increase in average temperatures worldwide. As a result of the higher temperatures, more of the ice on Earth has become liquid water, slowly elevating sea levels. The higher temperatures also introduce more energy into atmospheric systems, resulting in stronger and more frequent storms. Efforts are now under way in countries worldwide to reduce greenhouse gas emissions and to slow the pace of climate change.

CHALLENGE   Earth's Systems

Choose the word or phrase that makes each sentence true.

1. When rocks are subjected to heat and pressure, **(igneous/metamorphic/sedimentary)** rocks are formed.

2. Plant **(respiration/photosynthesis)** can take carbon dioxide out of the atmosphere.

3. **(Climate/Weather)** refers to average conditions over the long term; **(climate/weather)** refers to conditions that change from day to day.

4. **(Evaporation/Precipitation/Runoff)** takes water from Earth's surface and moves it to the atmosphere.

5. Molten rock above Earth's surface is called **(lava/magma)**, while molten rock below Earth's surface is called **(lava/magma)**.

CHALLENGE ANSWERS

Earth's Systems

1. **metamorphic:** When rocks are subjected to heat and pressure, metamorphic (or "changed") rocks are formed.

2. **photosynthesis:** Plant photosynthesis takes carbon dioxide out of the atmosphere to make food for the plant.

3. **Climate, weather:** Climate refers to average conditions over the long term; weather refers to conditions that change from day to day.

4. **Evaporation:** Evaporation takes water from Earth's surface and moves it to the atmosphere. Precipitation returns the water to Earth's surface.

5. **lava, magma:** Molten rock above Earth's surface is called lava, while molten rock below Earth's surface is called magma.

Earth and Human Activity

KEY TERMS: renewable, resources, sustainable

Human Need for Resources

Throughout history humans have been dependent upon Earth and the natural **resources** that Earth has to offer. Fresh water has always been vital for human survival. The earliest civilizations in Egypt and elsewhere arose near rivers that could be tapped for human use. River water is still used to irrigate land for agriculture. Away from rivers, people depend on rain or dig wells for their water supply. Many also use pipeline systems to tap distant water sources when local sources are inadequate or depleted.

Animals have been hunted throughout history for food, furs, and other products, and fish have always been another major food source. Today people depend heavily on raising livestock, a practice that also requires huge amounts of resources such as food crops and water.

Wood from forests has long been another vital resource. People use it in buildings, boats, innumerable manufactured products, and all kinds of paper products. Earth's remaining forests now require careful management to avoid depletion.

Fossil fuels have been in huge demand ever since the start of the Industrial Revolution in the eighteenth century. Coal, oil, and natural gas are extracted in enormous amounts from mines and wells. Today many of those wells are located not only on land but also offshore. Humans also mine huge quantities of minerals and metals needed for construction and manufacturing. Earth's overall supply of these resources remains vast, but today there are many areas where resources have been depleted or exhausted, or where resource extraction is no longer economically feasible.

Human Impact

Consumption of all these natural resources comes at a price. People who live near rivers or shorelines are at risk from flooding. Animal or fish species may go extinct due to overhunting or loss of habitat to pollution or human development. Cutting down forests leads to erosion, destruction of habitats, and poorer air quality. The burning of fossil fuels has raised the level of carbon dioxide in the atmosphere from about 275 parts per million (ppm) to about 400 parts per million. This increased level of carbon dioxide traps heat, impacting global weather patterns. Glaciers and polar ice caps melt, raising worldwide sea levels. Carbon dioxide in the air also induces the formation of acid rain, altering the pH of lakes and rivers. There is also the constant threat of catastrophic oil spills as huge quantities of petroleum are transported around the globe. Finally, there is uncertainty about the future: What will happen when more forests are cut down, when more animal and fish stocks are depleted, and when more species go extinct? And will Earth's supply of fossil fuels someday run low or even run out?

Sustainability

The answer lies in careful management of Earth's natural resources. Humans will need to practice conservation, reuse, and recycling on a very large scale. Also, there needs to be a shift toward the use of **renewable** resources, those with supplies that are constantly replenished. These resources also need to be **sustainable**; that is, the supply can be maintained at a steady level.

One way to reduce fuel use and carbon dioxide emissions is to drive hybrid and electric vehicles. Forests that are cut down for timber can be replaced by new planting. Solar panels can be installed on commercial and residential buildings to replace fossil fuel use with constantly available sunshine. Other sustainable and renewable energy resources are wind power and geothermal energy. New technologies will make these renewable resources affordable and easy to operate and install.

Livestock raising is another area that can benefit from resource management. Livestock farms require huge amounts of land, water, crops, and other resources. If people learn to decrease their demand for meat, the resources now used for livestock raising can be controlled and reduced.

Recycling of plastic, metal, and paper products is already widely practiced around the world. Many manufacturers have also reduced the packaging used with their products or have made the packaging biodegradable. As a result, fewer materials end up in landfills, and those that do cause less pollution.

A newer problem is pollution caused when batteries and outdated electronics (especially computer parts) enter the waste stream. Cities and towns are now starting to set up electronics recycling programs, and newer batteries are rechargeable and thus do not need to be thrown away.

In sum, making sure that Earth's natural resources are available in sufficient quantities in the future will require careful resource management, efficient usage, recycling, the development of new and effective technologies, reliance on renewable energy sources, and of course, a good deal of basic common sense.

CHALLENGE | **Earth and Human Activity**

Choose the word or phrase that makes each sentence true.

1. Human activity has caused the level of carbon dioxide gas in the atmosphere to **(increase/decrease/remain constant)**.

2. Renewable energy sources include **(coal/natural gas/solar energy)**.

3. Humans need to find resources that are **(sustainable/extractable)**.

4. Metal, paper, and plastic waste is managed effectively when it **(ends up in landfills/ is recycled)**.

5. Cutting down forests without replanting them can affect wildlife and people **(negatively/positively)**.

CHALLENGE ANSWERS
Earth and Human Activity

1. **increase:** Human activity has caused the level of carbon dioxide gas in the atmosphere to increase dramatically.

2. **solar energy:** Renewable energy sources include solar energy, wind power, hydroelectric power, and other resources that do not depend on the burning of fossil fuels.

3. **sustainable:** Humans need to find resources that are sustainable; that is, the supply can be maintained at a steady level.

4. **is recycled:** Metal, paper, and plastic waste is managed effectively when it is recycled.

5. **negatively:** Cutting down trees without replanting them can negatively affect wildlife and people.

Engineering

 Engineering Design

Methods for Problem Solving

The previous section looked at ways in which science and technology work together to make life easier and to tackle the challenges faced by people and the environment. The constant cycle of research and development enables people to make technological progress. But keep in mind that technology can have impacts that were not originally anticipated. There are a number of things to consider when designing solutions to real-world problems.

First, the problem must be analyzed. The analysis must take into account both potential benefits and potential costs. For example, one can ask if it makes sense to construct a new highway for economic development if the project requires cutting down a tropical forest that holds potential resources and helps mitigate air pollution. An analysis of this kind must include both qualitative measures (what is wanted) and quantitative measures (how much is wanted).

Managing Larger Projects

The best way to approach many large projects is to break them into smaller steps or phases, each with its own deadline. This can make the project more manageable and easier to accomplish. To take a small-scale example, if you are renovating a home, you might break the project into the following phases:

» Complete gutting of the interior
» Plumbing and electrical work
» Drywall installation
» Flooring
» Installation of cabinetry and sinks
» Painting and tiling
» Thorough cleaning
» Furnishing
» Placement of personal items

A contractor can provide a timeline and cost for each phase. Breaking down the project into smaller tasks allows for specialists to work on each phase of the project, making sure that each one is completed correctly.

In every large project a range of factors needs to be taken into consideration. There is a need to set priorities: which things are most important to achieve and which are less important? Some goals may be very difficult to achieve and require trade-offs or compromises. Costs, safety, environmental impacts, aesthetics, and other factors need to be considered. For example, a dam might be needed to stop flooding in an area. However, if few people live in the area, it might make more sense for them to relocate than to build an expensive dam that might adversely affect local fish and wildlife. To offset those negatives, the dam could include a hydroelectric plant to generate clean, greenhouse-gas-free energy. It's all about weighing the negatives and positives.

Computer-Generated Models

Computer-generated models are an effective way to predict the final results when planning a project. For example, a computer model can simulate what will happen when a breakwater is built to protect a beach. Will sand pile up on one side? Will sand wash away on the other side and leave the homes vulnerable to flooding? With accurate data input, a computer model can show what will likely happen over different spans of time. From such a model, engineers can refine their plans to make sure that the construction project achieves its intended goals.

CHALLENGE **Engineering Design**

Choose the word or phrase that makes each sentence true.

1. When planning an engineering project, engineers take into account **(only what people want/only what people need/the scope and scale of what is involved)**.

2. A homeowner builds a 30-foot-tall wind-power unit in his backyard. A drawback of the new unit could be that **(the neighbors find it aesthetically displeasing/it generates clean energy/it offsets some of the homeowner's electric bill)**.

3. A larger job can be made easier if it is **(broken down into smaller jobs/compared to other large jobs)**.

4. **(Computer-generated models/Small-scale wooden models)** can show the possible results of an engineering project.

CHALLENGE ANSWERS
Engineering Design

1. **the scope and scale of what is involved:** When planning an engineering project, engineers take into account the scope and scale of what is involved. This includes human wants and needs and what is good for everyone in the long run.

2. **the neighbors find it aesthetically displeasing:** A 30-foot-tall wind-power unit in a homeowner's backyard is likely to be considered an eyesore.

3. **broken down into smaller jobs:** A larger job can be made easier if it is broken down into smaller jobs.

4. **Computer-generated models:** Computer-generated models can show the possible results of an engineering project.

TASC Science Practice Test

47 questions, 85 minutes

The following test is designed to simulate a real TASC Science Test section in terms of question formats, number, and degree of difficulty. To get a good idea of how you will do on the real exam, take this test under actual exam conditions. Complete the test in one session and follow the given time limit. Answers and explanations begin on page 389.

1. What process is shown in the following reaction?

$$4\,^1_1H \longrightarrow\,^4_2He + 2\,^0_1e + energy$$

    Ⓐ nuclear fusion of the kind that occurs in the sun and stars
    Ⓑ nuclear fission of the kind that occurs in an atomic bomb
    Ⓒ an endothermic reaction that is absorbing massive amounts of energy
    Ⓓ gas formation from the eruption of a volcano

2. The diagram represents the bright spectra of four individual elements and the bright-line spectrum that is produced when three of the four elements are mixed together.

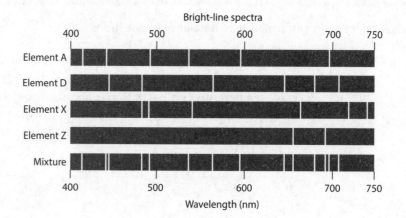

Which element is <u>not</u> present in the mixture?
    Ⓐ A
    Ⓑ D
    Ⓒ X
    Ⓓ Z

3. Which of these was most likely formed via the action and movement of a glacier of ice?

    (A) a V-shaped valley

    (B) a volcano

    (C) a U-shaped valley

    (D) a plateau

4. Water can cause weathering and erosion. Which product is <u>most</u> likely to form?

    (A) igneous rocks

    (B) metamorphic rocks

    (C) sedimentary rocks

    (D) fine sediments

5. Different places on Earth have various seasons throughout the year. The change in these seasons is easily predictable based upon the date of the year. The change in seasons is <u>most</u> dependent upon

    (A) the distance of Earth from the sun

    (B) the tilt of Earth

    (C) the amount of greenhouse gases in the atmosphere

    (D) the number of earthquakes that have occurred over three months

Use the following information to help answer questions 6–7.

The burning of fossil fuels has increased the amount of carbon dioxide, a greenhouse gas, in the atmosphere. This gas has caused average temperatures on Earth to rise because it traps heat that would normally escape back into space. The levels of carbon dioxide have been estimated at the following concentrations in parts per million over recent years:

Year	1960	1970	1980	1990	2000	2010	2013
CO_2 Level	315	325	340	350	370	390	400

In addition to the threat of rising global temperatures, carbon dioxide can also produce acid rain as raindrops mix with the carbon dioxide and precipitate to Earth's surface. The equation for this reaction is:

$$CO_2(g) + H_2O(l) \rightarrow H_2CO_3(aq)$$

6. Which of these is a way to combat the increase in levels of carbon dioxide in the atmosphere?

(A) using alternative energies that are renewable
(B) drilling for offshore oil
(C) cutting down trees in the Amazon forest
(D) shipping oil via pipelines instead of via oil tankers

7. When carbon dioxide reacts with rainwater, the end product is <u>most likely</u> to

(A) have no impact on the environment over time
(B) raise the acidity level of lakes and streams, producing a harmful impact on wildlife
(C) be a basic liquid that is harmless to the environment
(D) help in preserving marble statues

8. A thermostat in your home controls the heating and cooling. For example, during the winter you might set the thermostat to 68°F to keep the temperature of the home constant. If the temperature drops below 68°F, a signal is sent to the furnace telling it to produce heat until the inside temperature of the home is 68°F again. Similarly, when humans eat, blood sugar levels increase. This sends a signal to the brain that tells the body to release insulin into the blood to metabolize the added sugar. What does this feedback mechanism help maintain?

(A) only the person's body temperature
(B) a food web within the body
(C) a proper biome for humans to live in
(D) homeostasis in the body

Use the following information to help answer questions 9–11.

A plant captures light energy and uses it to produce glucose. The reaction for this process is:

$$\text{Sunlight} + 6CO_2 + 6H_2O \rightarrow 6O_2 \text{ and } C_6H_{12}O_6$$

The glucose produced can then be stored in the plant as starch. A rabbit then consumes the plant and uses the starch from the plant as energy. After eating the plant, the rabbit is preyed upon by an eagle. The eagle and its offspring feed on the rabbit's carcass.

9. The reaction shown in the passage is <u>best</u> described as

(A) cellular respiration
(B) a food chain
(C) photosynthesis
(D) ATP synthesis

10. Drag three tiles to form the reaction that is <u>most likely</u> to occur within the rabbit, the eagle, and the eagle's offspring.

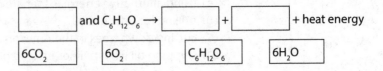

$$\boxed{} \text{ and } C_6H_{12}O_6 \longrightarrow \boxed{} + \boxed{} + \text{heat energy}$$

| $6CO_2$ | $6O_2$ | $C_6H_{12}O_6$ | $6H_2O$ |

11. The oxygen produced by the reaction in the passage can then be used by which organism?

Ⓐ an anaerobic organism
Ⓑ an aerobic organism
Ⓒ both an anaerobic organism and aerobic organism
Ⓓ neither an anaerobic nor an aerobic organism

12. Drag tiles to show the correct arrangement in the levels of organization within an organism.

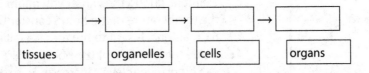

$$\boxed{} \rightarrow \boxed{} \rightarrow \boxed{} \rightarrow \boxed{}$$

| tissues | organelles | cells | organs |

13. The following graph represents a predator-prey relationship. The darker line represents the relative number of cheetahs in an ecosystem, and the dashed line represents the relative number of gazelles present in the same ecosystem. The *x*-axis shows the number of years that have passed. What is the <u>most probable</u> reason for the increase in the predator population from year 6 to year 8?

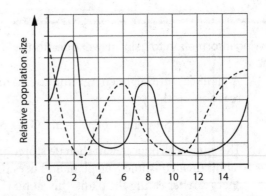

Ⓐ an increase in the prey population from year 3 to year 6
Ⓑ a predator population equal in size to the prey population from year 5 to year 6
Ⓒ a decrease in the prey population from year 1 to year 2
Ⓓ the extinction of the prey population in year 3

14. When comparing mitosis and meiosis, what can you say about both processes? Choose all that apply.

    Ⓐ Both produce the same number of daughter cells.
    Ⓑ Both produce sex cells with the exact same number of chromosomes as the parent cells.
    Ⓒ Both involve the replication of DNA.
    Ⓓ Both will have mutations.
    Ⓔ Both involve two rounds of genetic separation.
    Ⓕ Both begin with chromosome duplication.

15. In humans, dark hair color, D, is dominant over light hair color, d. If the egg cell of a blonde female who carries only the genes for light-colored hair, dd, is fertilized by the sperm cell of a male who carries only the genes for dark hair, DD, what are the chances that the offspring will have dark hair?

    Ⓐ 100 percent
    Ⓑ 50 percent
    Ⓒ 25 percent
    Ⓓ 0 percent

16. The diagram that follows shows the evolutionary relationships of some organisms:

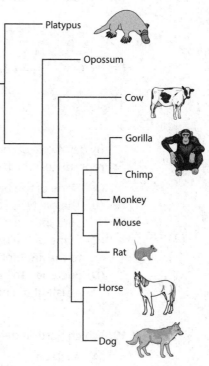

Platypus
Opossum
Cow
Gorilla
Chimp
Monkey
Mouse
Rat
Horse
Dog

Which two organisms would <u>most likely</u> synthesize the most similar enzymes?

    Ⓐ monkey and mouse
    Ⓑ cow and horse
    Ⓒ chimp and rat
    Ⓓ horse and dog

17. The DNA of three species of plants is sequenced using a gel electrophoresis. The results of the process show the following:

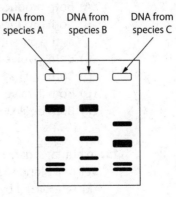

Which two species of plant are <u>most</u> closely related?

Ⓐ A and B

Ⓑ A and C

Ⓒ B and C

Ⓓ There is not enough conclusive evidence to determine which two are most closely related.

18. The diagram shows two types of bacteria being exposed to an antibiotic.

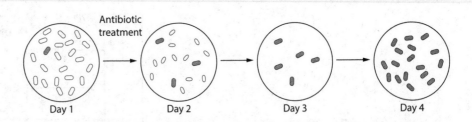

By day 4 one of the strains of bacteria was able to thrive and continue to reproduce. Which reason would explain why this took place?

Ⓐ None of the bacteria were able survive the exposure to the antibiotic.

Ⓑ The bacteria found a new food source, making them invincible to the antibiotic.

Ⓒ Some of the bacteria already had the genes that made them resistant to the antibiotic.

Ⓓ Bacteria can instantly change their DNA sequence to become more resistant to antibiotics.

19. Which particle defines what element an atom is?

Ⓐ nucleons

Ⓑ protons

Ⓒ neutrons

Ⓓ electrons

Use the following information to help answer questions 20–21.

Energy is needed to break the bonds between the atoms within molecules and the bonds that exist between molecules. The energy required to break these bonds can vary depending on the types of bonds involved and the types of elements involved. The chart shows the melting point for substances A, B, C, and D:

Substance	A	B	C	D
Melting Point (°C)	50	950	1350	1860

20. Which substance contains the strongest bonds?

(A) A
(B) B
(C) C
(D) D

21. Substance A is <u>most likely</u> made of which type(s) of elements?

(A) metals
(B) a metal and a nonmetal
(C) nonmetals
(D) a semimetal and a nonmetal

22. Which level in the energy pyramid is <u>most likely</u> to use carbon dioxide and water to make oxygen gas and glucose?

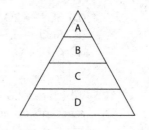

(A) A
(B) B
(C) C
(D) D

Use the following information to help answer questions 23–24.

The following reaction takes place in a reaction vessel:

$$\text{Heat} + A(s) + B(l) \longrightarrow 2C(s) + D(s).$$

The chemist who is carrying out the reaction in the laboratory repeats the experiment under various conditions to produce the maximum possible amounts of substances C and D.

23. This reaction can be classified as what type?

    Ⓐ endothermic

    Ⓑ exothermic

    Ⓒ at equilibrium

    Ⓓ a nuclear reaction

24. Which factor will <u>not</u> help the chemist change the speed/rate of the reaction?

    Ⓐ increasing the temperature of the system

    Ⓑ using powdered reactants

    Ⓒ increasing the pressure on the system

    Ⓓ adding a catalyst to the reaction

25. Choose the three equations that are correctly balanced.

    Ⓐ $C + O_2 \longrightarrow CO_2$

    Ⓑ $Na + Cl_2 \longrightarrow 2NaCl$

    Ⓒ $Ca + Cl_2 \longrightarrow CaCl_2$

    Ⓓ $3O_2 \longrightarrow 2O_3$

    Ⓔ $SnO_2 + H_2 \longrightarrow Sn + H_2O$

    Ⓕ $C_3H_8 + O_2 \longrightarrow H_2O + CO_2$

26. Which reaction needs the <u>most</u> manipulation to make sure that the reactants do <u>not</u> form from the products?

    Ⓐ $HCl + NaOH \longrightarrow NaCl + H_2O$

    Ⓑ $H_2(g) + I_2(g) \longleftarrow\longrightarrow 2HI(g)$

    Ⓒ $AgNO_3(aq) + NaCl(aq) \longrightarrow NaNO_3(aq) + AgCl(s)$

    Ⓓ $Zn(s) + 2HCl \longrightarrow ZnCl_2(aq) + H_2(g)$

27. What is a benefit of using nuclear reactions to produce electricity?

    Ⓐ Nuclear waste is safe and easy to dispose of.

    Ⓑ No harmful greenhouse gases are produced.

    Ⓒ Any radioactive materials released into the atmosphere by accident are harmless.

    Ⓓ The materials used to produce the energy can also be used to make harmful weapons.

28. In the carbon cycle, fossil fuels are produced from

(A) factory emissions
(B) photosynthesis
(C) animal respiration
(D) the decay of organisms that were once living

29. The population of humans on Earth has grown exponentially over time. It is believed that eventually the population will reach the maximum number that Earth's resources can sustain. This number is called Earth's

(A) carrying capacity
(B) extinction
(C) thriving population
(D) homeostasis

Use the following information to help answer questions 30 and 31.

A physicist is conducting an experiment regarding the momentum of objects in motion. She has a car, a baseball, a snowball, and a hockey player on ice skates ready to move. Each of the objects is set in motion, and its velocity is measured. The momentum of each object is then calculated. Next, the moving objects are set, two at a time, to collide with each other head-on (assume that no one is hurt).

---

30. Drag the tiles to order the objects from greatest to least momentum.

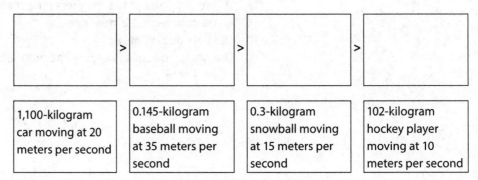

1,100-kilogram car moving at 20 meters per second	0.145-kilogram baseball moving at 35 meters per second	0.3-kilogram snowball moving at 15 meters per second	102-kilogram hockey player moving at 10 meters per second

31. Which pair of objects will demonstrate conservation of momentum when they collide with each other?

(A) the hockey player and the baseball only
(B) the car and the baseball only
(C) None of the objects will show conservation of momentum.
(D) All of the objects will show conservation of momentum.

Use the following information to help answer questions 32 and 33.

A child is playing with two magnetic bars. First, the child places the bars near each other with the poles in various positions. Then taking a long piece of copper wire, the child coils it and attaches the ends of the wire to a small, low-wattage lightbulb. The child then passes the magnets through the middle of the wire coil.

32. Which diagram could illustrate the field lines created around the poles of the magnetic bars when they are placed near each other?

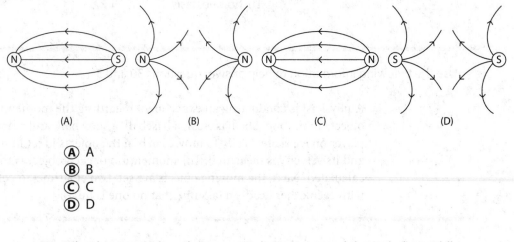

(A)   (B)   (C)   (D)

Ⓐ A
Ⓑ B
Ⓒ C
Ⓓ D

33. What happens when the magnetic bars are passed through the middle of the wire coil?

Ⓐ The south poles of the magnets attract each other.
Ⓑ An electromagnet is generated.
Ⓒ The lightbulb lights up.
Ⓓ The north and south poles of the magnets repel each other.

Use the following information to help answer questions 34 and 35.

A student accidently dropped a book that she had been holding up in the air. The book weighed 2.0 kilograms. It fell 1.8 meters to the ground, making a loud noise when it hit. Assume that the acceleration due to gravity is 9.81 m/s².

34. How much potential energy did the book possess while in the student's hands?

Ⓐ 35.5 joules
Ⓑ 6.0 joules
Ⓒ 13.6 joules
Ⓓ 2.73 joules

35. As the book fell through the air and eventually hit the ground

Ⓐ potential energy was destroyed and kinetic energy was created
Ⓑ sound energy was created
Ⓒ both potential energy and kinetic energy were destroyed
Ⓓ the energies of the system were converted from one form to another

36. A hockey player is hit in the leg by a puck. The trainer immediately takes an ice pack at 0°C and places it on the injured leg, which is at 37°C. This incident occurs in an arena with an air temperature of 14°C. Which of these best explains the direction of heat flow in this system?

Ⓐ The ice pack transfers coldness to the leg.
Ⓑ The only direction of heat flow is from the leg to the ice pack.
Ⓒ The heat from the leg is transferred to the air and to the ice pack, while heat from the air is transferred to the ice pack.
Ⓓ Heat from the air is transferred to the leg.

Use the following information to help answer questions 37 and 38.

A motorist stops at a gas station and buys a cup of coffee that he heats in a microwave oven. He then proceeds on his way, enjoying music on the radio in his car. Some miles down the road, he is involved in an accident. Paramedics take him to a nearby hospital for a CT scan.

37. What type of radiation will be used during the CT scan?

Ⓐ radio waves
Ⓑ microwaves
Ⓒ x-rays
Ⓓ infrared radiation

38. Of all of the types of radiation mentioned in the passage, which one causes the least amount of damage to living tissue and DNA with long-term exposure?

Ⓐ All types of radiation are equally safe.
Ⓑ radio waves
Ⓒ microwaves
Ⓓ the radiation used in the CT scan

39. Early in Earth's history, it is believed that Earth's atmosphere contained a number of gases. These gases combined to form the first large organic compounds. This is referred to as the "hot thin soup" concept and is illustrated in the following diagram.

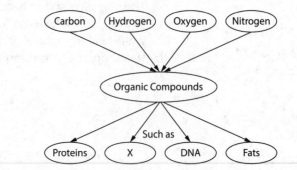

In the diagram, substance X is <u>most likely</u>

Ⓐ carbon dioxide
Ⓑ ozone gas
Ⓒ glucose
Ⓓ ammonia

40. A supermarket shopper approaches the exit door with a cart full of groceries. When the front of the cart approaches the door, a small red light on a sensor above the door turns on. The door then opens. What does this demonstrate?

Ⓐ diffraction of light
Ⓑ refraction of light
Ⓒ the photoelectric effect
Ⓓ destructive interference of light waves

41. A red shift of the light from a star indicates that the star

Ⓐ will soon explode in a supernova
Ⓑ will become a black hole
Ⓒ is moving toward Earth
Ⓓ is moving away from Earth

42. Drag each hydrologic process to its correct position in the diagram.

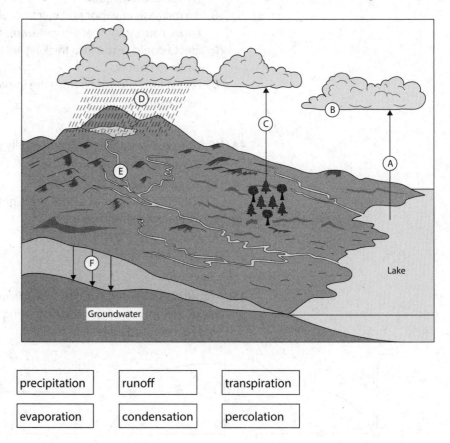

| precipitation | runoff | transpiration |

| evaporation | condensation | percolation |

43. The diagram shows a large meteor impacting Earth's surface.

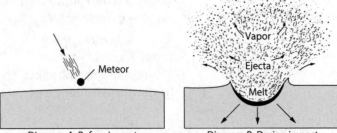

Diagram A: Before impact   Diagram B: During impact

The melt of the meteor is the material that melted during impact. The vapor is gases that formed. The ejecta are solid particles that were scattered into the air. Which statement <u>best</u> describes how the global climate could be affected by the meteor's impact?

Ⓐ The large quantities of ejecta could block sunlight, causing the global temperature to cool.

Ⓑ An increase in vapor and ejecta could reflect more sunlight from Earth, causing global temperatures to cool.

Ⓒ Ejecta could settle into thick layers and absorb sunlight, causing Earth to heat up.

Ⓓ Forest fires produced from the impact could raise global temperatures.

44. Which two events are cyclic and highly predictable?

Ⓐ a volcano eruption

Ⓑ an earthquake

Ⓒ Jupiter's movement across the night sky

Ⓓ an asteroid striking Earth

Ⓔ phases of the moon

Ⓕ landslides

45. According to the Big Bang theory, the relationship between time and the size of the universe from the beginning of the universe to the present is <u>best</u> represented by which graph?

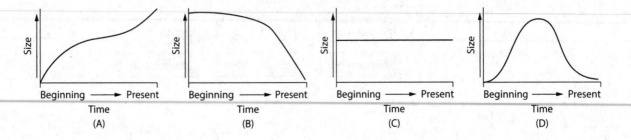

46. The map shows the tectonic plate boundaries near the Rift Valley of eastern Africa. The arrows show the movement of the plates. A region of Africa is crosshatched (▨). What is happening to the crosshatched region of eastern Africa?

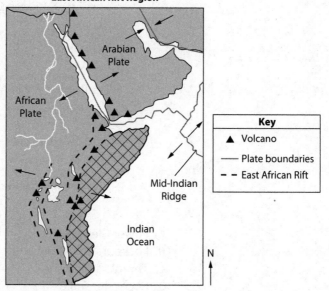

East African Rift Region

Ⓐ This region is colliding with the rest of Africa, forming mountains.
Ⓑ This region is colliding with the Arabian Plate.
Ⓒ This region is moving eastward relative to the rest of Africa.
Ⓓ This region is moving northward relative to the rest of Africa.

47. The diagram shows the sedimentary rock layers at Niagara Falls. Which type of rock layer appears to be <u>most</u> resistant to weathering and erosion?

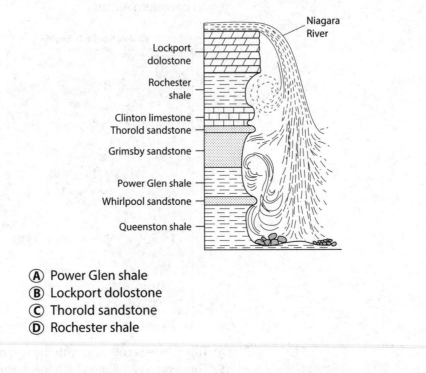

Ⓐ Power Glen shale
Ⓑ Lockport dolostone
Ⓒ Thorold sandstone
Ⓓ Rochester shale

This is the end of the TASC Science Practice Test.

TASC Science Practice Test
Explanatory Answers

1. A The reaction shows four hydrogen nuclei being fused together to make a heavier element and release energy. This is the process of nuclear fusion that occurs in the sun and in other stars.

2. C According to the diagram, the spectral lines that appear in elements A, D, and Z all show up in the mixture. Note that the lines that appear for element X in the 650–750 nm range do not show up in the mixture. Therefore, element X is not in the mixture.

3. C Valleys are shaped by weathering. A V-shaped valley is shaped by the movement of running water. A U-shaped valley is shaped by the movement of a glacier.

4. D Weathering can break down rocks. The smaller, weathered rocks are called fine sediments.

5. B While Earth can be at a range of distances from the sun during the course of a year, it is not this distance that determines the seasons. Instead, the amount of direct sunlight that an area on Earth receives determines its seasons. That amount of sunlight is determined by the tilt of the planet.

6. A Alternative energies that are renewable, such as solar, wind, and hydroelectric energy, are all methods for generating energy without burning fossil fuels and creating more carbon dioxide.

7. B The end product of carbon dioxide mixing with rainwater is acid rain. Acid rain can lower the pH of a stream or lake, making it more acidic. This can have a harmful impact on wildlife. Acid rain can also damage structures built with marble.

8. D Both the thermostat and the brain provide feedback so that the furnace and the body can make adjustments as needed. The adjustments made help maintain stability or homeostasis.

9. C The reaction shows sunlight reacting with carbon dioxide and water to form glucose, a simple sugar that can be used to supply energy. This process is called photosynthesis.

10. $6O_2$, $6CO_2$, $6H_2O$ The rabbit and the eagles will use glucose from the plant in a process called cellular respiration to produce energy that can be stored in ATP molecules for later use.

11. B Aerobic organisms need to use oxygen gas to stay alive. Anaerobic organisms and anaerobic processes do not use oxygen.

12. organelles → cells → tissues → organs

13. A In the chart, between years 3 and 6 the prey population (the gazelles) increases. That means that there is more food available for the predator cheetahs and their young. Because of this increase in food, the predator population (the cheetahs) begins to thrive and grow in years 6 to 8. All of the other choices do not make sense.

14. C and F While meiosis produces sex cells with half as many chromosomes as the parent cell, mitosis produces cells with the exact same number of chromosomes as the parent cell. However, both processes involve chromosome duplication and the replication of DNA.

15. A Set up a Punnett square for this problem. A parent with genes for light hair (dd) is crossed with a parent with genes for dark hair (DD).

	d	d
D	Dd	Dd
D	Dd	Dd

Because all of the combinations contain a D, there is a 100 percent chance that all of the offspring will have dark hair.

16. D For two organisms to synthesize similar enzymes, they must have DNA sequences that are similar. That is because DNA codes for the proteins that make up enzymes (and many other things). Because the dog and horse come from the same evolutionary line, they must have had a common ancestor that had a similar DNA sequence. That is why they will produce similar enzymes and other similar proteins as well.

17. A Looking at the gel electrophoresis, you can see that the DNA from species A is almost the same as that from species B. Species C's DNA fragments produced a sequence that does not match either of the other two.

18. C This is a classic example of survival of the fittest. Both strains of bacteria were exposed to an antibiotic, and one lived on while the other died. There was no new food source for the bacteria, because they were grown on the same Petri dish. Also, there was no DNA change over four days to create resistance, a change that could only take place over many years.

19. B Each element on the periodic table has a specific atomic number that matches the number of protons in the nucleus of an atom of the element. The number of electrons in an atom of the element often matches the number of protons, but the number of electrons can also be different because an atom can gain or lose electrons to form an ion.

20. D Substance D, with the highest melting point, will need the most average kinetic energy (temperature) to break its bonds. Therefore, substance D on the table has the strongest bonds.

21. C Substances made of all nonmetals will have lower melting points. For example, wax is made up of elements that are nonmetals. That is why a wax candle melts easily with a small flame. In contrast, iron, which is all metal, needs a blowtorch to melt it.

22. D The reaction described in the question is the one that occurs during photosynthesis. This reaction takes place in the leaves of plants. In the energy pyramid, the producers (or autotrophs) contain the most energy and are placed at the bottom of the pyramid. Choice D is where the producers can be found.

23. A This reaction is endothermic because heat energy is being added to the system as a reactant. If the heat were a product, the reaction would be an exothermic reaction.

24. C Increasing the temperature, using powdered reactants, and using a catalyst are three ways to speed up a reaction. Another way is to increase the pressure, but that works only with gases because only gases are compressible. In the reaction, none of the reactants is labeled (g), so there are no gases in the reaction. Because there are no gases present, pressure cannot be used to speed up the reaction.

25. A, C, and D According to the law of conservation of mass, what is on the left side of the arrow must add up to what is on the right side. Choice A has one carbon atom and two oxygen atoms on both sides. Choice C has one calcium ion and two chlorine atoms/ions on both sides. Choice D has six oxygen atoms on both sides.

26. B Of the four choices, only choice B is reversible (the products reform the reactants) and can reach equilibrium. Each of the other choices is a reaction that only makes the products and is not reversible.

27. B There are drawbacks to using nuclear reactions to produce energy that is then used to heat steam and produce electricity. These drawbacks are the opposites of choices A, C, and D, and none of those choices is true. However, no greenhouse gases are produced when nuclear reactions are used to generate electricity, and that is a benefit.

28. D The carbon cycle describes the movement of carbon within, on, and above the Earth. Respiration by organisms and emissions from factories and cars introduce carbon into the atmosphere. Photosynthesis introduces carbon into plants that are on Earth's surface. Fossil fuels are found deep underground. They were formed from the decay of once-living organisms.

29. A While estimates vary, it is believed that eventually Earth's human population will reach the maximum number that the planet's resources can sustain. This number is called Earth's carrying capacity.

30. car, hockey player, baseball, snowball To find the momentum of an object, multiply the mass of the object by its velocity.

31. **D** Momentum is always conserved when objects collide, regardless of their masses or velocities.

32. **B** The field lines around a magnet move away from the north pole and toward the south pole. That eliminates choices A and D. Choice C is also incorrect because it shows the field lines moving toward the north pole of a magnet. Only choice B shows the field lines moving away from the north poles.

33. **C** The movement of a magnet about a wire will cause an electric current to be produced. This current will flow through the wire and into the lightbulb, causing it to light up.

34. **A** The potential energy is measured by the equation $PE = mgh$. Multiplying (2.0 kg) (9.81 m/s^2)(1.8 m) gives 35.5 joules of energy.

35. **D** Energy is conserved; that is, it cannot be created or destroyed. Energy can be converted from one form to another. In this case, the potential energy became kinetic energy, which then became sound energy.

36. **C** The key to answering this question is to remember that temperature governs the direction in which heat will flow. "Heat will flow from high to low," that is, from a higher temperature to a lower temperature. Because the player's leg has the highest temperature, heat will flow from the leg to the ice pack and to the air in the arena. Because the air in the arena has a higher temperature than the ice pack, heat in the air will flow to the ice pack as well.

37. **C** Of the choices, x-rays are the most powerful type of radiation and are used for medical purposes when needed. The other types of radiation listed are much weaker and are reserved for everyday use in the home.

38. **B** Radio waves are the weakest type of radiation mentioned in the passage. The CT scan uses x-rays, which are harmful with long-term exposure. Microwaves carry more energy than radio waves and can be dangerous to a person with a pacemaker.

39. **C** The "hot thin soup" concept describes the early Earth's atmosphere, which is thought to have contained gases made out of carbon, oxygen, hydrogen, and nitrogen. Gases containing these elements were able to react to form larger organic molecules. Those are called the "molecules of life." They are DNA, fats, proteins, and sugars. Glucose is a simple form of sugar.

40. **C** Choices A, B, and D are all examples showing how light can act as a wave. Because of the wave-particle dual nature of light, light can also act as a particle. The sensor is one example of a device that uses the photoelectric effect of light acting like particles called photons.

41. **D** A red shift in the light spectrum of a star indicates that the star is moving away from Earth.

42. **A: evaporation; B: condensation; C: transpiration; D: precipitation; E: runoff; F: percolation** Letter A represents evaporation from the ocean. Letter B shows condensation in clouds, and Letter C represents transpiration, the loss of water from plants and trees. Letter D represents rainwater falling from clouds to Earth's surface. Letter E shows runoff of rainwater along the surface, and Letter F shows percolation through the soil.

43. **A** The ejecta from a meteor impact can create tremendous dust clouds that can travel several miles into the air. These dust clouds can block sunlight from reaching Earth's surface, causing global temperatures to fall.

44. **C and E** Because the moon and the planets have cyclic orbits, their positions and phases can easily be predicted by humans (sometimes with a little help from computer models). While there are warning systems in place to predict volcanic eruptions, landslides, and earthquakes, those events do not take place in regular cycles. Finally, asteroids and meteorites and other space objects orbit around the sun, but many are too small to detect until the very last moment before they collide with Earth, making them very unpredictable.

45. **A** The universe has been expanding since the Big Bang. The only graph that shows continual expansion of the universe is choice A.

46. C Plate tectonics is the movement of the continental plates due to convection within Earth's mantle layer. The arrows in the diagram show that the Rift region in eastern Africa (the crosshatched region) is moving eastward.

47. B All of the rock layers in the diagram have been impacted and rounded out by the falling water except for the topmost layer made of Lockport dolostone. Because that layer retained its shape, it is the most resistant to weathering and erosion.

Authentic TASC Test Sample Questions from the Test Makers

The makers of the TASC test at CTB/McGraw-Hill have provided the following authentic sample questions to illustrate the kinds of items that you can expect to see on the test. Because these questions come straight from the test makers, they offer the best, most reliable guide to the items you will see on the actual exam. Study them to make sure that you are familiar with the question formats in the different test sections.

Language Arts–Reading

Read this text. Then answer the questions.

THE DECLARATION OF INDEPENDENCE OF THE UNITED STATES OF AMERICA

IN CONGRESS, July 4, 1776

When in the Course of human events, it becomes necessary for one people to dissolve the political bands which have connected them with another, and to assume among the Powers of the earth, the separate and equal station to which the Laws of Nature and of Nature's God entitle them, a decent respect to the opinions of mankind requires that they should declare the causes which impel them to the separation.

We hold these truths to be self-evident, that all men are created equal, that they are endowed by their Creator with certain unalienable Rights, that among these are Life, Liberty, and the pursuit of Happiness.—That to secure these rights, Governments are instituted among Men, deriving their just powers from the consent of the governed,—That whenever any Form of Government becomes destructive of these ends, it is the Right of the People to alter or to abolish it, and to institute new Government, laying its foundation on such principles and organizing its powers in such form, as to them shall seem most likely to effect their Safety and Happiness. Prudence, indeed, will dictate that Governments long established should not be changed for light and transient causes; and accordingly all experience hath shown, that mankind are more disposed to suffer, while evils are sufferable, than to right themselves by abolishing the forms to which they are accustomed. But when a long train of abuses and usurpations, pursuing invariably the same Object evinces a design to reduce them under absolute Despotism, it is their right, it is their duty, to throw off such Government, and to provide new Guards for their future security.—Such has been the patient sufferance of these Colonies; and such is now the necessity which constrains them to alter their former Systems of Government. The history of the present King of Great Britain is a history of repeated injuries and usurpations, all having in direct object the establishment of an absolute Tyranny over these States. To prove this, let Facts be submitted to a candid world.

1. What rhetorical strategy does Thomas Jefferson, the principal author, <u>mostly</u> use to enhance the effectiveness of his argument?

   A. narration of a relevant story
   B. comparisons of different opinions
   C. analysis of a cause that drives actions
   D. questioning of what the audience values

Correct Answer: C. analysis of a cause that drives actions

2. Reread this excerpt from the Declaration of Independence.

   > . . . and accordingly all experience hath shown, that mankind are more disposed to suffer, while evils are sufferable, than to right themselves by abolishing the forms to which they are accustomed.

   How does Thomas Jefferson use this statement to develop the argument that some wrongs cannot be ignored?

   A. He provides a reason for the colonists' revolt, stressing the severity of the British rule.
   B. He provides a contrast to the colonists' intended actions that emphasizes the severe violation of their rights.
   C. He raises doubt about whether it would be wiser to endure the present distress or to revolt against repeated injustices.
   D. He criticizes the colonists' unwillingness to separate from British rule, even as they are continuously oppressed.

Correct Answer: B. He provides a contrast to the colonists' intended actions that emphasizes the severe violation of their rights.

3. What is the meaning of the word <u>impel</u> in paragraph 1?

   A. join as one
   B. force or urge
   C. cause to fall apart
   D. make an announcement

Correct Answer: B. force or urge

Read this text. Then answer the question.

Excerpt from "What to the Slave is the Fourth of July?"

Frederick Douglass

July 5, 1852

Fellow Citizens, I am not wanting in respect for the fathers of this republic. The signers of the Declaration of Independence were brave men. They were great men too—great enough to give fame to a great age. It does not often happen to a nation to raise, at one time, such a number of truly great men. The point from which I am compelled to view them is not, certainly, the most favorable; and yet I cannot contemplate their great deeds with less than admiration. They were statesmen, patriots and heroes, and for the good they did, and the principles they contended for, I will unite with you to honor their memory.

They loved their country better than their own private interests; and, though this is not the highest form of human excellence, all will concede that it is a rare virtue, and that when it is exhibited, it ought to command respect. He who will, intelligently, lay down his life for his country, is a man whom it is not in human nature to despise. Your fathers staked their lives, their fortunes, and their sacred honor, on the cause of their country. In their admiration of liberty, they lost sight of all other interests.

They were peace men; but they preferred revolution to peaceful submission to bondage. They were quiet men; but they did not shrink from agitating against oppression. They showed forbearance; but that they knew its limits. They believed in order; but not in the order of tyranny. With them, nothing was "settled" that was not right. With them, justice, liberty and humanity were "final"; not slavery and oppression. You may well cherish the memory of such men. They were great in their day and generation. Their solid manhood stands out the more as we contrast it with these degenerate times.

How circumspect, exact and proportionate were all their movements! How unlike the politicians of an hour! Their statesmanship looked beyond the passing moment, and stretched away in strength into the distant future. They seized upon eternal principles, and set a glorious example in their defense. Mark them!

Fully appreciating the hardship to be encountered, firmly believing in the right of their cause, honorably inviting the scrutiny of an on-looking world, reverently appealing to heaven to attest their sincerity, soundly comprehending the solemn responsibility they were about to assume, wisely measuring the terrible odds against them, your fathers, the fathers of this republic, did, most deliberately, under the inspiration of a glorious patriotism, and with a sublime faith in the great principles of justice and freedom, lay deep the corner-stone of the national superstructure, which has risen and still rises in grandeur around you.

4. Which of these statements from Douglass's speech is <u>most</u> similar to a central idea of the Declaration of Independence?

A. It does not often happen to a nation to raise, at one time, such a number of truly great men.

B. In their admiration of liberty, they lost sight of all other interests.

C. With them, nothing was "settled" that was not right.

D. Their solid manhood stands out the more as we contrast it with these degenerate times.

Correct Answer: C. With them, nothing was "settled" that was not right.

Read this text. Then answer the questions.

Excerpt from *Main Street*

Sinclair Lewis

That one word—home—it terrified her. Had she really bound herself to live, inescapably, in this town called Gopher Prairie? And this thick man beside her, who dared to define her future, he was a stranger! She turned in her seat, stared at him. Who was he? Why was he sitting with her? He wasn't of her kind! His neck was heavy; his speech was heavy; he was twelve or thirteen years older than she; and about him was none of the magic of shared adventures and eagerness. She could not believe that she had ever slept in his arms. That was one of the dreams which you had but did not officially admit.

She told herself how good he was, how dependable and understanding. She touched his ear, smoothed the plane of his solid jaw, and, turning away again, concentrated upon liking his town. It wouldn't be like these barren settlements. It couldn't be! Why, it had three thousand population. That was a great many people. There would be six hundred houses or more. And——The lakes near it would be so lovely. She'd seen them in the photographs. They had looked charming . . . hadn't they?

As the train left Wahkeenyan she began nervously to watch for the lakes—the entrance to all her future life. But when she discovered them, to the left of the track, her only impression of them was that they resembled the photographs.

A mile from Gopher Prairie the track mounts a curving low ridge, and she could see the town as a whole. With a passionate jerk she pushed up the window, looked out, the arched fingers of her left hand trembling on the sill, her right hand at her breast.

And she saw that Gopher Prairie was merely an enlargement of all the hamlets which they had been passing. Only to the eyes of a Kennicott was it exceptional. The huddled low wooden houses broke the plains scarcely more than would a hazel thicket. The fields swept up to it, past it. It was unprotected and unprotecting; there was no dignity in it nor any hope of greatness. Only the tall red grain-elevator and a few tinny church-steeples rose from the mass. It was a frontier camp. It was not a place to live in, not possibly, not conceivably.

The people—they'd be as drab as their houses, as flat as their fields. She couldn't stay here. She would have to wrench loose from this man, and flee.

She peeped at him. She was at once helpless before his mature fixity, and touched by his excitement as he sent his magazine skittering along the aisle, stooped for their bags, came up with flushed face, and gloated, "Here we are!"

She smiled loyally, and looked away. The train was entering town. The houses on the outskirts were dusky old red mansions with wooden frills, or gaunt frame shelters like grocery boxes, or new bungalows with concrete foundations imitating stone.

Now the train was passing the elevator, the grim storage-tanks for oil, a creamery, a lumber-yard, a stockyard muddy and trampled and stinking. Now they were stopping at a squat red frame station, the platform crowded with unshaven farmers and with loafers—unadventurous people with dead eyes. She was here. She could not go on. It was the end—the end of the world. She sat with closed eyes, longing to push past Kennicott, hide somewhere in the train, flee on toward the Pacific.

Something large arose in her soul and commanded, "Stop it! Stop being a whining baby!" She stood up quickly; she said, "Isn't it wonderful to be here at last!"

He trusted her so. She would make herself like the place. And she was going to do tremendous things.

5. Which of these sentences from the excerpt best emphasizes the difference between the character's expectations of Gopher Prairie and reality?

    A. It was unprotected and unprotecting; there was no dignity in it nor any hope of greatness.

    B. She smiled loyally, and looked away.

    C. "Stop it! Stop being a whining baby!"

    D. She stood up quickly; she said, "Isn't it wonderful to be here at last!"

Correct Answer: A. It was unprotected and unprotecting; there was no dignity in it nor any hope of greatness.

6. Read the excerpt from the text.

> It wouldn't be like these barren settlements. It couldn't be! Why, it had three thousand population. That was a great many people. There would be six hundred houses or more. And——The lakes near it would be so lovely. She'd seen them in the photographs. They had looked charming . . . hadn't they?

What do the character's thoughts as she nears Gopher Prairie indicate about how she is feeling?

    A. that she is curious but doubtful

    B. that she is reluctant and angry

    C. that she is excited and optimistic

    D. that she is uncertain but open-minded

Correct Answer: A. that she is curious but doubtful

7. Read this sentence from the text.

> Had she really bound herself to live, inescapably, in this town called Gopher Prairie?

Which feeling of the character in the text does the phrase "bound herself" best capture in the sentence?

    A. that she already feels tied to this town

    B. that she feels destined to live in this small town

    C. that she acknowledges that she decides her own fate

    D. that she recognizes her inability to make her own decision

Correct Answer: C. that she acknowledges that she decides her own fate

Language Arts–Writing

1. Read this sentence.

> Why my mom wanted me to clean up my room, there were many reasons; chief among them was the thick layer of dust on my table; there was also a multitude of candy bar wrappers covering the floor.

Which of these is the <u>most</u> accurate and effective revision to the sentence?

A. There were many reasons why my mom wanted me to clean up my room, but chief among them were the thick layer of dust on my table and the multitude of candy bar wrappers covering the floor.

B. My mom wanted me to clean my room for many reasons, but there were two that were chief among them: firstly, the thick layer of dust on my table and, secondly, the multitude of candy bar wrappers covering the floor.

C. In spite of the thick layer of dust on my table, there were many reasons why my mom wanted me to clean up my room; chief among them was the multitude of candy bar wrappers covering the floor.

D. Why my mom wanted me to clean up my room: chief among the many reasons was the thick layer of dust on my table, there being also a multitude of candy bar wrappers covering the floor.

Correct Answer: A. There were many reasons why my mom wanted me to clean up my room, but chief among them were the thick layer of dust on my table and the multitude of candy bar wrappers covering the floor.

2. Which of these sentences includes a misspelled word?

A. Bobby was ecstatic about heading into the city with his friends for a baseball game this weekend.

B. The spring weather was already getting warm but had not become miserably hot yet—perfect weather for a baseball game!

C. Bobby had promised his little brother that he would take pictures of some of the star players, as well as attempt to aquire their autographs.

D. He also reassured his brother that he would bring him an extraordinary souvenir from the ballpark's gift shop.

Correct Answer: C. Bobby had promised his little brother that he would take pictures of some of the star players, as well as attempt to aquire their autographs.

3. Read this sentence.

There was an effortlessness with which Barry played his guitar, and it was making it appear as if he and his instrument had—because of something almost impossible to describe—miraculously merged together into a single, music-producing unit.

Which revision of the sentence <u>best</u> expresses the idea precisely and concisely?

A. He and his instrument were merged together into a single, music-producing unit.

B. Miraculously merged together, Barry played his guitar with an effortlessness as if he and his instrument were a single, music-producing unit.

C. The effortlessness with which Barry played his guitar made it appear as if he and his instrument had miraculously merged into a single, music-producing unit.

D. There was an effortlessness in how Barry played his guitar—because of something almost impossible to describe—and it was making it appear as if he and his instrument had miraculously merged together into a single, music-producing unit.

Correct Answer: C. The effortlessness with which Barry played his guitar made it appear as if he and his instrument had miraculously merged into a single, music-producing unit.

4. Read the paragraph.

An everyday hero is the average person who responds out of a sense of urgency to a situation that demands immediate action. The everyday hero recognizes that complacency is not an option. Risk to self is considered, but generally only after the fact. A hero acts anyway.

Which sentence <u>best</u> concludes this paragraph?

A. The world is filled with many different kinds of heroes.

B. The actions define the hero as a giver, touching humanity in the process.

C. The everyday hero is the next-door neighbor who rescues the child from the oncoming car.

D. The size of the risk taken is of no matter to the hero because there is little time to consider the consequences.

Correct Answer: B. The actions define the hero as a giver, touching humanity in the process.

5. Read this excerpt of a draft of an essay. Then answer the questions.

> [1]All across the United States, there are cities known for their "specialty" dishes. [2]Each dish has a unique flavor and story, and people travel from all across the country just to try it out. [3]Chicago is famous for its deep-dish pizza. [4]New York–style cheesecake is one of New York City's claims to fame.
>
> [5]Pat and Harry were born in South Philadelphia. [6]Pat was born in 1907, and Harry was born nine years later. [7]When Harry was but a lad of three, the family Olivieri transported themselves to Italy. [8]The family stayed in Italy a short time before returning to Philadelphia. [9]Harry took up carpentry. [10]He worked after school. [11]He also worked at the Navy shipyard. [12]Pat began building sleds. [13]Harry and Pat wanted to earn a better living so they decided to open a hot dog stand and sell hot dogs at night. [14]In 1930, the brothers opened a hot dog stand at the corners of 9th Street, Wharton Street, and Passyunk Avenue.

Which sentence best completes the first paragraph in order to create cohesion between the two paragraphs?

- **A.** Pat and Harry Olivieri, who once lived in Philadelphia, invented the Philly cheesesteak.
- **B.** Philly cheesesteaks are Philadelphia's signature food and were invented by the Olivieri brothers.
- **C.** The Olivieri brothers invented the Philly cheesesteak in order to bring publicity to the city they called home.
- **D.** Thanks to two brothers, Pat and Harry Olivieri, Philadelphia has its own signature food as well: the Philly cheesesteak.

Correct Answer: D. Thanks to two brothers, Pat and Harry Olivieri, Philadelphia has its own signature food as well: the Philly cheesesteak.

6. Which revision most effectively combines the ideas of sentences 9 through 11 into one sentence?

- **A.** Because Pat built sleds, Harry worked at carpentry after school as well as at the shipyard.
- **B.** Pat built sleds, and Harry worked after school, taking up carpentry and working at the shipyard.
- **C.** The brothers worked after school at carpentry (Harry), at the shipyard (Harry), and at building sleds (Pat).
- **D.** Harry kept busy after school, taking up carpentry and working at the shipyard, while Pat began building sleds.

Correct Answer: D. Harry kept busy after school, taking up carpentry and working at the shipyard, while Pat began building sleds.

Write an essay to delineate and explain the qualities of an effective argument. Base your ideas on the two texts you have read: the excerpt from Thomas Jefferson's Declaration of Independence and the excerpt from Frederick Douglass's speech "What to the Slave is the Fourth of July?"

Before you begin planning and writing, read the two texts:

1. The Declaration of Independence (page 394)
2. "What to the Slave is the Fourth of July?" (page 396)

As you read the texts, think about what details from the texts you might use in your essay. You may take notes or highlight the details as you read.

After reading the texts, create a plan for your essay. Think about ideas, facts, definitions, details, and other information and examples you want to use. Think about how you will introduce your topic and what the main topic will be for each paragraph.

7. Now, write your essay. Be sure to:

>> Use information from the two passages so that your article includes important details. Introduce the topic clearly, provide a focus, and organize information in a way that makes sense.
>> Develop the topic with facts, definitions, details, quotations, or other information and examples related to the topic.
>> Use appropriate and varied transitions to create cohesion.
>> Clarify the relationship among ideas and concepts.
>> Use clear language and vocabulary to inform about the topic.
>> Provide a conclusion that follows the information presented.

Mathematics

The first two items demonstrate ways of assessing the test taker's understanding of rational and radical exponents by way of two different Common Core State Standards (CCSS). Both approaches are important to assess, as one involves algebraic reasoning skills and the other involves an understanding of how equivalent real numbers can be represented in different ways.

1. If $\sqrt[4]{64} = 4^x$, what is the value of x?

Correct answer: $\frac{3}{4}$

2. Consider this polynomial expression:

$$(x^2 - x + 1) + (2x^2 + x - 9)$$

What is the sum of the polynomial?

A. $x^2 - 8$
B. $3x^2 - 8$
C. $3x^2 - 2x - 8$
D. $3x^2 + 2x - 8$

Correct Answer: B. $3x^2 - 8$

3. When a spherical balloon is filled with air, it has a diameter of 6 inches. Which of these gives the <u>best</u> estimate for the volume of air in the balloon, in cubic inches?

A. 75.4
B. 108.0
C. 113.1
D. 150.8

Correct Answer: C. 113.1

4. Two rectangles are similar and the dimensions shown are in centimeters.

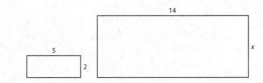

What is the measure of *x*, in centimeters?

   A. 4.0
   B. 5.6
   C. 8.4
   D. 11.0

Correct Answer: B. 5.6

5. Sharon made a scale drawing of a triangular park. The coordinates for the vertices of the park are:

   (−10, 5), (15, 5), (10, 12)

   Her scale is 1 unit = 1 meter.

What is the area of the triangular park in square meters?

Correct Answer: 87.5

6. What is the solution to the equation $2(x - 10) + 4 = -6x + 2$?

   A. $\dfrac{-9}{2}$

   B. 1

   C. $\dfrac{9}{4}$

   D. $\dfrac{5}{2}$

Correct Answer: C. $\dfrac{9}{4}$

7. The time, T, it takes for 2 people working together to complete a job is given by $T = \dfrac{1}{r_1 + r_2}$.

In the equation,

   r_1 is the work rate of the first person, and

   r_2 is the work rate of the second person.

Which formula could be used to find r_1 if you knew the values for T and r_2?

   A. $r_1 = \dfrac{T - r_2}{r_2}$

   B. $r_1 = \dfrac{1 - Tr_2}{T}$

   C. $r_1 = \dfrac{T}{r_2 - r_2}$

   D. $r_1 = \dfrac{Tr_2}{T + r_2}$

Correct Answer: B. $r_1 = \dfrac{1 - Tr_2}{T}$

8. The price of a certain sofa, S, is $900 more than the price of a chair, C. The total price for the sofa and chair is $1200. Which system of equations can be used to find the price of each piece of furniture?

A. $C = S - 900$
  $S + C = 1200$

B. $C = S + 900$
  $S - C = 1200$

C. $C = S + 900$
  $S + C = 1200$

D. $S = C + 1200$
  $S - C = 900$

Correct Answer: A. $C = S - 900$
  $S + C = 1200$

9. Water flows into a tank over a 10-minute period. The function $f(x)$ graphed models the flow rate, in gallons per minute (GPM).

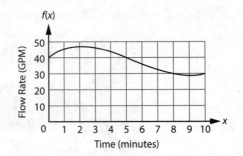

Over which of these intervals does the flow rate increase by the greatest amount?

A. $x = 0$ to $x = 1$
B. $x = 2$ to $x = 3$
C. $x = 4$ to $x = 5$
D. $x = 8$ to $x = 9$

Correct Answer: A. $x = 0$ to $x = 1$

10. Tom has two cubes each with numbers 1 through 6 on the sides. If he rolls the cubes at the same time and finds the sum, the sample space of possible outcomes is the set {2, 3, 4, 5, 6, 7, 8, 9, 10, 11, 12}. Tom rolls the cubes. One of the cubes shows a number less than or equal to 3. The other cube shows the number 4. Which subset of the sample space describes the set of possible outcomes for Tom?

    A. {5, 6}
    B. {4, 5, 6}
    C. {5, 6, 7}
    D. {4, 5, 6, 7}

Correct Answer: C. {5, 6, 7}

Social Studies

Study the political cartoon. Then answer the questions that follow.

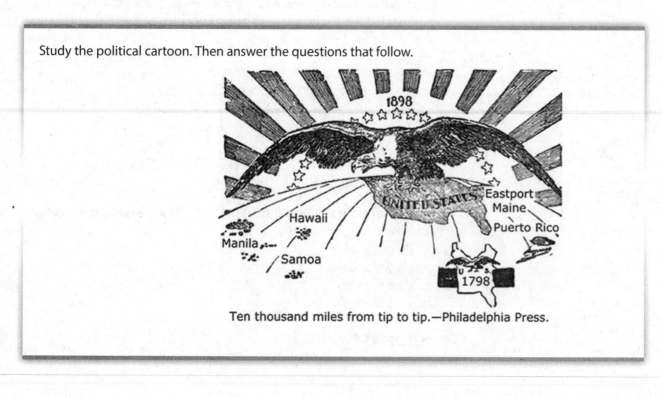

Ten thousand miles from tip to tip.—Philadelphia Press.

1. The United States acquired some of the island territories shown in the cartoon as a result of a

    A. war with Spain
    B. treaty with France
    C. treaty with Mexico
    D. war with Great Britain

Correct Answer: A. war with Spain

2. Which statement would the cartoonist most likely agree with?

   A. The United States should be cautious when acquiring new territories.

   B. The United States should only add territories that improve the American economy.

   C. The United States should only add territories when the native population needs assistance.

   D. The United States should continue to acquire territories in order to increase American influence.

Correct Answer: D. The United States should continue to acquire territories in order to increase American influence.

Read the information in the box. Then answer the question that follows.

> The powers not delegated to the United States by the Constitution, nor prohibited by it to the States, are reserved to the States respectively, or to the people.
>
> —*Tenth Amendment to the United States Constitution*

---

3. Which of these describes why the Tenth Amendment was added to the United States Constitution?

   A. to restrict state power over the people

   B. to limit the power of the federal government

   C. to allow citizens to participate in a direct democracy at the state level

   D. to allow states to invalidate federal laws that they felt were unconstitutional

Correct Answer: B. to limit the power of the federal government

Read the excerpt. Then answer the question that follows.

> When the legislative and executive powers are united in the same person, or in the same body of magistrates, there can be no liberty.
>
> There is no liberty, if the power of judging be not separated from the legislative and executive powers.
>
> —*Baron de Montesquieu, The Spirit of the Laws, 1748*

4. Which principle of the United States government is described by this excerpt?

- **A.** individual rights
- **B.** popular sovereignty
- **C.** separation of powers
- **D.** separation of church and state

Correct Answer: C. separation of powers

Read the excerpt. Then answer the question that follows.

> Baron de Montesquieu was an Enlightenment philosopher. Enlightenment philosophy in the 18th century challenged traditional authority and called for a society based on liberty, equality, and human reason.

5. Which statement describes an effect of the Enlightenment in Europe?

- **A.** It led to increased restrictions on individual rights.
- **B.** It led many countries to introduce democracy to their colonies.
- **C.** It led to increased peacetime cooperation between governments.
- **D.** It led many citizens to demand more rights from their government.

Correct Answer: D. It led many citizens to demand more rights from their government.

6. Read the list in the box. Then answer the question that follows.

> **?**
>
> - Ethnic conflicts
> - Militarism
> - Colonialism
> - Imperialism
> - Secret alliances

Which of these is the <u>best</u> title for the list in the box?

A. Causes of World War I
B. Causes of the Cold War
C. Causes of the Seven Years' War
D. Causes of the Russian Revolution

<u>**Correct Answer:**</u> **A.** Causes of World War I

7. Which phrase <u>best</u> defines the economic term *profit*?

A. the financial gain an employee earns in overtime, benefits, and bonuses
B. the financial gain from interest on bank loans, bonds, or savings accounts
C. the financial gain received through sales of products or services before expenses are subtracted
D. the financial gain an entrepreneur makes selling products or services after paying the costs of production

<u>**Correct Answer:**</u> **D.** the financial gain an entrepreneur makes selling products or services after paying the costs of production

8. What was the <u>main</u> reason England, France, Spain, and the Netherlands competed for colonies in North America during the 1600s?

A. to spread democratic ideals
B. to control trade routes to Asia
C. to convert native populations to Christianity
D. to gain control of valuable natural resources

<u>**Correct Answer:**</u> **D.** to gain control of valuable natural resources

9. Look at the graph. Then answer the question that follows.

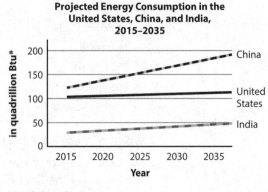

Projected Energy Consumption in the United States, China, and India, 2015–2035

* British thermal unit

Which of these explains how the changing demand for energy in China and India will <u>most likely</u> affect consumers in the United States?

A. Consumers in the United States will see prices for goods increase because the demand for energy will rise.

B. Consumers in the United States will have higher energy costs because the demand for energy will decrease.

C. Consumers in the United States will have lower energy costs because new energy resources will be created to meet the rising need.

D. Consumers in the United States will see prices for goods decrease because suppliers will need to use less energy to produce goods.

<u>**Correct Answer:**</u> **A.** Consumers in the United States will see prices for goods increase because the demand for energy will rise.

10. Read the list in the box. Then answer the question that follows.

> • Hot, dry climate
> • Low precipitation
> • Deserts created by mountains and winds
> • Large amounts of oil and natural gas

Which world geographic region is described by the list in the box?

A. Middle East

B. Great Plains

C. Southeast Asia

D. Amazon River Basin

<u>**Correct Answer:**</u> **A.** Middle East

Science

1. Which of these describes a role of DNA in a cell?

- **A.** DNA is the material that forms into the cell's membrane.
- **B.** DNA produces the energy needed for the cell's activities.
- **C.** DNA provides the information to make proteins for the cell.
- **D.** DNA is the building block for the other molecules in the cell.

<u>**Correct Answer:**</u> **C.** DNA provides the information to make proteins for the cell.

> **Rationale for A.** DNA is not the material that forms the cellular membrane.
> **Rationale for B.** DNA is not responsible for producing energy for a cell.
> **Rationale for C.** The nitrogenous base sequences of DNA provide the coded information needed to assemble different proteins for a cell.
> **Rationale for D.** Although DNA contains coded instructions for assembling proteins, DNA is not the building block for other molecules.

2. A certain plant species varies in the shape of its leaf edges. Some of the plants have wavy-edged leaves, and some of the plants have straight-edged leaves. In this plant species, the trait for leaf-edge shape is controlled by a single gene. The dominant allele is represented by L, and the recessive allele is represented by l.

A plant with wavy-edged leaves is crossed with a plant with straight-edged leaves, producing 421 offspring plants. Of these, 298 offspring plants have wavy-edged leaves, and 123 offspring plants have straight-edged leaves.

What are the genotypes of the parent plants in this cross?

- **A.** Ll and ll
- **B.** Ll and Ll
- **C.** LL and ll
- **D.** LL and Ll

<u>**Correct Answer:**</u> **B.** Ll and Ll

> **Rationale for A.** Crossing these genotypes would produce an expected phenotypic ratio of 1:1, whereas the observed phenotypic ratio is approximately 3:1.
> **Rationale for B.** The observed phenotypic ratio is approximately 3:1, which is consistent with a cross between two heterozygous parents.
> **Rationale for C.** A common misconception is that each parent is homozygous for its expressed phenotype. A cross involving a homozygous dominant parent would result in offspring that all have the dominant phenotype, even if the other parent was homozygous recessive.
> **Rationale for D.** A cross involving a homozygous dominant parent would result in offspring that all have the dominant phenotype.

3. A population of a certain species of mammal was studied over many generations. The graph shows the percentages of fur colors observed in the population over the generations.

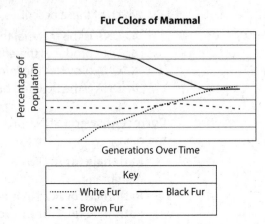

Fur Colors of Mammal

Which explanation is the most likely reason for the appearance of individuals that have white fur?

A. The mammals adapted to a change in climate by changing their fur color.

B. The mammals chose a different food source that resulted in a new fur color.

C. A mutation occurred in an individual's fur color gene and resulted in a new fur color.

D. A new predator moved into the area, which caused the individuals to change fur color.

<u>**Correct Answer:**</u> **C.** A mutation occurred in an individual's fur color gene and resulted in a new fur color.

Rationale for A. A common misconception is that organisms can choose to change their genotypes in response to selection pressures. A trait must exist in the population before selection can act upon it.

Rationale for B. The respondent may believe that food sources can produce new alleles within a population.

Rationale for C. New alleles (that can produce new phenotypes) are produced through mutations in gamete cells.

Rationale for D. The respondent may believe that predation pressure can produce new alleles within a population.

4. Which statement would <u>most likely</u> help explain the changes over time in the percentages of the fur colors within the population?

   A. The mammals with white fur had an advantage in producing offspring.

   B. The mammals with brown fur had an advantage in producing offspring.

   C. The mammals with white fur had a disadvantage in producing offspring.

   D. The mammals with brown fur had a disadvantage in producing offspring.

Correct Answer: A. The mammals with white fur had an advantage in producing offspring.

   Rationale for A. The percentage of the population with white fur increased steadily over time, which helps support the claim that white fur had a reproductive advantage.

   Rationale for B. The percentage of the population with brown fur was relatively stable over time, which does not support the claim that brown fur had a reproductive advantage.

   Rationale for C. The percentage of the population with white fur increased steadily over time, which does not support the claim that white fur had a reproductive disadvantage.

   Rationale for D. The percentage of the population with brown fur was relatively stable over time, which does not support the claim that brown fur had a reproductive disadvantage.

5. The sun produces tremendous amounts of energy. Some of that energy reaches Earth and affects Earth's systems.

Which statement explains how the sun produces this energy?

   A. The sun produces energy through fusion reactions in its core.

   B. The sun produces energy through radioactive decay in its core.

   C. The sun produces energy through convection cells on its surface.

   D. The sun produces energy through combustion reaction on its surface.

Correct Answer: A. The sun produces energy through fusion reactions in its core.

   Rationale for A. The sun produces energy through hydrogen fusion in its core.

   Rationale for B. A common mistake is that the sun's energy is from radioactive decay, which is a fission reaction (not a fusion reaction).

   Rationale for C. Although the sun does transfer energy toward its surface through convection, this does not explain how the energy is produced.

   Rationale for D. A common misconception is that the sun is a ball of fire, as a result of combustion.

6. The diagram shows a cross-section of an area where two tectonic plates of Earth's surface are moving toward each other. The leading edge of one tectonic plate has oceanic crust, while the leading edge of the other tectonic plate has continental crust.

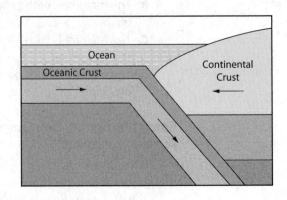

Several types of geographic features would be predicted to form over time in the area shown in the diagram. Which geographic feature would not be predicted to occur in this area?

A. volcanoes
B. mountains
C. ocean ridge
D. ocean trench

Correct Answer: C. ocean ridge

> **Rationale for A.** Volcanoes would be predicted to occur in this area, due to the subducting oceanic plate.
> **Rationale for B.** Mountains would be predicted to occur in this area.
> **Rationale for C.** An ocean ridge occurs where two oceanic plates are pulling away from each other, so this would not be predicted to occur in this area.
> **Rationale for D.** An ocean trench would be predicted to occur in this area, due to the subducting oceanic plate.

7. Which of these could explain the motion of the tectonic plates shown in the diagram?

   A. rotation of Earth's axis

   B. currents within Earth's ocean

   C. convection of material within Earth's interior

   D. gravitational pull of the sun and moon on Earth's surface

Correct Answer: C. convection of material within Earth's interior

Rationale for A. A common misconception is that Earth's rotation causes the movement of tectonic plates.

Rationale for B. The respondent may believe that currents within the ocean cause the movement of tectonic plates.

Rationale for C. The slow convection of material within Earth's interior could explain the motion of the tectonic plates of Earth's surface.

Rationale for D. The respondent may believe that the gravitational pull of the sun and moon cause the movement of tectonic plates.

8. An object at rest with a mass of 4 kilograms (kg) is acted on by a force causing the object to move. The table shows measurements recorded for the motion of the object.

TIME (S)	VELOCITY (m/s)
0	0
1	2
2	4
3	6
4	8
5	10

Based on the data, which equation correctly determines the amount of force, in newtons (N), that acted on the object?

   A. $4 \text{ kg} \times 0.5 \dfrac{s^2}{m} = 2 \text{ N}$

   B. $4 \text{ kg} \times 2 \dfrac{m}{s^2} = 8 \text{ N}$

   C. $4 \text{ kg} \times 5 \text{ s} = 20 \text{ N}$

   D. $4 \text{ kg} \times 10 \dfrac{m}{s} = 40 \text{ N}$

Correct Answer: B. $4 \text{ kg} \times 2 \dfrac{m}{s^2} = 8 \text{ N}$

Rationale for A. This equation incorrectly attempts to determine the force using the inverse of the acceleration (change in velocity over time).

Rationale for B. This equation correctly determines the force by multiplying the mass of the object by the acceleration of the object (change in velocity over time), according to Newton's Second Law of Motion.

Rationale for C. This equation incorrectly attempts to determine the force using the final time in the table rather than the acceleration (change in velocity over time).

Rationale for D. This equation incorrectly attempts to determine the force using the final velocity in the table rather than the acceleration (change in velocity over time).

9. Potassium chlorate ($KClO_3$) is a crystalline solid that can undergo thermal decomposition to form solid potassium chloride (KCl) and gaseous oxygen (O_2) when heat is added. The chemical equation for this reaction is shown.

$$2\ KClO_3 + heat \rightarrow 2\ KCL + 3O_2$$

ELEMENT	SYMBOL	MOLAR MASS (grams/mole)
Potassium	K	39.10
Chlorine	Cl	35.45
Oxygen	O	16.00

If 5.00 grams of $KClO_3$ (0.0408 moles) undergoes decomposition, which equation shows the predicted amount of oxygen that will be produced?

A. $0.0408 \text{ moles} \times \dfrac{2 \text{ moles}}{3 \text{ moles}} \times \dfrac{16.00 \text{ grams}}{\text{mole}} = 0.435 \text{ grams}$

B. $0.0408 \text{ moles} \times \dfrac{2 \text{ moles}}{3 \text{ moles}} \times \dfrac{32.00 \text{ grams}}{\text{mole}} = 0.870 \text{ grams}$

C. $0.0408 \text{ moles} \times \dfrac{3 \text{ moles}}{2 \text{ moles}} \times \dfrac{16.00 \text{ grams}}{\text{mole}} = 0.979 \text{ grams}$

D. $0.0408 \text{ moles} \times \dfrac{3 \text{ moles}}{2 \text{ moles}} \times \dfrac{32.00 \text{ grams}}{\text{mole}} = 1.96 \text{ grams}$

Correct Answer: D. $0.0408 \text{ moles} \times \dfrac{3 \text{ moles}}{2 \text{ moles}} \times \dfrac{32.00 \text{ grams}}{\text{mole}} = 1.96 \text{ grams}$

Rationale for A. This equation inverts the mole ratio, using 2:3 (instead of 3:2), and uses the molar mass of atomic oxygen instead of the molar mass of molecular oxygen.

Rationale for B. This equation inverts the mole ratio, using 2:3 (instead of 3:2).

Rationale for C. This equation uses the molar mass of atomic oxygen instead of the molar mass of molecular oxygen.

Rationale for D. This shows the correct mathematical equation to determine the predicted amount of oxygen produced from the given amount of potassium chlorate.